PEOPLE, POLITICS AND PAINTINGS

Cover photo © Nancy Durrell McKenna

Pencil portrait of the author by Saied Dai, 2009

People, Politics and Paintings

A journalist's life

Roger Berthoud

*For John and Jill
with many happy
memories
Roger, Jan '10*

ELSP

Published in 2009 by
ELSP
16A New St John's Road
St Helier
Jersey   JE2 3LD

Origination by Ex Libris Press

Typeset in 9.75/12.75 Caslon

Printed in Britain by
JF Print Ltd
Sparkford, Somerset

ISBN 978-1-906641-17-7

For my daughters Lucy and Lottie

Contents

Acknowledgements

I would like to thank the following for permission to use photos in their copyright:

The Observer/Guardian, Nigel and Maude Gosling with Henry Moore by Jane Bown
The Times, me with Mountbatten
Tony Gale of Pictorial Press, me with the Rolling Stones
The *Evening Standard,* The Londoner's Diary team
The *Bundesbildstelle*, me with Willy Brandt
Nancy Durrell McKenna, the cover photo
Tessa Smith, the great nieces

I have been unable to trace the family of Bryan Heseltine (Maurice and Ruth Ash with sculpture)

The Independent, for the three leading articles

Introduction

When I tell people I have been writing my memoirs, I usually feel a need to justify this seemingly self-regarding exercise. Well, I say, I persuaded both my parents to write theirs, and my three siblings and I are extremely glad they did. It's good to have a record of their deeds and thoughts, even better to be reminded of their personalities by the briefest dip into either volume: style really is the man (or woman). If they could make the considerable effort to dredge up their pasts, what excuse could I, a professional journalist and author of two biographies, have for not doing likewise?

It has on the whole been an enjoyable exercise, but of course sometimes painful. I wouldn't go as far as Laurence Olivier, who apparently said in as many words 'It wasn't till I wrote my memoirs that I realised what a shit I was'. But it has been distressing to be reminded how selfishly, even foolishly I sometimes behaved. Initially I favoured a high degree of openness and self-flagellation on the personal front. But I have two cherished daughters and a wife whom I still love even though we live apart. To sacrifice them on the altar of candour and readability would be, well, selfish.

This book is aimed not just at family, friends and ex-colleagues, but at anyone interested in what it was like to be a fairly prominent journalist on leading newspapers between 1960 and the early 1990s. Was I prominent enough? Having read many memoirs and autobiographies, and reviewed a few, I have detected an inverse ratio between success and readability. The more successful the authors have been, the more they want to emphasise just how central a role they played. Self-justification too often bulks large. Naturally there are plenty of exceptions, such as the memoirs of Denis Healey and John Major. But from the dense ranks of diplomatic memoirs, compare Sir Arthur Grimble's *A Pattern of Islands* (1952), a delightful and acclaimed account of his time as Resident Commissioner in the Gilbert and Ellice Islands, with Sir Frank Roberts' *Dealing with Dictators* (1990), which chronicled in excessive detail the important role that Sir Frank played at the Yalta conference and in the evolution of post-war Europe.

My career has been unusual in two respects. Not many broadsheet journalists have been successively diarist, stand-in art critic and saleroom correspondent, foreign correspondent, feature writer/interviewer, and chief leader writer. And very few have been professionally involved in the worlds of politics and international affairs on the one hand, and the arts on the other.

What is the difference between memoirs and autobiography? If a memoir depends largely on memories, this is an autobiography. My memory is not too bad, but – as has often been demonstrated – memories tend to be unreliable. My documentation has included an irregular journal, carbon copies of the many long letters I typed to my parents and siblings, notably my brother Martin, when they were abroad, letters from them (and some others) to me, and cuttings from much of my journalistic output.

I have not sought to make this book in any way a polemic. But I believe we Britons live in a country that has been consistently badly governed in my lifetime, by both main parties, though there is something to be said for Clement Attlee's post-Second World War government, and Margaret Thatcher's first term of office. Our electoral system is scandalously unjust; the country's infrastructure and public services are lamentable by West European standards; the gap between rich and poor, privileged and under-privileged is wider than in France, Germany, the Benelux countries and, especially, Scandinavia; to our detriment, successive governments have favoured the 'special relationship' with the USA over a closer relationship with continental Europe; we have a tabloid press that panders to the vilest and most chauvinist emotions of its readers, and reinforces their illusion that Britain is superior to the rest of the world; we imprison a higher proportion of the population than any other advanced country except the USA; the streets of our cities and our main roads are full of litter...and so on.

Yet, given a reasonable level of income, Britain is a very beguiling place in which to live. Its scenery is both beautiful and wonderfully varied, as are many of its villages, towns, cities, stately homes and gardens. On the whole we treat animals, including farm livestock, better than most of 'abroad'. We have integrated more people from racial minorities into public life than most western democracies, and London is a spectacularly multi-racial capital. The overall state and status of the arts is pretty good, and there is a (possibly related) streak of originality and delight in flouting conformity that is, by north European standards, refreshing. Our language is a delight, as is that cherished sense of irony and humour. There is generally a lack of vanity in the British that is endearing, despite its inevitable consequences: by continental standards we dress appallingly, and our obesity levels are second only to the USA's. That's enough generalisations, as my daughters would say – they accuse me of being far too 'lookist', not to mention judgemental, as no doubt I am. It runs in the Berthoud family.

If this book has a theme, it is my quest to achieve some sort of happy balance between work and family life on the one hand, and self-fulfilment on the other. 'Remember, Dad, facts boring, thoughts interesting', our elder daughter Lucy once observed with characteristic concision. I disagreed. As a journalist I have always found facts fascinating and the thoughts of columnists, even good ones, interesting only if supported by evidence. There are probably more facts than thoughts in the following pages, about some of the many people I encountered, places I visited and things I learned and enjoyed in the course of my work.

I would like to thank all those, mainly family members and especially my brother Martin and daughter Lucy, who have cast critical eyes over bits or all of these chapters. A local American lawyer friend, Alice Leonard, brought a fresh pair of eyes to my drafts, and made many helpful suggestions. I am also heavily indebted to my neighbour Martin Allen for his frequent and invaluable help on the IT front, to my omnicompetent and patient publisher Roger Jones and to Tracey Williams for PR advice.

Chapter 1

Early years and family background (1934-1943)

In early July 1940 my grandmother, my sister Elisabeth and I found ourselves embarking at Greenock in Scotland onto the *Monarch of Bermuda*, a former luxury cruise liner, for Halifax in Canada. Having been born on September 15 1934, I was two months off my sixth birthday, Lis was ten rising 11, Gran (my mother's mother) in her mid-60s. Our hastily organised odyssey was not exceptional. Hitler's Blitzkrieg in mainland Europe, the fall of France and the onset of the bombing of Britain in June 1940 had generated a real fear that Britain too would be invaded. Tens of thousands of children were despatched to Australia, New Zealand, Canada and the USA, while many from London were evacuated to parts of Britain (including, ironically, my grandmother's house in Essex) deemed less vulnerable to bombing. Robert and Sigrid Keyserlingk, friends of my parents from their days together in Berlin, had very generously offered to welcome the three of us into their home in Montreal.

Our boat was to be part of a large transatlantic convoy consisting of the battleship *Revenge*, the cruiser *Bonaventure*, two Free Polish former liners, the *Sobieski* and the *Batory*, and an escort of four destroyers, all under the command of a British admiral. In the previous two weeks, 28 Allied ships had been destroyed at sea. Needless to say, this escort was not to safeguard a bunch of evacuees. As was subsequently revealed, on board was perhaps the greatest combined load of treasure ever transported by land or sea. It included the entire gold bullion and securities normally held by the Bank of England, together worth an estimated £442m. Quite how this was distributed among the various ships is not clear, but it seems likely that the *Monarch* of Bermuda had its share. The bullion was destined for safekeeping in the vaults of the Bank of Canada in Ottawa. The Polish vessels carried treasures from the Wawel Castle in Cracow.

There is no evidence that the Germans knew anything of the convoy's cargo, though its size and the high speed at which it travelled must have aroused suspicion. My sister recalls that we had a boat drill very soon after departure. Later on the *Monarch* was violently rocked by an explosion. A German U-boat had apparently penetrated the convoy's defences, and a depth-charge from an escorting warship had found its mark. The captain came on the ship's loudspeakers to tell us not to worry – we had merely hit a shoal of porpoises. Some porpoises! That September, another British liner on the same route, *The City of Benares*, was less fortunate. It sank 30 minutes after being hit by a torpedo, with the loss of 248 lives, including those of 77 child evacuees. Thirteen of the 90 children on board survived 19 hours in the sea, holding on to bits of lifeboats, before the first rescue ship arrived. At the age of five I would almost certainly not have been among them. Most of the children on board our ship were unescorted, so we were privileged to have our grandmother with us.

Having made it safely to Halifax, we proceeded to Montreal and into the bosom of the Keyserlingk family. It consisted of Robert and Sigrid Keyserlingk and their children Bob, just older than me, Teddy, a year or two younger, and Cecilie (Cissy). Both Uncle Bob, as I came to call him, and Aunt Sigrid were of the German-speaking Baltic ascendancy, and sometimes lapsed into German at table. Bob Snr was also fluent in Russian. Although English had become their first language, Sigrid spoke it with a German accent. English was still the dominant language in Montreal.

Uncle Bob had been brought up in St Petersburg, Vladivostok, Yokohama, Kobe and Shanghai, his father having been variously an officer in the Russian navy and a pioneering whaler who escaped from the Russian revolution to Japan in 1917. Having attended a Canadian school in Japan, Uncle Bob settled in Canada, went to university in British Columbia, and before long found a job as a journalist for the United Press in Berlin. En route he had called on some relatives in the family's native Lithuania, where he met Sigrid and that very day asked her to marry him – which she did two and a half years later, in 1932. In Berlin the Keyserlingks came to know my parents, a friendship deepened after they were moved to London in 1935, shortly before my parents' own return to England in 1936. Of greater relevance to me as a five-year-old, they were a warm-hearted couple and made me feel part of the family, to which another son was before long to be added. As I later learned, Sigrid had as a teenager been forced to watch her parents being murdered by the Bolsheviks. Probably as a result, she was vulnerable to depressions, of which I was not then conscious.

I remember feeling acutely homesick on my first evening in this unfamiliar household. Happily, my grandmother was there to comfort me. But the Keyserlingks had evidently overestimated their capacity to absorb all three of us. Within a few days Gran was redeployed to some suitable friends of theirs, where she was humiliatingly dependent, being unable to extract her money from England. She soon retreated to the warmer climes of Bermuda, where access to funds seems to have been easier, returning to England in 1942. Sister Lis meanwhile was passed to an unmarried friend of the Keyserlingks in Montreal, an interior decorator called Edith Henderson. They seemed to get on well. We saw surprisingly little of each other, and after two years Lis was taken down to Cambridge, Mass., whence Ms Henderson came.

My memories of Canada focus on the 200-acre farm the Keyserlingks had fairly recently acquired. The property overlooked Lac Labelle in the Laurentian Mountains, some 80 miles north of Montreal. Much of the road was then a rough gravel track, and there was always a sense of adventure in our trips to the farm. These took place mainly in the long summer vacations. Although a generous sprinkling of fellow white Russians gradually settled or built holiday homes in the vicinity, the area was still largely undeveloped, having been opened up only 60 years previously. No human habitation was visible across the vast (as it then seemed) lake. Behind the log house where we stayed – a much larger clapboard house began to be built higher up the slope before I left – virgin forest stretched endlessly, home to bears, deer and coyotes, not to mention wild strawberries, raspberries and bilberries, which we were commissioned to pick for a small reward. Skunks and porcupines were frequently to be seen and smelt. From the birch-fringed lake came the eerie cries of loons (divers) and the croaking of bullfrogs. On the farm, which was managed by a resident farmer, were cows, pigs, sheep, chickens and turkeys, with whose feeding we became enjoyably involved.

Left: With 'Uncle Bob' Keyserlingk in Labelle;
Right: Feeding the pigs in Labelle with Ted Keyserlingk

I had a pet hen, which I used to put on my lap and stroke while it made a sort of purring cluck. One day it laid a shell-less egg on my thigh. I was very touched, and hopped, thigh parallel to the ground, to the kitchen so that it should not be wasted. Alas, it slipped off before I got there. One of the turkeys vanished into the forest one summer, and I was thrilled to witness its return leading a long line of chicks. A less happy memory is of the periodic slaughtering of a pig. We children took refuge down by the lake, and I expect I kept my hands over my ears to keep out its terrible squealing. I always liked pigs, and adored piglets. (So much contact with animals made me want to be a farmer. But a stay on my godmother Paddy Ullstein's farm in Suffolk in my early teens cured me: a boar attacked me when I was cleaning out its stall, and Paddy's husband Fritz seemed oppressed by bureaucracy, staff problems and the wrong weather).

Lac Labelle itself was an endless source of pleasure. In those days it teemed with fish. A stick, some string and a bent pin with a worm on it sufficed to catch as many as we could eat: grayling, trout, whitefish, perch, all delicious. I was less enamoured of the leeches and bullfrogs, which we cruelly threw as far as we could onto the water. At least one was shoved down my shirt, and once Bob and Ted dug a hole in the beach, filled it with frogs, covered it over, and then suggested a game of follow-my-leader. Needless to say I fell in and was a great deal less amused than they were. I've avoided frogs ever since. I soon learned to swim, albeit only a dog paddle, and we had a great time out on the lake in the canoe.

The Keyserlingks' house in West Montreal was less inspiring, but it was possible to ski and toboggan in the vicinity and on the slopes of Mount Royal. Winters, which we spent in town, could be exciting. The snowploughs threw up great walls of snow (as they seemed) on either side of the road. We would fortify sections near our house by pouring water on them. It soon turned to ice. The Keyserlingks were Anglicans in those days (they later converted to Catholicism), and from behind our fortress we would throw icy snowballs, sometimes spiked with small stones, at passing children from the Catholic school. This was after all Quebec, and most of the majority (in those days somewhat second class) population were French-speaking Catholics. When the Keyserlingks converted, their children had frozen snowballs thrown at them. Happily, Northern Ireland it wasn't. But I remember being chased by a youth: I had skilfully thrown a stick into the front wheel spokes of his bicycle, causing him to fly off. I just made it to the safety of our house at 47 Ballantyne Avenue North. Somehow a neighbourhood red setter was involved in the conflict, and I was deeply upset when it emerged from a fight with another dog with half its tongue bitten off.

My memories of the primary school I attended in Montreal are unscarred by any unpleasantness. Sigrid sent a copy of my first six-monthly report to my mother, which showed As for arithmetic, writing, effort and cooperation, and a B for reading. She told my mother how happy I was to have received a photograph of her. 'It hangs over his bed and after we have prayed, he often turns to it and gives it a kiss and says: "Now I will say goodnight to my dear mummy."' What an adorable child! A letter I wrote to my brother Martin on 15 March 1941 in large capital letters was admirably succinct:

'DEAR MARTIN
THANK YOU FOR YOUR LETTER WE STILL HAVE LOTS OF SNOW
MUCH LOVE FROM ROGER BERTHOUD'

To judge by the much smaller and greatly improved handwriting, a poem I sent my parents probably dates from the following year:

Before Thanksgiving morn.

There was a little turkey Who gobbled, gobbled, gobbled
He was roly poly He wobbled, wobbled, wobbled.
He grew so plump and beautiful Before Thanksgiving Day

He thought it would be safer for him to run away
                    Made by Roger Berthoud

This was probably when I peaked as a poet.

It wasn't just farm birds that appealed to me. The Montreal suburb where we lived had plenty of bird life, and I was thrilled by the scarlet tanagers and golden orioles. Birds were to be an interest for life.

It's odd that so little effort was made to bring my sister Lis and me together in Montreal. Perhaps it was thought it would be unsettling. However, in September 1941 we were both visited by my father in the course of his extended visit to Washington to discuss aid to the Soviet Union with, among others, its American supervisor Harry Hopkins, at the White House. We were very excited to see him.

The return journey

Because I would be nine years old in September 1943, my parents decided that – despite the hazards of the journey – my education at the prep-school my brother Martin was attending would suffer if I did not return for the autumn term. It was agreed that Uncle Bob should take me down to the eastern seaboard of the USA to catch a Portuguese liner called the *Serpa Pinto*. Portugal was neutral, which was supposed to make the ship safe from U-boat attacks, though the Germans must have known it would be stuffed with Britons. I was to be escorted by Bridget le Rougetel, daughter of Sir Ian le Rougetel, a diplomatic friend of my father from his earlier stint in the Bucharest embassy, though she was only 13. It's odd that Lis, who was also 13, did not come too: perhaps our parents did not want to risk both of us at the same time. She made the crossing a few months later.

I remember my excitement as we left Labelle in the handsome red Keyserlingk saloon, only to be held up for miles by a calf that had strayed onto the track and refused to get off. We must have taken a train from Montreal to New York, where we went to the top of the Empire State building. It was very windy up there, and somebody's hat got blown off, to my amusement. Uncle Bob bought me my first watch as a farewell present, saw me into my shared cabin on the *Serpa Pinto* in Philadelphia, and doubtless linked me up with my escort. Bridget was pig-tailed and very friendly, and found me 'a jolly, cheeky little boy.' The mixed bunch of passengers, she recalled, included a party of girls from Roedean escorted by a rather strict teacher. They were shut up early in their cabins each night, making us feel very superior. There was also an unfriendly German couple; and some cows, whose fresh milk and cream enriched the delicious food. We used to go and visit them, and greatly enjoyed scrambling up and down ladders. We took our meals with a very nice Mrs Galpin: she and her husband Michael, an oil man, had also been in Bucharest. The waiters, and crew generally, were very kind to us, and tried to teach us some words of Portuguese.

The highlight of the trip was the Captain's fancy dress ball. Mrs Galpin must have helped us with our costumes. I was a pirate and Bridget a spy. We discovered that the stand-offish German couple – who probably felt thoroughly guilty about being German in this context – were not attending and would be hiding away somewhere. Bridget takes the blame for the shameful prank we played on them. They had left their cabin door unlocked. We crept in and dressed up their pillows to look like monsters, using her makeup to give them a ghoulish look. Then we crept out and joined the party, proud to have made our contribution to the allied war effort. Bridget and I later hoped those Germans smiled and shrugged it off. (Bridget married a very Scottish diplomat, Arthur Kellas, and I spent some memorable days at their turf-roofed log cabin on the coast of the Ardnamurchan peninsula in Scotland. We remained in touch until her death in 2008.)

After stopping off at the (Portuguese) Azores, where I remember seeing a wheel fall off an ox-drawn cart, the *Serpa Pinto* docked in Lisbon. Our journey had given me a taste for sea travel, perhaps even sea legs. In Lisbon some kind people took us on a tour of the narrow, winding streets of the capital, which seemed very picturesque. Then we had dinner in a hotel before being whisked off to the airport for a very cold and uncomfortable flight in a Dakota to Bristol, and thence by train to Paddington.

I must have been told that England was a rather small and crowded country, since I was surprised and relieved to see so many fields with cows, sheep and crops in them, and even some woods. I was none too sure I would recognise my parents at Paddington, despite Dad's visit to Montreal. I asked one or two people if they were Mr and Mrs Berthoud – and then spotted the genuine articles some way off. I ran towards them, and fell over in my excitement. When we reached the family thatched cottage, of which I had no memory, I famously said in my broad Canadian accent: 'Gee, Dad, that's a cute little property you've got here!' I had an eye for it even in those days.

Tough though they were initially, I've come to regard my three years with the Keyserlingks as a great enrichment of my life. I later kept in touch by letter with Uncle Bob and Sigrid, went back to Canada a couple of times when they were alive, and on one happy occasion welcomed them to our home in Hampstead. I came to realise that as a couple they had a lot in common with my own parents. Uncle Bob was at least as dominant as my father, no less sure that his way was the right way and his views the right views, but he enjoyed debate more than my father, despite being more of a monologuist, and was perhaps less liable to lose his cool. Both could be enormously charming and convivial. Sigrid was superficially more self-effacing than my mother, but according to her sons was more likely to interrupt Bob Snr's flow with a bracing 'Nonsense!' Like my father, he also used her bouts of ill-health to his own advantage, under a veil of protectiveness.

The greatest gain was my lifelong friendship (school years apart) with Bob Jnr. We were to spend several holidays together, in Copenhagen and Paris for example and more recently with his wife Ela in Labelle and New Orleans, and at one stage I shared a flat with Bob in South Kensington for nine months. With nobody else have I had so many uproarious laughs. Even his deplorably conservative political views could not come between us.

I have sometimes wondered how I might have been different had I not been evacuated. Probably the experience of being taken away from a loving mother at the age of five made me even more self-sufficient than ten years of boarding school and two of National Service would have done. Self-sufficiency is not an engaging characteristic in a husband: most women like to be needed. Perhaps the experience made it more difficult for me to give a full emotional commitment to anyone (except my daughters). It may also have made me attach excessive importance to imposing my taste on my surroundings, as a means of defining my identity.

Family background: my father

It must be a mixed blessing to be the son of a famous person. It was difficult enough to be the son of Sir Eric Berthoud KCMG. Dad was a man of great intelligence, energy and charm (when so minded); and in his various careers he was pretty successful. But vis-à-vis his family – and sometimes to others – he could be hyper-critical, inflexible, intolerant and short-tempered. Fortunately he could also be affectionate, generous and supportive, not least to us children in our various careers.

His insistence that he was right probably sprang from an underlying sense of insecurity, deriving from his reaction to his own family background. Whereas his four siblings seemed to relish and cherish their partially Swiss and French origins, two of them marrying Swiss citizens, Dad reacted by being *plus anglais que les anglais*. He never joined family walking holidays in the Swiss Alps, carefully retained an English edge to his fluent French, and ended his career not just as a British ambassador but as the squire of an Essex hamlet dominated by our handsome Queen Anne house with its dozen or so bedrooms and as many acres. That element of insecurity helped drive him onwards and upwards. His siblings seemed to feel no such pressure.

Eric Alfred Berthoud (he became Sir Eric in 1954 as ambassador in Copenhagen) was born in December 1900 and could just claim to be a Victorian: Queen Victoria died a month later. In his own memoirs he traced the family tree back to 1592, when one Jaques Berthoud was enrolled as a citizen of Neuchâtel in Switzerland. It has always been assumed that the family derived from French Huguenots, probably from the Savoie region. Pride in this background once led Dad to say to Bob Keyserlingk Snr, a Roman Catholic convert: 'Of course my family has never been Catholic', to which Bob Keyserlingk responded: 'Eric, I never realised your family was so recent!' a master-thrust that Dad was happy to recall.

Our Swiss background

Key figures: Dad's grandfather Alphonse, his father Alfred, his mother Hélène.
Other players: his siblings Francis (called Bobby), Maysie, George, Oliver.

Our branch of the Berthoud family derived from the village of Boudevilliers, seven miles from Neuchâtel. The well-known 18th century clockmaker came from a different branch in Fleurier, as did the more recent US Army Captain Edward Louis Berthoud (1828-1908), who discovered the first pass over the Rockies in Colorado, called Berthoud Pass, and gave his name to the nearby town of Berthoud, both of which I have visited. Edward the engineer was brought to New York by his parents from Geneva aged two, had six siblings, and played a prominent part in bringing railways to the Denver area. There is also a major French agricultural machinery company called Berthoud and a Swiss supermarket, not to mention a restaurant in Paris and a Savoyard cheese sauce. In short, the name is far from rare.

Dad's grandfather Alphonse came to England when he was 18, in 1857. Eleven years later, when he was well-established in the London branch of a family-related merchant bank, he became a naturalised British subject just before marrying the daughter of a prosperous Exeter family: they would not allow their daughter to marry a foreigner. Their son, my grandfather Alfred, was born exactly nine months after that marriage, followed by three more boys and two girls. They had a substantial house near Walthamstow in Essex. Like many an upwardly mobile immigrant, Alphonse developed rather grandiose ideas. First he bought a small castle perched on a hill 12 miles from Neuchâtel, the Château de Gorgier, dating from the 13th century (my wife Joy and I were shown around it by its American owners in the 1970s).

Son Alfred (my grandfather), poor fellow, was sent to live there and attend secondary school in Neuchâtel, while his brothers went to public schools in England. He was presumably looked after by servants and wealthy relatives: the family bank derived from cousins called de Coulon, who had a large holiday home not far from Gorgier. Dad attributed some of his father's subsequent problems, which included drinking too much, to that lonely Swiss sojourn.

Alphonse gave up the Gorgier estate after 11 years, but then leased Dromore Castle in Co. Kerry in south-west Ireland. This was a large, castellated edifice with gardens leading down to an estuary and around 700 acres of parkland and forest rich in wild life. Dad spent many enjoyable holidays there. His father Alfred brought his fiancée Hélène Christ to Dromore when he married her in 1896. She was to prove tougher than him: shortish in stature, beautiful, energetic, intellectual in her interests, and a loving if demanding – and to my father, irritatingly French – mother.

Grandma, as we used to call her, was 20 when she married: Swiss on her father's side (from Basel) and Alsatian (from Mulhouse, where she was born) on her mother's. The common factor was banking, in which her father was successfully engaged. Alsace was

German at the time: it had been seized in 1871, four years before my grandmother was born, and she was to be fiercely anti-German and proudly francophile and francophone all her life. Though she spoke good English, her French accent and mannerisms were to be a source of embarrassment to Dad for much of his early life.

She and Alfred settled in Kensington, where their first three children were born: Violet, Francis, always called Bobby, and my father Eric. Violet died shortly after my father's birth in 1900. The family then moved to a spacious house in Wimbledon, where Maysie, George and Oliver were born. Their solid world was soon to be savagely disrupted. Alfred proved a disaster as a banker. In February 1914, three years after he had taken over, Coulon, Berthoud & Co suspended payments. If my father's memory was correct, creditors received no more than 10 per cent of their deposits. Alfred's siblings, most of them far from well off, lost every penny of their share of their father's £70,000 will (notionally worth some £3.5m today); and many of them, along with members of the public, must have said goodbye to such assets as they had entrusted to the family bank. Its failure was attributed to over-speculative investments, notably – as so often in that era – in Latin America.

All this was deeply shaming to my grandfather, at whom most of the odium for the collapse was directed. No doubt drink helped ease the pain. What little my father said about him suggests a somewhat weak, self-indulgent if affectionate and easy-going man. After the First World War, during which he served in the government's Press Bureau, he joined a firm of city stockbrokers. He died in 1920, aged only 50, at the Eccentric Club, where he had, as often, gone to play bridge. It seems he collapsed in a toilet and somehow suffocated: a sad and disappointed man, as my father (then a 20-year-old Oxford undergraduate) later commented, and the very antithesis of what Dad himself was to become.

Dad's fraught education

These dramas, in particular the crash of the family bank, had serious repercussions. Along with his older brother Bobby, Dad had been sent, aged 12, to a relatively progressive public school in Norfolk, Gresham's Holt, still flourishing. His mother disliked the emphasis at most public schools on team games, which the Gresham's ethos sought to replace by putting intellect above sport, encouraging the teaching of science and the pursuit of hobbies and other interests. The first headmaster of the new Gresham's (it had been a small local grammar school) was G.W.S.Howson, formerly a lowly assistant science master at Uppingham: a remarkable appointment.

Howson, a bachelor, had introduced the so-called Honour System, under which every new boy was obliged to promise first him, then his housemaster that he would avoid smoking, swearing and 'indecency'. Any boy who broke a promise was expected to 'own up'. If he discovered another boy breaking a promise, he should try to persuade him to confess or, failing that, report him to his housemaster. With its combination of the repression of adolescent sexuality, pressure to act as an informer while fearing being informed on, this vow – for such it must have seemed – had a devastating effect on many boys. In a rather dubious estimate, my father reckoned that among the most promising of his contemporaries at school, a third suffered mental or physical breakdowns, if only temporary and often after leaving school.

As Benjamin Britten, who followed his subsequent friend W.H.Auden to Gresham's, put it: 'It is no good trying the Honour System on boys who have no honour. Boys, small & rather weak are turned into sour & bitter boys, & ruined for life.' After a year at Gresham's, Britten became the object of my uncle Oliver's affections, Oliver having followed his brothers to Gresham's and by that stage become a sixth-former. The precocious Britten, who found bullying rife at Gresham's and was miserable there, confided early on to his diary: 'The only reason I don't want the end of term is because Berthoud is leaving. He has been marvellous to me, in spite of being a house pre[fect]…' Oliver was the only genuinely musical member of my father's family, becoming an accomplished viola player. My father would have thought Britten a wimp. Donald Maclean was another Gresham's alumnus, and Dad reckoned that the descent of this former model pupil (and Cabinet minister's son) into spying for the Soviet Union and alcoholism could have been attributable to the Honour System. So, perhaps, could some elements of Britten's genius.

Howson, the code's progenitor, was also the housemaster of School House, to which my father and his older brother Bobby were consigned. One of his sisters was the house matron, another in charge of the kitchen. Whatever the nature of Howson's repressed sexuality, my father undoubtedly aroused his affectionately protective and paternal instincts: all the more so since much of the Berthoud family had decamped to Neuchâtel for the duration of the First World War, when my father was aged 14 to18, leaving Bobby and Eric at Gresham's and their father working full-time in London. Thanks to the latter's role in sinking the family bank, no support was forthcoming from relatives elsewhere in England, leaving the two teenagers 'somewhat stranded', as my father put it, during holidays. Although their father did his best to help, it was Howson who tended to act *in loco parentis*. For example, he took them and other boys to fish in Yorkshire, initiating my father into the delights of wet-fly fishing.

With his energy, good looks, all-round athletic (captain of cricket and rugby, vice-captain of hockey) and intellectual abilities, my father was the son that Howson never had. Howson stepped into the breach once again in June 1915 when, as a delayed result of the family bank's collapse, it was decided that my father should leave Gresham's and complete his education in Switzerland. He was 14 and a half, and the prospect appalled him. It was considered too late to transplant Bobby, who was 16. The family finances were straitened, and his maternal grandfather had offered to pay for his education in Switzerland. But a month later my father was able to record in his diary: 'Papa has just written to tell me that Mr Howson is keeping me on by giving me an honorary scholarship. I am awfully grateful'.

Howson explained that at a time of terrible war casualties, 'I want to keep him as a British boy for his own benefit and for that of his country.' In subsequent talks with my father, Howson told him that he was not yet sure that his character was up to the standard of his work and games. He said he wanted complete frankness in their relationship, not least on the sexual front. Luckily, young Eric seems to have had nothing to confess: not even what he called solo indulgence, which was heavily frowned on and considered debilitating and deleterious to health. I was later to suffer painfully from the indoctrination he endured in this field.

The weight of the pressures on him may be gauged from an episode that caused him shame for the rest of his life. It involved a junior boy called Tom Garland. My father was captain of cricket and a school prefect, and found it necessary to address the assembled school on the need for the younger elements to take their cricket more seriously: presumably this was at the end of a school assembly. As he left the hall, young Garland clapped ironically and said 'Well done!' or something similar. My father considered this intolerable impertinence, and obtained Howson's permission to cane this subversive youth.

Caning of any sort was unusual at Gresham's, let alone a caning in front of the whole school, with my father flanked on the platform by the other broadly supportive school prefects. Unfortunately the number of strokes to be administered had not been agreed, and a red mist seems to have descended over my father once he got going. The number of lashes he inflicted seems to have considerably exceeded the normal maximum of six, and he probably had to be restrained. Garland's liberal housemaster complained, and Howson had to fight the rest of his staff to prevent my father from being demoted as a school prefect – which, he later admitted, he should have been. Dad was obliged to apologise to the whole school after morning prayers next day.

Tom Garland meanwhile emerged from the ordeal as a hero. Later he became a doctor in the Midlands, and was radicalised by the poverty and ill-health he found in the industrial slums during the Depression, becoming a Communist sympathiser and emigrating to New Zealand after the Second World War. My father eventually wrote to him to apologise and, in effect, seek his forgiveness. The resulting correspondence seems to have helped Dad live with his remorse.

One of Tom Garland's six children is the well-known political cartoonist Nick Garland, to whom I owe some of this information. When I discovered the link, I brought him and Dad together for lunch. Dad was then nearly 85, so not at his best, but the occasion went quite well. Some differing perspectives emerged, inevitably. Nick said his father had always associated the 'too many of the best' incident with rugger rather than cricket, which he loved. In the course of the subsequent school holiday Howson had, he recalled, uncharacteristically written his father a letter saying he hoped he had had a good holiday and was looking on life positively – clearly feeling guilty about what his protégé had done.

A discussion ensued over the lunch table about the damaging effects of public schools on the emotional lives of those who attended them. Nick said his father had become something of a womaniser once he got going after university. My father said that Howson's anathematising of sex had caused him serious problems in later life (probably he had little experience between university and marriage). He reiterated his conviction that he was unusually highly sexed as a young man. I said an awful lot of men thought that of themselves. To me, the chief legacy of boarding schools, with their lack of social contact with girls and enforced sexual abstinence, was to make ex-public schoolboys – initially at least – even more prone than other young men to regard women primarily as sexual targets rather than companions and friends.

Dad eventually rewarded Howson by winning various exhibitions to Magdalen College, Oxford. He was in Cheshire on a tutoring job when, in January 1919, he read in the *Times* that Howson had died suddenly. Without him my father would have completed his education in Switzerland, and his subsequent life would have been very different.

Sir Herbert Warren, the President of Magdalen College, where my father read chemistry, was a noted snob, and among the college's 180 graduates were numerous Old Etonians as well as many war veterans. When a Japanese envoy sought to enrol Prince Chichibu, the second son of the Emperor of Japan, the envoy stressed that the prince was worthy of every respect, being descended from the Almighty. 'We are accustomed to receiving the sons of distinguished people', the President is said to have replied.

Some of Dad's regard for Britain's aristocracy may have stemmed from the atmosphere at Magdalen. He said it was friendly and unsnobbish, even towards someone with a foreign name from an obscure public school who was studying science, not a strong combination in those days. He was also influenced by his tutoring jobs. Two were with the family of Lord Clinton, who had three country estates; another with the vastly wealthy Marquis of Bute on the family's estate in Andalusia, for which Dad rather ruthlessly dumped the Clinton boy. The additional income was useful, and he was impressed by the grandeur of it all, if not always by the food.

At Oxford, Dad devoted most of his afternoons to playing rugger, hockey or cricket for the college and, in the case of hockey, for the university. He was also made commander of the Magdalen corps of the Oxford Office Training Corps. All this helped build his self-confidence and his powers of leadership, but in later years led him to believe that what had been good for him would be good for his two sons. As a teenager, no word was to induce in me a greater sense of loathing than 'leadership'. I wonder whether his faith in the character-building attributes of team games would have survived today's revelations about the off-pitch antics of some leading footballers. One can have team spirit, say in the workplace, without having excelled at team games.

On leaving Oxford, Dad opted for a post in Vienna with the Anglo-Austrian Bank. Banking was after all in the blood. The Austrian Bank had ended the war owing the Bank of England some £3m (multiply by 50 for today's equivalent), and the latter had taken it over in conjunction with Glyn, Mills of Lombard Street. A very enjoyable two years ensued in rump-Austria's empire-sized capital, where my father learned German, made many friends, savoured Furtwängler conducting at the opera house and the cuisine of the Sacher Hotel.

After a spell in Milan and at head office in London, he joined the Anglo-Persian

Oil Company, which became British Petroleum. He started as personal assistant in Paris to the leading director of its French subsidiary. The experience in banking was valuable: Dad was always a shrewd investor, and judiciously generous with such money as he could spare.

In the summer of 1926, between the two jobs, he met my mother Ruth Bright at a house party in Ugley, Essex. They were married in Great Hallingbury, near Bishop's Stortford, on New Year's Day 1927, when they were both just over 26. After a honeymoon in Cap Ferrat, they settled in Paris. A cousin sent them a photograph taken at the wedding, inscribed on the back: 'Eric and Ruth Berthoud are one, and that one is Eric Berthoud.' Dad used to tell the story with pride.

My mother's family background

Key players: the Gosling tribe, including her mother Isobella (known as Isabel), and her father Charles Bright (Jnr), later knighted but not to be confused with his father Sir Charles Bright (Snr).

Gran was among the youngest of the 16 children of Robert Gosling, who owned 6,000 acres of tenanted farms near Stansted and the Essex/Hertfordshire border. Much of the family fortune came from the long-established Goslings Bank at 19 Fleet Street, notably from its merger in 1895 with Barclays Bank, when it became merely Goslings Branch. First came six girls, one of whom died aged 30, then eight boys, one of whom survived little more than a year, interspersed with two more girls, among them our splendid grandmother.

To accommodate this vast brood, Robert Gosling pulled down the handsome old family home and replaced it with a vast Victorian pile called Hassobury, so large it later became a prep-school. They also had, for the 'season', a fine Adam house at 28 Portland Place, W.1. now the headquarters of the Royal Institute of Health and Hygiene. The older girls were educated at home, but the two younger ones, including my future grandmother, went to boarding school. The boys inevitably went to Eton, where there were at one stage five at the same time. Several were outstanding athletes. Cunliffe, for example, played cricket for Cambridge and Essex, and football for England on five occasions. Despite being, like most of his brothers, more than six feet tall, he was notably quick on his feet. Another, Ben, co-led the scientifically very successful Alexander-Gosling expedition to the Niger and the Nile (1904-6), towards the end of which he died of blackwater fever, aged 33. Three brothers survived the Boer War, and several became masters of foxhounds. Shooting was high among family pastimes. A certain closeness with money was a Gosling characteristic.

The male Goslings of that generation tended to be buttoned-up and inarticulate: probably, as my mother surmised, because they spent a lot of time in each other's company. As she observed: 'One does not invite a family of 15 to tea or tennis or croquet.' So, apart from the explorer Ben, they remained in some ways immature, their

Gran

interests restricted to 'country pursuits.' Their wives must have had a tough time. My grandmother was very down-to-earth and, in large matters, a generous and supportive woman with wonderful violet blue eyes. She inspired a great deal of affection, not least in her son-in-law and grandchildren, but my mother found her hard to communicate with. Gran remained remarkably fit till her death at the same age as her mother, 93.

My mother Ruth and her brother Geoffrey spent many school holidays at Hassobury, accompanied by Gran's parlour maid, Alice. On arrival from the station in the brougham, my mother would be transported with delight by the smell in the great hall of burning logs, furniture and floor polish. Inevitably she was spoiled by her unmarried uncles, one of whom taught her to play the pianola, and befriended by various members of the vast staff. Among them was the head groom, Bird, a special favourite, whose equine charges included the mowing pony, which wore special leather shoes when pulling the mower.

My grandmother had been forbidden by her father to marry anyone worth less than £1,000 a year, equivalent of some £50,000 today. So she waited till he died, and at age 30 married Charles Bright, whose love of cricket had brought him to Hassobury as guest and player. The Bright family came from Yorkshire. Charles Bright's father, Sir Charles Tilston Bright, was an outstanding figure in the history of electrical engineering. He and his elder brothers went to school at Merchant Taylor's and were intended for Oxford. But for financial reasons Edward and Charles had to be withdrawn when they were 16 and 15 years old, and joined the Electric Telegraph Company. Within a year both became inventors, soon joining separate and rival telegraph companies.

By the age of 20, Charles Bright had patented 24 separate inventions (many still in use) and become chief engineer of the Magnetic Telegraph Company. In 1858, when only 26, he was knighted for his key role in laying the first Atlantic cable, more than 2,000 miles long, between the United States and the westward tip of Ireland, a feat attended by appalling difficulties and regarded by many scientists as impossible. It was hailed at the time as the greatest scientific achievement of the century, and Sir Charles was certainly among the youngest men to be knighted in the industrial era. Why is he not better known? After many further submarine cable undertakings in the Mediterranean, Caribbean and Indian oceans, he became an MP at the age of 33, dying in 1888, aged 55. The *Times* commented: 'Few men have ever done more useful work for his country and for commerce within less than forty years.'

Unfortunately Isabel's intended, confusingly also called Charles Bright and also eventually knighted, was not made in the same heroic mould, to put it *mildement*, as my brother and I used to say in our teenaged proto-franglais. His problem, at least as my mother saw it, was that his father's frail wife adored and spoiled her only son, despite also having two daughters, one of whom, Beatrice Bright, became a distinguished painter. The younger Charles followed his father into electrical engineering. If he expected to be spoiled by his robust Gosling wife, he must have had a (non-electric) shock. Perhaps as a reaction, he became hypochondriacal: his doctor later described him as the most neurotic man he had ever known. It can't have helped

Charles Bright when knighted aged 26

that once our mother Ruth and her brother Geoffrey had been born, Gran ended such sex life as they had had. My mother remembered meals as an endless stream of complaints and marital bickering.

Yet the second Charles Bright must have been a more effective and less weak man than my mother portrays him in her memoirs. The first 15 years of his career were devoted to continuing his father's marine cable work. He subsequently turned his attention to the application of wireless telegraphy, first to shipping and coastal wireless stations, and then to aeroplanes. Thanks in part to his far-flung work as a cable engineer and broad knowledge of and interest in the Empire, he sat on many government commissions and committees. He also wrote six books, including *Science and Engineering during the Victorian Era*, and was knighted for his services to engineering. He died in 1937, when he was 73 and I was three.

The unhappy home atmosphere and their parents' emotional inadequacies took their toll on my mother, and more particularly on her brother Geoffrey. During his late teens at Eton (an uncle paid the fees), he and his father were not on speaking terms. His housemaster was a bachelor, the school food was terrible, and he began a long slide into anorexia, probably aggravated by a tubercular appendix and untreated concussion from a fall in the school gym. He made it to Hertford College, Oxford, but before long was taken first to hospital, then – when the hospital explained that death was bad for other patients' morale – to a nursing home. After many months and many visits from his mother and sister, he died of pneumonia. For the rest of her life my mother felt she had failed to give her adored brother adequate support, though she seems to have done her best. She laid Geoffrey's death at their father's door. Criticising the illogicality of pacifist attitudes in a letter to me at school in 1950, she said: 'My father for instance killed my brother, indirectly perhaps but far more painfully than ever happens in war time' – an overstatement of course, but it showed how bitter she felt, and why she came to scorn her father.

A complementary union

Given their respective backgrounds, the dice seemed to be loaded against my parents settling into a happy relationship. Yet they were in many respects quite well matched. My father was an optimist, my mother a pessimist. My father liked to dominate; my mother was naturally quite diffident. It was less than ideal, however, that whereas he greatly enjoyed social life,

My mother in her 50s

she preferred it in small doses, despite her gift for genuine friendship. In later life he would use her various minor ailments, notably headaches, to go to parties alone, saying: 'I don't think Mother is quite well enough to come out this evening.'

Their marriage soon ran into tragedy in Paris. When their first-born son Julian was almost one year old, my mother was obliged by their social life to take on a nanny. Julian soon developed intestinal trouble, probably due to insufficiently boiled milk, and had to be put on a milkless diet. While out with his nanny he subsequently fell, and a tooth pierced his inner cheek, initially unnoticed. His blood would not coagulate, and he died of haemorrhage within a few days. Coming two and a half years after Geoffrey's death, this was a cruel blow, especially for my mother. A move from their sunless flat to a villa overlooking a park helped restore morale, and my mother was soon pregnant again.

BP reckoned that a change of scene might be helpful, and they were sent to Berlin in 1929, before the birth of my sister Elisabeth on December 13, and around the time of the Wall Street crash of that October, which heralded the Great Depression of the 1930s. Although during the previous five years life in Germany had improved considerably and foreign businessmen were once again investing there, the country had been morally as well as financially eviscerated by the hyper-inflation of 1923. That provided the rich seedbed for Hitler's rise to power, in part because Jewish financiers were easily blamed for both causing it and profiting from it. Yet by 1928 Hitler seemed to be fading into oblivion: in the May elections of that year, the National Socialist party won only 2.6 per cent of the vote, entitling it to 12 Reichstag seats. Hitler was saved by the Wall Street crash. Before it, some two million Germans were out of work. By January 1930, they exceeded three million and by 1932 the official figure stood at six million, in reality probably nearer nine million, or one in three of the workforce. Many put their hopes in Hitler, who promised action and seemed able to deliver it; others in communism, of which Germany's industrialists were deeply afraid.

Doubtless day to day life in Berlin did not reflect all this, but my father would soon have been abreast of the political situation, which was to lend his job a ghastly fascination. BP held a 75 per cent interest in a German oil company called Olex, which in turn had some 10 per cent of the domestic market, with a network of petrol pumps across the country. My father was to be the senior representative of the parent company, BP, with an office next to the general manager's, and to report independently on all policy developments. It cannot have been easy to be a sort of head office spy without inspiring resentment in his German colleagues.

Hitler was appointed Chancellor on January 30 1933. The most direct effect of his regime on Olex was the obligation before long to fire anyone who had as much as one Jewish grandparent. A substantial proportion of Olex's management fell into this bracket. Being subject to German law, BP could do nothing to spare them (except generously compensate those who managed to go abroad). The law had to be enforced from top to bottom. It was, my father said, a terrible experience.

Happily, he was able to make a valuable contribution to British intelligence about Germany's rearmament, which flouted the terms of the Versailles treaty. Increased military activity necessitated increased supplies of oil. Olex was a favoured source for the air force, the oil being notionally channelled through the civilian airline Lufthansa. Demand increased noticeably from mid-1934 – in part, my father discovered, thanks to the setting up of large numbers of new aerodromes, allegedly for the training of additional civilian pilots. He was able to establish the location of some 40 of them, and their oil consumption. He passed the information to the air attaché at the British embassy, where he had good contacts. He also elicited information from a senior German naval official about the new and secret pocket battleships, for whose engines Olex was supplying oil; and also about Germany's ambitious plans to extract oil from bituminous coal and lignite.

My father spent a good deal of his spare time indulging his regrettable passion for shooting game large and small; and he rode regularly in a local park with Bob Keyserlingk Snr, a friendship that

Dad in his early 50s: he collected glass
(Nordisk Pressefoto)

27

was to bear such unexpected fruit. My mother was meanwhile preoccupied with looking after Elisabeth and producing first my brother Martin, in August 1931, and then me, in September 1934. I was nearly aborted, because my mother was ill and lost a lot of weight during her pregnancy. Fortunately she stuck it out, and I emerged weighing a hefty nine and a half pounds. These births took place in England: my parents were already convinced that Hitler was bent on war, and that 'Place of birth: Berlin' would not look good in a passport.

I was born in a friend's house in Chiddingstone, Kent, while my father was out 'cubbing' nearby. Back in Berlin I acquired two of my four godparents: my cousin Nigel Gosling, who was an attaché at the embassy, later became the *Observer*'s art critic, and was one of the loveliest men I have known; and Paddy Guinness, who was studying the piano out there. She was a member of the Guinness tribe, and bravely married Fritz Ullstein, whose (Jewish) family owned the Ullstein publishing house. They later settled in Suffolk.

My mother's health was not improved by a fall from the top bunk of a train that lurched suddenly while she was holding Martin in her arms, throwing her to the floor. The resulting concussion, ignored for several days while moving house, may have helped cause her headaches and sleeping problems for the rest of her life. She protected Martin so effectively that he did not even wake up.

At the end of 1935 my father was transferred back to Paris to run the BP office's finance and administrative departments. Of Berlin I have no memory, and precious little of Paris, where we lived in Neuilly, opposite the Bois de Boulogne. It must have been a wonderful change from Nazi Berlin. My father rode in the Bois, played tennis with Jean Borotra, who remained a friend (several decades later he took my father and me to Wimbledon, where he had won the men's singles in 1924 and 1926), and went to work in a chauffeur-driven car. My only, somewhat inconsequential memory is of a mouse running along the top of the garden wall.

In late 1938, after two years in Paris, Dad was offered the top job as managing director of French BP. Courageously in many ways – certainly financially – he turned down this flattering offer. He could see that war with Germany loomed, and did not want to risk being caught in Paris with the family. BP was not pleased, reluctantly finding him a job in the distribution department at head office in the City, at the heavily reduced salary of £2,000, just double what he had earned when he first went there 12 years earlier. This salary was to stick with him right through the Second World War, when he was seconded to the Ministry of Fuel and Power in association with the Ministry of Economic Warfare.

His decision was strongly supported by my mother. She was keen to get back to England and settle in the thatched cottage they had had built in the orchard of her mother's house opposite a flour mill at Hatfield Heath, near Bishop's Stortford, on the Essex side of the border with Hertfordshire. This was intended as a refuge from war, and there we all happily gathered late in 1938.

Shortly after war was declared in September 1939, my father was sent to Bucharest as an 'oil attaché' at the embassy. There he was to be a senior member of a small team dedicated to denying Romanian oil to the Germans. Initially Rumania was a quasi-ally of Britain's, and British, American and French companies controlled more than 80 per cent of the Romanian oil industry. Dad's main task was to organise the pre-emptive purchase of as much petroleum as possible, its removal by tanker via Istanbul, and the leasing of every available Danube river tanker, to reduce supplies to the Germans. There was also an associated team of military and technical personnel with the potential to blow up the Ploesti refineries. In the event, Ploesti was bombed in 1943 by 176 Flying Fortresses based in Libya, with mixed success.

In September 1940 General Ion Antonescu and the fascist Iron Guard seized power in Romania and the persecution of the Jews began: my father saw stacks of naked corpses, with three men checking the names and numbers of the discs around their necks. Then German troops poured in, notionally as a military mission. Some Jews were given visas by the British Legation and passage to Palestine. My father helped extract an oil company employee of exceptional talents, Louis Eisinger. He went initially to the Middle East, later becoming a successful merchant banker in the City. He and my father became friends, and I eventually met him during my unhappy spell in the City. My father left Romania when Britain broke off diplomatic relations in February 1941, shortly after he had supplied the Foreign Office with valuable intelligence about future German intentions, based on a build-up of oil dumps towards Bulgaria and Greece.

Dad's wartime service did him great credit: perhaps all those team games and character-building activities at Gresham's and Oxford really did foster the enterprise and courage he showed. His many missions took him variously to Athens, whence he escaped just before the Germans took over; to Beirut, then in the hands of the Vichy French; to Iraq, Iran, Palestine and several times to Cairo, where he briefed an unresponsive General (Archibald) Wavell, the commander in chief of the British army in the Middle East; thrice to Moscow, where the ambassador Sir Stafford Cripps wanted him to stay as Minister at the embassy in charge of economic aid to the Russians (the appointment was fortunately quashed by Lord Beaverbrook, Minister of Supply, who wanted his own man there).

In the Kremlin he attended a dinner hosted by Stalin, and was – as on several similar occasions in Moscow – appalled by the lavishness of the refreshments, given that many Russians were starving outside. Immediately following the allied victory he was appointed head of the economic division of the UK element of the four-power Control Commission for Austria back in his beloved but battered Vienna, with the equivalent rank of Major-General; and at the Potsdam conference was able to observe Churchill, Stalin and Truman together at close quarters.

Back at home, the outbreak of war had found our sister Elisabeth unhappily at a boarding school in Cambridge, our brother Martin packed off to prep school in Northamptonshire, and me at a private primary in Bishop's Stortford, about four miles away. My mother records me as having been a very easy child, whereas Martin had been through a phase of tantrums. To judge by a report from my kindergarten for the summer term of 1939, I was a little paragon, achieving 'good' or 'very good' for every subject, among them nature and poetry. For the first I was said to be 'very observant', for the second to have shown 'great appreciation of rhythm.' Lis however remembers me being chronically anxious about who was going to give me my evening bath.

The new cottage had been let, possibly for financial reasons, and we had moved into my grandmother's house at the other end of the orchard. Both Lis and Martin remember going to see our grandfather in his study: a kindly man with a white beard often stained by Heinz tomato soup. According to my mother, Gran was – though this seems out of character – terrified of being bombed, a fear that apparently infected us children. Those anxieties must have helped Mother decide, after much telegraphic consultation with Dad in Bucharest to send me, Lis and Gran off to the Keyserlingks in Canada, as earlier described.

Chapter 2

To school at Maidwell Hall and Rugby (1943-1952)

Life in Hatfield Heath

My memories of life at Forbetts, the cottage to which we returned from Canada, are fragmentary. A few minutes walk away were some disused gravel pits interspersed with broom and brambles, around which I used to wander alone with our retriever, Grumps. He lived down to his name, specialising in 'dive-bombing' any dog significantly smaller than himself. Across the huge village green was the genial Mr Reynolds the butcher. He was like something from the old card game Happy Families, with his red face, gap-toothed smile, bloody apron and nicked fingers. He was a very good butcher, and I was often sent with the necessary ration cards to collect an order from him. Nearby were the Wordsworths, with one of whose sons, Ben, I was friendly. Mrs Wordsworth was rather formidable, but held the family together (her husband drank). At the far end of the village lived Nancy, or 'Auntie' Henry, as she liked to be called. She was a professional glove-puppeteer, if that is the term, and thus potentially a good thing. But she had a rather cloying personality. Perhaps, being lonely, she wanted too much to be loved, and I felt uncomfortable with her.

Immediately behind our cottage was a prisoner-of-war camp, with whose inmates, mainly Italian, I used to chat over a fence. They seemed to be well-treated, and were probably relieved to be in such a safe place. After the Italian government joined the Allies in 1943, they were allowed a measure of freedom before being repatriated. One of them turned out to be a doctor. We discovered this immediately after I had fractured my left arm above the elbow, trying rather uncharacteristically to emulate Ben Wordsworth by jumping over a barbed wire fence: my foot caught in the top strand and I fell hard. The friendly Italian volunteered to look at it, suggested I had dislocated a shoulder, and offered to put it back in place. Fortunately my mother, who was escorting me, showed her usual scepticism of foreigners, thus saving me some excruciating additional pain. An X-ray in Bishop's Stortford's hospital confirmed that I had, as we had expected, fractured my arm.

The drone of 'doodle-bugs', those motorised German bombs that cut out shortly before they fell, was often heard, and later occasionally the sinister whine of V2 rockets. One or two of each fell in the neighbourhood, including one on the village cricket pitch. My sister Lis was particularly spooked by the doodlebugs. They periodically cut out above her when she was riding: like many country girls of her age, she was going through a prolonged horsey phase. Her education being considered less important than Martin's and mine, she was attending the Herts and Essex High School in Bishop's Stortford, of which she rose to be head girl.

Living in a small flat above the garage adjacent to the cottage was Dorette, the slim, attractive widow of my uncle George. With her were her son Luke and daughter Anne, who was one year old when I returned from Canada. George was the only one of my three uncles young enough for active service. He joined the RAF, starting as a wireless operator and gunner (he was too old to be a pilot), and becoming a flight sergeant. In June 1943, a couple of months before my return, he was killed with his fellow crew members when their bomber crashed on a practice flight in Norfolk.

Forbetts, built in the late 1930s

George had been the only one not to go to Oxford. After King's College School, Wimbledon, he was despatched aged 17 to study textiles under the wing of a family friend in his mother's home city of Mulhouse. He seems to have been the most open, genial and adaptable of the four brothers (not going to Gresham's may have helped), and was much mourned. Dorette came from Basel, but her family had moved to Mulhouse, where she and George met. After he had volunteered for the RAF at the outbreak of war, Dorette managed to extract herself from France to join him. My parents took them in, though George was inevitably away at his base most of the time. (Dorette left England in 1946, settling with her two children in Lausanne, Switzerland. Four years later she married a charming and handsome French architect, Jacques Marozeau, and went to live with him in Rabat, Morocco, where he worked. Tragically, he died of a cerebral haemorrhage in 1964, when the two children were in their early 20s and he was only 54).

My younger sister Belinda, known in the family as Binnie, was born at Forbetts in early November 1944, a few weeks before my mother's 44th birthday and after an earlier miscarriage. Allegedly, when I received a telegram at school stating 'Belinda has arrived and has blue eyes', I was disappointed to learn that she was not a puppy. I had surely noticed my mother's difficult pregnancy. Belinda was just under 10 years younger than me, and her eyes have long been more green than blue. I don't recall feeling 'dethroned' as the youngest, probably because of my long absence in Canada.

Maidwell Hall, a fine prep school

I probably realised I was to be sent to a boarding school soon after my return to England. Nonetheless it was a shock once again to find myself in strange surroundings, aged barely nine, at the start of the autumn term of 1943. Fortunately Martin had already been there for three years, though he cannot have been too thrilled to be chaperoning me. Happily, Maidwell Hall in Northamptonshire was a well-run school in an idyllic setting.

The original building dated from 1637, but was destroyed by fire in 1896, and rebuilt in neo-Jacobean style in honey-coloured stone, with two turreted towers. It overlooked an hourglass-shaped lake some 300 yards long and 50 yards across, on which we skated in the cold winters that were then so much more frequent (in January 1947 the temperature sank to minus 11 degrees F). The founding headmaster and owner, Oliver Wyatt, was more urbane than most of his breed, and a serious horticulturalist and naturalist. Maidwell's gardens were visited by specialists from far and wide, and even we children were not blind to their beauty. Behind them was a small wilderness good for mucking around in, and playing fields were in the grounds. With the war still raging and rationing in place, the food was pretty revolting after the plenty of Canada – I came to hate dried egg in its many forms, not to mention tapioca and rice puddings – but the school's overall atmosphere was good. There were a couple of bullies, but nothing too serious. Beak, as Wyatt was known, could be formidable, but he was liked as well as respected. He made frequent but not very heavy use of his cane. 'Your little brother is an obstinate mule', he wrote to Martin in October 1944 (did he write to many of his charges, I wonder?). 'He is in my form, so I know. He is not being allowed to be mulish to me: I'm 'larning' him.' I was often 'swished'. 'I am sorry to say that the latest score is that Roger has been wacked (sic) 8 times', my father wrote to Martin a month later. 'I really think they do it too frequently. He says it is always feeble.'

I must have regarded those minor beatings as part of life's rich pattern: until reminded by those letters, I had forgotten they took place. Beak, essentially a benevolent figure, would play a round of cards or show us how to make cat's cradles out of string before closing down our dormitories at night. He fanned the interest in birds that was to give Martin and me so much pleasure. I was particularly thrilled when a pair of kestrels nested in one of the towers (there is still a resident couple 60 years on, I was glad to learn.) One of their young fell out before it could fly, and became a pet. I remember it with the tail of a mouse that it couldn't quite swallow sticking out of its mouth. By the time I left Maidwell, I could recognise the song and call notes of all garden birds, and used to enjoy mentally ticking them off as I lay in bed listening to the morning chorus. My letters to Martin after he left were full of the species I had seen or heard, including nightingales.

To my subsequent regret, I also started collecting butterflies. These were asphyxiated in a 'killing jar', an old jam jar partly filled with compressed young laurel leaves, which emit lethal fumes. That hobby did not last long, though I remember the thrill of chasing a silver-washed fritillary, a truly beautiful butterfly, down one of the rides in Hatfield Forest, not far from home. I fear I caught it. There were some strange, usually short-lived 'crazes' in the school. One was for knitting. For a term or two any outside visitor to the school library would have been surprised to see half a dozen boys, me sometimes among them, plying their needles rather inexpertly. I read voraciously in the same comfortable library: P.C.Wren, P.G.Wodehouse, Jack London etc, moving through them from left to right.

Maidwell Hall

The penetrating reports that Beak wrote about every boy (there were 70 or 80 of us) at the end of each term make frustrating reading. The same refrain runs through most of them. Despite being considered mature for my age, my work disappointed many of my teachers. In some subjects, like French and Latin, I was fast but careless. I rushed into things without thinking. I was good at 'unseen' translations (from Latin and French), interested in art and music, terrible at geometry. In short, I was thought to be erratic and slapdash, to have talent yet lack the determination to fulfil it. Probably worse in my father's eyes, I loathed criticism and being made to do something again.

Outside the classroom, by contrast, I was considered friendly, pleasant and well behaved. Even after my first term, Beak described me as 'devastatingly amusing, and this is in great danger of making him much more popular with all ranks than he should be.' A discriminating man indeed! My parents tended to stereotype me as idle. My mother wrote in her memoirs: 'Roger was at Maidwell, proving lazy after the state school in Canada, where he kept up without exerting himself at all.' Not a very *nuancé* reading of Beak's far less simplistic reports.

The masters, on whose own comments much of this must have been based, were a varied and probably pretty typical lot. I disliked the main maths master, G.W.I.Greenish, aka Gwig, who seemed to take my incomprehension personally. He was understandably irritated by my habit of beating him at ping-pong with my left hand in my pocket (I ended up as the school champion). I admired the English master, P.L.Masters, aka Plum, because he was good-looking, consistently genial, and once handed me back an essay with the friendly injunction: 'Polish it, Bertie.'

Among my friends was Richard Cobham, who had large sticking out ears and shared my interest in birds. He invited me to the family home in Yorkshire one holiday (my first sparrowhawk, but a plague of flies which I described to Martin as 'the utter dregs'). I deliberately caught mumps off him so we could be in the sick-room together. Another, more glamorous, was Geoffrey Holland-Martin, whose father was a test pilot and owned a magnificent Armstrong Siddeley car, in which he took us for a spin on a local disused airfield. And I developed a crush on John Lucas, a pretty youth with whom I was to resume contact as a journalist. I was still naïve about sex, and remember being surprised when a contemporary, Roger Gibbs of the banking family (later Sir Roger, chairman of the Wellcome Trust), told me that if in a year or two one rubbed one's penis for long enough, white stuff came out.

One contemporary to whom adolescent ejaculation would probably not have been news was Jeremy Wolfenden, who must have been one of the cleverest boys in England. From Maidwell he won the top scholarship to Eton (we had an afternoon off school to celebrate), later gaining a congratulatory First in Politics, Philosophy and Economics at Magdalen College, Oxford, with straight alphas in every paper, and a prize fellowship of All Souls. His was to be a sad decline into alcoholism, aggravated by the tension of working for both the *Daily Telegraph* and MI6 in Moscow, and being bisexual. He died in Washington, aged 31. At Maidwell he was in the top form within a year (no wonder his life was haunted by boredom). I remember him as a slight, blond boy of some charm with a nice complexion. Our worlds did not overlap much, though I beat him in the finals of the table tennis doubles.

My stammer

At Maidwell I was for the first time afflicted by a stammer that caused me much grief in my teens. It took the form not of tripping on an initial syllable (which I call a stutter), but of failing to get anything out. I would suck in breath, with my shoulders rising in sympathy, while everyone waited for words to emerge. It generally happened when I had something fixed to say, as when attempting to read out loud, give in my marks and so on. If I could choose my own words, the stammer was less likely to strike, unless I was under pressure. It proved to be a handicap later in my journalistic career.

The first time it seized me could scarcely have been more Freudian (if I invoke that name correctly). I was about 11 years old, Beak was taking us for a scripture lesson, and we had to come forward in turn and recite part of the catechism. I knew what I was supposed to say, but I couldn't get it out, to my acute embarrassment.

The causes of stammering are, in the jargon, 'multifactorial'. It is often stress-related, and there may be a family tendency. A typical internet entry by a speech and language pathologist says: 'Some common precipitating factors are: change of school, moving home, birth of a sibling, separation of parents, conflict in the family... and demands exceeding the capacity of the child.' There were no other stammerers in the wider Berthoud family, and I was reasonably happy and settled at Maidwell. True, we had recently moved to a much larger house, of which more later, but that was pure gain. True too that I had acquired my younger sister Belinda in November 1944, as mentioned, but with minimal impact on my psyche. My school reports do not suggest I was striving stressfully hard to fulfil expectations. On the other hand, my father was a very demanding as well as somewhat authoritarian figure, and I did feel under pressure from him.

Leaving aside my rather unsatisfactory efforts in class, I knew the importance Dad attached to athletic achievement. But I seemed unlikely to impress him on that front. My strongest suit among team games was hockey, in which my strong wrists and good eye were an asset. In cricket my batting was of the agricultural but often effective variety, and I fancied my leg breaks. I was average at rugby and football, though handicapped by flat feet. My tennis was promising. I excelled only at ping-pong, a minor game, as my father hastened to point out when I started beating him.

Despite the occasional stammer at this stage, I think of those prep-school years as happy. My relationship with my brother Martin, unaffected by his remaining at home while I was despatched to Canada, gave great pleasure and support. We had wonderful ping-pong games at home, at first on a tiny table: very good for ball control. One of the stranger things we did was to sit opposite each other in shorts, legs crossed, and attempt to slap each other's exposed thighs as hard as possible, to see how much pain we could bear. No doubt the eternal desire for physical contact played its part in this masochistic fun – as it did in some activities at Maidwell: 'Just before tea we had the most corking rough-and-tumble', I wrote to Martin, 'and we all went bright puce after it. My hair slicked wizardly with perspiration.' Martin and I also had mock sword fights with wooden staves. No lasting damage was done.

Gaston House

In 1945, shortly after the war had ended – how well I remember the *News Chronicle* headline announcing the atomic bombing of Hiroshima – our lives had taken a qualitative jump. A couple of miles from Hatfield Heath, off the road to Bishop's Stortford, lies the village of Little Hallingbury. It includes Gaston Green, a hamlet dominated by a classic early 18th century mansion, Gaston House, built around 1730, architect unknown. Together with three cottages by the top entrance to its drive, it belonged to a great friend of my parents, Rhoda Barclay. Her husband Robert, a public-spirited director of the clearing bank, had died in 1939, aged 70. During the Second World War, the house had been used as a children's hospital, with Rhoda living in the nearest cottage.

She decided to sell Gastons, as we came to call it, when my father had taken up his post in the four-power Control Commission for Austria in Vienna. By letter, he gave the go-ahead to the purchase of this 14-bedroomed house, plus the three nearby cottages and nine acres of grounds, including the village cricket pitch across the road. That was pretty brave, but big houses were then at a discount: people were afraid they would be too expensive to heat, and my mother reckoned the top floor and wing, as well as the cottages, could be let. Dad was probably on a bit of a high in Vienna, what with his ranking as a general, and I'm sure he fancied himself in the role of village squire.

Gaston House: watercolour by Hubert Williams, 1967

Gran came to live on the upper floor of the two-storey wing, and probably added the proceeds from the sale of her house at Hatfield Heath to what we got for our old cottage. Gran and I used to do things together. Once we went off in our pony and trap to deliver her visiting card to a substantial house a couple of miles away. If you delivered such a card yourself, perhaps depositing it on a silver salver in the entrance hall, you turned down the top right corner. Otherwise it was assumed someone else, perhaps a chauffeur, had delivered it.

True to her origins, Gran spent much of the hunting season following the local Essex Hunt, initially on a bicycle, later in her splendid black Lanchester car with pre-selective gears: you chose your gear with a lever off the steering column, then punched in the clutch to engage it. She was very down to earth. When one of us once asked her what she would like for Christmas, she replied: 'A pound of mixed nails would be very useful.'

To one side of this wonderfully handsome Queen Anne house was a fine stable block with a hay loft, a wood-clad bothy ideal for a handyman, and a substantial walled kitchen garden. On the far side of the latter my parents built a house for Fred Parker, Gran's gardener since his teens, and his wife Marjorie. Fred kept us supplied with fresh vegetables and honey, of which he was one of Essex's leading producers. On the ground floor of the wing, under Gran's premises, lived the Oakleys, with their attractive daughter Elsie. Oakley, as I'm afraid we knew him, looked after the livestock, which soon ran to a Guernsey cow, some pigs, large and rather fierce rabbits called Flemish Giants, which sometimes ate their young, to my distress; ducks, briefly some noisy geese, even more briefly some goats, and of course chickens.

All this was intended to supplement the wretched post-war rations (meat, butter, cheese, sugar and sweets were among items rationed until the early 1950s, bread rationing was actually introduced in 1946, for two years). Half of any home-reared pig had to be sold to the government. The other half we had cured at one of those establishments for which that part of Essex, notably Dunmow, used to be famous. If Oakley was away or ill when I was at home, I used to milk the cow and feed the livestock. The cow, whose encrusted tail had to be washed periodically, not an enjoyable task, had an engaging habit of leaning against me. Thanks to this smallholding, we lived a life of plenty, if only – where Martin and I were concerned – during school holidays. How well I recall the sensual pleasure of pouring Guernsey cream onto my Frugrains at breakfast. We made our own butter and cream cheese. After two or three years the Oakleys left, as did the cow and her calf. The big room on the ground floor of the wing was temporarily given over to a billiard table, on which I used to challenge the visiting postman.

It's hard not to look back on those innocent years with a touch of nostalgia, coloured by my deep love of Gaston House, its garden and surrounding fields and walks. Cart-horses, whether of the Suffolk Punch variety or otherwise, were still to be seen at work during hay-making, and I sometimes helped toss the hay onto haystacks on the farm that bordered our large garden. Is the numinous aura that haystacks seemed to possess purely a figment of this nostalgia? It lingers on: I have an oil painting of a haystack by a Polish artist that seems to exude just that quality. In nearby Bishop's Stortford, shops had devices that now seem quaintly charming. It was a treat to stick one's feet into one of those X-ray machines (later deemed a health hazard) in shoe shops that showed one's feet and all their bones inside new shoes; and I used to marvel at the pneumatic ('Lamson') tubes widely used in big shops to convey bills, cash and receipts to and fro between shop assistants and cashiers, with a wonderful sucking-whizzing sound.

In that era we had a lovely labrador of an unusual coppery-golden hue called Tigger, who was as bouncy as his name suggests and whom I adored. We used to go for long walks together, and I have a photo of myself lying on the lawn reading *David Copperfield*, with my head on the prone Tigger's strong ribs. He would be sent in to wake me in the morning, sticking his soft muzzle under my bedclothes and emitting a wide range of excited and lovable cries. He was an exceptionally articulate beast. I have loved dogs ever since, but know I would be their slave should I own one.

Tigger as pillow,
1949

Less nostalgia-inducing was the difficulty of heating a very large house. Bad luck decreed that the winter of 1946/7, a year after we moved in, should be of record-breaking cold and snowfalls. Fortunately I was at Maidwell during most of the worst weeks, and have happy memories of skating on the lake there, and also on the large lake in nearby Hatfield Forest during the preceding Christmas holiday. Once, out walking from school in early 1947, I broke through the crust of the snow and found myself on top of a hedge. At home, my mother and others clustered around a log fire in the smaller sitting room.

Dad was spared those rigours, being abroad much of the time on various missions. In January 1946, his mandate in Vienna having run out, he had switched to full rather than seconded membership of the Civil Service. At first he stayed at the Ministry of Fuel and Power, but in 1948, more momentously from our point of view, switched to the Foreign Office in Whitehall. This move followed his lengthy involvement with the US-financed Marshall Plan for the reconstruction of war-ravaged Europe, of whose crucial central committee he was a vice-chairman. He entered the FO as an assistant under-secretary of state and No 2 on the economic side, under the very demanding Sir Roger Makins, later Lord Sherfield. Nobody before or since has, I believe, joined the FO at such a senior level, if one excludes political appointments to senior ambassadorships. Ernest Bevin was Foreign Secretary at the time. My father admired him greatly.

Although Dad would have earned vastly more had he gone back to BP, his new diplomatic status meant that our school fees were largely paid from public funds. Without such a perk, the children of diplomats who changed posts every three years or so, often serving in developing countries, would have no continuity of education. This held good even when the diplomat concerned was based in London, as my father was throughout my nine years at boarding schools, a very unusual stint.

Five years at Rugby

For reasons unknown to Martin and me, our parents – meaning Dad – had decided that we should proceed from Maidwell to Rugby, as did two other sets of contemporary

Maidwell brothers. Eton and Winchester were more common choices, not that I would retrospectively have wished to go to either. Martin paved the way to a well-located and relatively recently built (1930) 'house' at Rugby called Sheriff House. My parents had met and liked the admirable housemaster, but sadly he died in early 1950, in Martin's second term, aged 42. He was succeeded by R.H. ('the Mick') Walker, an emotionally deficient martinet. A startling amount of the Mick's impressive head of white hair grew out of his ears. He had a very clear mind, spoke in clipped and curt tones, and was an exceptionally good German teacher. But as a shoulder to cry on or confide in he was useless, and his pleasant, rather gauche wife, whom he once told his class he used 'purely for breeding purposes', was too much in awe of him to be of any help.

Sheriff House was a pretty bleak building after the cosiness of Maidwell, and there was some strange vocabulary to pick up. The lavatory, with its doorless cubicles, to prevent any hanky-panky, was called the topos (Greek for place, as in topography); our curious hip baths were called toshes; waste paper baskets were waggers, and so on. But there was no beating by prefects, and by masters only for what were considered serious offences; no ghastly initiation ceremonies; and as far as I could detect, in Sheriff at least, no bullying. There were plenty of irritating regulations, however. We had to wear house caps outside house premises, sports jackets and grey flannels, Van Heusen shirts with collar studs and separate white collars.

Entry was highly streamed: one could pass into one of six forms, none of them parallel. Despite my alleged idleness at Maidwell, I had only just missed a scholarship and did well enough in the entrance exam to pass into the form just below the scholars, five forms up from the bottom form and – to my considerable satisfaction – one higher than Martin had passed into. This was cheering and even useful. Rugby was, contrary to the stereotype perpetuated by *Tom Brown's Schooldays* and film versions thereof, a meritocracy based on brains. So I got a study to myself sooner than most, after two years of sharing. Later, one became a prefect by reaching the sixth (top) form.

The transition from primary to secondary school is proverbially traumatic: from large fish in small pond to small fish in big pond. It was softened for me by having a brother there who was very much a twin soul. The old institution of 'fagging' lingered on, obliging new boys to carry out small tasks, such as shoe-cleaning, for their 'fagmaster'. Martin had persuaded the new head of house, Giles Talbot Kelly, to take me on. Giles's father, R.B. Talbot Kelly, was head of the school's excellent art department and a seriously good bird artist. Giles was himself often mistaken for a master. He was losing his hair prematurely, wore thick spectacles, and seemed top-heavy, having massively developed his chest and shoulders doing the butterfly breast-stroke. His feet were small and, like his father before him, he was a very fleet winger at the game the school's William Webb-Ellis was credited with inventing. He later played rugby for the Harlequins.

I soon developed a serious crush on him, which was reciprocated. I used to rush to his study on weekday evenings to listen to *Dick Barton, Special Agent*, when I heard that thrilling signature tune. He would come and chat to me in my dormitory before lights out, and I would hold his hand under the bedclothes: nothing more. He introduced me to his parents, and once he ill-advisedly sent me a box of chocolates during the holidays. My parents summoned me to their bedroom to account for it. I was thoroughly embarrassed, but fortunately they accepted my explanations. He later had a relationship with my sister Elisabeth, and became a designer, writer and very large father of seven children. For me he was, I think, a maturing and mind-broadening influence.

An admirable aspect of Rugby in those days, as I believe now, was the standard of music, thanks partly to the high proportion of boys who learned an instrument. No doubt its musical reputation attracted burgeoning talent and good teachers, though I found mine irritating. The world-class oboist Neil Black, a very nice fellow and already a brilliant player, was one year ahead of me in my house, and in the school there were several seriously good pianists, violinists, 'cello and French horn players. In addition to the school orchestra there was a school band, in which before long I found a niche as one of several clarinettists. Martin featured on trumpet in orchestra and band. One house even had its own band. There were inter-house instrumental and singing competitions, the latter known as the 'house shout', in which I much enjoyed taking part. Among songs we tackled, in German, were Schubert's *Erlkönig* and Schumann's no less wonderful *Ich grolle nicht* (I do not complain). Since I was learning German, Neil Black asked me to help with the pronunciation of the German lyrics. To my intense frustration, my stammer prevented me from getting anything out, and someone with a lousy accent took over. I felt humiliated by such episodes.

Yet, to Rugby's credit, I was never teased or mocked for my stammer. The fact that I was reasonably well-liked and had a potentially sharp tongue no doubt helped. Even so, to be pitied is not pleasant, nor to feel waves of sympathy tinged with impatience coming towards one. Trying to read out loud in class was an ordeal. I found it difficult even to state my marks when essays, proses or 'unseen' translations, my strongest suit, were given back to us. I was limited to a back-stage role in the house play. The teachers were generally sympathetic, but no one ever suggested I should seek some form of remedial treatment. My mother took me once or twice to a useless elocution teacher during holidays.

Six of the best, with consequences

Fortunately my stammer did not greatly inhibit normal social intercourse, nor my burgeoning sexuality. Once the benign influence of Giles Talbot Kelly had been removed (he was to survive a grim spell as a subaltern in the King's Own Scottish Borderers in the Korean War), I found myself drawn into a small circle of boys a year or so older than me who met in one study or another to savour the delights of mutual masturbation. Even though it was some time before I achieved ejaculation, I found these sessions very exciting. To some extent I was being corrupted by my elders, but I wanted to be corrupted. The sense of forbidden fruit gave an added frisson. Had there been girls around, our sensual urges would have been directed at them (back home I quite fancied a girl called Edna in the village, though she was slim and boyish).

Inevitably, with some 10 of us involved off and on, the beans were liable to be spilled, and it may even have been me who innocently spilled them to a prefect I thought I could trust. We were summoned to be lectured one by one by the Mick, and then given six of the very best by our respective tutors. In my case this was the Rev. Jack McDonogh, a wiry Irishman. He was said to have played hockey for Ireland, and as centre forward to have – uniquely – scored a goal straight from the initial bully-off. Anyway, he had wrists of steel, and even took a few steps before each vicious stroke with his cane. No doubt he felt he was doing God's work. The pain was excruciating, but I felt somewhere between a hero and a martyr when I emerged into the main corridor to murmurs of sympathy.

The episode served to reinforce my rebellious streak. The outcome could have been serious. The Mick wrote a somewhat apocalyptic letter to my father: 'I am extremely sorry to have to tell you that Roger has got himself into serious trouble…He has been punished, and that will be the end of it, as far as we are concerned, if he pulls himself together…But it is only fair to add that the Headmaster [Hugh Lyon still] bids me say that if a further lapse of this kind occurs, it will not be possible to keep him in the school…I am distressed, too, to hear that he has, or is, adopting a cynical attitude to his misdeeds and our discovery of them and the beating he had last night from his tutor.… We'll do all we can, but I'm afraid there will be a lot for you & his mother to do in the holidays to get Roger straight.'

My father's brainwashing at Gresham's about the evils of masturbation and suchlike 'smutty' goings-on ensured that his reaction would be no less apocalyptic. He wrote me a letter that so enraged me that I tore it up. But Martin kept the one he wrote to him at Rugby. Not only did it emphasise the threat of expulsion should any such episode recur, but it dwelt on the morally debilitating effects of masturbation. 'I have told him that if he goes on, it leads to decadence and lunacy which is no exaggeration. It is vital for his whole life that he should stop all forms of masturbation, and like all habits it is difficult to break.' Did he speak from experience? How many forms of masturbation did he know of? It's extraordinary that an intelligent man should have clung to such beliefs.

'He must be really contrite as a basis for a new start', Dad continued to Martin. 'Unless he changes his outlook on life, we will remove him from Rugby without hesitation. We can't risk expulsion and the H.M. has said there won't be a second chance.' My own response, suitably apologetic though it was, probably didn't help much. 'I want to say that the whole affair was not as serious as it may have sounded from the Mick's letter, and Martin will bear me out on this', I wrote. 'The Mick heard the story so many times that he got an exaggerated idea of the whole thing.' Nonetheless, I said that after the beating I felt a different boy, 'and I promise faithfully that I shall never (underlined three times) get into such an unpleasant affair again, and I apologise as wholeheartedly as possible.' I did not say I wouldn't engage in similar practices again. Further explanations resulted in my father calming down, and the generally friendly and chatty tone of his letters was resumed.

To his credit, the Mick wrote on my rather patchy end of term report: 'I would rather be writing next term's report: shall we leave it at that, and hope that I shall be justified?' Self-centred teenager that I was, I don't think I appreciated how much genuine distress I might have caused my parents. I was more concerned with the disproportionate punishment, as I saw it, that had been meted out to me, and my father's initial over-the-top reactions. Given his history of suppressed sexuality at Gresham's, it was hardly likely that he would say: 'What you've been doing is perfectly natural in a single-sex community, just don't get caught again' – which was my own resolve. Henceforward I ensured that my encounters were one-on-one and with boys, usually near-contemporaries, I could trust. For most of the time I was happy with unfulfilled but often passionate crushes.

One 'crushee' was my very own fag when I became a prefect: a very pretty, slight, blonde youth. When I bumped into him in Hampstead some 20 years later I would not have recognised him had he not hailed me. He was living with his parents next to our local pub, in which his sadly bloated appearance suggested he had spent a great deal too much time.

More trouble with Dad

The sexual episode added to my father's general unhappiness with the way I was evolving. My school reports for at least the first two years at Rugby continued the Maidwell theme 'could do better if he tried harder'. Both Martin and I were crazy about New Orleans jazz ('the good noise', as we sometimes called it), for which Dad naturally had no time. I spent every spare penny on buying the old shellac three-to-four minute 78s of Louis Armstrong, Johnny Dodds, Jelly Roll Morton and so on. I used to go for record-playing trysts with a 'townee' at his flat (such visits were forbidden by school rules). And I helped form a house jazz band in which I sought to emulate Johnny Dodds, but was hampered by my ignorance of chords.

Dad thought my obsession with jazz was excessive, as in some ways it was. At home I spent a good deal of time reading novels, mainly classics, though I was keen on tennis, at which I was soon better than Dad though less good than Martin. I think Dad saw me evolving as a self-absorbed quasi-intellectual. I may even have reminded him of his 'over-intellectual' mother, which would have counted against me.

Despite all this and the sometimes bitter, often petty rows our differences generated at home, both my parents wrote me regular and affectionate letters at school chronicling life at home, the misdeeds of our two Labradors, Tigger and Kanga, the cow's fluctuating health, sister Binnie's progress at school and so on. My mother periodically sent me a cake, eggs and butter from home. Such parcels were laid out for us on a table, and hers were usually embarrassingly badly wrapped. Dad could be affectionate in a practical way: in the summer of 1948 he took me for a day at the Olympic Games at Wembley. There we were thrilled to see Fanny Blankers-Koen, Holland's 30-year-old 'flying housewife', win one of her four gold medals, in the 80 metres hurdles final. I was glad to read that this remarkable woman, who set 20 world records, lived to the age of 85.

The opening paragraph of a letter Dad wrote me after a visit to Rugby in July 1950

43

shows him at his most sympathetic, even almost retrospectively apologetic: 'What a lovely day last Sunday was, and I enjoyed it all, not forgetting your clarinet solo! And it was a real pleasure to find that you are qualifying as an "enjoyer of life". What a difficult period those adolescent years from 13 and a half to 15 and a half or so are, and I do think (and agree with the Mick) that you are emerging from them very creditably.'

I blush now when I read some of the ridiculously intemperate things I wrote in a journal when I was a year or so older. I had criticised my current history master at Rugby, J.B.Hope-Simpson, as ineffably tedious, and Dad had objected. 'To Dad and most of his generation', I wrote, 'to condemn anyone so much older than myself is a heinous display of presumption and conceit. In his day, of course, they used to "respect their elders without questioning". It is precisely this state of intellectual dishonesty, apathy and aridity that is sapping the fibre of this complacent isle. We must question, we must search for the truth.' Fine sentiments, but oh dear, the pomposity of youth! How insufferable I must have been at times.

Maurice and Ruth Ash

When I was about 16 a man came into my life who was destined to encourage the very interests that least appealed to my father. I remember the moment vividly. I was playing tennis on our grass court at around teatime on a glorious summer day. Down from the house came my parents with three decidedly glamorous-looking people. They turned out to be Maurice and Ruth Ash, and Ruth's half-brother, Michael Straight. Maurice was dark, could have been Celtic or French; Ruth was attractive rather than pretty, with a lovely smile, voice and laugh and a pert bottom; Michael Straight was tall, blond, charming, handsome. The Ashs had recently moved into a large house and farm in the next village, Great Hallingbury, and my parents had probably been told they were interesting and well-off: if so, a notable understatement.

Maurice was an economist and graduate of the London School of Economics. His father, Gilbert Ash, had been a successful building contractor, and had coincidentally sent Maurice to school at Gresham's Holt, where he overlapped with his later friend Benjamin Britten. Maurice had two other things in common with my father: he had been a brilliant hockey player, and had a great knowledge and love of fine wines. Otherwise he could scarcely have been more different. He was soft-spoken, diffident, ruminant, yet with an inner strength and a definite twinkle. His interests – and they tended to be intense – ranged from town planning (he was soon to become chairman of the Town and Country Planning Association) to philosophy, the environment, contemporary art, which he collected, and classical music.

The Ash money came mainly from Ruth. She was the daughter of Leonard and Dorothy Elmhirst, the founders of the many-faceted Dartington estate near Totnes in Devon. Dorothy's American father had established the Whitney fortune, and her mother was from the seriously rich Payne family. Dorothy's first husband Willard Straight, who had many abilities but little money, was killed by the influenza epidemic of 1918. One of their sons was Michael Straight, who when I met him was editor of the radical magazine, *New Republic*, that Dorothy had founded. It later transpired that while at Cambridge he had been recruited as a rather reluctant and short-lived Soviet spy by Anthony Blunt, whom he later helped to expose.

Seven years after being widowed at age 31, Dorothy married Leonard Elmhirst, a self-confident Yorkshireman of 'good' family who had been studying agriculture at Cornell University in the USA (he had earlier gained a Third in history at Cambridge). Once destined for the church, he combined a keen social conscience with an interest in both agriculture and India, where he had spent some time. At Dartington the Elmhirsts founded an estate that combined agriculture, forestry, a school, an arts college and some light industry. One aim was to arrest the depopulation that was damaging the fabric of rural life in the mid-1920s. Another was to revive the old concept of the estate as a genuine community.

I was immediately drawn to Maurice and Ruth, and they seemingly to me. They were in their early 30s, thus half way between me and my parents in age, and I'm sure they sensed that all was not well between me and my father. I soon became a regular visitor to Howe Green Moat, their house a couple of miles away. It was a haven of contemporary art, good music, relaxed discussion about anything and everything, and delicious food and wine. Before long a large two-piece reclining figure by Henry Moore took its place on a revolving plinth on their front lawn. No doubt Maurice had already met the sculptor through Dorothy Elmhirst, a great patron and collector. He soon became one of Moore's closest friends, and before long introduced me to him over lunch.

The Tosswill and fforde effect

Back at school, I was beginning to do much better. Martin had left after my second year, and entertained me with letters about the rigours first of basic training with the Rifle Brigade near Winchester, then of being an officer cadet at Eaton Hall, near Chester. Later he was commissioned into the Bedfordshire and Hertfordshire regiment. Much of our weekly correspondence was about jazz, the latest records we had bought – and about when we might next see each other.

By the age of 15, I had reached the form just below the Sixth form, in the 'block' that embraced languages, history and English. The other two were devoted to classics and science. In the old School Certificate exam in December 1948 I had gained three distinctions, in English language, English literature and Latin; credits in French and German, and a pass in history. In maths I failed, but gleaned the necessary pass at the second attempt. Commenting on that first failure, the Mick told me: 'I realised you were bad at maths, but I didn't realise you were abysmal.' I had no idea what a bismal was, and was surprised not to be able to find this evidently pejorative noun in the dictionary. Despite that disappointing result in what were thought among my best subjects, I decided to specialise in French and German. It was known to be easier to gain a place at Oxbridge for languages than for English.

At this stage I encountered the first teacher who took took me seriously, a lanky, corduroy-clad poet of high seriousness but some humour called Tim Tosswill. He taught us English, scripture and history, and took great trouble marking our essays, the first teacher to do so. His comments on my reports were generally encouraging, for example (for English): 'His work is always smooth and attractive in style: he has a sense of humour, and the capacity to think clearly is emerging.'

He also encouraged me to have faith in my own judgement. On one seminal occasion he was walking past my desk and noticed that I had written the word CANT in pencilled capitals across a paragraph in a book of religious essays we were studying. He peered over, read the paragraph concerned, then laid a hand on my shoulder and murmured: 'Good boy'. By such vital moments is intellectual self-confidence formed. Tosswill and his German wife had a rather scruffy house not far from school, to which he occasionally invited me for tea. That too was heartening.

I was also much encouraged during my last two terms by the headmaster, Sir Arthur fforde, a solicitor who to everyone's surprise had been appointed in 1948 to succeed the lightweight Hugh Lyon (no doubt partly to shore up the school's finances). I was by then in the small and select Upper Sixth, with five others. We adjourned to Sir Arthur's study for English and scripture. For the latter we were reading the then fashionable American theologian Reinhold Niebuhr's *Beyond Tragedy*. For English we did T.L.Peacock's satirical novel *Gryll Grange*. As a composition he asked us to write a parody of the latter, and at the top of my effort wrote in his red ink: 'A very distinguished piece of nonsense.' How enormously pleased I was. On my final report he wrote: 'It is difficult not to think he's a much better man than he thinks he is. I have much enjoyed his presence in the 'B' UB English set, to which he has unfailingly contributed the right ingredients, once he got rid of a certain facetiousness, not native to his genius. I can really say he has come to the end of a good run.' In an earlier comment, he reckoned I was 'happier with Samuel Butler than with Niebuhr', a nice understatement (I was a fan of the author of *The Way of All Flesh*, which is an assault on a difficult father, and that great satire *Erewhon*. Later I cherished Butler's *Notebooks*).

Sir Arthur and I had one rather touching encounter beyond the confines of his study. My dreaded turn had come to read the lesson in chapel in front of the whole school, masters and all. Having experienced my stammer, he kindly offered to give me a trial run. We met outside William Butterfield's handsome striped-brick school chapel. Inside someone was playing the organ and had to stop, an inhibiting factor as I envisaged his frustration. I mounted the podium where the bible reposed on a brass eagle, and attempted to read out the appointed text. Not a word emerged. We had to agree there was no way I could do it. Sir Arthur was very understanding, and even my failure felt like a bond between us. I later had some journalistic contact with him when he was chairman of the governors of the BBC. He was a person of exceptional quality.

Sadly, no one remotely of his or Tim Tosswill's stature was to be found on the languages side. For all too many daily lessons of both French and German during my last five terms I had a plump and deeply boring teacher nearing retirement known as Porky Slater. He was conscientious enough, but burnt out. So Corneille, Racine, Molière, Goethe and Schiller became swathed in tedium, with Molière surviving best. For prep we learned endless chunks of verse, none of which I remembered for more than a few weeks. I got my A-levels (they were not graded then) and then a state scholarship. This was means-tested, but good for morale, and the minimum payment was worth a tie and a few jazz discs a term at university.

My modest sporting career reached some sort of apotheosis in my last year. Although I wasn't really good at any one game, I played for the school at Rugby Fives, which led to some entertaining trips to such rivals as Oundle and Marlborough. We were invariably beaten. I was considered a creditable hockey and tennis player for my house, and the opposition tended to move to the outfield when I came in to bat at cricket. In my best match I was using an 80-year-old bat that had belonged to my maternal grandfather. As I told my father in one of my weekly letters: 'Our side was in a precarious position when I went in at No 5. My first four balls I smote for healthy fours…In all I faced 13 balls, and scored 47 (including three sixes, all the others were fours except one single). That bat is quite terrific.' Most of the boundaries were scored off the school's temptingly slow spin bowler. It was admittedly a smallish field.

In the game to which Rugby gave its name, I played in practically every position in the scrum and three-quarter line, except wing. Being cautious, or generally gutless, about tackling, I would sometimes notice that my knees had remained spotlessly clean, and would furtively drop into the mud. The team game at which the school excelled in my day was hockey: at rugby we were regularly thrashed by such schools as Oundle and Uppingham. We also shone at tennis and racquets.

Looking ahead, my father having gone to Magdalen College, Oxford and Martin being destined to follow him thither, I decided to try for Cambridge, which my mother's family had favoured and I loved as a city and where the modern languages faculty was said to be more flexible and progressive that Oxford's. But which college? I liked the sound of King's (small, brainy and non-sporting), and tried unsuccessfully for an exhibition there. The only gain was meeting the harpsichordist Colin Tilney, a fellow candidate. Since I would still be young enough to try the following year, I was told to try again then. I decided to play safe. There was a link between Rugby and Trinity Hall, where Charles Crawley, father of my contemporary John Crawley, was senior tutor. The Hall had a good reputation and was well located on the river between Clare and Trinity colleges. I took the entrance exam, and was accepted.

Despite the largely free education that Martin and I enjoyed at boarding schools, courtesy of the Foreign Office, the family finances were far from flush in those school years. It must have been expensive to run such a large house and garden. My frequent requests to my parents for subsidies were often turned down, and produce from the kitchen garden was sold locally to raise extra cash. Holidays were generally spent at home, but there were exceptions. Aged around 16 I once accompanied my parents to an admirable hotel melodiously called The Lands of the Loyal in Alyth, Perthshire, from which we visited the Highland Games in Blairgowrie. One day we went shooting. Dad had given me a 16-bore shotgun, with which I occasionally eliminated a pigeon at home. In Scotland we went out with a keeper and a Labrador, and I somehow shot a hare that was racing across a field some way off. It was screaming when the dog brought it to my feet. I had nightmares about it afterwards, and vowed never to shoot again. Nor did I.

On at least one earlier occasion Mother rented a caravan at Walton-on-Naze on the Essex coast, a claustrophobic experience that Dad wisely avoided. Martin and I much enjoyed a week at a Centre for Field Studies based at Flatford Mill in Suffolk, which Constable painted. It was run by a charismatic bird artist, E.A.R.Ennion, who took us on trips to local estuaries to tone up our wader identification or to hear the elusive stone curlew in the Suffolk heathland. We camped on that occasion, and I remember being disturbed by the proximity of one or two attractive girls in nearby tents.

Sexual confusion

My sexuality was in a state of confusion, essentially because I had spent so many years in a predominantly male environment – and was destined to do so for another two years of National Service. But I never thought I might turn out to be more homo- than heterosexual. There was good evidence for this from an Iberian holiday with a group of some 20 girls and boys from an ultra-progressive school where sister Elisabeth was then teaching. Called Long Dene, it was located in Chiddingstone Castle in the very village where I had been born.

In the spring holiday before my last summer term at Rugby, a Long Dene school party was going to Spain in a converted truck. Inside there were two long, padded bench seats facing each other; outside, rolled-up tent flaps that could be unfurled and pegged down, providing shelter for boys on one side and girls on the other. The master who mainly drove this vehicle was having an affair with the most beautiful of the girls who came along, and ripely gorgeous she was. He later married her. I was invited to fill a spare seat, as was an up-and-coming soprano, Anne Dowdall, a friend of a member of staff. Lis was naturally of the party. While waiting at the school for our postponed departure, I had the novel experience of being thrashed at ping-pong by Humphrey Burton, the future BBC classical music presenter, whose mother was the school's colourful cook.

My chief memories are of the unspoilt beauty of the Costa Brava, the smell of orange blossom one evening near Valencia – and, most of all, the excitement of sitting for long hours in close proximity to one or other of three attractive girls. Often they would be wearing short shorts, at least one pair of which my straying hand explored under cover of darkness. No less memorably, at one camp site, the teacher's busty beloved jumped on my back and cried: 'To the woods!' Sadly, I had neither the courage nor the strength to bear her off. As a crash course in heterosexuality, the holiday could not have been better. The attractions of one of the younger boys were quite eclipsed.

Rugby is now among the most comprehensively coeducational of all public schools. In that respect I was unlucky in my timing. I have no great feeling of loyalty or affection for the old school, have only been back twice (once for an article), yet don't reckon I was unhappy there. Although we were snobbish about the local day boys in Town House, generally pronounced Tahn Aas, it was a far from upper-class establishment. The sons of professional people – doctors, lawyers and so on – predominated, and Midlands business was well represented. It was bad luck that my contemporaries in my house were pleasant rather than interesting, since only in the upper school was it easy to make friends in other houses. Mercifully, we were not often told we were future leaders of men, though a few boys were clearly qualifying themselves. Among the stars of the school cadet force, which I loathed in its entirety, was the genial, red-headed Tom King, a future Conservative defence minister who was also head of my house.

It was generally a tolerant place. One of my best friends was an Indian, Ronnie Pillai, whose father Sir Raghavan Pillai was a senior Indian civil servant. Ronnie, a gentle soul, was a brilliant flautist and artist, and widely liked – hence my suspicion that Salman Rushdie, at Rugby somewhat later with fellow novelist A.N.Wilson, was a victim of unpopularity rather than the racism of which he has complained. There were quite a few Jewish boys, and they fared according to their talents and personalities. One was said to have been disciplined for selling his birthday cake slice by slice, in the grand entrepreneurial tradition. He probably was teased, since he was also fat and charmless.

An outstanding boy in my era was Robert Ogilvie, a brilliant classicist, head of school, top scholar to Oxford and Fellow of All Souls. He shot himself when the educational and scholastic worlds seemed at his feet. Another was Ewen Fergusson, as brilliant an athlete as he was a scholar. He passed top into the Foreign Office, played rugby for Scotland, ended his high-flying diplomatic career as ambassador in Paris, and then became a ubiquitous chairman, inter alia of the Savoy Hotel group, the Henry Moore Foundation – and Rugby's governing body. My contemporary Geoffrey Owen was an exceptionally good tennis and hockey player, and became editor of the *Financial Times*. One youthful master, Mike McCrum, married the headmaster's daughter, Christine fforde, rose to be headmaster of Eton and then Master of Corpus College, Cambridge. A number of my contemporaries died young, one or two during National Service.

Financial considerations apart, I would never have dreamt of sending my own children to a boarding school, unless obliged by some circumstance to do so, and certainly not to a single-sex one. My main regret about Rugby is that it so retarded my contact with girls. Despite that Spanish trip, my sexual confusion lasted several more years, and made me anxious to make up for lost time once I shed my virginity. In that respect at least I felt I was emotionally not just immature but stunted. That did not make marriage any easier (apologies, Joy). No doubt Rugby also reinforced my Canada-induced tendency to self-sufficiency: likewise not usually helpful in marriage, but valuable in the ordeal by military service that lay ahead.

Chapter 3

National Service in Oswestry, Germany and Korea (1952-54)

The prospect of doing two years of National Service in the army filled me with dread. I had, as mentioned, loathed the school cadet force, and had passed a test known as Certificate A only at the second attempt. This was of a piece with my stereotypical teenaged tendency to be anti-authority and to deplore officious contemporaries who actually enjoyed marching, wearing horrible rough uniforms and bossing other people around.

This was one field in which having an older brother to pave the way was of no use. Indeed, Martin's letters describing the horrors of basic training and, even worse, of officer cadet training had reinforced my sense of foreboding. The lucky fellow had got off with 18 months, which he spent mainly and unthrillingly as a second lieutenant and instructor at the School of Infantry in Warminster. The outbreak of the Korean war in 1950 had resulted in National Service being extended to two years: Britain was contributing substantially to the Commonwealth forces that had come in on the American (notionally United Nations) side in this hot section of the Cold War.

I followed Martin's example by applying initially to be sent to the Rifle Brigade, only to receive instructions to report on October 2 1952 to the main training unit in Oswestry, Shropshire, of the Royal Artillery, which in those days constituted almost a third of the British army. I decided that the grisliness of the impending ordeal might be alleviated if I went up on the little motorcycle, a Royal Enfield 125cc, that my father had ceded to me. I was the only new recruit to arrive with his own transport. When trying to find somewhere to park the trusty vehicle I was surprised to see a large sign saying: Out of Bounds to ORs, letters that meant only one thing to me. Surely that is carrying prejudice against Old Rugbeians a bit far, I thought for a second or two. I was soon told it meant Other Ranks, i.e. non-officers. Such was the stratified world I was entering.

The first fortnight was spent, in a state of horrified daze, in a 'selection' regiment, in which we were sorted out and initiated into the joys of bullshit in its proper meaning: blancoing webbing (gaiters, belt etc); Brasso-ing the shiny bits of same; 'bulling' boots to a high shine with spit and polish; ironing the trousers of our uniform, 'squaring off' our blankets at the end of the bed, and so on. Our hair was cut unpleasantly short, and we began to realise how important normal clothes are to comfort and self-expression. Our 'civvies' were taken from us. All this was part of the army's notorious desire to strip recruits of their sense of individuality and make them obedient machines.

Those of us who came from the more or less one-class world of boarding schools found the assembled company wonderfully varied and the language richly colourful. It was good to tune in to accents from all over the UK, since the Gunners were in no way regional. I don't suppose I'd ever heard a Geordie, Scouse or Brummie accent before. There were one or two natural and very funny raconteurs, including an agricultural worker. In one of his stories he described how he met up for a drink with a mate, who arrived with one hand in his pocket, and – bizarrely – kept it there. It transpired that several fingers thereof had a short while earlier been exploring his 'taggie's' private parts. Suddenly he whipped it out, thrust the privileged digits under our raconteur's nose and triumphantly cried: 'Meet the missus!' This was also my first encounter with the delightful acronyms with which soldiers used to emboss envelopes to their girlfriends: SWALK (sealed with a loving kiss); BOLTOP (better on lips than on paper); CAPSTAN (can a prick stand twice a night?) and NORWICH (Knickers off ready when I come home).

Initially we were not treated too badly, and those of us from public schools were naturally less traumatised than those who had rarely or never left home. The regime became less benign when we were moved to the adjacent training regiment, in which potential officers were separated from the rest. Our new sergeant, name of Williams, was a Yorkshireman and a real class warrior. He took a strong dislike to me and, to a lesser extent, to the two Old Marlburians who soon became my friends, Richard Bateman and Howard Baveystock. Dickie Bateman in particular became a major source of support. Sgt Williams would intone our names with deep loathing: 'Bateman, Baveystock and bloody Batoo', as he called me. Fortunately our (National Service) second lieutenant had also been at Marlborough, and defended us against our persecutor, who once or twice came near to striking me.

Sometimes an utterly exhausting day of training, involving 'square-bashing' and gun-drill with 25-pound brass-encased shells, would be followed by fatigues (chores like coal-heaving or cleaning). Once we were called to the cookhouse at 5.30pm to fill a bath with peeled potatoes. It took us five hours. On such occasions Dickie Bateman's sense of humour was a great comfort. Our beds became not just a blessed, positively voluptuous escape from physical weariness, but a zone of privacy, a refuge in which to think of home, family, friends and post-military delights. I amazed myself by my ability to fall asleep at around 9pm in a barrack room full of noise and conversation, with top lights blazing.

It was a great comfort to receive regular bulletins from civilisation, mainly from my parents and Martin, but also from Maurice Ash ('My dear Gunner') and a school friend or two who were undergoing the same ordeal. Maurice was often in my thoughts, especially during the long, chilly ordeal of guard duty. How passionately I longed for all the culture and well-heeled civilisation that he represented.

Dad as ambassador

For my parents this was also a time of dramatic change, upwards rather than downwards. In mid-November my father had taken up a new post as H.M. ambassador to Denmark. Their letters were full of first impressions of that delightful country, of the embassy residence and (problematical and largely foreign) domestic staff, descriptions of presenting letters of credence to the King and so on: a painful contrast to my lowly world of barrack room and parade ground. It was bad luck for the parents that not long after their initial warm welcome, the Danish Queen Mother died, official mourning was declared, even sister Elisabeth had to wear black when she went out, and places of entertainment were off limits. Lis was even not allowed to attend a ball with an attractive count. However, my mother loved being cosseted in the residence, and not having to do any domestic chores, apart from planning meals. Unfortunately her favourite and very attractive maid soon went off with the no less good-looking Danish chauffeur.

Mother had some friends who lived near Oswestry, and on my first available weekend I went to see them – in uniform, alas – on my motorcycle. At some stage of the day I was following their car, perhaps to a restaurant. We came down a minor road to a T-junction. They turned left. Anxious not to lose them, I took a risk in following, and was knocked off my m.c. by a car coming from the right. Fortunately the m.c. was worse affected than me. I continued to see mother's friends from time to time, and to venture into the glorious countryside with Dickie Bateman when possible.

My leadership deficit

Despite my poor posture and lack of aptitude either for shooting or stripping and reassembling Bren guns ('Imagine it has hair around it' was the standard exhortation), I wasn't too incompetent overall. But my attitude of bored and slightly amused tolerance did not endear me to my superiors, least of all when after six weeks or so I went off to the War Office Selection Board (WOSB) to have my officer potential assessed. This two-day ordeal involved obstacle courses, group discussions, interviews and lecturettes.

At all of these one was expected to show qualities of leadership and, above all, enthusiasm. As may be imagined, the idea of simulating enthusiasm went against just about everything I thought I stood for. Was I prepared to pretend I was enjoying basic training? I was not. Or that I relished discussing the merits or otherwise of flogging, a subject itself (in that era) flogged to death? Again, an emphatic no. There was an element of integrity in this: unto thine own self be true, and all that. But also a lot of stupid cussedness. I used to claim that I was observed yawning while going over an obstacle course, but in truth it was during a lecture by one of the adjudicating officers. He was not amused. And I was useless at seeing how my group could be got over a ditch that was too wide to jump, with boards that were too short to span the gap. When it came to the intelligence tests, I scored outstandingly high on those involving words and outstandingly low on those involving figures: the gap was said to be unprecedented. As for working out who D is sitting next to if A is sitting next to C and B next to E: my brain froze over.

In short, I failed a test passed by most young men of comparable background and qualifications. I had assumed a mantle of abnormality.

As P.G.Wodehouse might have commented, the parents were a considerable distance from being gruntled by news of my rejection, which I presented as a kind of achievement. My father admired success, and his elevation to H.M.'s envoy extraordinary and plenipotentiary reinforced his tendency to take questions of status seriously. He did not reckon failure was character-forming. He would have to go on addressing letters to me as 22724421 Gnr Berthoud (Gnr for Gunner). A terse correspondence ensued. My reactions were considered regrettably arrogant: they angered even my mother. I defended my corner doughtily, and no doubt counter-productively.

I had two fall-back strategies. I could take WOSB a second time; and I could apply for the armed services' notoriously intensive Russian course. With my A levels and state scholarship in French and German, I would surely be accepted for the latter, which usually ended with commissioned status. Meanwhile I was off to Trinity Hall to try for an exhibition, for which I was still young enough. I didn't expect (accurately) to get one, my brain having atrophied and my knowledge withered over the past two months, but it meant missing the last week of basic training, including the passing-out parade (my squad came last). Instead I had a blissful few days in Cambridge, and liked what I saw of Trinity Hall.

On my return to Oswestry I was categorised as 'awaiting disposal', as if I were a bit of garbage. Fortunately Dickie Bateman was too. A few days of fatigues awaited us. We decided that coal-heaving was less humiliating than washing floors. 'Don't think you're on your Daddy's fuckin' yacht', Sgt Williams sneered at me when I was on my knees scrubbing away. A couple of days later I virtually was.

Respite at the residence

To our great joy, we were given a fortnight's Christmas leave. After a night or two chez Ash and a rough sea crossing to Esbjerg, I was greeted at Copenhagen railway station by a radiantly welcoming mother and the chauffeured official car, a large Austin Sheerline (the Rolls came later). We purred to the embassy residence, a handsome mansion in central Copenhagen, where Lothar, the German butler, eased the overcoat off my shoulders. Sgt Williams, if only you could see me now, I thought.

It was a glorious and refreshingly sedentary interlude. My sins were at least temporarily forgiven, though Dad was initially a bit tense. Martin, who was enjoying his time at Magdalen College, Oxford reading Greats (classics and philosophy), was there. Our sister Elisabeth arrived soon with Belinda, now aged eight. Lis was still teaching at

Long Dene school, and Binnie was spending a year there under her watchful eye. Our parents had little choice but to send Binnie to boarding school, but she was much too young to enjoy embassy life during holidays.

The residence was genuinely palatial – its formal name was the Lindencrone Palace – with a ballroom and numerous reception rooms, though not many bedrooms. It breathed an atmosphere of opulence and plenty. There were two main snags: it had no garden, and stood at the top of Bredgade, the smart but noisy thoroughfare leading to the main city square where the opera house and Hotel Angleterre are prominent features. Martin and I shared a bedroom outside which trams plied late into the night, which didn't matter, since we talked at least till midnight. Less welcome was the resumption of their creaking and grinding at 6am.

It was good for my battered morale, as I noted in my journal, to come down at around 8.45am and say: 'Good morning, Lothar! Could we have grapefruit juice today; and about the eggs' (pause for thought) 'could we have them scrambled?' He must have thought us insufferably spoilt. We weren't very enterprising: just one trip outside Copenhagen, to Elsinore Castle, impressive as a building but ruthlessly and very well modernised within (it was nice to imagine Hamlet enjoying peach-coloured loo paper); and a couple of uninspiring diplomatic parties. There were no heartening contacts with the opposite sex, for which we both yearned.

This sybaritic existence could not last, and soon it was back to avoiding as many duties as possible ('skiving') at Oswestry. One interesting task was to escort back to camp a Scottish soldier who had gone absent without leave: he wanted to spend New Year's Eve in his native Glasgow. I went up with an NCO (non-commissioned officer, probably a sergeant). Towards the end of the journey some young men got into our compartment. What language are they talking, I wondered. They were Glaswegians. As we approached the city, we were enveloped in a smog so yellow and dense that it made the eyes prick. This was just under a month after the great London smog that lasted five days, killed some 4,000 people, stopped all transport, closed theatres and cinemas because stage and screen were no longer visible, and led to the first successful anti-pollution laws anywhere. Somehow we found our man, and made our way back to salubrious Shropshire.

Having failed WOSB, I had been interviewed by an officer who outlined the various alternatives, or 'trades', for which I could opt. This being the artillery, several involved an ability to calculate the correct trajectory to connect a shell with its target. For such tasks my incompetence at maths disqualified me. Among the alternatives was becoming a clerk, which I imagined would be fairly undemanding.

Learning to be a clerk

Before long I found myself proceeding by train to the RA's headquarters depot in the grimy south London borough of Woolwich (the Arsenal and all that) for a six-week clerks' course. I was the only member of my batch to have attempted WOSB. The company was adequately congenial, the barracks appalling: they were said to have been condemned in the Crimean War. There were some gains from being in London. The West End was accessible in the evening, and in six weeks I saw 25 films and three shows, including *Porgy and Bess* with the great soprano Leontyne Price, her first big success.

I was also able to get home every weekend but one, so I could report back to my parents in Copenhagen on developments at Gaston House, where the main part was being let. I also spent a good deal of time with Maurice and Ruth Ash. Maurice took me out to dinner one evening in London (I had to wear uniform, humiliatingly), and we called in at Dorothy and Leonard Elmhirst's picture-filled house in Upper Brook Street, Mayfair, then reckoned about the poshest address in London. What a strange life of light and shade it was.

Public duty called one weekend, when we rose at 5am and found ourselves carrying one hundredweight bags of cement on Erith Marshes, part of the army's contribution to flood relief following the disastrous but little remembered storm of 31 January 1953. This left a trail of destruction starting in Scotland and travelling down the East coast. Hundreds died at sea and on land. Many were drowned in their beds, notably in Lincolnshire and on Canvey Island. The Netherlands was even worse affected. It was probably the most physically testing weekend of my life. We later learned that the gap we had plugged was re-opened by the next high tide.

The long-term gain from the Woolwich course was that I acquired good typing skills. Admittedly these can be picked up by anyone without too much difficulty, and we were not, regrettably, taught to touch-type. But I would probably not have got up to the same speed had I been self-taught, nor have used typing so extensively to write essays at Cambridge, letters to my far-flung family, periodic journals and so on. All these were, unlike my handwriting, wonderfully legible, and carbon copies of the letters – I never wanted my life to trickle into the sands of time – have been invaluable in putting this record together. At Woolwich we also grappled with army records and procedures. I passed the relevant tests – I was now a Clerk B3, heady thought – and volunteered to join one of the many RA regiments in Germany, with a view to improving my spoken German.

My hopes of being accepted for the army Russian course were dashed. The interview at the War Office (as it then was) had seemed to go well enough, but I reckon that one word dished me. As I was about to leave, the interviewing officer observed matter-of-factly: 'You realise you won't necessarily end up with a commission if you get through the course.' This was genuinely news to me, and I said: 'Really?' in a surprised tone of voice. Perhaps if I had said: 'Of course', I would have been accepted. He may have thought that, having failed WOSB, I was desperately trying to get a commission by a back door. Alternatively, the board may have felt, reasonably enough, that my stammer would severely limit my usefulness as an interpreter or interrogator. I was never given an explanation. Hindsight suggests that if I had genuinely wanted to do the Russian course I should have applied for it immediately on reporting to Oswestry, if not before.

I have occasionally wondered how different my life might have been had I emerged from National Service speaking fluent Russian. I would probably have dropped German in favour of Russian at Cambridge. I might have become a foreign correspondent in Moscow rather than in Bonn. More immediately, I would have spent 18 months with intellectual equals or superiors, such as Michael Frayn, a contemporary who did the course. That would no doubt have been very stimulating, but less 'broadening' than what actually lay ahead.

Posted to West Germany

This was, in the short term, grim enough. True, I was sent to Germany as requested. The posting was to the 42nd Field Regiment RA based, rather unusually, in a suburb of Essen called Essen-Kupferdreh, near the former headquarters of the armaments manufacturer Krupp. Most of the British Army of the Rhine (BAOR) was further north. Essen, an industrial city on the Ruhr, had been heavily bombed by the allies, and the destruction was still very visible.

Life in the ranks in Germany was frustrating and often humiliating. Whereas junior officers could swan around in civilian clothes and regimental vehicles, other ranks had no access to transport and were obliged to wear uniform for their first six months in the army, even when sallying forth into central Essen or the surrounding countryside. We were an army of occupation, we had helped destroy their city: the vibes from the Germans were not good. My difficult but ever helpful father had used a connection to persuade a local BP executive, Nikolai Jahr, to befriend me. He and his wife took me out to meals and to local places of interest. I was deeply grateful, but felt my uniformed self was an embarrassment to them in public places. I spoke a good deal of English with them, and practised my German mainly on the odd-job men who worked within the camp.

Worse, although my fellow soldiers were genial enough, there was no one with whom I could bond and share my thoughts, interests and aspirations. I was paying a high price for my arrogant assumption that I would get onto the Russian course and therefore didn't need to take WOSB too seriously. I had fallen neatly between two stools. 'Never before have the pangs of remorse struck me so deeply', I wrote in a self-pitying outpouring in April 1953. 'Loneliness and a sense of hollow failure and negation are my most common emotions, and I try to live over again the sweeter moments of freedom, either those nectared days on leave, or the pre-enslavement era.'

Work in the office was generally undemanding, and the chief clerk, Sgt Roy Kinsley, was youngish, with a good sense of humour and vivid vocabulary. On one occasion he was wistfully recalling some woman he had fancied, and said: 'I could have sucked her shit through a sweaty sock!' Disgusting, of course, but also in its way pure poetry. It was that sort of outlandish humour that kept me going.

When I had served the requisite six months, I had to show my 'civvies' to a sympathetic lieutenant. 'Try not to look too much like an officer', he said wryly when I showed him my sports jacket and grey flannels. Since my whole demeanour and drawling voice had 'public school', and thus officer, written all over them, that would not be easy. My voice often caused me embarrassment, notably on mobile exercises. Once we were up north near Fallingbostel. I had just helped dig a command post in the dark (three hours of gruelling work, and we dug two on this exercise), and needed to pass on some message to our regimental sergeant major (RSM). Hearing my officer-like tones cleaving through the night, he saluted and addressed me as Sir – only to discover I was an unpipped, unstriped clerk. He was not amused. That was not the only time it happened.

To South Korea, via Plymouth

In early 1953 we were told the regiment was to be posted to South Korea, to relieve 20th Field Regiment RA. The Korean War had started in June 1950, when North Korea, heavily armed by the Soviet Union, invaded the lightly armed South. The Americans sent in troops to defend the regime of the dictatorial Syngman Rhee. Following a UN resolution supporting their action, 16 member states including Britain and several Commonwealth countries contributed contingents. This vicious war raged the length of the country, involving much hand-to-hand fighting. When the Chinese joined in on the North Korean side, human wave onslaughts were common. The war was to cost some 4,000,000 military and civilian lives, including those of 1,078 British troops. Eventually a stalemate was reached near the 38th parallel and negotiations began that lasted for some two years. We were due to embark in late November 1953. The armistice was signed that July. In effect, we would have a bit of an adventure without any real risk to our lives, accidents apart (and in the army there are always plenty of those).

But first, late that summer, I had another go at WOSB. Surely, after all those regrets, I must have been trying. Whether it was my natural aversion to displays of factitious enthusiasm, my aura of languor or my stammer that caused me to be failed a second time, I never discovered. But fail I did, no doubt to my parents' disgust. By this stage, I think I was relieved to be spared four months of officer cadet training at Mons, which notoriously made basic training seem like a holiday camp. The prospect of going to Korea was quite appealing. I would certainly be wringing the maximum of travel out of my two years of military service, and it would be quite an experience.

The preliminaries were banal. Before we could embark for the long sea journey to the Far East, we had to spend three weeks in transit in the UK, where the regiment would be brought up to strength numerically (at the risk of being sent the offscourings of other RA regiments), and we would be inoculated and kitted out. I was among those fingered to form an advance party to our transit camp, Plumer Barracks in Plymouth. There we toiled for two or three weeks, installing hundreds of beds, cleaning floors and so on. The barracks were grim, as was Plymouth, which had not recovered from serious war damage.

This time it was Maurice and Ruth Ash who provided a lifeline, in the shape of

Isobel Cabot, deputy head of Dartington School not many miles away. She was a charming yet motherly woman, and had two lively sons of roughly my age, David and Murray, plus a younger daughter of exquisite beauty, Lally. In my six weeks in Plymouth I spent two restorative weekends in the spacious Cabot home on the edge of Totnes. One evening we attended a jam session at the school, and I was dazzled by the skills of the clarinettist and saxophonist Dick Heckstall-Smith, who was to be a significant figure on the national jazz scene. My friendship with the Cabots endured, and I never forgot Isobel's beauty, the warmth of her voice and the loving embrace in which her blue eyes seemed to enfold me.

The regiment departed for Korea in November, perversely from Liverpool. Our troopship was the *Empire Pride*, presumably named with no sense of irony, built in 1941 but seeming vastly more ancient. We could hardly believe our eyes when we were shown the troop decks in which we were supposed to sleep for the next five weeks – not in beds but hammocks. These were thoroughly uncomfortable and very difficult to get in and out of.

Our first night at sea was extremely rough, as was the following morning. Of the 800 or so soldiers on board, a good 90 per cent were sick. The smell in my troop deck in the bowels of the ship was nauseating. Fortunately, and perhaps thanks to my journeyings to Canada and back and to Denmark, I was able to eat a nourishing breakfast. Up on deck I'm afraid I was cheered to see the high wind splattering the fat, pompous, unloved RSM with a nearby soldier's vomit.

On the ship's only deck we regimental clerks were installed in a smallish office, where I slept on a table or the floor until it was balmy enough to sleep on deck. Our first stop was Port Said, where we were not allowed ashore: there had been trouble between British troops stationed in the Suez Canal zone and Egyptian nationalists. To the former we waved as we made our way through the canal into the sweltering Red Sea. 'Get your knees brown!' they shouted back derisively, as we would on the way home.

There was clerical work to do in the office, some shooting practice (at targets launched from the rear of the ship), and a few menial tasks. 'So they call this a Sunday!' I wrote in my diary on November 29. 'Up at 6.15. Queue for 15 minutes for a wash. After perfunctory ablutions, queue up for breakfast for 10 minutes, eat breakfast then wash up, scrub floor, table etc (it is my unhappy lot to be mess orderly this week). All with sweat pouring off one's body like so much water'. That was when we were passing through the Red Sea, a seriously humid zone.

There were compensations, as I noted next day: 'An amazing sunset tonight. A great blue rift above the horizon, half blotted out by a cloud of deepest black, from behind which pressed a great mass of red glory. The surrounding sky was almost every possible colour – golden, silver, grey and blue. A staggering sight to all but the most insensitive', I concluded sententiously. The language of my fellow soldiers continued to delight. One late afternoon I was in the toilet peeing between two Geordies when the following conversation took place across me (you have to image the broadest Geordie accent):

First Geordie: 'What's for fuckin' supper, mate' (pronounced meeyut).

Second Geordie: 'Duff.'

First Geordie: 'Fuck'

Could Pinter have improved on it?

Never having been to the East, I was fascinated by the sights, sounds, smells and women in our three main stops: Colombo, Singapore and especially Hong Kong, where the cheongsams were a highlight: close-fitting dresses slit up to the upper thigh. Aden was furnace-like and grimly austere. By this stage I had become friendly with a fellow National Service clerk called Ivan Hughes, an intelligent and civilised fellow from Banbury. We tended to spend these three-to-four hour stops on shore together, along with a diminutive regular soldier known as Sheff, a fellow regimental office clerk.

In the South China Sea we found ourselves on the edge of a typhoon. 'Mon Dieu, this is really rough', I wrote on December 10. 'We are making practically no headway against a very strong headwind, and the boat is pitching about 20 degrees either way at the bows and stern. The fo'c'sle (bow) is perpetually submerged and the spray is colossal. At 6.15 this morning, as we lay peacefully sleeping here in the office, a dirty great wave swept in through the open hatch and soaked Ivan and Sheff as they slept on the floor. Being on the table I remained comparatively dry.' We were blown a day or two off course, and at one stage crockery flew around the canteen.

After some five weeks en route, we docked at Pusan, on Korea's southern tip, welcomed by an American military band and a sign announcing: 'Pusan, the busiest military port in the World' (the Americans love such slogans. We would soon see an education corps train labelled 'A Moveable College of Useable Knowledge'). On the way by lorry to yet another transit camp we passed shacks built of cardboard and smelt the stench of acute poverty, inspiring feelings of guilt as we spent two days being kitted out with, *inter alia*, superb parkas in which to face the rigours of the Korean winter. We then staggered on to a vastly long train, complete with full backpacks, two kitbags each, a bedding roll and a rifle. There was a seminal moment in which a junior officer ponced past carrying just a pistol. Never had the full injustice of social divisions struck me so personally. It has not occurred to me to vote Conservative since.

Life in our tented encampment

The train's seats were wooden. For the first few hours I watched the impressive scenery roll by – a foreground of paddy fields against a backcloth of mountains. Come nightfall I repaired to a vacant spot on a luggage rack and, with my head on a bedding roll, achieved more than five hours sleep, to my great satisfaction. After 18 hours we reached Tokchong, and were taken along steep, powdery roads in a fleet of Canadian army lorries to our base camp some 50 miles north west of the capital, Seoul. There we were separated into our four component units: it would be a five-mile circuit from regimental headquarters, in which I served, to the three batteries and back. Our camp was on flat terrain set against a backdrop of mountains, dominated by Mount Kamaksan, with the river Imjin not far away. We were three miles from our dug-out positions nearer to the 38th Parallel, on the so-called Kansas Line, to which we were supposed to 'scramble' should hostilities resume.

We worked and slept in tents, though there were a few prefabricated Quonsett huts around, for the officers' and sergeants' messes and the canteen. The tents were lit in the evening by paraffin-fuelled Tilley lamps and heated by a steel stove fed (via a thin pipe) with petrol from an inverted jerry can outside the tent. The flow was controlled by a carburettor that tended to freeze up over night, during which the stoves were supposed to be turned off. Sparks from the chimney periodically set a tent alight. The speed at which a tent could burn down was frightening: after a couple of minutes, only red-hot metal bedsteads were left. The previous regiment was said to have suffered a few fatalities when soldiers, faced with a fire, failed to get out of their sleeping bags fast enough. No doubt they had kept their stove on: rashly but understandably, since the nights were cold enough to freeze the blankets over one's head. The nearest latrine, an eight-seater, was 50 feet away up a hill. To be stricken by diarrhoea in the middle of a freezing night was not an amusing experience: the temperature was down to zero Fahrenheit when it happened to me. By contrast, winter days tended to be bracing but sunny.

As a Christmas Eve treat we were taken to a Commonwealth Division building called the Coliseum to see a show put on by Maori elements of the New Zealand forces, plus four professionals fresh from New Zealand. They sang, danced and manipulated their *poës* – bead-filled woven spheres on the end of a woven thong – with mesmerizing skill. A duet version of *You Wonderful One* brought the house down. Never had I heard a popular song so well sung. On Christmas day we were woken by two sergeants bearing tea well laced with rum. It was hard to believe that a year previously I had been at the breakfast table in Copenhagen opening Christmas presents. The change was good for me, I told my journal, adding 'Too much comfort softens the moral fibre', a sentiment my father could have uttered.

A considerable enrichment of my life in Korea was a burgeoning friendship with a fellow clerk called Bernard Hickey. He worked for the Quarter Master not far from our tented office, had been to art school and had a good sense of humour. There were other very pleasant people around, and I developed a crush on a charming young Scot, a driver called Ian Grant. It lasted the duration of my time in Korea, and I used to chat to him most evenings. Where is the borderline between a sustained crush and love? I yearned to stroke or embrace him, but there was no such thing as privacy in that set-up, leaving aside his possible reactions. There are some things in life best left untested.

In contrast to the set-up in Germany, it was no great disadvantage to be a private in Korea. With relatively few officers in each of the regiment's four officers' messes, their choice of company was more limited than mine, and there was often bad blood between the older regulars and the National Service subalterns. Several of the latter befriended me, and one even took me on an expedition or two. One day one of

Bernard Hickey and Ian Grant

my closest friends from Rugby, John Hamilton, paid a visit from an RA unit on the far side of the Imjin: we had also overlapped at Oswestry. He appalled me by saying he was thinking of signing on as a regular officer and giving up Cambridge. Fortunately he changed his mind, and was on the same troopship going home.

There were other cheering elements, among them the beauty of the countryside, especially in spring. One fine day in late April three of us walked two thirds of the way up Mt Kamaksan, following a stream full of boulders and little waterfalls. Wild azaleas, violets and flowers I could not identify covered the hillside, to be followed by wild roses. Then there was the interest of being in an ancient if war-ravaged country. Many villagers had been evacuated from the military zone, but elsewhere it was common to see old men with their quaint horsehair stove-pipe hats and long, thin pipes. Seoul was still badly damaged, and bore no resemblance to today's prosperous metropolis (I went back fairly recently for the *Times*). Such artefacts as were available were often fashioned

from brass shell casings. There were also some handsome pots: Korea's ceramic pedigree is even longer than Japan's.

The poverty in the villages was sad to see. Houses were made of mud and generally thatched, sometimes tiled. In the paddy fields, ploughs were drawn exclusively by oxen. The smell of 'night soil', the only available fertiliser, was often heavy in the air. There were even some women around, for us a rare sight, fleetingly visible in the villages through which we passed on manoeuvres (static in winter, mobile in summer). I saw my first bare breasts when we passed a woman washing: 'Talk about the hanging gardens of Babylon!' I crassly noted in my diary. Scrambling to our positions on the Kansas Line was exciting. They were about 2,000 feet up steep and winding tracks, and the views on the ascent and descent were inspiring. This is life with a capital L, I periodically thought to myself. Tedious and restrictive though the regimental office itself was, there were enough compensating elements to make Korea overall a positive chapter in my life.

On leave in Tokyo

Another new experience was 'rest and recuperation' (R & R) in Tokyo. This had been off the menu for months because the transport involved, USAF Globemasters, was being used to carry supplies to French forces in Indochina. Being well-placed in the office, I was able to secure two of the first vacancies, for me and my chum Bernard Hickey. Our destination, after a hot, cramped and bumpy flight, was Ebisu leave camp, which we reached in pouring rain. It proved to be a well-run establishment, catering for all allied troops, with excellent food and accommodation. 'The only flaw', I censoriously told my diary, 'is the behaviour of the less admirable elements of one's fellow soldiers, whose main idea is to get drunk and to indulge with the to me almost wholly unattractive Japanese girls, amongst whom the VD rate is the highest in the world.' That was probably an exaggeration. But one of my minor tasks in the office had been to handle the results of the medical officer's checks for sexually transmitted diseases, and I had noted the high incidence of gonorrhea. So I was not tempted: no blobby knobs, as they were called, for me, thank you. My virginity did not yet feel burdensome. As for Japanese women, my attitude to them later changed.

Once again the Berthoud contact service had been in action, and after a few congenial days shopping, relaxing, sunbathing and talking to Bernard, off I went for a weekend in the British embassy compound with a diplomat friend of my father's, John Chadwick, his pregnant wife and their two children. If it was wonderful to sleep in sheets at Ebisu leave camp, it was even more wonderful to be cherished by this lovely family. John Chadwick had coincidentally been to Rugby, and his brother Owen was Dean of my future college, Trinity Hall. They encouraged me to go and see the Great Buddha, a vast bronze at Kamakura, some 30 miles from Tokyo, in front of which hundreds of adorable schoolchildren were having their photographs taken. Meanwhile Bernard, more enterprisingly, was visiting Kyoto. Feeling guilty that I had missed this key sight,

I consoled myself that I was only 19 and would surely come back to Japan in later life. I never have, though my wife Joy went there solo a few years ago. Tokyo has of course changed almost as dramatically as Seoul.

The Korean summer could be as torrid (if less humid than Japan's) as the winter was cold, and at one stage we had to dig ditches around our tents to protect us from being flooded by monsoon-like rainfall. Temperatures were often in the 90sF, in spring swooping down to the 30s at night: on May 26 1954, the maximum temperature was 99°F, the minimum 38°F. Our main escape was to swim in the Imjin, making sure to avoid the reputedly deadly black water-snakes. Bernard saw one at close range: it was about four foot long and as thick as his forearm. From time to time a great skein of geese would fly above the river, honking gloriously.

Among the perks of being on active service, as we notionally were despite the armistice, was a free ration of cigarettes and chocolate, the former at least unthinkable today. Since Dad had bribed me not to smoke until I was 21 (£100 was at stake), I swapped the cigarettes for chocolate, to the severe detriment of my teeth. *A propos* my father, there was a nice moment in the regimental office in early June 1954 when the charming deputy adjutant perched on my trestle table desk and said: 'Well, Berthoud, I see your father's got his K.' Dad's KCMG had been announced in the Birthday honours, and I felt a glow of filial pride. He was fortunate in his timing. Nowadays, when knighthoods are less liberally dished out, an ambassador to Denmark might not rate one – however good, and I believe Dad was a very good ambassador in all important ways, even if he was not liked by some of his staff. He had been awarded the CMG in 1945, for his wartime service.

For being in Korea on active service, we humble soldiers gleaned the United Nations medal. It consisted of blue and white vertical stripes, and was consequently dubbed 'the butcher's apron.' I have never had occasion to wear it. There was a tastefully matching war medal for those who had been there during the action.

Thoughts on Mother

A word here about my mother, whose letters to me were a considerable comfort. She was not naturally gregarious, though her strong sense of duty had involved her in village affairs: wolf cubs, youth clubs, adoption committees and so on. She did not relish the idea of being an ambassadress, feared she would miss her English friends and fail to make good Danish ones. In the event she did find the proliferation of cocktail and dinner parties tedious: imagine a long dinner sandwiched between, say, the Romanian and Chinese ambassadors, neither with more than a few words of English. But, like my father, she made many very good Danish friends. Her interest in psychology led her to study and interpret the tales of Hans Christian Andersen, Denmark's most famous son.

Like her own mother, she could be very down-to-earth (on my childhood passport, she entered my colour of hair as 'mouse', and under Other Distinguishing Features put 'long pointed nose'). She was a great believer in humility, never my strongest point. Shortly before I left Korea I must have made some rather smug and competitive remark in a letter about having had a more interesting and formative time in the army than Martin. 'Yes, I hope the army has done you good', she responded, 'but I think it's unwise of you to feel you start ahead of Martin. Certainly he came out of the army bumptious & pleased with himself apparently, but it was only a veneer & soon wore off. It's his enthusiasm, energy & courage coupled with determination that get him somewhere'.

She went on: 'Humility really is the basic quality because without it we can learn nothing for we don't see the necessity for anything. Because I am full of fear & sense of inferiority I have put on lots of self-protective coverings, but gradually they are getting ripped off & exposing the bareness. Courage is a terribly necessary thing in life & one which you & I both need badly...so many people appear conceited because they are inflating themselves against a sense of inferiority.'

How wise she could be. A week later, after a discussion of the differences between philosophy and psychology (she had been dipping into Martin's books on Greek philosophy) she wrote: 'The great mistake of religions is to impose patterns on people rather than help them to find their own pattern by canalising certain inner experiences or feelings.' Yet despite her wisdom and her humility, she could be crudely anti-Roman Catholic, more than a touch racist and somewhat snobbish, as indeed could my father. In that they doubtless reflected their upbringing and generation. It's sad, however, that all those years abroad and their experience of Nazi inhumanity to the Jews did not make them react against such prejudices – especially as they claimed to be Christians. Nonetheless, a loving mother she was, and I often felt very close to her. A not untypical letter from her at around this period ended: 'Now I'm going to have a lovely introverting (sic) hour writing my journal, so goodnight darling. Much love Mum.'

Her vulnerability was also touching. In the spring of 1954 she wrote from Copenhagen at a stage when being an ambassadress had evidently been taking a heavy toll: 'My one objective at the moment is to get through the next month, so you might support me with prayer or loving thoughts or anything you can lay on. Since I've been back from England I've been fighting something like a breakdown and have literally not felt myself at all. Now after three weeks I suddenly feel I am back in my usual skin, but I have had such a shake-up and fright that (a) I didn't mention it to you because I feared to emphasise it in my mind and increase my own fear and (b) I am still a bit nervous that things may slip again and expose my jangled inner machinery.' Fortunately she recovered.

Some plus factors on the way to demob

Among other compensations of life in Korea was a good library service, and there was plenty of time to read, as well as talk. There were frequent film shows, during which Cockney wit from among my fellow soldiers was often in evidence. Showers were infrequently available at a divisional shower unit some way off. Local Koreans provided a minimal laundry service. We washed our own socks. Rather surprisingly, I joined a bible-reading and discussion group led by the regiment's (National Service) medical officer, the evangelical but gentle Dr Mervyn Rosser, with three or four friends. Bernard Hickey and I used to go to Sunday services, which rotated around the regiment's four component parts, giving us a pleasant walk. They were a reminder of normal life.

In summer the air was loud with the sound of frogs from nearby marshland. There were mosquitoes aplenty. From spring to autumn we used mosquito nets at night, and took our unpleasantly large anti-malarial Paludrine tablets daily. There was the occasional nasty accident: our signals sergeant, a very nice man, was fatally electrocuted when the long aerial of his jeep touched a power line. I was shocked to see his charred body being unloaded. The face of a not very bright soldier was badly burnt when he put a match to the orifice of a jerry can to see if there was any petrol left in it.

Above all, we counted the days before demob. That, as I knew from my office experience, would be a long process, but towards the end of July 1954 it wondrously began. After saying goodbye to everyone in RHQ – it was a wrench to part from my beloved Ian – our batch headed on the same agonisingly uncomfortable train back to Pusan, whence we had come eight months previously. From there, by sea to the major Japanese port of Kure, adjacent to Hiroshima, where we arrived in torrential rain after a very rough journey. In Kure we wasted six days in a transit camp in torridly humid weather, doing nothing very much: the odd parade, some desultory fatigues, a trip or two to outlying islands, some shopping in Kure, a lot of ping-pong in the NAAFI, writing letters and reading. I vaguely recall an oppressive sense of being near the scene of the terrible (if perhaps militarily justifiable) tragedy of the atomic bombing of Hiroshima.

The ship that was to bear us homewards was the *Dilwara*. Built in 1936, it was five years older than the *Empire Pride*, but must have been refitted, or perhaps built to a higher, peacetime specification: it seemed more modern, and there were bunks with sheets and pillows. Apart from the odd chore – I had to polish a long length of brass handrail and 14 brass portholes every day for a fortnight and then do regular stints of fire-watch – we had no duties. It was like a month-long cruise: nothing much to do but talk, read, sunbathe, admire the sunsets, watch the dolphins and flying fish, consume a bit of beer and enjoy the same ports of call as on the outward journey. Morale fluctuated according to the state of the sea (often stormy), the heat and the tedium factor.

We were heading towards freedom! 'Get overseas', we duly shouted to the Canal Zone troops watching our progress through the Suez Canal. Bernard was not with me: he had needed to be home earlier to catch the start of his art college year. Fellow clerk Ivan Hughes was, however, an excellent companion, and I made some new friends.

We docked at Southampton on September 10, just under five weeks after leaving Kure. Those among us from the Royal Artillery then proceeded by train to Waterloo and thence to the RA depot in Woolwich. It was a Saturday morning, and to our great joy a genial sergeant said we could buzz off until 0750 hrs on Monday morning. I was back home in time for tea, greeted by a radiant sister Elisabeth, her new husband Richard

Pentney, and dear old Gran. Richard was a handsome and charming schoolmaster whom Lis had met in Copenhagen while he was tutoring the son of a (visiting) junior minister. He taught at Sedbergh, the Spartan and hearty public school in Cumbria.

My delight at being home was muted by tragic news from Lis that Marcelle Bennett, an old family friend who had lived upstairs at Gastons until recently with her husband Gordon and daughter Zoë, had committed suicide by throwing herself in front of a local train. Zoë was staying in Copenhagen with Binnie at the time. Marcelle, who was almost part of the family, was a beautiful and charismatic French woman married to a very intelligent but somewhat uptight Englishman. A French friend of hers had taken her life in the same way not long previously.

After three days back at Woolwich, I was finally demobbed on September 16 1954, one day after my 20th birthday, by which time my mother and brother Martin had joined the reception committee at Gaston House. It was not to be a complete break with the military: we were obliged to spend a few weekends a year with our allotted Territorial Army unit , and therefore could not shed our uniforms, webbing and so on. It was in the dreaded khaki, much less comfortable than our kit in Korea, that I returned home.

To my surprise and pleasure, I left the army on a positive note. My adjutant must have written quite warmly about me in an 'end of National Service' report to my parents. 'We were, of course, all very delighted with your release report & I shall treasure it greatly', my mother had written just before I embarked for the return journey. 'If people who know you so comparatively little feel you've developed & improved, we shall feel it more profoundly I am sure.' Back in the bosom of the family I remember having to try to get a grip on my swearing. At dinner one evening I inadvertently said 'abso-fucking-lutely', which everyone kindly ignored.

Was my adjutant right in thinking I had developed? Certainly my view of the world had been greatly widened. My sympathy for the underdog and any resentment he might feel for those born privileged (such as me) had been aroused. I had dwelt among people from varied walks and stations of life from all over Britain, of whom I would otherwise have had little first-hand knowledge. I like to think I had learnt to treat people as equals. My experiences would provide a bond with most of my contemporaries, from wherever they might come. And I had seen a slice of the Far East before it was heavily westernised. Thanks to all that, I would surely extract more from university life than if I had gone straight to it, aged barely 18, from school.

Chapter 4

Cambridge (1954-57)

I went up to Cambridge on October 3, two years and a day after joining the army. The trip to basic training in Oswestry had been long, the prospect bleak. The trip to Cambridge and higher learning was short, the prospect of the rosiest.

Trinity Hall is one of the university's smaller colleges (some 350 undergraduates and graduates in those days), beautifully located on the river between Trinity, the largest, and medium-sized Clare. I was on tenterhooks about the accommodation I would be allocated in college for my first year. I had been told it might be wise, well in advance, to butter up Bert Stearn, the clerk to the senior tutor. Bert called the shots. This I had done when trying for an exhibition back in autumn 1952. I may even have stooped to mention that my father was an ambassador. There was a limited number of single rooms, of varying vintage and quality, available to freshmen: a majority were obliged to share, usually with someone not of their choice, which I was desperate to avoid.

I could hardly believe my luck when I climbed to my allotted room at the top of O staircase, which lay through the main courtyard in a relatively modern extension by the river. It was spacious, perhaps 30 x 18 feet, with a view over a lawn and past a beech tree to the Cam. It may well have been the best room in the college. I never saw a better. My only immediate neighbour was an eminent and elderly law don, J.W.C.Turner, who lived elsewhere and gave few tutorials there. From him there would be no noise. I could not have had a better start, and thanked my benefactor profusely. In this room I first expressed my burgeoning interest in contemporary design, fostered by visits to Copenhagen. I bought a number of pots (one by Bernard Leach) at Primavera, a craft shop on King's Parade, some fabric for a screen at Heal's in London, and a coloured etching by Gwen Raverat, author of that classic memoir *Period Piece*: my first picture.

At the Hall I had two useful contacts. While at school I had, as mentioned, been in the same house as the sons of the senior tutor, Charles Crawley, a distinguished historian. My near contemporary among them, John, was a brilliant musician (piano and violin), a classical scholar and a friend. He had wisely gone to Oxford, but because I had known him well I was periodically invited to the Crawley home for tea and advice. Rather surprisingly, given his slightly out-of-this-world aura, John became a senior figure in the Inland Revenue. I once even received a cheque signed by him.

Then there was Owen Chadwick, the college Dean and ecclesiastical historian, whose brother I had stayed with in Tokyo. He was widely tipped as a future Archbishop of Canterbury, but eventually chose the more scholarly and lower profile role of Master of Selwyn College in Cambridge. It was the more extrovert but less overtly impressive Robert Runcie, his successor as the college Dean after my second year, who gained the archbishopric after his later stint as Bishop of St Albans. Coincidentally and slightly improbably, Runcie's spirited wife Rosalind was the daughter of my sober-sided legal neighbour, Cecil Turner. I both ate and played squash periodically with Owen Chadwick, who as a pre-war undergraduate had played rugby three years running for Cambridge and had shoulders to match. A lovely man.

There were also numerous Old Rugbeians around: not that I felt I needed them, having every confidence in my ability to make friends. But as a source of twin souls, Trinity Hall proved to be less than ideal. Legal and medical students predominated, and the arts students were far from uniformly interesting. The most engagingly eccentric was Adrian Taylor, a major scholar in English who did no work, failed his exams, then came back to study law, did brilliantly and became a lecturer in law at Kent University. He was on my staircase, and very amusing in an anarchic way.

On the plus side, what school anyone had attended was a matter of little or zero interest, in contrast to my brother Martin's experience at Magdalen, Oxford, where he was an uneasy member of the 'smart set'. When he stood for President of the Junior Common Room (JCR), he was defeated by the (surprisingly) larger and better organised grammar school faction. This upset him considerably. At Tit Hall, as it was sometimes known, the atmosphere was friendly, not least during meals (uninspiring) in the high-ceilinged, portrait-bedecked dining hall. The JCR was scarcely a concept.

Some of my friends

Among the few historians in the Hall was a childhood acquaintance, Robin Hooper, whose family had earlier lived on the edge of Hatfield Forest. We recognised each other in the Porter's Lodge on day one. He had a slightly glamorous aura, having been the army's skiing champion during his National Service in the Rifle Brigade. Through him I met a number of the more interesting Old Etonians, mainly at nearby King's or Trinity colleges.

Robin's father Ian was a charming shipping executive who was to die aged 56. His formidable mother Alison had had a relationship with *Picture Post*'s founder, Stefan Lorant, father of Robin's attractive sister Gini, who periodically appeared on the Cambridge scene. Alison had helped found and edit *Lilliput*, a famous small-format magazine of the late 1930s and 40s. Robin had a great deal of his father's charm. At the end of our first term we went to a young people's dance in Notting Hill co-hosted by his mother, Mrs Malcolm Muggeridge and Mrs Ronald Searle. Both of the latters' husbands were famous at the time, as journalist/ broadcaster and cartoonist/artist respectively: I briefly felt I was entering the glamorous media world. Robin and I gave several parties à deux at Cambridge, including one in our last year for 130 people, and holidayed together in France.

The most engaging medic among my contemporaries was Adam Lawrence. He was not only unfairly good-looking, but had a perfect physique: 6ft 2in tall, broad shoulders and so on. He excelled at tennis, and earned some useful extra funds modelling. More to the point, he was very good company, vastly popular, and very keen on jazz. His father, Dr Robin Lawrence, had been a pioneer in the treatment of diabetes, from which he suffered: he experimented on himself. Adam's mother Anna, a wonderful woman who was to die all too young, had been a professional pianist.

Bobbie Lawrence, Nicholas Barrington,
Adam Lawrence, somewhat later

One evening Adam and a fellow medic waylaid the blues singer and guitarist Big Bill Broonzy after a London concert (Broonzy's manager had been given some warning) and invited him back to the Lawrences' flat in Devonshire Place, W.1. for supper. For more than an hour, about 10 of us subsequently enjoyed wonderful talk and music from the great man. Around 1am there was a loud twang as one of the 12 steel strings of his guitar snapped, and Broonzy roared: 'I must go now.' Did he contrive it, we wondered? As Adam drove him back to his hotel, Broonzy said with feeling: 'That was the first time I've been in a private party during all my European tours.'

After qualifying as a doctor, Adam became a specialist in sexually transmitted diseases, little suspecting how big a field this would become thanks to the Aids pandemic. Like Robin Hooper, he has remained a close friend. A bond between us was our friendship with a postgraduate law student, Bernard Josien. He was your ideal Frenchman: handsome, highly intelligent, witty, and with a gift for friendship, especially with women, though he never married. Later I often stayed with him in his attic flat in the Rue Bonaparte, off the Bd St Germain. When he began earning lots of money as a corporate lawyer, he acquired a large penthouse atop the 31-storey Tour Perspective near the Eiffel Tower, with dizzying views over the Seine. We were to see a lot of each other when I later found myself working in Paris, and subsequently when I visited Paris with the family. He was a wonderfully generous man.

Before long Clare College, next door, yielded three good friends: Richard Kershaw, later a prominent BBC radio and TV journalist; Nicholas Barrington, who

Left: Robin Hooper; Right: Bernard Josien

ended his diplomatic career as High Commissioner in Pakistan; and Roger Norrington, a versatile musician who later became famous (and knighted) as a conductor, though at Cambridge he was reading English. Two other Clare contemporaries became friends shortly after leaving Cambridge: Philip Hughes, later co-founder and chairman of Logica, the software company, who is also a remarkable painter; and Peter Barbor, a paediatrician of great charm.

Language and literature

Having done my A-levels in French and German, I had decided to stick with languages at Cambridge: Dad reckoned history would have been more valuable, but I had no talent for it, and a poor memory. Because Trinity Hall had just one linguist among its Fellows, those of us doing languages were farmed out for supervisions to dons or even post-graduates in other colleges. One of the latter took me for first year French. He seemed a bit of a class warrior, did not like me, and gave me discouraging marks. I fared better when I was switched to the charming and sophisticated Douglas Parmée. My German supervisor, Dr Ronald Gray of Emmanuel College, was by contrast the Tim Tosswill of my Cambridge career. He thought my essays pretty good, grading them somewhere between beta double plus and a straight alpha. He once even said: 'I wish I could feel confident I would have written it as well.' Graham Storey, my college 'tutor' (*in loco parentis*), observed: 'There seems to be a curious dichotomy between the views of your French and German supervisors. One expects you to get a 2:2, the other thinks you might get a first.' This was more of a reflection on my supervisors: I tried harder for Ronald Gray because he was a man of high calibre, a recognised authority on Thomas Mann, Kafka and Rilke, took a lot of trouble with my essays, and liked me. [He followed my career, invited me back for a posh dinner at Emma when my first book was published, and even put me up for the night].

In reality, I was better at both speaking and writing French, a much less grammatically complex language, and enjoyed the literature more. To my mind, German literature has no poet to compare with Baudelaire, though some might argue the case for that all-round genius Goethe, or for Heine or Rilke; and no pre-20th century novelists to compare with Stendhal, Balzac and Flaubert. But German writers are arguably stronger on ideas (Thomas Mann, Kafka, Brecht, not to mention the great philosophers), and so perhaps easier to write about. For my 16th century French paper, I relished Montaigne, that great advocate of tolerance and the middle way in an intolerant age, but found the supposedly rumbustious Rabelais tiresome.

We had exams at the end of each academic year: hence the Tripos. Only two of them counted towards one's BA degree. With modern languages, Part 1 was generally taken after the first year, with the emphasis on linguistic competence, plus two papers on literature: a bit like the last few terms at school. For Part 2 we had to select five periods for their literature and history, and write an essay in one language: I naturally chose French.

Since I find self-discipline easier within a fairly regular routine, I worked every morning from around 9am till lunchtime, and then from around 4.30pm till supper. If I had an essay to write, I would continue after supper and/or over the weekend. Lectures varied in quality. If the same material could be better acquired from books, I avoided them. I probably went to about five a week, including Ronald Gray's. A brilliant French woman called Odette de Mourgues lectured on Montaigne. She had written a novel entitled *Hortensia Bleu* (*Blue Hydrangea*), and her lectures were intellectually pellucid.

Lectures had their social aspects. Via 19th century French literature I met another life-long friend, Jo Frampton, who was at Corpus. I was still impressed by male good looks, and Jo had them in spades. He was a natural linguist, and for his other language was tackling Russian after only a year of it at King's Canterbury: most of his fellow students were fluent veterans of the armed services' Russian course, onto which I had tried to clamber. Jo later became fluent in Spanish and Italian (he lives in Tuscany), had goodish German, excellent French, could get by in most East European languages thanks to his Russian, and acquired a modicum of Greek. He learned and practised most of these languages as a salesman, mainly of specialised printing machinery – and with his many female friends. He was to be a great travelling companion. He had the languages to cope with all the hassle, and his relaxed personality was undemanding.

As a bonus, his appetite for culture while holidaying was roughly the same as mine.

Looking back at my essays on literature and philosophy, I'm amazed at how long they were – around 1500 words – and how knowledgeable they seem. We were not expected to reveal our sources, and it's hard now to disentangle my own judgements from those of heavyweight critics. I was certainly good at weaving it all together. I remember feeling guilty about my debt to Bertrand Russell's *History of Western Philosophy*.

Jo Frampton,
with granddaughter, 1990s

Left: Merete by the Cam; Right: Richard Kershaw

Unfortunately my memory was poor both for poetry and the names of characters in novels. But I worked hard, hoping I might get a first. In the event, I was nothing if not consistent, scoring a 2:1 in all three parts of the Tripos. Ronald Gray lost a ring or two of his halo at the end by failing to warn us that in our German papers we would be obliged for the first time to answer one question on history: he surely should have known. In French, history remained optional.

Social life and holidays

My social life at Cambridge involved tea-time encounters with friends old and new, squash, tennis, the occasional lunch or supper in town, lots of films (40 in 1955, for example, plus nine plays, three operas and three ballets, not all in term-time of course), a jazz club, and occasional meetings of the French Society. This last was the only non-college society I joined, mainly in the hope of meeting a desirable woman. In those days all colleges were single-sex. There were around 7,000 male undergraduates and 700 female ones. I can't imagine how I failed to meet more of the latter. There were other young women in circulation, notably from the town's language school, its hospital and teacher training college, and I was not without some contacts.

On the beauty stakes, help was at hand. In Copenhagen, where I spent at least part of most vacations for my first 18 months, I had the rarity value of being the British ambassador's son, though that created certain constraints. There I soon met the very beautiful Merete Topsøe-Jensen, daughter of a distinguished engineer (a much higher-status profession in Denmark than in England). Miraculously, she was coming to Cambridge as an up-market *au pair*, and I was soon seeing a good deal of her in Cambridge, though not all the parts I wanted to see. Maddeningly, Martin was meanwhile having a fulfilling relationship at Oxford with a student from the Ruskin School of Art.

Holidays in Copenhagen were a joy, especially when Martin was there – or Bob Keyserlingk from my Canada years, now tall, charismatic and very entertaining. He came to Copenhagen for Christmas 1954, and we went to Paris together the following spring. Rarely have I enjoyed myself so much. On one rather lamentable occasion we had to be escorted out of the gardens of Versailles by uniformed attendants after trying to insert an empty wine bottle into the outstretched hand of a female sculpture.

In Copenhagen Dad had inherited a short list of young people with whom his predecessor's offspring had been friendly. To these we soon added the children of my parents' new friends. In no time a very jolly and attractive group was formed, and I soon had a good grip on their often double-barrelled names. Copenhagen being a smallish world, many knew each other, and Denmark being an egalitarian country, they had sometimes been to school with the maid who opened the door to them. Danish girls seemed better educated than their English counterparts, more socially adept, walked better and aged gracefully. Other diplomatic offspring were part of the scene, most memorably the amusing and energetic Suzie Heap, daughter of the U.S. naval attaché, who introduced us to the sardonic songs of Tom Lehrer and to her two droll Afghan hounds.

Occasionally I accompanied Dad to some official function if Mother was not feeling up to it. One such was dinner with the great, Nobel prize-winning physicist Niels Bohr in his impressive home. He was then in his early 70s, silver-haired and a bit stooped. I remember him as quite reserved. His wife Margrethe, a lovely woman, was more outgoing. [Not long after Michael Frayn had written his very successful play *Copenhagen*, about Bohr's encounter in 1941 with the German physicist Werner Heisenberg, I told Frayn at a party that I had once had dinner with Bohr. For once I felt I had his full attention].

We held a dance or two in the embassy ballroom, as well as a sumptuous dinner party for my 21st birthday. At one such event my father showed the shortness of his fuse. The room was getting rather hot and stuffy, and one of our guests, Tom Federspiel, son of a prominent Danish lawyer and later MEP, took it upon himself to open a window. My father was furious that he had done so without consultation, and upbraided him in a most unpleasant and indeed undiplomatic way. The atmosphere was ruined.

John Hamilton, the school friend encountered again in the army and currently at Corpus with Jo Frampton, came to stay for a week and, being low-key, failed to impress Dad, though he was polite to him. When John had left, my father said: 'I must say, John Hamilton was very, how shall I put it' (pregnant pause) 'unexpected.' I knew exactly what that loaded adjective meant: clever and athletic he may be, but he will not go far. In the event John became a country solicitor. Fortunately Dad loved Bob Keyserlingk, who (leaving aside the family links) was extrovert, a good listener, and exuded energy.

During vacations, when not in Copenhagen, I tried to get around the Continent, especially France. Trips included a long drive to the Riviera, camping en route, with Robin Hooper

Bob Keyserlingk by the Seine, 1955

and Richard Kershaw; and an unpleasant fortnight in a forestry-oriented international youth camp, succinctly called an *Internationaljugendgemeinschaftdienstlager* (literally: international youth community service camp) in Bavaria's Fichtelgebirge not far from Bayreuth. This was intended to boost my German and my CV. It rained persistently among those gloomy pines while the rest of Europe had record sunshine. I made friends with a genial Frenchman called Philippe. One day we hitched a lift on the back of a lorry to nearby Bayreuth. When both of us suffered what the army called convoy cramp (vibration-induced erections), Philippe said memorably: '*Je bande comme un Turc*'. *Bander* was a welcome addition to my vocabulary, and the tribute to Turkish virility was mind-expanding.

It was common practice, at least among the better off, to reserve major trips for one's second year long vacation. I have kept those two memorable months for the next chapter.

Dad is posted to Warsaw at a key moment

Over in Copenhagen my parents were in the throes of a round of farewell parties, Dad having been told in the spring of 1956 that he was being posted to Warsaw. Eastern Europe was becoming increasingly restive under the Soviet yoke since Nikita Krushchev's secret speech of 25 February 1956 denouncing the crimes against humanity of the Stalin era and Stalin's 'cult of personality'. On 28 June of that year the most serious riots in post-war Poland took place, resulting in the deaths of 50 people in confrontations between workers and the police and militia. There were growing calls for a more Polish, less Soviet form of socialism, and the rehabilitation of Wladislaw Gomulka, a former leader then spending his second term in prison.

Gomulka was coopted onto the Communist Party's Central Committee at a crucial meeting in Warsaw on October 1956, prompting the arrival in Warsaw of much of the Soviet Union's political and military leadership, including Krushchev and Marshal Koniev. Meanwhile Soviet military units within Poland were moving towards Warsaw, and those in East Germany towards the Polish border. The Poles made it clear they would fight, and workers from Warsaw factories were armed and deployed. The Russians backed down, made numerous concessions, and Gomulka once again became First Secretary – and vastly popular. This heroic Polish defiance helped spark the subsequent Hungarian uprising, starting on October 23 with mass demonstrations in Budapest in sympathy with the Poles. Then came Suez. A week later the Israeli army began its attack on Egypt, and the following day the air forces of Britain and France began bombing Egyptian airfields. It was hard to criticise the Russians for aggression when the French and British were helping invade a country whose government had merely nationalised a foreign-controlled asset, the Suez Canal..

October 19 1956 came to be seen as a key date in Poland's post-war history, so Dad was lucky to arrive in Warsaw on October 16. He was also lucky to find an old Magdalen College contemporary, fellow cricketer, left-wing Socialist and former Labour Minister of War, John Strachey, in Warsaw as a guest of the Polish government and thus well-placed to brief him about those dramatic events. Dad's tour of duty in Warsaw was to last until the spring of 1960, shortly before he reached the retirement age of 60.

Sadly, the Polish 'spring' of October 1956 did not last. My first visit to Warsaw was for Christmas that December. It felt like what it was, an impoverished police state: a far cry from Copenhagen, but in a grim way more interesting. The ambassadorial residence (soon afterwards replaced by a new building which I visited in 2009) was a smallish house with a tiny garden: larger scale entertaining had to be done at the embassy office building (Chancery). The house and official car, an elderly Austin Sheerline, were bugged.

At the entry gate was a soldier in a sentry box. Knowledge that they would be noted and monitored discouraged all but the most politically secure or courageous Polish visitors. Our own cars were followed by the secret police, often in wonderful old black Citroëns. Winters were very cold and deeply gloomy. The city, most of which had been systematically blown up by the Germans before they were driven out, had been only partially rebuilt. Shops were pathetically thinly stocked. Outside Warsaw, horse-drawn carts were a hazard on the roads, especially at night, when their drivers were often drunk and asleep, relying on their horses' homing instincts. After one expedition I wrote to Martin: 'One feels strangely disembodied, speeding in the Austin Sheerline through dilapidated villages full of strolling people in their Sunday best, who stare as if one was from Mars.'

I was fortunate to be merely dropping in on this melancholy scene for two or three weeks at a time. But thanks to the diplomatic party circuit I made a number of friends, mostly diplomatic offspring or junior staff. When I left after those first few weeks, I gave a party for 30 young people, including four Poles, two Brazilians, one Finn, one Norwegian, one Turk, two Canadians, one Dutch, one Swede, three Italians, three French and four English. It was all good training for the important journalistic skill of making contacts. Of the Poles, a lively cancer specialist, Czesław Gørski, became a close friend. In the summer of 1957 he invited me to join him and a friend or two for a sailing holiday in the (north-eastern, formerly Prussian) Mazurian lakes, but sadly I couldn't make it. He later came to England for six months to work in a hospital near Manchester, and spent some time in London, enabling me to invite him home several times. He was to die young.

An unfortunate accident

During that first visit my relations with Dad were bumpy. They were not improved when, driving the family Rover back from a diplomatic party at around 1am, I hit full-on a raised slab of concrete that passed for a tram stop. I had been travelling at around 45mph, and was definitely the worse for wear. There was a loud report. 'Goodness me', I thought as I heaved the car to the kerb, 'I didn't realise a puncture had such a drastic effect.' On emerging I found that all four wheels were virtually square. The police were soon on the spot, and I had to explain – one of them spoke German – that I hadn't seen the poorly-lit tram stop. I then had to wake my father from a deep sleep and confess. To his credit, his first question was: 'Was anyone else involved?' Next morning, a Sunday, we walked to the stricken vehicle and removed the Union Jack from the little flag mast (it had been furled and covered). It seemed a symbolic moment, and I felt decidedly ashamed. Four new wheels were flown out from the UK, their cost more than covered by the roguish chauffeur's sale of the battered originals. Such was the level of Polish shortages. Astonishingly, the Rover's steering and suspension were unaffected.

My parents later took delivery in England of a new model, the P4 105S, once described as a wolf in sheep's clothing, with a silky six-cylinder engine. We drove it out from England, via Switzerland, where we stayed with Dad's mother at La Tour de Peilz; Austria, where we dined with the engaging ambassador Sir Geoffrey Wallinger in the embassy residence in Vienna at a table that could seat 34; and Czechoslovakia (pretty landscape and lots of geese). Our stay in Switzerland proved to be my last sight of Dad's mother. Grandma died some 18 months later. Maddeningly fussy though she could be, I always felt she was on my side, and her pleasure in my enjoyment of French literature was heart-warming.

The only significant trips I made within Poland were with the parents to Sopot, a resort on the Baltic coast where it rained continuously, and to Cracow, that lovely and largely undamaged city in the south. This was with a brave friend of my parents, Stefan Garzinski, the Polish translator of Aldous Huxley's novels. He and a friend of his showed me around the beautiful Wawel Castle. Unaccustomed as he was to travel in a powerful, up-to-date car, Stefan commented as we sped back to Warsaw along a dead straight road: 'I never realised one really could feel drunk with speed.' En route we were stopped by a policeman, who took Stefan's details and asked for my papers. Stupidly, I hadn't even brought my passport with me. Stefan had to explain that I was the British ambassador's son. We were waved on, with me feeling thoroughly guilty. Stefan did not, I believe, suffer from his contacts with me or my parents.

I also found a close friend among Dad's staff in Dick Joseph, the third secretary. Dad disliked him. Dick was tall, Jewish, ex-grammar school, non-athletic, intellectual, amusing, deeply interested in music, liked whisky – all of which meant we got on very well. He moved on to Oslo, where the ambassador appreciated his qualities.

A shadow over the last lap at Cambridge

Back in the normally tranquil world of Cambridge, those of us entering the crucial last year of our studies found our concentration impaired by the momentous events of October 1956 in Suez and Budapest. Some brave undergraduates went on missions to Hungary to smuggle young Hungarians out of the country, and more than a dozen refugees were found places at Cambridge, including one at Trinity Hall. He was of aristocratic lineage, and had had a tough time in prison.

I had spent my second year in digs (lodgings) a longish bike ride away in suburban Milton Road. Probably mistakenly, I had opted for a decent room further out rather than a scruffy one nearer in. My landlady gave me smoked haddock with a poached egg on it for every breakfast, until I mustered the courage to ask her to omit the egg. Why didn't I also delete the haddock? For my last year I was thankfully back in college, and once again, thanks to my benefactor Bert Stearn, in a splendid new room above the Master's premises near the river. There was an accessible bit of roof where, in fine weather, I could revise in the sun – if not on a bank of the Cam below King's chapel, a favourite perch, trying not to be distracted by passing punts. What a privileged existence, and I really did appreciate it: even work was exciting, with novels to read by Balzac, Zola, Gide, Thomas Mann and Kafka, and poems by Baudelaire and Rilke among many others. I also managed to read T.E.Lawrence's *Seven Pillars of Wisdom*, which I found riveting.

My brother Martin recently sent me a large swatch of the letters I wrote him in his first diplomatic post (see next chapter) roughly every fortnight. I had quite forgotten how clothes-conscious I was in those Cambridge days, forever hymning the delights of some new shirt or tie I had bought at Bays on the King's Parade: I sent him several, along with many other items not available in Iran. I winced when I read the following, in my then sub-Wodehouse style, about a suit I was having made: 'I enclose a piece of the cloth that is even now being hewn by our delightful little cutter. I think it is rather subtle, though of course a small piece like this is not ideal to judge from: 17 and a half inch trousers, one vent (lo! a convert) and also – subtle enough – a raised seam (with turn-ups, of course). Waistcoat plain. 3 buttons. I think the result should be pleasing enough to warrant a small launching party 'to meet my new suit." No such party was held – but what vanity! Dad had given me some money to have the suit made, my first and, it transpired, penultimate.

A propos the great PGW, I quoted with relish Bertie Wooster saying: 'Lay out durable raiment, Jeeves. I am going to mingle with the hydra-headed.' And I started one letter: 'It is a wearyish sort of quill that I raise, after a taxing day spent on the infinitely hermetic symbolist Mallarmé...'

I had forgotten too that I popped home for the weekend from time to time, often with a friend or two, to check up on Gastons, see Gran and the Ashes, by whom my friends were always entranced. And there was the occasional party in London, where attractive women were always much more numerous than at Cambridge parties. Promising!

When it came to the dreaded finals, I felt I had just about done myself justice, aside from those obligatory history questions in the German papers. But I had some trouble with my beloved Montaigne. I had got his ideas so neatly potted that I had difficulty planting them out. Euphoria struck when it was all over, and I took a beautiful girl, Caroline Garnett, to a May Ball. I had met and danced with her all evening at a London party. She was highly intelligent, despite having been a model, and was then working at the Foreign Office. We remained close for some time, but she probably sensed the distance I was from anything resembling commitment. A letter to me in which she made clear her Christian proclivities may have taken its toll of my feelings for her.

The shadow over those last months was the ineluctable need to pin down a job, preferably before leaving. I thought of journalism, but knew that budding journalists were expected to mortify their flesh for a good 18 months on some provincial newspaper.

Short-sightedly, I was determined to work in London. Furthermore, I had done nothing journalistic at Cambridge. Like many a quasi-intellectual undergraduate I fancied publishing, but that was known to be a lottery, and poorly paid: you had to put your foot in the right door at the right moment. As for those five or so glittering traineeships at the BBC: what chance did I have compared with those who been involved in drama, film societies or journalism at university? *Faute de mieux*, there was business. As we used to say, the road to Shell is paved with good intentions. I even thought of Harrod's!

I didn't so much as toy with trying for the Foreign Office, which had a remarkably WOSB-like entry test. What's more, I would dislike the constraints of diplomatic life, and surely two diplomats in the family were enough. Several people I knew did get into the FO, including friend Nicholas Barrington, who passed in second. One who didn't was a splendid mathematician I knew called Dolf Mootham, who when asked: 'What do you think of the lower classes?' answered: 'Would you mind asking me a rather more intelligent question?'

In those days the need to pad one's CV with impressive activities did not bulk large in the undergraduate psyche. My naively cocky attitude was probably widely shared: 'I'm intelligent, not without charm, well connected, got a 2:1 at Cambridge, and speak French and German: how can they resist me?' It was in this spirit, destined to be short-lived, that I presented myself to the Cambridge Appointments Board. I soon realised that having failed WOSB and done nothing showing leadership or initiative at Cambridge (barring perhaps my big trip) I was eminently resistible.

I wasn't even short-listed by the BBC. I had a genial interview at publishers Chatto and Windus, but they had no vacancy, ditto the Cambridge University Press and Penguin, whose founder Sir Allen Lane kindly saw me (he had stayed with Dad in Copenhagen). My friend Giles de la Mare said the same went for Faber & Faber, where he worked in the footsteps of his father, a founding director. I knew that the big oil companies, which more than a dozen friends or acquaintances joined (generally not for long), would not deem me executive material. ICI and Courtaulds gave me the thumbs down. Even Dad's friend Louis Eisinger at merchant bankers Samuel Montagu, whom he had rescued from the Germans in Romania, could not conjure up a slot for me after I had seen the managing director. Another family friend and Essex neighbour did however come up with a possible opening in the City: a classic case of the old boy network.

He was Sammy Allsopp, a very large and genial banker (he had been with Dad in Vienna) whose sons had been at prep-school with me. Among the companies on whose board he sat was the Northern Assurance Co. He thought I might make it onto their graduate trainee scheme. Insurance! More or less a synonym for tedium. Everyone would say: 'Surely not, Roger. It's the last thing I would associate you with!' I suppose I could have hung on and continued the search. But the pressure to get the matter settled and then have a last long summer holiday was strong. Moreover, spring was the time for graduate recruitment, and it seemed unwise to miss that boat.

The Northern was a medium-sized company, more correctly a group of a dozen companies, covering the full field of insurance, including life assurance. Among its earlier management trainees was a far from stupid and notably athletic contemporary of Martin's at Rugby, so the job couldn't be all that bad, I told myself. I was interviewed at the company's head office at No 1 Moorgate, near the Bank of England, and deemed acceptable. They said they wanted to use my languages: I might go off after a couple of years of training to be an underwriter in French-speaking West Africa. I was warned I was likely to find the training rather boring: probably an understatement. But at least I had nailed down a job. I could go off to the Ash villa in Cap d'Antibes with Robin Hooper (Shell-bound, like so many) and Nicholas Barrington, and then to Warsaw via Switzerland and Vienna with my parents, as described, knowing I was on my way. The prospect of living in London was exciting.

Looking back on my Cambridge years, I realise how relatively immature, mixed-up and low on self-knowledge I still was, despite those two years of National Service. I should have at least tried to penetrate the world of university journalism. I should have joined a few more arts-oriented societies. So what had I gained, apart from a good degree? I had made a lot of friends and acquaintances, half a dozen of whom have remained close to me. I was not so far a high achiever, but I was good at spotting those who were. I had taken on board a lot of knowledge of French and German literature. I'm sure my writing skills in English were improved by translating into and out of French and German, which forces one to examine nuances of meaning. In addition to giving me great pleasure, those studies would often prove a useful bond when forging relationships with the French and the Germans. My stammer had receded, but still inhibited me from anything resembling public speaking.

It was not a very impressive tally.

Chapter 5

To Tehran with my brother (1956)

I owed the big adventure of my second long vac, a two-month trip to Iran and back, to Martin. Having emerged from four years at Oxford with a good second and passed into the Foreign Office, he had opted to learn Persian at the School of Oriental and African Studies in London. In the days of the Shah's corrupt, often brutal and, for a Muslim country, provocatively pro-Western regime, Tehran was considered a very desirable posting. The climate was good, the scenery beautiful, the civilisation ancient. Whereas Arabists faced spending much of their careers in Arabic-speaking countries of varying desirability, Persian was spoken only in Iran and Afghanistan. The F.O. was not worried how Martin got himself to Tehran by mid- August 1956, and was happy to give him the price of an air ticket if he wished to drive. He reckoned that would be enough to cover my costs as well as his, providing we camped all the way. I would only have to pay for my journey back.

It was an exciting idea. Martin bore the brunt of the planning, and Dad, who loved not only to help but to show how extensive his contacts were, wrote to friends and acquaintances along our putative route, warning them that we would be passing by and would be grateful for any help.

We left Gaston House on July 10 1956, having loaded Martin's new, green Ford Consul with our camping equipment, plus some provisions and a minimum of clothes. Such of Martin's possessions as he wished to export would follow. Our start was not propitious, though it reflected the then state of the British car industry. About four miles from home the Consul's engine began to lose its pulling power. Mechanics at several garages gave varying diagnoses, with much shaking of the head at the enormity of the task. Eventually we limped down to a Ford dealer in Folkestone, who said there was trouble with the tappets and pushrods, whatever they were. It took almost three hours to fix, but eventually and without much sleep we caught our boat at Dover. Martin was understandably a touch nervous about my driving. I had only recently passed my test in Cambridge. The journey would be a baptism of fire.

By the time we camped near Soissons, my poor bum was itching intolerably from the aftermath of an operation in Copenhagen, and we were assailed by mosquitoes. Morale rose as we headed south and sampled the glories of Reims, Auxerre, the peerless Romanesque cathedral of Vézelay, the Palais des Papes in Avignon and the Roman amphitheatre in Arles. On the Riviera we had to compromise our integrity with a night at a camping site, rather than pitching our tent in a field (all too often stubble). When we failed to drive our tent pegs into the adamantine ground, several Germans leaped to our aid with gleaming instruments and much advice. It was good for my German.

After crossing into Italy we headed down to Genoa, which we found uninspiring, and then, rather too rapidly perhaps, swept in a glorious arc through Piacenza, Cremona, Brescia, past Lake Garda (Italy's largest), into Verona and on to Venice. I feel sure we stopped at Padua too, but my diary doesn't mention it. Cremona and Verona were the highlights. I castigate myself for not having revisited those lovely north Italian cities, where the architecture and people are so handsome and the food so good. Venice was well up to expectations, the mildly hilarious low point being provided by a bald little priest with appalling halitosis who gazed at our thighs with ill-concealed interest, tapping them periodically to emphasise some point about the Veronese ceiling of the church of San Giovanni e Paolo. I wrote a poem about him, which began

> We met him in Venice
> This Titian-lover's menace
> Queer priest with halitosis
> Bane to cultural osmosis
> Heaving great pungent sighs
> Yearning for golden thighs...

Pushing southwards towards Ravenna, we were dining in a little restaurant in a hill town called Argenta when a motorcycle roared up and in came a Cambridge chum, Hugh Dunphy. A small world moment. He camped with us after we had dined together: another night plagued by mosquitoes.

We seem to have had no decent guide to Italy with us. Ravenna, we thought: it's well known for something cultural, but what? Thus did Europe's most famous (early 6th century) mosaics escape our attention. But we enjoyed the city's old streets, and found a lovely beach nearby. Dining in Guilanova after admiring the beautifully simple cathedral in Ancona, a genial young waiter showed us how to eat spaghetti the Italian way with a fork and spoon: a lesson for life.

Heading south and across Italy's mountainous spine, we were stared at in some hilltop towns as if we were from an alien planet. In a charming little

Martin with the inquisitive mule

town called Zagarolo everyone seemed to be sitting on their doorstep, sewing, peeling vegetables, and so on. It was a golden evening. An old man was scratching the tummy of a piglet on his lap. The piglet had a look of ecstasy on its face and was grunting at the sheer bliss of life. In other villages we saw pigs being led on leads, as if they were dogs.

We spent just one very hot day in Rome, where we had the car serviced cheaply and efficiently, and Martin lost a second pair of sunglasses, taking the edge off his enjoyment of the Roman Forum and the Colosseum. In my experience, on long car journeys big cities seem very stressful after days or weeks in mainly rural surroundings. We were glad to be out and camping at 6.30pm by a river, in which we bathed next morning. There we encountered a handsome and inquisitive mule. After gazing at us from behind a bush, long ears pricked with interest, it came over and allowed us to fondle its soft muzzle. We rewarded it with some bread.

Another U-bend-fraught drive across the country brought us to our final Italian destination, the port of Bari, where we put our car on a boat destined for Istanbul. Martin managed to leave his new sunglasses in the car, which was then battened down in the hold. The men's cabin in which we found ourselves was frowsty, but the people interesting and the food excellent. A day and a half later we docked at Piraeus and joined a conducted tour of the Parthenon and its environs. In those less image-saturated days, the beauty of those honey-coloured pillars against a deep blue sky came as an uplifting shock.

The voyage through Turkey

To approach Istanbul by sea on a lovely evening is quite an experience, with the minarets of Santa Sophia and the Blue Mosque piercing the air like huge sharpened pencils. We watched nervously as our car was winched ashore, and found our patience sorely tested at customs: rather than come out to inspect our car, an official insisted we bring the entire contents into the customs shed. Our faith in the Turks rose when someone volunteered to escort us to the consulate. There the consul told us he had booked us into a nearby hotel. Alas, we said, that's beyond our means. How about the tennis court? he suggested. And there, after an evening visiting a nearby district of the city guided by an embassy security guard, we erected our camping beds.

The embassy staff divided their time between the (inland and boring) official capital, Ankara, and coastal and cosmopolitan Instanbul. Next morning, after a good night's sleep, we saw in turn a not very helpful consul, then the charming second secretary Tony Parsons, later Sir Anthony Parsons, Britain's notably effective Permanent Representative at the United Nations, and finally the widely loved ambassador, Sir James Bowker. He was relaxed and informal, and seemed genuinely anxious for our welfare. Plying us with advice and maps, he invited us not just to dinner but to spend some time with his family (his wife was Syrian) on their boat. We had to decline in the interests of our schedule.

'Thought for the day', I wrote sententiously in my diary, inspired by this lovely man, whom I was to meet again later in London: 'Formality is an attitude of mind.

The same man cannot be alternately formal and informal. He is either one or the other. Formality implies rigid standards, and a spirit of criticism is the corollary.' Of course I was contrasting Sir James with my father, probably unfairly. Dad could be pretty relaxed, but one was never sure how long it would last.

We were advised not to flog across arid and baking Anatolia to the Iranian border (it was now August 1), but to head north east from Ankara to Samsun on the Black Sea coast, along which we could then dawdle to Trabzon, aka Trebizond, the subject of Rose Macaulay's recently acclaimed novel, *The Towers of Trebizond*. We would then cut inland over the Zigana Pass and past Mount Ararat, through a military zone (potentially tricky), before bearing left into Iran. The roads were said to be adequate, though the only Tarmac road (of a sort) in Turkey in those days was between Istanbul and Ankara.

With a full tank of diplomatic petrol we headed over the Golden Horn and Ataturk Bridge into old Istanbul, where we were staggered by the vastness and very different beauties of the two great mosques we had seen from the sea: Santa Sophia and the Blue Mosque, in which many Muslims were praying on superb carpets, our first contact with Islam.

Could this be the right road, we wondered as we set out for Ankara. It was asphalted only in parts. Some stretches were gravel, others cobbled, some very dusty, most of them pot-holed. Would the car's suspension withstand several more weeks of such punishment? We passed a man leading a performing bear, and some impressive hills. A rather sinister-looking fellow observed us eating our lunch under a tree. He disappeared, and came back to give us a huge and delicious tomato. Our car got stuck as we turned off in search of a camping site. Two lorry drivers helped us extract it. We were warming to these helpful Turks. Even some soldiers who came over with an officer to check us out as we erected our tent seemed anxious only that we should be warm enough in it.

The First Secretary at the embassy in unlovely Ankara, Ronald Arculus, was rather condescending. Giving advice to travelling Brits was clearly a bore, even if one of them was a fellow diplomat. But he did furnish us with a letter to help us through the military zone around Erzerum (beyond Mt Ararat). We set off northwards after dinner: a mistake, we soon decided. Overtaking trucks through a dense swirl of dust on gravel roads felt suicidal. We decamped next morning at 5.30am and covered the remaining 300 miles to Samsun in 12 hours. The secret of dealing with the washboard-effect roads was, we discovered, to crank our speed up to around 50 mph, creating a 'floating gait' that ironed out the bumps. It also seemed, improbably, to reduce the danger of skidding. We were sobered to see a car that had come off the road and lay upside down, its roof boxed in.

It was great to reach the (Black) sea, but the coastal region beyond Samsun was highly cultivated. Unwisely exploring a tract of firm-looking ground in our quest for a camping site, our car sank up to its belly. A minute later a busload of cheerful Turks saw our plight. Out they cheerfully poured to help us, half lifting, half shoving the car some 15 yards back onto the road. We eventually found a grassy if ant-infested site right by the sea.

The next few days were bliss. The coastal scenery was magnificent: hills often clad with hazel groves (apparently a major source of nuts for British and German chocolate), mountains beyond, some impressive cliffs, glorious beaches and a steeply shelving, remarkably unsaline sea perfect for bathing. However tucked away our chosen camping site, our *levée* was always well attended. We would emerge from our tent in our pyjamas (mine were pink) to find it ringed by up to 10 small boys a dozen yards off. They watched fascinated as we performed our ablutions – shaving and cleaning our teeth were highlights – occasionally exchanging words of appreciative commentary. Lighting the larger of our two primus stoves, the Major Trauma, was also a favourite.

Blond West Europeans were still a rarity up there. When we arrived in a small town called Kesap early one evening, much of the male population turned out to follow us as we did our shopping, guided by a teenager who spoke good English. About 70 of them posed for my camera, looking rather sheepish. The only hazard were the roads: narrow, twisty, rutted, dusty and punctuated by bridges of terrifying flimsiness. Several times we were nearly written off by trucks coming around corners on a virtually single-track road.

There was an acute shortage of petrol throughout Turkey at the time, thanks to a foreign currency crisis. 'Yok Benzin' (no petrol) was the usual greeting at petrol stations. Not far from Trabzon we nearly ran out, and pulled up behind a lorry whose driver appeared to be reassembling its engine on the grass verge. He had none to spare, but his mate took us to a power station up a nearby hill, where they gave us three gallons, refusing all payment.

In Trabzon itself, following unanimous advice in Ankara and Istanbul, we called on the British consul and his wife, the Harrises, at their residence: the finest house in town on the best site, a cool hill overlooking the sea. He was ex-RAF and enormously genial, and both had the typical wry consular humour. When we asked what they thought of Trabzon, she replied: 'Better for a holiday than eight years.' We stayed for an enjoyable lunch.

A storm seemed to be brewing, an alarming prospect with a couple of mountain passes ahead. Sure enough, by tea time, when we had been climbing in second gear for an hour or so on a well-engineered road, visibility was reduced to nearly zero by mist, fog, cloud and drizzle. So we pitched camp on a mountain meadow with the sound of a rushing stream in our ears.

Conditions were better when we continued early next morning. It was a memorable moment when, some 40 miles inland from Trabzon, we reached the top of the Zigana pass, over which Xenophon had once marched (from the opposite direction), allegedly crying 'Thalassa!' (the sea) when it hove into view. Mile on mile of mountains stretched on all sides, with the road snaking through the valley below. As a touch of local colour, a dozen or so picturesquely accoutred Kurds were resting by the roadside with their horses and donkeys.

The scenery became more prosaic towards Erzerum, where we had to take on a military escort through the militarised zone for some 50km. Our escort not only civil but cheerful. Next day we lunched on a breezy hill near the snow-covered slopes of Mount Ararat, which rises to some17,000ft. Like Mount Fuji, it is a finely symmetrical mountain, with what looks like a smaller adjacent understudy. Ararat's peak, regrettably, was swathed in clouds.

Into Iran

At the Iranian frontier a corporal who looked like a screen convict thumbed dumbly through our upside-down passports. Then a dapper, efficient and charming officer took over, and all was well. Martin was able for the first time to exercise his Persian, which sounded impressively fluent. But initially he tended to become rather agitated, and thus even more liable to leave things behind: like his wallet in a café, for which we turned back, recovering it intact.

That night, our first in Iran, we camped on dead flat, barren terrain. Next morning Ararat was revealed in all its glory, its snowy summit gleaming in the sun. We soon discovered that our novelty value was even higher in Iran than in Turkey. Large and friendly crowds gathered around us in Khoi, Marand and all subsequent towns in which we stopped. In Turkey the women had been veiled. In Iran then were cowled to the eyeballs, of which frequently only one was visible. We adjudged Iranian men better looking and more openly friendly than the Turks, but reckoned the latter more reliable and more genuinely anxious to help. Neither in Turkey nor Iran did we see a single non-Western woman in a restaurant.

After a very comfortable night, by arrangement, in the otherwise empty British consulate in Tabriz, the last lap to Tehran had its nightmarish moments. The landscape varied from some extraordinary moonscapes to what our AA guide understatedly called 'impressive gorge scenery'. In Kasvin, where we stopped to shop, Martin began to feel faint, and developed both a splitting headache and diarrhoea, probably because of the altitude. As we pressed on, we reached a stretch of road that was merely the foundation for a new road. It was composed of loose stones, some of them alarmingly large, and deeply rutted. Periodically the bit between the ruts was too high for the car's clearance, so our Ford Consul took a series of sickening belly blows. When a truck approached from the other direction, one had to get out of the ruts, involving dangerous skidding and near loss of control. Martin was in no state to drive, and my knees felt weak with fear.

At one stage a hurricane-like wind sprang up, making the whole world a dust cloud. Our hair was thick with it, it grated between our teeth and cracked our lips. Camping was out of the question, and it was in this harrowed and ailing state that we arrived in Tehran a day ahead of schedule. We just about managed to drag our possessions up into Martin's temporary flat, to which we were shown, ate a frugal supper and collapsed onto our beds, vastly relieved to have made it in one piece. We had covered 4,450 miles in 33 days, without even a puncture (five or more were normal on that route). The car had more than redeemed itself.

Next morning, after sending a telegram of safe arrival to our parents, we found central Tehran to be pleasantly full of tree-lined avenues, cosmopolitan in atmosphere, and overlooked on one side by the magnificent Elburz mountains, including the snow-capped Mount Demavend, at 19,000 feet a notch taller than Ararat. Architectural standards were poor, however, and most of the buildings were built in local bricks of a sour yellow hue. The British embassy occupied a large site in the city centre, full of trees and with a blissfully cooling swimming pool. There was another pool at the residential compound a good mile away at Gul Haq, plus some tennis courts.

Martin was lucky to start his career with a first-class ambassador, Sir Roger Stevens, who was later Vice Chancellor of Leeds University at the time of the 1968 student troubles. As ambassador he was both liked and respected. Lady Stevens contrived to be both eccentric and rather grand. In Tehran she had a tame sheep, which joined us in the drawing room of the residence after we had lunched there. The Stevens' son Bryan was in evidence. He later became a good friend.

Two interesting experiences in Tehran sprang from a chance encounter with an Iranian called Dr Akaberian, who befriended me after I had asked him the way to the Lebanese embassy (I needed a visa for the return journey). He took me there on his motorcycle, then invited me to tea at his house. It turned out he had spent four years at King's College, Cambridge – despite which he treated his wife like a servant, while deploring the backwardness of his compatriots and their religious fanaticism, of which he was to show me an unnerving demonstration.

Off we went on his motorcycle, and in the vicinity of the large, tasteless tomb of Reza Shah we came upon one of the flagellant processions found in Shia communities during the peak days of the holy month of Muharram. A chanting line of men dressed in black were rhythmically raising a sort of cat-o-nine-tails of light chains aloft in their right hands, then cracking them down onto their backs. Their shirts were largely worn away, revealing bruised and bloodied backs. In the middle of the column walked a man in red brandishing a knife and representing the murderers of Hussain, the grandson of Mohammed, and his small band of followers in the 7th century. In front of him was one in black, representing the victims. Some of the men were chipping their foreheads with knives. The look of burning sincerity on their faces was unnerving, as was the way they glowered at us. We did not dally.

Two days later, thinking the days of mourning were over, Martin and I went to the bazaar to take some photographs. We were surprised to find everything shut in the endless series of arcades lined with shops and booths. Instead, the narrow paths were lined with chadored women and children and men of all ages. When we had gone too far to retreat, we found ourselves sandwiched between two chanting processions, this time smiting their chests rhythmically and with alarming vigour, glaring at us as they passed. Compared with us, trapped rabbits would have felt carefree.

We had heard stories of an American who had tried to photograph one such procession and had not survived. It did not help that we were blond, dressed in white and toting cameras, which we tried to hide. Fortunately help was at hand in the stocky and reassuringly well-armed shape of a policeman, who escorted us out. Shortly after we had emerged a friendly young student approached us near a medium-sized mosque and asked: 'You want to take photograph of God-house?' No thank you. We had had enough of Islam for that day.

One evening when Martin, now full recovered, was busy, Dr Akaberian took me to see the film *The Robe*, a biblical epic. In lieu of dubbing, a large chunk of Persian script was flashed onto the screen every ten minutes or so to bring the all too talkative audience abreast of events. Half way into the film, a tremendous row started just behind us: it seemed a man had begun to make advances to the woman next to him, only to find (surely rather predictably) that her husband was on her other side. About a quarter of the audience followed the screaming trio out to see how the drama would end.

In retrospect, I should have made more of my 10 days in Tehran. But all the major sites – Persepolis, Isfahan, Mashad, the beautiful Lar valley and so on – were too far for a quick trip, Martin was working, and no other company available. Furthermore, my finances were low, and the journey home promised to be taxing.

Back the hard way, via Baghdad

For two days, that promise was richly fulfilled. But first I bade a fond farewell to my dear brother. We had not had a single row on our three-week journey. We treasured our relationship, and ahead of us loomed a stretch of separation much longer than those imposed by National Service.

I was scheduled to catch the ill-reputed Tehran to Baghdad bus, used mainly by Iraqi pilgrims returning from holy Shia sites in Iran. My heart sank when I clambered aboard. Noise and odour levels were high, the bus itself was primitive and uncomfortable, and soon began to leak dust. Fortunately I was befriended by a couple of young Iraqi schoolmasters who spoke some English, and sat next to a sweet old Arab who kept on asking me if the sights we passed were 'good or not good'. 'Good', I usually reassured him.

Each time we went over a mountain pass or had some brush with death the assembled company chanted a prayer to Mohammed for our well-being, watching keenly for my reaction. The driver was, surprisingly, somewhat craven, perhaps a fault on the right side. Progress was slow, and punctuated by tea breaks every two hours. This enabled me to see a bit of village life from the wayside cafes where endless small glasses of milkless tea were drunk. In one we stopped by a holy water stream whose shape replicated a stream in an old miniature I had bought in Tehran (not nearly as old as claimed, it transpired). The water in this stream was used for everything, from washing feet to drinking. It was after all holy. No wonder we were accosted by so many blind beggars, eyes staring sightlessly upwards. We also saw them from the bus. One scene could have come from Bunuel's *Los Olvidados*. A man was standing atop a hill against a mountain background, one arm outstretched in anguished supplication, the other holding a baby aloft. More prosaic roadside sightings included vultures, shrikes, rollers, bee-eaters and fox-like wild dogs.

We did not reach that day's destination, Kermanshah, till 10.30pm. There we stayed in a loathsome hotel run by the bus company. The corridors were full of sleeping Arabs, the courtyard with noisy camping families. I notched some three hours sleep.

The last restaurant in Iran, at Khosravi near the Iraq border

Next morning we set off at short notice: no time for a wash, shave or breakfast. Luckily I had some sandwiches left, and there were all too many stops for tea. At midday we had a dubious lunch at the last restaurant in Iran, reaching the frontier at 2pm. Needless to say the relevant officials were having their siesta. We had to hang around in the scorching heat in this grim townlet till they emerged at 4pm, only to discover that the driver had no visa for Iraq. This proved to be a blessing. The non-pilgrims among us were transferred to a rather better Mercedes bus on which there was, *mirabile dictu*, another European. His name was Gian Pennacchio, he was 25, worked in the Italian embassy in Tehran, and spoke fluent English, German and Farsi (Persian), plus some Arabic and Turkish. He was on his way to Baghdad to collect a new ambassador, and his genial company transformed the ensuing customs ordeal – before we could leave they went through every suitcase – from the infuriating to the tolerable.

By now a scorchingly hot wind was parching our throats. A slice of water melon was bliss. We pulled away from customs only at 7.30pm, and stopped for some dinner at 10.30. Never has a drink tasted as good as those iced Pepsis, and the kebabbed lamb was delicious. We reached Baghdad not as scheduled at 6pm but at 12.30am. My new Italian friend found a hotel, with only the prospect of a bath keeping us going. Never have I been so dirty. My shirt collar was literally encrusted. Our double room was hot and noisy, but the main agony was over.

My luck held next morning. A British embassy contact helped me sort out a visa problem, I clinched arrangements for the next leg of my trip, and returned to the hotel to find a message from Gian: would I like to join him and a friend for lunch at the (very smart) Khayyam Hotel? The friend, Carlo Ando, turned out to be the Middle East rep. of Alitalia, the Italian state airline. He was 30 years old, had an English wife (not present), was as charming as Gian, and lived in Beirut. Within a few minutes of meeting me he offered me the use of his flat for the two nights I would be spending in the Lebanese capital. Such good fortune comes, arguably, only to those who travel alone and thus meet more people.

And what of Baghdad, of which I saw a bit on my travel-related taxi rides and a walkabout? It was certainly an improvement on Tehran. Palm trees abounded, the river Tigris ran through the middle, the rather handsome men wore colourful headdresses and flowing garments, and the children looked even more adorable than their Turkish and Iranian equivalents. The buildings too were more interesting and varied than Tehran's. But being on a plain it was a great deal hotter: 110°F in the shade that day.

I was to travel that evening and overnight across the desert to Damascus on the once-famous Nairn bus, in first class, nothing cheaper being available. It was quite a contrast to the agony wagons of the previous two days: an air-conditioned silver trailer some 20 metres long, with a powerful tow vehicle up front, and a toilet at the back. We passed some primitive mud villages, plenty of camels, and a few men looking magnificent on horses. This driver meant business. There was just one stop for tea. So bumpy did the ride become that sleep was elusive: my third night of three hours or less. It was beginning to tell.

The Nairn bus

We reached Damascus around 9.30 am and changed without more ado into a normal-sized bus, driven ruthlessly by a Boris Karloff look-alike. The 'fertile crescent' between Damascus and Beirut is beautiful, a bit like the hinterland of the French Riviera. Our driver overtook private cars on steep inclines. Peering over, we were not surprised to see assorted wrecks, and we passed the aftermath of five recent collisions.

Carlo Ando's flat was as tastefully modern as I expected. There was even a Lebanese lady called Wadiah to look after me, and a good selection of operatic LPs. I felt the fatigue seeping out of me as I listened to Mario del Monaco and Renata Tebaldi.

It was refreshing not to owe a seriously useful contact to my father, for once. But needless to say Dad had provided me with an acquaintance in our Beirut embassy, a charming, soft-spoken fellow called Robert Tesh (later ambassador in Ethiopia). After running me past the Beirut ambassador, George Middleton, definitely a heavyweight, he invited me to spend the afternoon at the family's summer house in the hills outside Beirut, where they 'estivated'. It was gloriously cool up there. Jean Tesh had been at Girton College, Cambridge, and was very welcoming, and there was a sweet young daughter with amazing blue eyes, plus a very pink son. A soothing interlude.

Legend has it that before it was rent asunder by civil war, Beirut was the Nice of the Levant, a fairly modest compliment. I was not much impressed by what I saw: Damascus glimpsed from the bus had looked a more interesting mix of old and new. I was sorry not to have had time to visit the famous Roman temples at Baalbek, some way off in the Bekaa valley.

Carlo Ando returned next morning from Baghdad. How kind and trusting he had been, and how grateful I was to him. After our farewells his driver took me to the port, where I boarded the Greek ship *Aeolia*. This would take me to Marseilles via Port Said, Alexandria, Piraeus and Genoa. I shared a four-man cabin and spoke a lot of French to some colourful people. Of our ports of call, much the most interesting was Alexandria, with its glorious crescent-shaped sea front, an excellent museum, ancient casbah and sophisticated shops: a great mix.

Just over a month earlier, on July 26, the Egyptian leader Gamal Abdel Nasser had seized control of the 'strategically vital' Suez Canal, and announced its nationalisation (it had been run by a Franco-British consortium). Although the ill-starred Israeli, French and British invasion of the canal zone would not begin until late October, the British Prime Minister Sir Anthony Eden was already making belligerent noises, comparing Nasser's nationalism to that of Mussolini and Hitler. Notwithstanding all this, Alexandrians shouted cheerfully to me in English as I wandered around taking photographs. I also had no problems visiting the vast palace of the pro-British ex-king Farouk, who had been overthrown by a military putsch four years earlier.

Our penultimate stop, Genoa, revealed an attractive main square that Martin and I had missed all those weeks ago. The approach to Marseilles along the Riviera and past the Château d'If was lovely in the early morning light, and even Marseilles looked picturesque from a distance, crowned with the cathedral of Notre Dame de la Garde. The train to Paris was packed with soldiers just off a troopship from Algeria. The three in my uncomfortable carriage chain-smoked for virtually the entire 10 hours of the journey, so I emerged kippered. On the plus side, it was wonderful to see green fields again after the browns of the Middle East, even if many of them around Lyon were badly flooded.

A Berthoud does not willingly stay in a hotel if a friend is available. In Paris I had arranged to spend two nights chez Geoffrey Hoare and Clare Hollingworth, who I had got to know quite well through my father (he had met Clare during the war in Istanbul). Geoffrey was Paris correspondent of the not yet defunct *News Chronicle*, an admirable liberal daily belonging to the Cadbury family (it merged with the *Daily Mail* in 1960). Clare was an outstanding war correspondent and famous for her fearlessness in covering the Algerian war. She and Geoffrey were devotees of contemporary art and great friends of the Greek painter Ghika, whose work decorated their Paris flat in the Rue du 4 Septembre. I had seen something of Clare in Paris in March 1955, when she had arranged for me to stay in an auberge in a village near Meaux, to do some concentrated study and speak French. I think I may have appealed to a maternal streak deep in that fearless breast. Her outspokenness was refreshing.

So it was distressing to get no reply to their doorbell. They may have tried to alert me to their plans, but I had failed to pick up my post in Beirut. Hotel after hotel said regretfully: '*Malheureusement nous sommes complet.*' Eventually the poky Hotel Victory permitted me to flake out between damp sheets. When I described my itinerary of the past two months to Madame next morning, she said in a notable understatement: '*Ah oui, les Anglais aiment beaucoup se déplacer.*' Next day God was back in his heaven and Clare and Geoffrey in their flat. A varied cultural and diplomatic day ensued before I caught the cross-Channel ferry at Boulogne next morning for an exceedingly rough crossing. The great journey ended in time for supper at home with dear old Gran. It was sad for the first time not to have Martin around to share such moments.

Chapter 6

From insurance into journalism (1957-1967)

Life at the Northern

That trip, it may be recalled, was in my second long vacation while at Cambridge. After leaving university and before starting work, I fitted in a lesser trip around Spain embracing, among other highlights and doubtless not in this order Toledo, Cordoba, Burgos, Seville, Avila and an unspoilt little fishing port called Marbella. The moving spirit was my school and Cambridge friend John Speed, who brought along an entertaining American friend of his.

Then it was off to the Northern Assurance Company. I went with low expectations, and they were to be amply fulfilled. That year there were two of us management 'cadets', rather optimistically described on the recruitment brochure as 'keen, ambitious young men of exceptional ability in the 20/25 age group.' My companion in tedium was Roy Hitchman, who was pleasant company if not exactly a twin soul. Our starting salary was £600 (£9,000 in today's money), about the norm for graduates in the business sector in those days.

The aim of the two-year training scheme was to give the cadet a fairly detailed overview of the theory and practice of the various branches of insurance by visiting the Northern's many departments for between one week and two months. Knowledge was to be gained through a blend of reading, talks from members of the company, and actual practice. In addition one was expected to take the exams of the Chartered Insurance Institute (not difficult). In reality, four fifths of the time was spent reading, one fifth in being briefed about underwriting policy and dealing with applications etc.

As I eventually wrote in a report to the board of directors: 'The procedure in each section has a certain uniformity. The cadet is greeted by the section leader, usually with the words: 'Well, Mr Berthoud, I'm afraid you've come at a bad time.' One is then seated at a desk with a pile of the relevant proposal and policy forms, a copy of the branch manual for the particular class of business…If the period is one or two weeks, the cadet will sit there at his desk brooding in bitter inactivity until the last couple of days, when the section leader will grant him a brief spell of questions and perhaps a short résumé of underwriting policy ('though it's all there in the branch manual.')…The condolences of the rest of the staff do little to mitigate the oppression of enforced sloth. The most routine work would be vastly less humiliating and appreciably more instructive…The general attitude to trainees of all sorts is that they are a cross to be borne, rather than an integral part of the future prosperity of the company.'

There were some parallels with National Service. The main aim of the average soldier was to spread a minimum of work over a maximum of time. For the lower ranks within the Northern, work was a tedious prelude to the evening/weekend. Pleasure or pride in one's job did not come into it. How could it, when most of the work was so routinely clerical and boring? The Fire Department was much the best-managed. I was even allowed a trip with an underwriter on a cold, wet winter's day to Thames Board Mills at Dagenham, a memorably grim experience. The Northern's management was not impressive (it later became part of the Commercial Union group), with the exception of the youngish head of the investment department. When three of us trainees complained to the general manager, he told us: 'The important thing to remember is that you are absorbing atmosphere and background, and learning far more than you realise.'

Fortunately there were some pretty young women around with whom to flirt: 'Indeed', I wrote of them in my journal, 'sitting here in the Motor Department I am in an almost permanent state of erection, and am acquiring an almost owl-like flexibility of the neck from following their straining limbs around the room. Cathy McGill appeals particularly – a lovely slender figure with pertly rounded buttocks and excitingly mobile breasts. She smiles at me invitingly every time she passes my desk.' My fellow trainee Roy Hitchman went so far as to marry one of these angels, and very charming Margaret was.

Former trainees who had stayed the course and were now abroad seemed by contrast to enjoy their work. John Gardner, the Old Rugbeian, wrote to say that he had had a 'most satisfying' year in Hong Kong, adding 'Certainly if insurance is to be one's life, the Northern is without doubt the only company for such as us.' The genial Breon Rawlings, who had breezed into the office once or twice, wrote me a long screed from Dakar, mainly justifying his choice of fiancée, to whom I had apparently not taken and for whom he was resisting the gorgeous women of Senegal, who 'all expect one to bed them almost at once, as far as I can see.' Given that my virginity was still hanging albatross-like around my neck, that was a mouth-watering thought, though scarcely justification for staying on.

Meanwhile I could fantasise about a beautiful woman with a magnificent figure who frequently swayed towards and past me as I walked to work along Moorgate, always well-dressed and often with a plunging neckline. How did any of her immediate colleagues get any work done, I wondered, especially if she were leaning forward? (Was that why Goldsmith called his tiresome play *She Stoops to Conquer*?) I never mustered the courage to engage her in conversation.

A taste for posh addresses

Finding the right accommodation in London did not prove easy. I had hoped to share a flat with Dickie Bateman, but he was being despatched to Birmingham by his industrial employers. Roger Norrington seemed briefly to be a possible alternative, but that idea came to nought. So a solitary bed-sitter it had to be. Rather than scanning newspaper ads, I consulted Universal Aunts, better known as a source of nannies and the like. They provided four very smart addresses, and I eventually opted for a room in Cliveden Place, off Eaton Square, at three and a half guineas, provided by a Mrs Gunn. Only a few evenings after I had moved in I invited a female friend – perhaps Caroline Garnett, whom I had taken to that May Ball – around for a drink. No sooner had Mrs Gunn opened the door to her than she informed me that members of the opposite sex were not permitted on her premises. What a different era that was. So I moved out swiftly, to a spacious first floor bedsitter in a terraced family home in Abingdon Villas, off Kensington High Street.

Surveying passers-by from above, I was struck by the number of women who had seriously thinning hair. After some six months there, the possibility arose of sharing a house in Ebury Street, a classy but noisy road on the edge of Belgravia, with Jeremy Leigh-Pemberton. He was the younger brother of the future Governor of the Bank of England, Robin Leigh-Pemberton, and of Nigel Douglas (as he restyled himself), the opera singer. Jeremy had been at Oxford with my school friend John Watt, and we had clicked instantly. A third member of the household was to be Antony Snow, destined to become chairman and chief executive of the Charles Barker public relations agency. Jeremy had been at Eton, both had done their National Service in the Guards, Antony was suavely handsome and had a modellish girl-friend. Both moved in the smartest social circles and were a great deal better off than I was.

Jeremy was a real opera buff, and I learned a great deal about opera and vintage opera singers from him and his huge collection of old 78s. He was very good company, and invited me down to the family's 5,000 acre estate near Sittingbourne in Kent for four days. His father was rather quiet and distinguished-looking; mama was lively. In their woods was a working model railway, large enough to travel on, and I took my turn in driving it around its two and a half mile track.

Although we did not have to pay much for the Ebury Street house, I tended to feel like a poor country cousin with Jeremy and Antony, and found some of their upper-class friends hard to take, notably a few empty-headed, under-educated, snobbish women. I was not unduly distressed when the owners of the house, part of the Hong Kong trading Swire family, reclaimed it.

From Ebury Street I moved to Swan Court in Flood Street, off the King's Road in Chelsea, not far from the old Chelsea Town Hall. This ground floor flat belonged to the parents of the afore-mentionedfriend John Speed. John was gay, somewhat camp in manner, exceedingly amusing and liked to shock – despite which he was a budding barrister. His father, Sir Robert, was a senior government lawyer, rather quiet and sober-sided. John took after his lively and entertaining mother, whom he adored: a classic gay background. Among his friends was the notably handsome Paul Danquah, son of the leader of the opposition to Nkrumah in Ghana, Dr J.B. Danquah, and later a friend of the painter Francis Bacon. John's hands would sometimes stray towards my pyjama trousers, but I resisted his advances. His parents spent the odd night there, bringing their loudly snuffling pug, which liked to dance on the sitting room desk, inflicting deep scratches.

John had a destructive streak. Soon after Joy and I had married (which he might have resented) we asked him to dinner with Joy's boss at the *Daily Mail*, the formidable Iris Ashley, and her rather younger lawyer husband. For some reason discussion turned to the boundaries of rudeness. John turned to la Ashley and said: 'Now would you consider it rude if I said you might be taken for your husband's mother?!' A chill fell over the dinner table, and the evening never recovered. We lost touch with John who became an early Aids victim.

My life too could have ended one sunny day in 1959, when I was walking down a street in South Kensington. I heard running behind me, and a cry of 'Stop that man!' from two men chasing a

John Speed

well-built male who was about to pass me at speed. I could have stuck out my foot and tripped him. That might have been fatal, since it transpired he was carrying a gun with which he shortly afterwards shot one of the plain clothed policemen following him. He could have fired at me out of sheer irritation! His name was Guenther Podola, a German-born petty thief, and he was the last man to be hanged for murdering a policeman. His claim that he was so shocked by his arrest that he had no memory of shooting anyone did not impress the jury.

Convinced though I had been virtually from the start that insurance was not for me, I had decided I would give the Northern 18 months, just to stop people saying: 'But you never gave it a chance.' So in February 1959 I started putting out feelers for alternative employment, along much the same lines as my earlier attempts. This time it was Shell and BP from the industrial sector who turned me down after interviews. I came tantalisingly close to securing a job with art book publishers Thames & Hudson, being shortlisted with two others and interviewed twice. One of the other two was preferred, and I think rose to be managing director.

Journalism belatedly calls

My father was reasonably understanding about my decision to quit the Northern, and helpful with my oil industry applications. It was Maurice Ash who gave me the crucial impetus towards journalism. On one of my many weekend visits to his home I said I was thinking about it as a career. With unusual incisiveness he commented: 'I think that's the first intelligent remark you have made about your future.' He had, moreover, a friend called James Shand who owned a local newspaper, the *Harlow Citizen*. Maurice said he would speak to him about the possibility of my joining them on an unpaid basis for a few weeks experience. This was duly arranged for some time ahead in the autumn.

Once my decision had been taken, Dad – nearing the end of his stint in Warsaw – swung into action in his usual wonderfully supportive way. He had remained in intermittent contact with a friend from Berlin days, the once famous *Daily Express* foreign correspondent (and wartime black propagandist) Sefton Delmer, who had retired to Suffolk. Tom Delmer gave me an introduction to Edward Pickering, the *Express*'s very civilised editor, who as Sir Edward was to become the elder statesman of Times Newspapers. Meanwhile Clare Hollingworth, alerted to my hopes, did the same with a friend of hers, Jack Nener, then editing the *Daily Mirror*. I went to see both, and both offered me their next vacancy for a trainee reporter on their Manchester edition. It cannot have done my cause any harm that Ted Pickering ~~was~~ also owned a flat in Swan Court. Vastly cheered, I opted for the *Daily Express*, then a Beaverbrook-owned broadsheet with a reputation for good reporting marred by tendentious views and petty hate-campaigns (notably against Lord Mountbatten and the British Council) inspired by its proprietor.

I left the Northern at the end of April, and signed up for a Pitman's shorthand course near Russell Square. Inevitably I was the only man in the class: the other 20 or so were budding secretaries, though physically in full bloom. As the weather grew hotter their clothes became more revealing, not least when we sunbathed with a lunchtime sandwich in Russell Square's public garden. But it was a case of 'so near yet so far'. I was no good at chatting up the ladies, and common ground was hard to discern.

I found shorthand hard to learn and easy to forget. I had got to a point where it was faster than normal writing – though sometimes even harder to read back – when the call came to join the *Harlow Citizen*. So it was farewell to Swan Court and the pleasures of London, and back to Gastons (about 15 minutes drive from Harlow) until the more drastic move to Manchester. The main part of the family home was let to a couple called Whitaker and their youngish son. Sheila Whitaker was attractive in a gamine way, very friendly and much younger than her husband, and he was away a lot. Sex-starved though I was, even I could see that getting involved with the tenant's wife might have a near-terminal effect on relations with the parents.

Before long I was getting near to base with the full-breasted daughter of a local poultry farmer, but she remained unlaid. I was also seeing a lot of, and was at least half in love with, a nurse called Julia, whom I had met at a dance. She had a beautiful face, lovely hair and an adorably sweet and affectionate nature. The snag was that I didn't really desire her. She was on the plump side, and when I went to her home in East Molesey, her vast mother loomed behind her like a dreadful prophecy, in George Eliot's memorable phrase in *Middlemarch*. I suspected our relationship would not survive separation, painful though parting eventually was.

At home I had the company of Gran, in her 80s but remarkably fit, and her middle-aged, upper class Polish companion Anna de Breza, whom my parents had rescued from a miserable life in communist Poland. Classical music was a great bond with Anna, and we spent many an evening listening and chatting, generally in French, in which she was still more at home. When Gran followed the local hunt in her Lanchester, Anna went too.

The Harlow initiation

I was nervous about taking my first infant steps in journalism, but there could not have been a less daunting environment than the *Harlow Citizen*. It was a weekly, so the pace was gentle. The editor, Trevor Davies, was relaxed and anxious to help. The staff was small and genial. Although Harlow was only a few miles from home, I was unfamiliar with its new town, whose population was predominantly ex-London working class. It was well-planned (by Frederick Gibberd, with whom Maurice Ash was friendly), but too much of the architecture was uninspiring, as were the shops. The population was not yet large enough to sustain a cinema.

My first assignment involved checking a tale that had reached the editor's ears: late in the 19th century, a corpse had been buried facing north to south rather than the traditional east to west (towards Bethlehem). A local church warden, Herbert Mace, reckoned this gripping tale was true. In the 1880s, he said, an act of parliament had made it legal to bury people of all denominations in Church of England burial grounds. The vicar of St John's disapproved, and as a gesture had buried this non-conformist sideways. Anti-climactically, the grave itself had recently been levelled. The story made a paragraph in the mighty 'John Citizen' chat column. What a debut.

There followed a good deal of worthy stuff involved with local meetings, not least of the nearby Sawbridgeworth Urban District Council, said to be the smallest in England. I reported on the plans of the Harlow Development Corporation to build a further dozen tall blocks of flats; on pressure for a traffic warden to guide children across the A11 on their way to school; and on accusations that there was nothing for young people to do in Harlow (too true).

I wrote a longish and quite sprightly piece on the pros and cons of holidaying abroad, but my first proper feature concerned the Harlow Arts Trust, of which Maurice Ash was a moving spirit. The trust had already endowed the new town with a dozen pieces of sculpture by as many distinguished sculptors, including Henry Moore, who lived nearby. My principal informant and guide, in her splendid old Bentley, was an intelligent and sympathique local lady, Pat Fox-Edwards, who before long married Freddie Gibberd. This piece was of course right up my street, and was well-received. I was beginning to enjoy myself, and felt I had at last found my true vocation. The act of writing was satisfying, as was seeing the product in print. My six weeks on the *Citizen* helped me come to terms with the basics of journalism – largely overcoming my stammer-induced fear of the telephone, developing skills in questioning people thereon while taking notes, trying to appeal to the reader and so on – in an undemanding environment. I was lucky to have had the company and advice there of a plumply genial young reporter, Ruth Maglouf. She was appallingly paid, as most provincial journalists always have been.

To Manchester and the Daily Express

In mid-January 1960 I was due to take up my appointment as a trainee reporter on the Manchester edition of the *Daily Express*. I had sold my Austin 7, and was driven up through snow and slush by Mr Johnson, who lived in the Bothy at Gaston House and was helpful to my grandmother in practical ways. The journey took seven hours, ending at the deeply depressing Waverley Hotel, recommended as potentially subsidisable by the *Express* for a night or two. The radiators in my cream and brown room were purely ornamental, the bathroom had a pane of glass missing, and there was a pungent smell of dust *passim*. Fortunately I soon found an adequate bedsitter in a convenient location.

The *Express*'s offices were a replica of the splendid 1930s building that housed the paper's Fleet Street headquarters. The printing presses on the ground floor were dramatically exposed to public view, whirring away behind a glass wall. There was a staff of some 25 reporters, plus sub-editors and photographers. Features, the main political news and foreign news were retained from the London edition, but local news dominated the domestic inside pages, including much of the William Hickey social diary. The northern edition sold an impressive 1,500,000 copies.

I was the third graduate trainee to join the staff. The other two were John Lucas, on whom I had had such a crush at prep-school, and one Jeremy Hornsby, both ex-Winchester but otherwise totally dissimilar. John was clearly well-liked and respected, but due to leave in March for a stint in Glasgow. Although initially he gave me much good advice, he seemed anxious not to be too closely associated with someone as obviously 'public school' as myself. To me – if not presumably to the noted soprano Dame Anne Evans, whom he much later married *en deuxième noce* while on the *Observer* – John seemed a curiously impersonal fellow. But he did me a great service before long by passing on to me his flat in Didsbury, the Kensington of Manchester, which was a great improvement on the bedsitter. Jeremy Hornsby was by contrast open and loquacious, but a bit of a bullshitter. He even persuaded me to share his taste, briefly, for Ray Conniffe's brand of schmaltzy big-band music.

Most of the staff had been in journalism since the age of 17. Generally they were friendly and helpful. At first I merely accompanied them on stories to see how they operated – which was often in a rather formulaic way: for example, if covering a big fire, find a hero. Before long I was given minor tales to handle. One such not untypically began: 'A new life began yesterday for Rufus, the black-and-tan mongrel who was found staked out to die on the Yorkshire moors last week.'

I described one escapade in my first letter to my parents from Manchester, as an example of the typical blend of hard work and skulduggery that characterised 'big' stories. 'We were doing a follow-up of a woman whose youngest daughter had been kidnapped by her separated husband and taken to Scotland. We called at three police stations to see if there was any more news, at the courts to check whether she had legal custody, then around to her. No news of baby. To a pub for 2 hours (they drink a fantastic amount here – alarming). Then back to mother. Still no news, but suspect he is in Glasgow. Phone news desk. They say collect mother and daughter and take to Glasgow. Opposition now closing in (D. Mail etc). Reporters pretend to go away, hang around in side streets of this slum area, switching off lights. We get back first and stick to them. Woman can't make up mind to go with us. Boy friend arrives and says will come too. News comes that baby is safe in Glasgow. Big reunion still the order of the day. They pack up. Off to the office for photograph (we have been phoning the news desk every hour or so). Opposition in full pursuit – about six cars or so. Real cloak and dagger stuff dear to the heart of the news editor Tom Campbell. Huge limousine spirits family and two reporters to Paisley, Glasgow. Glasgow edition prepares to produce decoys to fox the opposition, still in hot pursuit, and strong-arm boys to deal with the husband should he produce a knife, as he did when kidnapping the kid. A good strong story – inner page headlines three days running.' One of the reporters sent to Glasgow had been due for a day off. 'This will mean divorce!' he cried. In such an exercise I was seeing aspects of Britain that not even the army had revealed.

I was soon found to have some talent for writing William Hickey diary stories, which gave more scope for stylistic flourishes. 'Always remember, Roger', the deputy news editor told me, 'when you're writing for Hickey, flick up the dirt in the first par.' On one occasion I refused, despite considerable pressure, to include something that I had been told off the record. 'Look here, don't get bloody ethical', I was told by someone on the news desk. I was also frequently chided for trying to put both sides of a story, thus making it less dramatic.

'Pubmanship', I was advised by John Lucas, played an important part in establishing one's credentials. But I soon decided I would rather be thought a bit stand-offish than waste time and money propping up the local bar with colleagues. At that stage I disliked drinking more than a pint of beer (I still do). And although I had stupidly taken to cigarettes at Cambridge, just when their deleterious effects had been established, I found the smoky fug in the open-plan office, let alone pubs, hard to take. Practically everyone seemed to smoke at least 20 a day.

Social life got slowly underway. Dad produced introductions to Sir John Barbirolli, a little bird of a man of great charm, and his oboist wife Evelyn Rothwell, who took me to a Hallé concert conducted by Sir John. I also met the vice chancellor of Manchester

University, Dr William Mansfield Cooper. Both had been guests in Warsaw. An economics lecturer at the university and his charming and voluptuously endowed wife befriended me and invited me to a party at their home. And there were some genial journalists around, working for the *Guardian* (it had just dropped Manchester from its title) or Granada TV. My journal laconically records: 'Met a chap called Mike Parkinson, who is joining the features section [of the *Daily Express*] in London from the *Guardian* and ITV up here. A pleasant man.' I like to think I am normally good at spotting those who will go far. Parkinson's potential seems to have eluded me.

By mid-March I could feel my stock rising in the office: in one week I had three medium-sized stories in the paper on consecutive days. Another milestone: in early April I at last shed my virginity, aged 25. Angela had a lovely figure, even if her skin was not as silky as I might have wished. She had been having an affair with an older man, and was thus relatively experienced. I was now anxious to make up for lost time. But although I met some very pleasant women variously at my local bus stop and the Ritz Ballroom and enjoyed some delicious embraces, they drew a line short of my goal.

In mid-April, after I had been in Manchester barely four months, I had a life-changing stroke of luck. I was pecking away at a typewriter in the office one Friday afternoon when in walked a friend from Bishop's Stortford, John Clarke, the highly-regarded cricket correspondent of the London *Evening Standard* (and father of Nick Clarke, the much lamented BBC broadcaster). John had come up to interview the Lancashire fast bowler Brian Statham. I was about to drive home to see my parents, who had returned on Dad's retirement to resume life at Gaston House. 'Would you like a lift home this evening?' I asked Clarke. 'Door to door service!' On the five-hour drive we got to know each other much better. Not a word from me about hankering for a job on the E.S. So it was a wonderful surprise when he rang a few days later and said: 'I have been talking about you to the editor here, and he would very much like you to join us.'

This proved to be an over-statement. A couple of weeks later I went down to London for a short but gruelling interview with the *Standard*'s editor, Charles Wintour. He came across as inscrutable, impersonal and as wintry as his name. It was difficult to raise more than a frosty smile from him. He asked me what I thought of the present state of the Labour Party, what my politics were, whether I thought Poland would be likely to come over to the Western side, whether I went to the theatre a lot, what I was reading at the moment: very good questions, except the one about Poland, which was stuck behind the Iron Curtain. He summed up: 'Well, you are obviously a pretty suitable candidate, but we would like to see your cuttings. If they are up to scratch, you must come down again and meet Nick Tomalin, who is away at the moment.' Nick was the editor of the Londoner's Diary, for which I was being considered. A painful period of uncertainty impended.

Meanwhile a weekend at Gastons with the repatriated parents produced a short but epic row with my father. As usual with family rows, it had a trivial beginning. Dad had commented during dinner how gratifying it was that cousin Susan (eldest daughter of his brother Bobby) had been playing lacrosse for Scotland. I agreed, but added, rather insufferably, that it would be better for English girls in general to concentrate on more feminine sports and interests. Dad went into a tirade about my la-di-dah tone of voice and over-intellectual approach, and when I picked up the wine decanter to fortify myself, he said: 'Put down that wine! It's my wine and this is my house. Obviously you can't take your drink.' To which I countered: 'How puerile can one get!' Martin joined my protests, and Mother and Binnie also seemed to be on my side. After the meal Dad stumped up to his room. Before long Martin and I went up on a peace mission. We eventually got him to agree he had over-reacted, and talked the matter out.

I had of course goaded him, and I think part of me enjoyed exposing the shortness of his fuse and his need to dominate. In retrospect, our rows were a useful experience. I think he respected me for standing up to him, and after facing his wrath it was hard to be daunted by anyone else. Martin tended to take a more emollient line, even when both parents criticised his generally rather young girl-friends. Fortunately they approved of the one to whom he was now engaged: Marguerite Phayre, daughter of the military attaché in Tehran, Brigadier Desmond Phayre, and a relatively elderly 18.

My first encounter with Nick Tomalin, editor of the Londoner's Diary, ex-Trinity Hall and a man of enormous energy and charm, went well. When we met for lunch at Rule's in Maiden Lane he amazed me by saying: 'Please don't think that whether you get this job depends on the impression you make on me, as the editor thought you were marvellous.' That wasn't my impression, I said with a relieved smile. Somebody more experienced was being considered, Nick said, but might prove too expensive. My suspense was destined to continue.

Chapter 7

The Evening Standard (1960-1967)

I joined the staff of the Londoner's Diary in early June 1960, and immediately found myself a round peg in a round hole. The *Evening Standard* was still in its somewhat down-at-heel premises in Shoe Lane, off Fleet Street, on or near which all the national dailies were then located. The editorial staff sat in one vast room, with the Londoner's Diary's block of eight desks at the lightest end, beyond which were ranged the feature writers, an outstanding bunch including Maureen Cleave, Tom Pocock and Anne Sharpley, the fashion editor Barbara Griggs (later succeeded by Suzy Menkes), off and on the cartoonists Vicky and Jak, the political staff (when not in Westminster), occasionally a star such as George Whiting, the revered boxing correspondent. Then came the sub-editors and finally, on the far side of the room, the news staff, headed by the stylish and immaculately dressed news editor Ronald Hyde (when dismissing the playwright Michael Hastings after a trial stint as a reporter, he said: 'I'm afraid there is no longer a niche for you on the *Evening Standard*, Mr Hastings.') The editor sat on the far left when not in his small office near the Diary staff, where the morning conference was held at 9am, with each section going through its proposed topics.

Exceptionally for the world of journalism, the hours were a regular 9am-5pm, though the Diary editor and one staff member had to be there around 8am to put to bed the early edition of the Diary, in the so-called Racing Edition. The material for this 'overnight' edition of the Diary was cobbled together the previous afternoon, some of it from freelance contributors. Most of it was thrown out at noon and replaced by that morning's stories, written in the preceding three hours.

It was normally the Diary's editor who went down at noon to the print room, or floor, to work with a printer inserting the various stories, set in metal type, into the space for the Diary. For visual reasons, one had to make sure that the mini-headline ('crosshead') at the top of each story neither lined up with one in the adjacent column nor came less than three or four lines from the bottom. The first time I went down to the 'stone', as it was called, I picked up two lines of type for which the printer was searching, thinking this would be helpful. I was promptly told it was forbidden for any member of the editorial staff to touch a line of type, and that I could have caused a strike there and then.

There was a further, minor update of the Diary at 1.30pm. Only if something cataclysmic happened would the Diary be 'replated' at 3pm. I recall one instance. The editor rang, exceptionally, on his hot line to the Diary to tell me (I was by then its editor) that Vicky, the great but depressive cartoonist whose work appeared top centre of the Diary page, had killed himself. He gave me 20 minutes to write a few paragraphs of tribute. I had had a particularly liquid lunch, but the devastating news sobered me instantly: Vicky used to come around every morning to seek reassurance that his cartoon was OK.

Taking over the art slot

Lord Beaverbrook, whose newspaper group then owned the *Evening Standard* along with the *Daily* and *Sunday Express*, took a fond interest in the *Standard* in general and the Diary in particular. He would frequently phone Charles Wintour with tip-offs. A keen art collector, he liked to read in the Diary about the London art scene and the big sales at Sotheby's and Christie's. A genial reporter called Richard Walter was our specialist in such matters, but soon after my arrival he moved on to join the press staff at Christie's, and I was asked to take over. Bliss! It was thus my task to get to know all the major dealers and artists in London, to do mini-interviews with the latter, chronicle such events as a sell-out private view, and cover the major sales at the big auction houses. That was on top of the normal diary tasks of interviewing visiting celebrities, and helping to chart the rise and fall of authors, publishers, diplomats, senior civil servants and politicians, in whom our readership was presumed to be interested. An earlier *Standard* editor had memorably defined the ideal diary story as: 'an exclusive news story that lends itself to comment, preferably malicious'. Of malice there was rather little, however. Then as now arts stories were valuable publicity for impending events, exhibitions, publications, films, plays, operas and so enjoyably on.

One of the Diary's stand-bys was the weekly list of celebrities staying at the Savoy and its sister hotels. Among these in my first fortnight was the great Swiss playwright Friedrich Dürrenmatt, whose chilling parable *The Visit* was about to open in the West End, with the Lunts in the main roles. Nick Tomalin said something on the lines of: 'Roger, you've got Swiss blood, pop along to the Savoy and interview Friedrich Dürrenmatt. He'll probably be having lunch, but don't let that worry you. I'm sure he'll be delighted to see you'.

No doubt a press officer pointed the elderly author out to me. He was at the coffee stage, and probably happy to have a plug for his play. It transpired that he lived in or near Neuchâtel, home of the Berthouds, and he was reassuringly avuncular. Did I know that Neuchâtel had once been part of the Prussian empire, he asked. I did not. It would be hard to imagine today's Londoner's Diary taking an interest in such a figure. A few months later I met the other great Swiss-German playwright Max Frisch, who caused my jaw to drop by observing: 'I think the English and the Swiss have a similar sense of humour.'

It was typical of the civilised nature of the *Standard*'s staff that when, in those first few weeks, I attended a party at the Institute of Contemporary Arts I found six other staff members there. The occasion was a major Picasso exhibition at the Tate Gallery.

I was thrilled to be mingling with such stars of screen and stage as Gregory Peck, Antony Quinn, Laurence Harvey and Margaret Leighton, not to mention the Duke of Edinburgh, surprisingly.

One of my first mini-interviews was with the composer Michael Tippett. The man was a verbal Niagara! I remember thinking: if everyone talks as fast and as much as this, taking notes is going to be purgatorial. I was deemed to have done well soon afterwards in 1960: when John F. Kennedy was elected President of the USA, I flushed out and interviewed Jackie Kennedy's sister Lee Radziwill, who was then married to a London estate agent, Prince Stanislas Radziwill.

Through a series I wrote on artists' wives I met the painter Ceri Richards, a lovely man whose work I instantly admired: so much so that I bought one of his watercolours, a substantial study for his *Rape of the Sabine Women* series, for £50 (around £700 in today's money: wow! I may have paid in instalments) at a Whitechapel Gallery exhibition. It was my first serious acquisition, and remains a prized possession.

Among the Diary's staff was, for a brief spell, Adrian Mitchell, later a major poet and playwright. One day my phone rang and a muffled voice said: 'You don't know me, Mr Berthoud, but I'm an attendant at the Tate Gallery, and I thought you might be interested to know that someone had just taken a chip out of Rodin's The Kiss.' 'What part did they chip?' I asked. 'I'd be too embarrassed to tell you', said the voice, improbably. At this I became aware of some suppressed giggling around me, and looked up from my notebook to see Adrian with one hand over the mouthpiece, fighting his own laughter. A couple of weeks later he rang from outside. When I answered he said: 'Roger, I'm in a telephone booth near King's Cross and I think I'm having a breakdown.' 'Come off it, Adrian, you can't pull my leg twice', I said. But he was in serious trouble, and another colleague, Tilly Laycock, who had a car nearby, sped off to help him. In later life it was always a pleasure to bump into Adrian and his wife Celia in the Hampstead zone where we both lived.

Surely only on the *Evening Standard* of those days could an interest in art have been a pathway to advancement. Charles Wintour was almost as interested in art as he was in the theatre (he was soon to found the *Evening Standard* drama awards), literature and politics. Chilly though his manner was, and poor though he was at small talk, he was a wonderful editor: crisply decisive, totally loyal to his staff, and as ready to praise as to criticise. It was a joy to work for someone I admired unreservedly: I wonder if the staff of American *Vogue* have any of the same feelings towards his celebrated and even chillier daughter Anna. Charles inspired awe tinged with affection. For example: after a good lunch together at the Garrick Club in Covent Garden, he offered the cartoonist Frank Dickens a lift back to Shoe Lane in his office Ford Cortina. Dickens had parked his new Rolls Royce around the corner from the Garrick, but felt it would be churlish to refuse the lift. So he went back to the office with Charles, then returned to Covent Garden to collect his Roller.

First feature articles, and Douglas Cooper

My first big feature, on the prized page opposite the Diary, was triggered by the marriage of one Katharine Worsley to the Duke of Kent. Her father, Sir William Worsley of Hovingham Hall in Yorkshire, collected pictures, and had revived the local village's annual music festival. He seemed slightly startled to be confronted with someone so young and so relatively unknowledgeable about old masters: two fine Poussins and a Rubens sketch were his *pièces de résistance*. But he was kind to me. His particular interest was in the 'Norfolk' school of watercolourists: Cotman, Towne, Girtin, with a Turner or two thrown in. He must have been pleased with my flattering piece. It concluded: 'Sir William is a man of action who finds pleasure and mental solace in the arts. It is delightful to find a Royal wedding throwing such a man into prominence.' That proselytising tone was a feature of my stuff in those days. Journalists were then more deferential than nowadays, and keener to build up than to knock down their subjects. They did not practise amateur psychology on their interviewees.

I may have been under pressure to be kind to Graham Sutherland, who in November 1961 was the subject of my second substantial feature: he was a Riviera friend of Lord Beaverbrook and the Beaver's favourite contemporary artist. The 'peg' was the first monograph on Sutherland's work, by the contentious art historian and collector Douglas Cooper: 'Peter' Norton, a co-founder of the Institute of Contemporary Arts and a friend via Dad (her husband had been an ambassador), later warned me never to be too closely associated with Cooper. I interviewed the charming but touchy Sutherland at his home in Kent. My piece was more a summary of his career, lifted from Cooper's book, than a probing interview. Nonetheless, Sutherland sent me a flattering telegram of congratulations and thanks. Little did I suspect he would be the subject of my first biography.

My initial telephonic contact with Cooper was not promising. He lived near the Pont du Gard in Provence. The telephone line was appalling. Douglas had a high-pitched voice, and I had no idea he was gay. 'Is that Mrs Cooper?' I kept on asking. 'May I speak to Mr Cooper?' I'm surprised he didn't hang up. When we eventually met (he was curating a major exhibition for the Edinburgh Festival), I couldn't help finding him very amusing, which he was in a camp, bitchy way. Douglas either liked me, or thought me useful, or both. Eventually he urged me to come and see him at his home, the Château de Castille, should an opportunity arise. I took him up on this a year or two later on my way back from a Greek cruise that ended in Marseille. The temptation to see his famous collection of Picassos, Légers, de Staëls and Braques was strong. He met me in Avignon, and I was duly stunned by his collection, especially a great bird by Braque in his bedroom. In the one I was allotted were 11 small Miros.

Staying with him was his gay friend of those days, (Lord) Basil Amulree, a genial geriatrician with a pronounced stammer. Off we went to dinner at a famous restaurant in Les Baux, the Beau Meunière. Douglas's first, characteristically unsubtle move was to order a bottle of whisky (death to one's palate) and plonk it down on the table between us. I had drunk no spirits for weeks, and when the quail I had stupidly ordered as a starter arrived, head still on, I had to rush to the loo to throw up. Otherwise a great evening.

Douglas urged me to stick around for a couple of days and go to a bullfight with him and Picasso. But I was due back at the office, and reckoned Picasso could easily cancel. So I motored back via Boulogne with Basil Amulree in his convertible Sunbeam Talbot. A few days later the editor came over and said very coolly: 'Reuter is saying your friend Douglas Cooper appears to have been stabbed in the stomach by an Algerian soldier he picked up in his car. It seems he crawled a couple of miles to the nearest house, and is now in hospital on the danger list. Would you care to write a few paragraphs about him for the next edition?' I was genuinely shocked by the news: Douglas had evidently tried to fondle the soldier, not a wise move, especially with a Muslim. I struck a studiedly neutral note in what I wrote. Cooper made a remarkable recovery, and before long I received a letter in his inimitable green ink (on blue paper), starting: 'You are the first person I am writing to from my hospital bed...' How many other letters had he begun thus, I wondered. He and Sutherland soon quarrelled, and Cooper switched from being his greatest protagonist to being his most vicious detractor. Peter Norton was right: he was a dangerous man, but I used to like a whiff of danger.

The *Standard's* art critic was the no less camp but far more charming and witty David Carritt, who had the keenest eye in England for a misattributed old master painting. Before long he too left to join Christie's, then lagging way behind Sotheby's ('the first known case of a rat swimming out to a sinking ship', one of his friends remarked). I was asked to take over as art critic, though I was not labelled as such, alongside my Diary duties. I had to review the blockbuster exhibitions, but did not feel qualified to pass judgement on contemporary artists. So I devised a format blending interpretation with an interview, with my own views implicit rather than explicit. These pieces meant that my name ('byline') was frequently in the paper. I also did (anonymous) pocket interviews with artists for the Diary. Throw in private views, and it's not surprising I came to know most leading London-based dealers and artists, and not a few foreign ones. Among these were Leon Golub, with whom I remained in correspondence, the amusing Larry Rivers (one of the first practitioners of Pop Art), both American; and the diminutive, Paris-based surrealist and photographer Man Ray. When I cheekily asked the French artist Bernard Buffet whether he agreed with the critics that his success had affected the quality of his work, he replied: 'I think my success has affected the quality of the critics.'

The commercial gallery that did most to shape my taste was Gimpel Fils, then in South Molton Street, W.1. Peter and Charles were the sons of a famous Paris art dealer, René Gimpel. A third brother, Jean, had been a diamond dealer before specialising in medieval technology: see his seminal book *The Cathedral Builders*. Peter, a bachelor, had some engagingly eccentric views, suggesting for example that NHS dental treatment should be withheld from anyone who did not use a water-pick. He shared a small yacht, moored at Antibes, with Maurice Ash and the French mustard king, Jo Poupon. I interviewed a disproportionate number of the Gimpels' artists.

Another useful source was the more roguish Eric Estorick of the Grosvenor Gallery in Davies Street, W.1, a former economist who had written a biography of the post-war Labour Chancellor, Stafford Cripps. Estorick had a major collection of contemporary Italian art (which now has a permanent home in Islington). He did pioneering work in bringing over good contemporary Russian graphics, two of which I bought – at 'family' prices, of course, a perk of the job. Of my various purchases I wrote to my sister Elisabeth: 'I can't tell you how enriching it all is, and it gives one a terrific bond with people who share this interest. Like music. And writing about art one does feel a certain missionary sense of spreading the good word.'

Outside the London art world I had memorable encounters with, among many others, the great film director Jean Renoir, who commented at length on his father Auguste's currently soaring prices, and the former French prime minister, Pierre Mendès-France, an impressive man; the American writers Gore Vidal, Jerzy (*The Painted Bird*) Kosinski, Richard (*The Manchurian Candidate*) Condon, the humourist S.J.Perelman and a pioneer of the 'police procedural', Ed McBain (sitting in the sun in Green Park); the mime Marcel Marceau, the sopranos Régine Crespin (formidable) and Birgit Nilsson (genial), and the tenor Mario del Monaco. The latter resulted in a ticket to the Royal Opera House where he was singing with Tito Gobbi, surely the greatest operatic baritone of the mid-20th century. Why didn't I interview Gobbi? Richard Condon was one of the most delightful men I interviewed. He signed my copy of his latest novel 'To Roger Berthoud and spiked orange juice', which we had consumed in his room at the Savoy. I was later to meet his daughter Debbie, a leading fashion model married to the playwright Kenneth Jupp.

Some of my political and diplomatic encounters impressed Dad. Rather sadly, I have always – and perhaps wrongly – dated the change for the better in our relationship to the weekend when I came home and said: 'By the way, Dad: Rab Butler, Peter Thorneycroft and Lord John Hope (pillars of the then Cabinet) send their regards.' He was touchingly delighted by this reminder of his past glories. From then on, perhaps, he ceased to regard me as a failed version of himself, and saw me more as a person in my own right whose interests and talents were at last beginning to form the basis of a worthwhile career. As proof of which, I was even moving in the right circles, circles in which he was a concept. He was a great admirer of success, and it was hard not to be affected by the same prejudice. As he might have said, people who have achieved something are more likely to be interesting than those who haven't (though of course they are often egotistical bores).

Before long, however, the spectacle of my having a wonderful time proved too much: Dad was soon telling me my life was self-indulgent, selfish, egocentric and narrow. No doubt there was something in what he said, but jealousy probably played a part. I did not take these parental strictures lying down. 'Do you really think I lead a narrow life?' I asked my mother in a rather insufferable letter in February 1962. 'Painting, music and literature, and much friendship both male and female, seem to me to add up to a pretty rich life. But if you rate these things low, no doubt it is natural that you should think it narrow. Aside from a direct participation in politics or charitable work, I can't see how it could possibly be broader. Any suggestions welcomed.' There was more fighting talk in this vein.

Saleroom dramas

Covering the big sales at Sotheby's and Christie's for the Diary was sometimes tedious (most porcelain, furniture, jewellery and silver sales), sometimes dramatic and exciting, as when the prices of Impressionist and modern works were going through the roof. That process had started in 1956 with Sotheby's record-breaking sale of the Goldschmidt collection, which had helped bring Christie's to its knees. Revelations about some major collection coming up for sale were keenly contested by the broadsheet papers, but I held my own. Coverage taught me a lot, and I made a few exciting purchases at Sotheby's (five Japanese 'prints', and a couple of Gauguin woodcuts printed by his son, all since sold).

Personal relations with the chief press officers of the two auction houses played an important role. Both were very good company. Sotheby's was a chunky ex-brigadier called Stanley Clarke who had worked his way up through the army's ranks. He was much shrewder than his kindly, overweight and bonhomous exterior suggested, and could not have been more different from his master, Sotheby's chairman. Peter Wilson was tall, suave and ruthless: it was said he once saw the Christie's chairman lunching with a well-known collector, phoned the collector's solicitor, secured the collection, then enjoyed his own lunch, happy in the knowledge his rival was wasting his time and money. Stanley's favourite watering hole was the Westbury Hotel in nearby Conduit Street. How I managed to do much work after a stiff Campari and soda and half a bottle of wine I'm not sure, but work was too demanding to doze off.

Down at the more gentlemanly Christie's in St James's, the humourist A.P.Herbert's son John presided over a press office handicapped by a touchy, portly, pink-faced chairman, Peter Chance, and a sense of being outclassed by Sotheby's. John favoured a wider range of restaurants, but was no less generous a host. Somewhat embarrassingly, saleroom correspondents would receive for Christmas a case of spirits from Sotheby's and a case of good wine from Christie's, discreetly delivered to their home address. It seemed unduly moral to cart it into the office and share it out, as I should have done. My annual sense of guilt was short-lived.

The most testing episode in my saleroom coverage came in 1965, when a baronet called Sir Francis Cook and his seventh wife consigned a valuable group of Old Masters to Christie's. By this stage Christie's, thanks largely to David Carritt's expertise and contacts, was recovering lost ground. But the sale of Rembrandt's *Portrait of Titus* (his son), the most important of the Cook pictures, proved a mixed blessing.

The millionaire Californian food manufacturer, Norton Simon, was known to be interested in buying it for his foundation, preferably anonymously. Mr Simon, a very tough cookie, was met at Heathrow on the eve of the sale in a hired Rolls Royce, and a ridiculously complex code was concocted, defining how and when he would be bidding. It read: 'Portrait of Titus. When Mr Simon is sitting down he is bidding. If he bids openly when sitting down he is also bidding. When he stands up he has stopped bidding. If he then sits down again he is not bidding until he raises his finger. Having raised his finger he is continuing to bid until he stands up again.'

This was presented to the chairman shortly before he mounted the rostrum. A big sale is a testing occasion even without five television crews, a host of reporters and a very important and difficult customer. Confusingly no doubt, Norton Simon almost immediately started bidding verbally for *Titus*, and continued to do so. He then stopped bidding, and the picture was knocked down to Marlborough Fine Art for 740,000 guineas (it was typical of Christie's that they clung to this outmoded monetary unit, a guinea being one pound and one shilling). Mr Simon objected, claimed he was still bidding, and got his dealer to read out the agreement. Chaos ensued. *Titus* was put up for sale again, despite understandable protests from its first purchaser, Marlborough Fine Art's David Somerset (later the Duke of Beaufort), and knocked down to Mr Simon for 760,000 guineas. A press conference followed, in which John Herbert tried to justify what had happened.

I was battling to catch the *Standard*'s main edition for what was bound to be a front page story, handicapped by my usual failure under stress to get everything down legibly, and unsure whether I could afford the time to go to John's press conference. Fortunately Reuter's had as usual done a good job, our two pieces were neatly grafted together by a sub-editor, and the resulting front-page story was soon on the streets. I can be seen scribbling away just behind Norton Simon, who is scowling at Peter Chance, in a photograph in John Herbert's entertaining Inside Christie's, to which my account of this episode is indebted.

Most of the Diary's talented staff were around my age (mid-20s), but Bruce Page, tall, red-headed and laconic, with an enviably good shorthand note, was only 23. He was part of a growing Australian influx into British journalism, and soon left to play a leading role on the *Sunday Times*'s Insight Team, later editing the *New Statesman* magazine. One evening a couple of us had been having a grog or two, as Bruce put it, and listening to jazz at his flat (my introduction to Charlie Mingus), along with his girl-friend. Next morning he came into the office limping. What happened? we asked solicitously. 'Well', he said blushing, 'in my animal way I was about to slip it to this girl on the floor, and just at what I can only call the most important moment, my foot got caught in the electric fire.' Convulsive laughter around the Diary. 'And did you carry on with the good work?' we inquired eagerly. 'There was no question of picking up the thread again,' he replied with a croak. Bruce was a very useful fast bowler, and came down to Gastons with me one weekend to play for the Little Hallingbury village cricket team. His performance impressed Dad.

My Venice and Paris stints

I was lucky to be working in an era of plump expense accounts, though lunches were expected to produce worthwhile stories. Publishers made particularly congenial lunching partners. I was also friendly with several MPs, including Labour's notorious Tom Driberg (no one was quite sure which side he was spying for), the charming Maurice Edelman, a goodish novelist, the former actor Bryan Faulds, a talented self-publicist; and a number of London-based diplomats. I was, unsurprisingly, good at getting advance news of top diplomatic appointments.

Could this extraordinarily agreeable life, marred only by the occasional ghastly editorial mistake, get any better? It could and did. First, Maurice Ash offered me the use of his London *pied-à-terre* in Duchess Mews, off Portland Place and near the BBC's headquarters, for a very modest rent. Second, I was sent to Venice in 1962 and 1964 to cover the art Biennale. Third, for three consecutive summers I went to Paris for five weeks to write the weekly *Paris Newsletter* while its famous incumbent Sam White was on holiday. Fourth, I got married. Fifth, I took over as editor of the Londoner's Diary.

The Ashs' pad was just off just off Portland Place and near the BBC headquarters. The bottom half was let to a young Catalan couple. Maurice and Ruth Ash used the top flat, which had two bedrooms, for the night about once a week when they went to a play or concert, or out to dinner. The deal was that they could continue to use it if I moved in. I was almost embarrassed by their generosity. The flat was both luxurious and central: I could walk to most gallery private views after a quick bath. The modest rent meant I could spend more on pictures and entertainment – roughly one concert a week, the odd play and lots of films. I had my own small bedroom, and Maurice and Ruth did not impinge too much.

Before my first stint in Paris in July 1963 I had an entertainingly gossipy assignment involving a glamorous ball hosted by the Queen and Prince Philip at Windsor Castle to mark the engagement of Princess Alexandra and Angus Ogilvy. I was asked to find someone (preferably both observant and well-informed) who had been invited and would agree to be de-briefed immediately the ball finished. I would then write my piece and dictate it by telephone by 7am that same morning. I can't imagine how I found my contact, at whose home I waited for his return at around 3am. His eye and memory proved as good as hoped. We concocted the piece together on my portable Olivetti Lettera 22, complete with a waspish reference to Princess Margaret and Lord Snowdon as 'the shrimp cocktail', a phrase coined by a fellow guest. This caused Charles Wintour some difficulty with Lord Snowdon. The piece was in all other respects a howling success. At my request, it was bylined 'Evening Standard reporter.'

My six days at the 1962 Venice Biennale were a great experience, apart from the stress of producing a flow of lively stories and battling with poor telephone lines. The Biennale was then uniquely influential as a shaper of reputations, and much of the London art world repaired to Venice for the week-long jamboree, each nation's pavilion vying for attention from the press, critics, dealers and so on. The British Council's pavilion featured one of my favourite artists, Ceri Richards, and he was there with his two daughters. He won the second painting prize. Most evenings I dined with some 20 painters, sculptors, dealers and their partners. Sadly, Venetian food is less than wonderful, unless you know where to go, which generally we didn't.

After three days the editor sent me a 'herogram' saying: 'Your Diary coverage has been really top class. Congratulations.' When the Biennale finished the new editor of the Diary, a genial *Daily Express* veteran called Donald Edgar, suggested I should proceed from Venice to Rome to report on the filming of *Cleopatra*. Starring the world's currently most famous show-biz couple, Richard Burton and Liz Taylor, this had been attracting much press attention. Once in Rome, where some Italian friends showed me around, I discovered that filming had moved to the island of Ischia, near Capri. Should I proceed thither by train and boat, I asked the office? Happily, yes.

It was a very hot July day, but I suffered little in Ischia by comparison with Richard Burton and several other soldiers about to be involved in the battle of Actium, most of them wearing a Roman leather uniform and working under six hot arc lamps. I watched them for an hour and a half, in which they went over the same scene eight times, producing perhaps a minute of film. I was sitting close to Liz Taylor, who was, inevitably, disappointing up close. Vastly more attractive, indeed enchanting, was the young Francesca Annis, whom I interviewed at her family's posh home on my return. Her small part in the film did not test the talents that were to make her a star of West End theatre. A seductive shot of her reclining by a pool illustrated my feature, which was given half a page and my biggest byline yet. She attended one or two of my subsequent parties, and asked me if I would show her around the Tate Gallery. Crazily enough, I never did.

My second stint in Venice, two years later, produced one of my few scoops. Travelling into the city by *vaporetto* with the Gimpel clan, Kay Gimpel said: 'You ought to talk to the American collector Jo Hirshhorn. He's thinking seriously of giving his collection to Britain, if they'll build a new gallery for it in Regent's Park.' I duly pinned down the tiny millionaire, of whom I had not heard. Hirshhorn came from the humblest origins and owed much of his fortune to the mining of uranium. He confirmed that he had indeed been having talks with the Treasury about London as a possible destination for his collection, which then numbered some 4,000 paintings and 416 sculptures 'as of this month'. But Zurich, California and Italy were also in the frame.

Charles Wintour put my piece on the front page, date-lined Venice and headlined 'Vast new art collection for England?' The effect was gratifying. Within a few hours of my dictating it, every British correspondent or art critic was chasing around trying to follow it up, and Charles sent me a telegram saying: 'Warmest congratulations your very fine world exclusive jestarday (*sic*) stop good followup in classy papers today'. After touting his collection around several countries, including Israel, Hirshhorn decided that Washington would be the right destination. It was eventually housed in the doughnut-shaped Hirshhorn Museum, custom-designed by the architect Gordon Bunshaft, which

I visited in the 1980s.

There was a memorable moment at the 1964 Biennale when someone tapped me on the shoulder at a party and said: '*Roger, est-ce que je peux vous présenter Monsieur Giacometti?*' And there he was, that deeply-lined face as sculptural as any of his creations. For once I was at a loss for small talk.

By contrast with my success in Venice, I found the Edinburgh Festival of 1962 very hard to deal with: there was just too much going on. Where should one strike? But I had a memorable hour with the Russian cellist Mstislav Rostropovich and his wife, the soprano Galina Vishnevskaya, who were in the throes of an argument. I was thrilled by their subsequent concert.

Standing in for Sam White to write the weekly *Paris Newsletter* during his summer holiday, from 1963 to 1965, was daunting. His reputation was based on a steady flow of revelations about scandalous goings-on in French government circles and the higher reaches of Parisian society. His tentacular network of contacts was firmly rooted in the bar of the Crillon Hotel. Inevitably he took his five weeks of holiday (always on the Ile de Ré) during the dead days of July and August, when even he might have been pressed to flush out much of great interest. Even so, the prospect of five weeks in his flat in the Rue de Grenelle, just off the Boulevard St Germain, was delightful. I knew Paris quite well, spoke goodish French, had some contacts at the British Embassy; and my Cambridge chum Bernard Josien, now a successful commercial lawyer, lived not far off in the Rue Bonaparte. I had the use of Sam's office near the Louvre, his secretary and even his chauffeur-driven car. It was quite a step up for a mere particle of the Londoner's Diary.

The challenge each week was to find a story strong enough to lead the column. To follow that with four or five reasonably entertaining items, including interviews, was less difficult, and a good chance to meet a film star or two to 'lift' the page. My first effort in July 1963 opened with a tale about a feud between (President) General de Gaulle and Gaston Monnerville, the black, flute-playing President of the Senate who would notionally stand in for de Gaulle should the latter meet an untimely end. Both had recently given large and highly political parties, omitting with studied and much discussed rudeness to invite the other. Monnerville had come to France from French Guiana to study, aged 15, and had stayed on. That just about 'stood up' as the lead story. My picture interview was with the enchanting Corinne Marchand, star of the film *Cléo de Cinq à Sept*, in whom I discovered a keen interest in bees. One week, instead of a female film star, I had the actor Harold Lloyd, of silent film fame, a very entertaining interviewee. It was the time of the Profumo affair, and that newsletter featured a one-liner that tickled the editor: 'According to a current jest, de Gaulle's reaction to the Stephen Ward trial was 'That will teach the English to try and behave like Frenchmen.'

One of the most interesting people I interviewed was Dr Frank J Malina, since the mid-1930s one of the pioneers of American rocketry and one of the co-founders of the Jet Propulsion Laboratory. Unlike his two colleagues, he had held onto his shares in

Aerojet, the manufacturing spin-off from JPL and its predecessor, the Galcit Rocket Research Project, from which NASA's programme of inter-planetary exploration ultimately derived. He had taken refuge in Paris, working initially for Unesco, after falling foul of the FBI thanks to a youthful interest in the Communist Party. Since then he had devoted his life to a complex form of kinetic art that he had invented. In the sitting-room of his home in the suburb of Boulogne-Billancourt, I saw dozens of screens onto which moving forms that he had painted were projected. The effect was eerie and beautiful. Dr Malina (his parents were Czech) was modest, bearded and charming. He has remained virtually unknown outside the world of aerospace. Yet of the hundreds of people I have interviewed, few can have had as much influence on the modern world.

On one flight to Paris I found myself sitting next to Maurice Girodias, whose notorious Olympia Press first published works then considered pornographic, by Nabokov, Beckett, William Burroughs and J.P.Donleavy among others. He was a great companion for a short flight. Once or twice I drove my convertible Triumph Vitesse onto one of the Superfreighters that plied in those days (1953 to 1970) from Lydd airfield in Kent to Le Touquet, surely the most painless and quickest way ever to cross the Channel.

A pleasure of the annual Paris exercise was the spectacular July 14 military parade down the Champs Elysées, headed by General de Gaulle. It was followed by his press conference and an evening of communal revelry. De Gaulle always spoke without notes and had a surprisingly genial presence. No doubt he had memorised his opening statement, which no actor could have delivered with more subtly modulated intonation and timing. It was a joy to hear the French language so beautifully handled, and he answered questions with great fluency, charm and humour. I was able to savour all this because, miraculously enough, the *Evening Standard* was happy to take agency reports of anything he said of note.

Allegedly, when de Gaulle retired to Colombey-les-deux-Eglises, he had some urinary problems. Referring to his penchant for saying 'La France, c'est moi', his wife Yvonne is said to have quipped: '*Ah, Charles, tu étais la France, maintenant tu es incontinent!*'. It's a joke better spoken than read.

My first stint in Paris came shortly after meeting my future wife, a fashion

Joy

journalist on the *Daily Mail* called Joy Tagney. I owed the introduction to Judy Innes, who had been both at Cambridge and on the Diary with me. When she left to become the *Daily Mail*'s youthful fashion editor, I urged her to look out for someone for me: 'slim, full and without hairy arms', I specified. One evening, she and her then husband Johnny Moynihan, editor of the *Standard*'s In London Last Night column, invited me around for a drink, and there was this lovely woman who not only answered my description but radiated beauty and charm. True, she was engaged to the son of a notorious Rhodesian minister, Desmond Lardner-Burke. But it seemed the engagement was crumbling. I was, it transpired, a great deal more impressed by Joy than she was by me. Nonetheless, we agreed to meet up in Paris at the cosmetic queen Helena Rubinstein's party that traditionally marked the opening of the Paris fashion collections, to which she and Judy were shortly heading. We did so, dined together afterwards and saw a good deal of each other subsequently. I began to feel my enjoyable quest was drawing to a close.

Staying with Somerset Maugham in Cap Ferrat

One of my tasks back at the Diary was to chronicle the activities of two old men in whom Lord Beaverbrook took a personal interest: Somerset Maugham and John Paul Getty, the oil billionaire who, like Maugham, was also a picture collector. It was a Diary tradition to interview Maugham on his birthday in January, for which he forsook his home in Cap Ferrat on the French Riviera (not far from Beaverbrook's) for the Dorchester Hotel on Park Lane. My first encounter was in 1961. On a beautiful Sunday morning I swished through the leaves in Hyde Park and was ushered into Maugham's hotel room by his secretary Alan Searle. Maugham, 88 that day, had a dehydrated look, and his speech was constrained by his stammer, with which I naturally sympathised. Searle was a complete contrast: pink, plump, chatty and amusing. A delicious lunch was brought up, and Maugham seemed to warm to me as we discussed Balzac, Flaubert, Maupassant and other French writers he admired.

A year on, Lord Beaverbrook heard that Maugham had decided to sell his collection of Impressionist and post-Impressionist paintings at Sotheby's. I was eventually authorised to release this story in the Diary. The modest stir it caused was nothing compared with the aftermath, on most of which I had an iron grip. Not long after the paintings had fetched more than £500,000 at auction, Maugham's daughter by his marriage to the interior decorator Syrie Maugham, Lady John Hope, sued for the proceeds from nine paintings, valued at £231,750. These, she claimed, had been assigned to her in a legal document. It helped the story that her husband, Lord John Hope, was the Conservative government's Minister for Public Buildings and Works

Maugham countered, not very lovably, by seeking to disown her as his daughter and to adopt Alan Searle as his son (the adoption was eventually annulled by a French court). All this was of course meat and drink to the Diary. It was my task to keep abreast of the developing scandal, and to maintain friendly contact not just with Searle but also with Lady John Hope's supporters. Mainly old friends of her mother, they included the photographer Cecil Beaton and the writer Rebecca West. They seemed to regard me as reasonably objective.

These shenanigans brought me into frequent contact with Searle, who liked me but showed no sign of fancying me ('rough trade' was more his line). It was no doubt thanks to him that I was invited to spend a few days at the Villa Mauresque, Maugham's home in Cap Ferrat since 1925. Charles Wintour agreed that an article about life chez Maugham, who had been so much in the news, would make a good feature, and I could perhaps interview one or two other people on the Riviera.

Thus one evening in March 1963 I was greeted at Nice airport by Searle and Maugham's elderly chauffeured Rolls. At the Villa Mauresque I was shown to a large bedroom, its adjacent bathroom a bower of lotions and essences. Flinging open the shutters next morning, I found row upon terraced row of fruiting orange, lemon and tangerine trees, leading down to mimosa, fir and eucalyptus trees among which goldfinches twittered – and then the sea. Paradise!

The house was run by a staff of seven, with three more in the garden of 60 sculpted acres. The cook could operate for three weeks without repeating herself, and the food was delicious: my first dinner opened with a memorable oyster soup. Maugham and Searle were touchingly solicitous for my welfare. Did my bedroom lack anything? Was there anything I would particularly like to eat? Or anyone I wanted to meet? I suggested Graham and Kathy Sutherland, and on my second day they came to lunch, I had tea with Lord Beaverbrook and drinks with Jean Cocteau, before returning to dine with Maugham and Searle. After dinner I typed up all that had transpired on this goodish day.

If seeing Graham Sutherland again was an act of consolidation, tea chez Beaverbrook was one of *politesse*. The *Standard*'s proprietor was taller, less wizened and even more twinkly than I expected. He asked me a stream of questions, even pressing me about my time in South Korea. I felt gruelled when I emerged into the sunshine.

Cocteau, who lived nearby, was also exhausting, and this was meant to be an interview. He talked incessantly and amusingly, in a fine spray of paradoxes and quotations, and was full of the honorary degree that Oxford had latterly bestowed on him, not to mention a recent lunch with Princess Margaret. He did not come across as a man with serious artistic achievements to his credit (plays perhaps, films certainly, art possibly), more as a social butterfly.

The best moments with Maugham came after supper, when we relaxed in the sitting room in front of a fire and talked, sometimes through the intermediary of the dachshund George, a charming beast who seemed to welcome my relatively youthful company. One evening Searle and I were sipping whisky after Maugham had retired to bed when we heard a dreadful moaning sound from upstairs. Searle rushed up and asked what was the matter. 'Nothing, it's just death stalking', Maugham replied. Searle told me some touching stories. Once Maugham had been wandering off the leash on a railway platform. Someone came up to Searle and said: 'Are you with that old man?

He seems to think he's Somerset Maugham.' I left the Villa Mauresque with a feeling of real affection for both Maugham and Searle, who told me I had had a rejuvenating effect on the old man.

Lord Beaverbrook seemed pleased with my feature, which was rather crassly headlined 'The paradise that Maugham bought for £7,000.' 'Certainly some intimate touches', he messaged the editor.

From Cap Ferrat I drove to Vallauris to interview Lord Astor of Hever, a sad man who had been exiled from England by some recent trust fund legislation; and then to the Grasse area to spend 36 hours with the editor's friends, Yvonne Mitchell and Derek Monsey. Yvonne Mitchell was a distinguished actress of stage and screen, remembered for her title role in the film *Lady in a Dressing Gown* and, in her 40s, still lovely. Derek Monsey was the film critic of the *Sunday Express*, and a touch bitter about her greater fame. 'Have one of Yvonne's cigarettes', he urged at one stage. But they made me very welcome, and Yvonne told me some hair-raising stories about the physical ordeals of making films.

The success of my five days in the south of France gave me the ludicrous idea that I could make a plump living as a freelance based in that area. With the arrogance of youth, I failed to realise that without the guaranteed outlet of the *Evening Standard* (or another major newspaper), I would amount to very little. The status of all but a few freelance journalists is close to zero, as would later be brought home to me. I soon abandoned the idea.

I returned to the Villa Mauresque for a weekend in January 1964, the excuse being Maugham's 90th birthday. I was shocked by the degeneration of his mental faculties: mild dementia had set in. When I had been there for 24 hours, he cried out as I came down for dinner: 'Aha, who have we here?' and several times after meals he extended his hand and said 'Goodbye, I don't suppose I shall see you again.' On one occasion he said: 'Would you mind speaking up, if what you have to say is of the slightest interest.' Far from being crestfallen, I realised I would be able to dine out on this, as intermittently I have. Searle was depressed at being trapped by Maugham's dependence on him in the gilded cage of the Villa Mauresque. This time I left it with a feeling of relief, and had some difficulty cobbling together a piece on 'Life with Maugham at 90'. He died the following year, not many months after Lord Beaverbrook went the same way.

I visited Jean Paul Getty at his home, Sutton Place in Surrey. As mean as his son John Paul was generous, this proverbially wealthy oil man was notorious for having a pay phone for his guests. All I remember is being ushered into his gloomy, cadaverous but very polite presence in a beautiful room panelled in pale oak and hung with seriously good Impressionists. He would then have been in his early 70s. His staff were by contrast rather jolly. They included two lawyers, Robina Lund and the Danish-born Claus von Bülow, who later moved to New York. In a sensational trial in the 1980s, he was found guilty of the attempted murder (by insulin injection) of his wealthy and diabetic American wife, but subsequently cleared on appeal: a film, *Reversal of Fortune*, was made of the case, starring Jeremy Irons. As a young man, Claus was excellent company.

Late in 1962, Maurice and Ruth Ash decided to move down to Devon, where Maurice would become chairman of the trustees of the Dartington estate. They bought a large, austerely handsome Palladian mansion, Sharpham House, and its estate of several hundred acres 20 minutes drive from Dartington. It stands on a hill overlooking a broad bend in the river Dart (tidal at that point), with Totnes visible in the distance: a magnificent location. 'One would never get planning permission for it nowadays', Maurice once wryly commented.

Last flats and flings

As a consequence, the Ashes sold the house in Duchess Mews, and I moved to a flat in Roland Gardens, South Kensington. This I shared for about a year with Bob Keyserlingk, who had come to the metropolis to take a history PhD at London University. It was for me a time of culture, women and laughter. Then the friends who owned it wanted to take it over themselves, and I moved to my last bachelor flat. This was a first floor apartment (two rooms, k & b) leased from the Church Commissioners in a house at the less plush end of Blomfield Road, overlooking the Regent's Canal in Little Venice (part of Maida Vale). The house had been freshly converted into three flats, so I could furnish it from scratch, which I greatly enjoyed. The first floor was sunny, the view over the canal and its various houseboats was a joy, and it was the first area I had lived in since those early days in Chelsea where it was a pleasure to wander around. There were even two charming young women in the flat above me.

It was probably a sign of my emotional immaturity, or excessive hedonism, that – even though well into my relationship with Joy – I took a three-week solo Club Méditerrannée holiday in Israel in September 1963. This was based on the northern coast, near the border with Lebanon, but had the option of an extended trip to Galilee, the Negev and Eilat in the south, which I took. I swam in both the Dead and the Red seas (better Red than Dead: the latter's greasy salinity is unpleasant). That was a time when Israel's achievements in conquering arid land rather than Palestinians were widely admired. The kibbutz was regarded as an enlightened and very effective experiment in agricultural socialism, while the less famous moshavs were transforming agriculturally ignorant immigrants into productive Israeli citizens. It was a moving experience to spend my 29th birthday on a kibbutz, where a birthday cake was conjured up in minutes.

I had stayed at a Club Med in Elba a few years previously, so I realised that, although I enjoyed several passionate embraces with single but married women, the eternal quest would not necessarily be successful. In Israel I was not entirely disappointed, the French girl involved being pleasingly surnamed Sépulchre.

There was perhaps something slightly desperate, or pathetic, in my *chasse au bonheur*. If my inner need was for intimacy, I was not going about fulfilling it very sensibly. I had been quite seriously involved with four or five girls, but I had not really shared much of my life with any of them. Some had grown fonder of me than I of them. Was

Sharpham House

Maurice and Ruth, with Henry Moore's Two Piece Reclining Figure
(Bryan Heseltine ?)

I congenitally emotionally shallow? Did my vanity need a stream of conquests? Was I collecting women rather as I collected pictures? Was my common enough yearning to stroke and be stroked fuelled by a cuddles deficit when I was in Canada?

No doubt all these factors played a part. Where Joy was concerned, a further set of difficulties loomed. She had a classless aura and accent, but was mysterious about her background. When she left Camden School for Girls (as it then was) she had to find a job rather than continue her education: her father had become schizophrenic, and her mother needed support, financial as well as emotional. She had long wanted to be a journalist, and through a school friend's father, started work on a horticultural magazine he ran called *The Grower*, from which she had graduated to the *Financial Times*, and thence to the *Daily Mail*.

To upper middle-class people of my parents' generation, 'background' was a matter of great importance. Joy had to fend off some unpleasant grilling about hers from my father when I took her home – as did I. I defended her doughtily, not least when Dad asked her over dinner: 'May I ask what wine you think you are drinking?' 'Dad, I think that's an unfair question', I interposed. Such traumas drew me closer to my loved one: my parents' whole-hearted approval of one or two earlier girlfriends had been near-fatal.

Joy and I tested our relationship, which had had its bumpy moments, with a holiday in and around Connemara on the glorious west coast of Ireland and, despite last minute doubts, were married at Marylebone Register Office in November 1964, followed by a small party at Durrants Hotel in Baker Street. Joy's mother and sister Eileen attended, as did my two sisters (Martin was in the Philippines), plus a few friends. My parents boycotted the occasion, to my distress and disgust. Their attitude to Joy changed before long, not least because their friends seemed to like her so much; and when we came to buy our run-down house overlooking a sliver of Hampstead Heath, my father very generously provided almost half the asking price of £10,500 (some £131,000 in today's money: we had to spend around £5,000 re-vamping it). Joy nobly put in several thousand pounds worth of savings, and we took out a mortgage, tiny by today's standards, to finance the refurbishment.

The five-storey house, part of a cream-brick terrace in Christchurch Hill, had been on the market some six months: Albert Finney's ex-wife had just withdrawn as a potential purchaser. The house had a 'sitting' tenant, the elderly Nellie Headford, in the rear room of the first floor, paying a minuscule controlled rent, with the statutory right to remain (and to pass on that right to family, which she fortunately did not have). She smoked, and liked to keep her door wedged open, with a whistling kettle generally on the boil. The basement had for years been used to store the ladders of the owner, a builder, and was waterlogged. We had originally planned to spend only around £5,000 overall, probably on a flat. That was then about the norm for a young professional couple. So a total of £15,000 seemed a lot to take on, despite the splendour of the location. Joy was by now a lynchpin of the *Daily Mail*'s fashion desk, and I was quite well paid.

Christchurch Hill: our house was behind the willow

As we were leaving after our first inspection, we heard a loud tapping on the window of the next-door house, and saw someone waving at us to come in. It was Jeremy Hadfield, the charismatic publicity chief of publishers Weidenfeld and Nicholson, whom I knew well. It was like seeing the same house before and after. They had knocked the two rooms on the first floor together to make a spacious L-shaped sitting room, and inserted dormer windows in the attic to make two extra bedrooms. The basement had been turned into a separate flat, the rent helping to pay their mortgage. We decided to go for it, and could not have made a better investment. Our mortgage broker turned out to be a member of a Peking-oriented cell of the British Communist Party. He recommended an architect, Colin Penn, who lived nearby and (we later discovered) belonged to the same group. Penn was pleasant and did a decent if uninspired job. Later he had the rather more challenging task of modernising the huge Chinese embassy in Portland Place, no doubt a reward for loyal support.

Back at the Londoner's Diary, Donald Edgar had departed as editor, to be replaced by one of our number, Laurence Marks. Laurence was a talented writer and interviewer, more interested in the arts than Edgar, but too buttoned up emotionally to extract the best from the Diary team. I was quite frequently asked to edit on Saturdays, sometimes on weekdays, felt nervous, but enjoyed it. In 1965 Marks departed for the Observer, and I was appointed to succeed him.

Editing the Londoner's Diary

I had been worried about prolonging my time as a diarist. Fun though it was doing pocket interviews with interesting people – I had latterly encountered, among others, Alan Jay Lerner, Harold Pinter, who was kind to me, and Katharine Graham, publisher of the Washington Post, with whom I naively felt I had clicked – there was something trivial about it. On the other hand, as art critic I was agreeably stretched by writing a review of, for example, a major Goya exhibition in London; and I had loved my stints in Paris. But there could be no refusing this job: editing the Diary was a well-known route to greater things, and no doubt my salary would be suitably increased. Less gratifyingly, I would have to be in the office by 8am to see the early edition to bed and attend the morning conference at 9am with a list of possible stories. I would be desk-bound, and I would no longer see my name in the paper.

To my surprise, I found I loved being in charge. We aimed to be first with the news of changes in publishing, the art world and, to some extent, politics and Whitehall; and to interview people in or behind the news. In my two years at the helm, the Diary staff included such future stars as Max Hastings, Magnus Linklater, Mary Kenny, Paul Callan and Andrew Duncan. Max had grown impatient with Oxford and wanted to launch himself into the profession in which his illustrious parents, Macdonald Hastings and Anne Scott-James, excelled. He was headstrong, astonishingly confident and, virtually from the start, a brilliant operator. I would give him some tricky task, and two hours later he would plump his story in front of me and say: 'How about that, Roger!' We tried to stretch the Diary envelope, for example by treating one of the first black fashion models, Donyale Luna, as an intelligent woman and getting an intelligent interview. It was enormous fun.

Only occasionally would I write something myself, perhaps a telephone interview with someone I knew like Rab Butler, by then Master of Trinity College, Cambridge, or Henry Moore. I was pleased with a riposte I wrote to a campaign by General de Gaulle to defend the French language against Anglo-Saxon verbiage. One paragraph will give the slightly laboured flavour:

> My position vis-à-vis this cause célèbre is one of hauteur. Anything, I say, for a rapprochement. As the soi-disant chauffeur of the French nation, de Gaulle is, in his bourgeois, blasé way, driving down a cul-de-sac towards a non-existent venue.

We had a lively discussion as to whether the words of French origin should be italicised or not. We decided that not to italicise them would emphasise their integration into English usage.

I look back on my yellowing copies of the Diary with pride. It still reads as a lively, informative and entertaining column, written about interesting people by and for intelligent people, with a sprinkling of exclusive news stories that were followed up by the broadsheets the following morning. The editor was pleased. He even invited us all to dine (black tie) with our wives at the very posh Stafford Hotel one evening 'because the Diary is so very good'. Donald McLachlan, since 1961 the cerebral editor of the new *Sunday Telegraph*, observed in the *Spectator* that the Londoner's Diary was probably the best of the current crop of diaries.

The Londoner's Diary 1967: (L to R) me, Max Hastings, Magnus Linklater, Paul Callan, Mary Kenny, Philip Whitaker, with Charles Wintour on the piano (Evening Standard)

Before long I was approached by *The Times* to start up something similar on their 'op-ed' (opposite the editorials and letters) page. That august organ, previously owned by the Astor family, had been taken over by the Canadian Roy (later Lord) Thomson. Its new editor, William Rees-Mogg, was busy recruiting fresh talent from across Fleet Street. I responded to his offer by saying I felt I owed it to Charles Wintour to stay another nine months at the Standard. *The Times* was, flatteringly, happy to wait.

How different the history of British journalism in the 1970s and '80s might have been had Charles Wintour rather than Rees-Mogg been chosen to edit the Thomson-owned Thunderer. Apart from being a brilliant editor with a great eye for talent, Charles was essentially a Social Democrat. With more centrist attitudes and reactions to world events, the paper could perhaps have achieved a broader and younger readership, eating into that of the *Guardian* and closing off the gap subsequently left for the *Independent*.

Chapter 8

The Times Diary (1967-1969)

Transferring to *The Times* was not the only event that made 1967 a testing year for Joy and me. Joy's mother died that January, aged 56, shortly before our first daughter Lucy was born. Not long after our marriage in 1964, Joy's mother had begun to notice a tingling in her toes, accompanied by a loss of sensation that became progressively worse: the first symptoms of what was before long diagnosed as motor neurone disease (MND). This involves a relentlessly progressive degeneration of the nerves and muscles controlling speech and movement. The survival time from the disease's onset is usually three to five years (Stephen Hawking's variant form is rare).

We tried to make what remained of her life interesting. When she was still just able to walk, we took her to Paris, which she greatly enjoyed. Towards the end, she came to live with us. The inexorable progress of the disease was horrifying. Three years after its onset, she died in Joy's arms.

Lucy was born just two months later, in an under-equipped cottage hospital some 200 yards up the hill from our Hampstead home. Joy's labour was protracted, and eventually an obstetrician had to be summoned during the rush hour from the parent hospital in distant Whitechapel. Lucy was dragged out with forceps, with a large, short-lived bump on her head to show for the ordeal. Joy was just about OK. My mother generously paid for a (wonderful) trained nurse to help us for the first fortnight. When Charlotte (Lottie) was born 18 months later, it was in the safe confines of the Middlesex Hospital, but even with a saline drip to help she was slow to arrive.

Of course Lucy's arrival changed everything for Joy, and a great deal for me. I was a doting dad, did my bit on the changing nappy front, and loved taking Lucy out onto the heath in her pram. Her first word as she gazed up into the foliage was 'twee'. When she was joined by Lottie, and as they both grew older, we tried not to push them in any particular direction, and I treated them as I would have treated boys, for example playing catch as soon as possible. Lucy soon showed a preference for boyish toys – a bionic man was a favourite – while Lottie favoured softer playthings. The heath was a perpetual joy for us all, and our back garden was big enough for the girls to crawl or run around in (there was also a small patch in the front, on the wall of which our ancient sitting tenant sometimes sat, looking like a life-sized garden gnome).

We did not have to look far for friends and entertainment. Our terraced section of Christchurch Hill, the less expensive end, was full of compatible people. In the Hadfields' next door basement flat was a female Japanese philosopher called Hidé, soon replaced by a well-known literary agent, Ilse Yardley. John and Ann Tusa soon took the house one up from them. They had been leading thespians at Cambridge, where I had known John slightly. His was a formidable combination of intelligence, energy and determination that was to take him to the top of the BBC as reporter, current affairs presenter and managing director of the Overseas Service, not to mention subsequently running the Barbican Centre, for which he was knighted. He shared my interest in contemporary art, and we frequently played tennis together. He was keener to win, and I think I only beat him once.

Slightly down the hill in the same terrace, though not for very long, was Maurice Temple Smith, another publisher (he was soon to start his own imprint). At one of his at home launch parties, the American novelist and short story writer Bernard Malamud said to me: 'Has anyone ever told you that you look a bit like John Updike?' I wasn't sure whether this was a compliment, but it sounded good. Across the road were the gardens of houses that fronted onto Gainsborough Gardens, in one of which lived John le Carré, with whom I would eventually sometimes chat. Among numerous actors in the immediate vicinity were Jeremy Irons and his wife Sinead Cusack.

I moved the to *The Times* in the spring of 1967. The way I was initially treated at Printing House Square was heartening. I was greeted by Jim Bishop, the features editor who lived in Willow Road, just down the hill from us, introduced to senior staff members, and shown to the Diary's spacious and carpeted room facing towards the Thames and adjacent to the offices of the deputy editor and other honchos. My staff of four reporters and a secretary (unthinkable nowadays) initially included Hugh Noyes, a descendant of the poet and a very professional journalist. He had worked for the Diary's predecessor, a smaller affair whose title, As It Happens, conveyed its peripheral status. He soon moved to the political staff.

The Times was then located in a handsome modern block at Blackfriars, which it shared with *The Observer*. It was in every respect very different from the scruffy and friendly *Evening Standard* in Shoe Lane: more compartmentalised, and much more hierarchical. But morale seemed generally positive. Under Rees-Mogg there was the deputy editor (and Communist affairs expert) Iverach MacDonald. He was a rather gentle and very polite Scot, of whom it was said when he was at the helm 'The editor's indecision is final.' The No 3 was the very posh Oliver Woods, a former Commonwealth specialist, who had sounded me out. He was soon succeeded as home affairs editor by John Grant, a good administrator. Also near the top of the hierarchy were the senior leader writers, in terms of intellect and knowledge genuinely impressive people.

The Diary was to occupy two full columns down the right hand side of the 'op-ed' page, and would be devoted to much the same mix of news and interviews as the Londoner's Diary. After much debate, it was to be signed 'PHS' (for Printing House Square): naturally I would have preferred 'edited by Roger Berthoud'. Despite the anonymity, I felt a heavy weight of expectations pressing on me, and was anxious to secure a strong story to top the first issue. Well in advance I said as much to the then director of the Tate Gallery, Norman Reid, with whom I had long been friendly. Could he, I wondered, come up with something for me that would create a bit of a stir? Thus it was that I was able to announce that Mark Rothko, the American abstract painter, had decided to give the Tate around 20 paintings spanning his career. In the event, the Tate got rather fewer (nine) of his mystically throbbing canvases, but that's still quite a lot of Rothkos. The story was picked up from the early editions by *The Daily Telegraph*, a sound yardstick of its news value. Rees-Mogg was pleased with our debut

I was lucky he realised that a newsy diary needs a good staff: some editors assume that specialists within the paper will have a constant flow of stories to offer. In practice, it's only the political staff who are likely to be effective contributors. Since I had indicated I did not want to do the job for more than two years, I needed a No 2 who would succeed me. He came in the reassuring form of Ion Trewin, son of the drama critic J.C.Trewin. Ion is a charming fellow, and was a very reliable operator, if not a particularly inspired wordsmith. He later became a very successful publisher, with a particular talent for spotting winners (such as Alan Clark's diaries), and outstandingly good with people: latterly he has been administering the Man Booker prize. A more entertaining writer, with an engagingly subversive streak, was Stuart Weir, a committed Socialist who later edited the *New Statesman*. In the early days there was also Tony Aldous, subsequently a pioneer environment correspondent. He was followed by Robin Young, a sterling ex-Liberal parliamentary candidate. Perhaps the one who influenced me most, though he was a far from elegant writer, was an Australian, Paul Martin, of whom more later.

On the Times Diary we assumed a reasonable attention span in our readers: whereas those perusing the Londoner's Diary were likely to be hanging onto a strap on the Tube, PHS's would more likely be at the breakfast table or on a train. So we had fewer and often considerably longer items, especially if they were interviews, many of which I did myself. Much the longest, at some 750 words, was with Sir Oswald Mosley, whose zig-zag political career had ended with his leadership in the 1930s of the British Union (fascist) party and his internment during the war. He was then 70, writing his memoirs, and every bit as engaging as I had been warned he would be. The chief leader writer, the esteemed Owen Hickey, told me he was sorry I had seen fit to give so much space to such a man.

A few weeks after seeing Mosley I was ushered into the presence of Sir Harold Macmillan at his eponymous publishing house. The former Tory Prime Minister was off to Canada and the USA, and treated me to some fresh yet mellow reflections on his links with those countries: he would for example be visiting Indiana, where his maternal grandfather had studied medicine and been a small-town doctor: astonishing to think, he mused, that Indiana was then a territory rather than a state. He remembered meeting Dad in Algiers during the war – 'a most delightful man', he commented. Although Macmillan is nowadays sometimes seen as a bit of a fraud, a sense of history was very much part of his considerable style. I also interviewed that dubious ex-minister Lord Boothby, who had been Lady Dorothy Macmillan's lover and friend of the notorious gangsters, the Kray twins. Boothby subsequently wrote a letter to *The Times* accusing me of misquoting him in criticising Winston Churchill. Fortunately I had taped the interview, a fact I was not allowed to append to the letter.

I was interested to meet Field Marshal Lord Montgomery, whom I had missed on his visits to the embassy in Copenhagen: he had been prominent in the liberation of Denmark. In Copenhagen he had lived up to his reputation for egocentricity: he once put my small sister Belinda on his uniformed knee and urged her to count his medals. My contact came through Denis Hamilton, by now editor-in-chief of Times Newspapers, who rang me one afternoon to say he had his old friend Monty upstairs: it was his birthday and perhaps I'd like to have a brief chat. So up I went, and a somewhat stilted conversation took place, with no doubt some tactful allusion on my part to his Copenhagen visits. A paragraph or two resulted.

Editors are always pleased when an article generates controversy within the letters column. The Diary succeeded in doing so periodically, once by defending the Russian poet Yevgeny Yevtushenko, who was a candidate in 1968 for the Oxford chair of poetry and under attack by the novelist Kingsley Amis. I reckoned that Yevtushenko, flawed though his record might be, was basically on the side of freedom of expression and the Soviet Union's dissident writers. Amis had described him in the *New Statesman* as a 'squalid pseudo-liberal'.

The detailed and complex argument turned partly on the authenticity of a telegram that Yevtushenko was said to have sent to the Soviet leader, Leonid Brezhnev, about the Soviet Union's suppression of Czechoslovakia's moves towards democracy. Amis wrote two long letters seeking to rubbish my arguments in defence of the Russian poet. I wrote three pieces rebutting Amis. I conceded that Yevtushenko was vulnerable to attack, but suggested that Amis and his friends (Bernard Levin, Robert Conquest et al) were too one-sided. I quoted Paul Johnson who, writing about the controversy in the *New Statesman*, found the Amis cabal much more culpable than Yevtushenko – for their unqualified support for the American war in Vietnam.

I was proud to have put the Polish novelist and playwright Witold Gombrowicz slightly more firmly on the English map. I first wrote about him in 1967, when he won the valuable (£6,000, then a lot of money) Prix Internationale de Littérature. *L'Express* had nicely dubbed him *le plus grand des inconnus*. Two years later we were holidaying in Cap d'Antibes, and I went to see him in Vence, where he was living, having by then read his remarkable novels *Cosmos* and *Ferdydurke*. He was racked by asthma, but made clear his bitterness at his neglect in Britain. I hoped I had helped correct this.

I am sometimes asked who was the most impressive person among those I have interviewed. Three I met through the Times Diary would be candidates. One was J.P.Narayan, a tall, rather gaunt Indian with piercing eyes who had once been seen as a possible successor to Pandit Nehru as Indian Prime Minister. A follower of Gandhi and a socialist of the most principled variety, he believed that, in his own words, 'society should be made up of smaller communities.' He was a persuasive and early advocate of what would now be called 'communitarianism' (horrible word). Narayan had been a Marxist. Perhaps it was this sort of item that led the then Roman Catholic Archbishop, Cardinal J.C.Heenan, to say to his fellow Catholic Rees-Mogg: 'You realise that you have a Marxist on your paper?' Rees-Mogg expressed surprise and asked for his name. 'Roger Berthoud', said the notoriously reactionary prelate. I laughed incredulously when Rees-Mogg told me the story.

By what criteria does one assess impressiveness? All such terms as spiritual force, sense of humanity, humour, even intellectual grip are inevitably subjective. Two other men who seemed to have that touch of greatness as human beings were the American social philosopher and expert on cities, Lewis Mumford, a deeply humane man; and the American-Japanese sculptor and designer Isamu Noguchi. A lithe and handsome 63-year-old, Noguchi seemed to radiate the life force. He told me that he had had a design for a radio turned down because it would never go out of fashion. It took a very long time for those once-ubiquitous hanging paper lampshades, which I believe he designed, to do so, and I am told they are now making a come-back.

Middle East attitudes – and more interviewees

To revert to my Australian colleague Paul Martin: he had lived in the Middle East, and was unequivocally pro-Arab. He helped show me the extent to which Israel's creation had been at the expense of the Palestinians: an initial ethnic cleansing subsequently perpetuated by the occupation of East Jerusalem and the West Bank and Israel's transformation into an oppressive, constantly expropriating, expansionist and racist colonial power. The terrible suffering of the Jews at the hands of the Nazis had led to the lesser but appalling and continuing suffering of the Palestinians.

Paul had excellent contacts in the Arab and pro-Arab worlds. He (or sometimes I) interviewed visiting Arabs, and also Israelis who were disturbed by their government's policies. We evidently succeeded in getting under the official Israeli skin: when I was introduced at a party to the then Israeli ambassador as the editor of the Times Diary, his face changed colour and he launched an angry attack on various recent items we had carried. The embassy later sent the editor a long list of Diary stories that it considered evidence of our anti-Israel bias. Paul went to another job before long, and I continued to mine the same vein. Among the pro-Arab MPs with whom I became friendly was Labour's Christopher Mayhew, a genial fellow who subsequently switched to the Liberals and became a life peer.

Looking back on those two years of editing the Times Diary, I realise what a privileged position I enjoyed. Our sanctuary was far removed from the stresses of the main reporters' room and the home news desk. Since the Diary 'went to bed' relatively early, I could be home in time to see Lucy (and after 1968, Charlotte) before she was tucked up – or get to a concert, film, theatre, private view, dinner or party without too much trouble. The Sixties were still swinging, and we went out a great deal – at least before the girls were born. I have a letter to brother Martin saying: 'We went to Robert Carrier's restaurant in Islington [then all the rage] for our third anniversary. Unbelievably good, really original food. There is a prix fixe, £2 10s for three courses, or £3 for four. We had four and enjoyed every one tremendously.'

One potentially memorable party I attended was given in the King's Road, Chelsea by the Duke of Bedford for the then hugely successfully black singers, the Supremes. A photograph, reproduced in the 1990s in *The Observer*'s colour magazine, showed me at this event, standing near a bearded Mick Jagger, (the late) Brian Jones and Marianne Faithfull, a slice of whose memoirs *The Observer* was publishing. 'I didn't know you knew the Rolling Stones', said a colleague. 'Never met them', I replied. As they say, if you remember the Sixties, you weren't there.

Rolling Stones observed: Mick Jagger, Marianne Faithfull, Bryan Jones
(Pictorial Press)

Interviews sometimes led to social contacts. I liked some freshly published poems by Ruth Fainlight that her publisher had sent me. We got on so well when I interviewed her that Joy and I invited her to dinner in Hampstead with her husband – who turned out to be Alan Sillitoe, author of *The Loneliness of the Long-Distance Runner* and many other seminal novels. We had a lovely evening, and they asked us back. Another socially productive encounter was with one Edmund Brudenell, who was hoping for a plug for the stately home he was about to open to the public. Brudenell was a descendant of the 7th Earl of Cardigan, who led the Charge of the Light Brigade at Balaklava and, more importantly, a very amusing fellow of 38. He liked my piece, and pressed me to come for a weekend with Joy to his 80-room Georgian pile, Deene Park in Northants.

When we arrived, Brudenell and his chums had just come back from a shoot. We were ushered into a vast Elizabethan hall with a table as long as a cricket pitch, at which were seated large men in hairy jackets and plus-fours. We were introduced. 'This is Lord Dilhorne' (yes, the oft-execrated ex-Attorney General and Lord Chancellor, Reginald Manningham-Buller), 'this is Lord Clarendon, this is Lord Stormont and his sister Lady Maria, this is Count Kinsky'…and so on. London's most successful antiques dealer, John Partridge, was also of the party: his wife was the daughter of the immensely rich Lord Brownlow.

Conversation included such cries down the table as 'How many woodcock did we get today, Reggie?'; 'What's your record bag here, Edmund?'; and 'Are you spending much time in Roaring River (in Jamaica) this winter?' The youngish Lady Maria's nickname was Tiddler, a euphemism in our family for the vagina. So when someone later asked her 'How many times a week do you open to the public, Tiddler?' Joy and I had to suppress our mirth. Brudenell had an endearing inability to pronounce both his r's and his th's, as in 'We now have 12 bafwombs, I fink'. Altogether a very surreal weekend, which made upper-class life of the stuffier sort seem deeply undesirable and tedious.

Lavishly staffed though the Diary was, we did not find it easy to fill those two long columns with good material. I still have nightmares about not having enough to cover the white paper. In March 1969 we were shunted to the bottom of the page across five columns, losing a few inches in the process. It felt like a demotion, but reduced the pressure on us and made designing the main features page easier for the sub-editors.

Family events

An update on the family: while Joy's two labours/births were painfully slow, one of my sister Elisabeth's was far too quick. In 1958 she was travelling, heavily pregnant, to London by train from Sedbergh in Cumbria, where her husband Richard Pentney was still teaching. Perhaps the jolting of the train made her go into labour. With one of her two daughters she was taken off at Nuneaton, where her third daughter Catherine was very soon born. This drama delayed her departure for Tanganyika (as it still was), where Richard had been appointed as the first lay headmaster of a missionary school, St Andrew's, Minaki. Mother remarked that it was auspicious, given the big-cat hazards of Africa, that the drama had taken place at Nuneaton.

The school at Minaki was a challenging assignment. It was in the developmental stage, with a mere 180 boys, a few mud and wattle buildings, no electricity and a dubious water supply. When the country's Governor, Sir Richard Turnbull, paid a visit, he likened it – with that gossamer colonial touch – to the last days of the House of Usher. Tanganyika, a British, though formerly German colony, was heading towards internal self-rule and then, in late 1961, independence: it was renamed Tanzania after its merger with Zanzibar.

Julius Nyerere, a politically active teacher from a school not far down the road with whom Lis and Richard had become friendly, was soon to become the country's chief minister and then President. The new government poured money into St Andrew's, and under Richard it became a substantial establishment with 400 pupils, a more advanced curriculum, numerous new buildings, electricity and good running water. But out in the bush lions still roared in the night, giving a new dimension to Lis's production of Shaw's *Androcles and the Lion*.

Julius Nyerere was a warm and very engaging human being and rare among African leaders in being modest and uncorrupt. It was typical of him, Lis recalled, that he should take to the great Uhuru (freedom) Ball in Dar-es-Salaam the Scottish landlady who had been kind to him when he was at Edinburgh University. Unfortunately these human qualities did not prevent him from progressively bankrupting his country by nationalising the 'commanding heights' of the economy and (often forcibly) regrouping the rural population in so-called socialist villages. Another impressive local personality was Father Trevor Huddleston, later famous as the President of the Anti-Apartheid Movement. He was then Bishop of Masasi and, as chairman of the governors of Richard's school, a valuable supporter and friend, with whom they remained in touch.

Post-independence Africanisation resulted in Richard losing his job after six strenuous years. He spent a year teaching at Oundle, and was then appointed headmaster of King's College, Taunton. There he was popular with the boys and much of the staff, not least for introducing girls into the sixth form. With Marlborough, King's Taunton was the first public school to do so. But to ease stress he drank too much, and after four years was retired 'on grounds of health'. After drying out he sought salvation as Warden at Toynbee Hall in Whitechapel, London, a focal point for social services in the East End, where John Profumo, the former Conservative minister, had gone to redeem himself after the Christine Keeler scandal of 1963. Richard became the first warden of a new addition to Toynbee Hall called Attlee House. Lis moved with her daughters to Sherborne, where the girls went to school and she taught for two years at Sherborne School for Girls. Deciding that Richard and his rehabilitation needed her support, she then joined him in multiracial, traffic-ridden Whitechapel, quite a shock to the system. Later they moved to Kent, where Richard taught English at a comprehensive in Maidstone. Lis meanwhile secured a part-time job teaching drama at Queen's Gate School in Kensington, which she did for 29 years with great success. They remained in Kent and East Sussex until Richard's death from cancer in 1990.

Meanwhile our younger sister Belinda (Binnie), to whom I had been *in loco parentis* while the parents were abroad, was trying to throw off the handicap of a childhood spent oscillating between embassy residences and boarding schools that failed to inspire her. At 16 she was 'withdrawn' from Downe House, where she was considered idle and rebellious. After some *Wanderjahre*, she knuckled down to a secretarial course at the House of Citizenship in Berkshire, where Martin's wife Marguerite had preceded her.

In some respects my father had a tougher time with Binnie than with me. She was by ten years the youngest in the family, and he both adored her and wished to control her: a vain ambition, since she naturally rebelled against his authoritarianism, using all her curly-headed, green-eyed charm and engaging sense of humour to mitigate his anger. She was also his last hope that one of us would marry someone really suitable, that is of equal or higher social status as defined by him. Richard Coote, the handsome young man who seemed to offer her an escape from family bondage, failed to fulfil Dad's criteria, despite his looks and considerable sporting abilities.

The Cootes lived locally, and papa Coote was in cork. Richard had gone from school into the family business. In the hope that distance would make the heart grow less fond, Binnie was urged to take a slow boat to Canada and spend a few months with the Keyserlingks. She enjoyed her time there, but married Richard not long after her return and her 21st birthday. As happened not infrequently, Dad was to some extent proved right. The marriage lasted only ten years. By the time it ended, Binnie had become a dealer in ceramics, first (her apprentice years) in Kensington, then on her own in Hartley Wintney, Hampshire. The failure of her marriage and her responsibility for her daughter Tabitha and son Daniel had brought her sharply into the real world, and she proved to be a very good businesswoman.

Eventually she moved into reproduction tapestries and commissioned fabrics, and employed seven people. I suspect that tertiary education would have killed her commercial instincts. She was a great risk-taker, happily running up huge overdrafts. Sensing the market and taking commercial risks are attributes that a cerebral weighing of pros and cons tends to eliminate. Few of those who become millionaires by starting up new companies have been to university.

Meanwhile our brother Martin, his wife Marguerite and their growing family (eventually three sons and a daughter) moved in 1967 from the Philippines, probably their least enjoyable posting, to South Africa, where domestic life was complicated by the government's annual switch from Pretoria to Cape Town. Diplomats had to follow. As for Dad, he was formidably active in retirement. His old company, BP, had appointed him to its Swiss, Belgian and French boards of directors, and he had the use of an office at their headquarters in London. The first two directorships proved short-lived, but he continued his monthly visits to Paris, where he had served BP between the wars, for some 10 years. He would return with chocolate truffles, soap and eau de cologne, and tales of delicious meals. But he once commented poignantly (to Binnie): 'They aren't interested in my views. They just want my name on the notepaper.'

He also made numerous trips to east Europe to drum up scholarships for Atlantic College, the international sixth form boarding school then being set up at St Donat's Castle, on the coast of South Wales, as the first of numerous United World Colleges. It was an inspiring idea that by bringing together impressionable 16-18 year olds from often antagonistic countries, Israelis and Arabs for example, mutual understanding could be engendered.

To increase the children's bonding, they were to be involved in various forms of community service, such as sea and cliff rescue operations. Dad also advised on the setting up the national committees that were to choose entrants. When he had done the groundwork, Lord Louis Mountbatten, chairman of the International Council, would formalise arrangements. Dad did not seem to mind Mountbatten getting most of the glory. Thanks to their relationship, I was able to

With Lord Mountbatten, 1976 (The Times)

interview Mountbattten twice, first for the Times Diary and, much later as a feature, specifically about Atlantic College. After Dad's death I even developed a relationship of my own with St Donat's, as a notably ineffective member of the governing council: the only time I have sat with the 'great and good'. My stammer still tended to silence me in such contexts.

In 1967, the children having flown the 14-bedroomed nest and Mother suffering from severe arthritis, our parents decided to move from Gaston House to a smaller home in the village of Little Horkesley, on the Essex side of the border with Suffolk. Colchester and the new Essex University were just a few miles away. Dad soon became involved in various committees and the university's council. He was friendly with the Vice-Chancellor, Albert Sloman, an engaging linguist, who bore the brunt of the student troubles for which the university became notorious. These peaked in November 1973, shortly after Dad had resigned from the council.

Dad was also involved with Sue Ryder, a difficult woman whose work for displaced Poles and other East Europeans he wished to support. He helped set up, and became vice-chairman of, the Sue Ryder Foundation, and backed her (unsuccessful) nomination for the Nobel Peace Prize. His relations with her husband, the no less selfless but better organised ex-Group Captain Leonard Cheshire VC, OM, DSO, DFC, founder of the Cheshire Homes charity, were easier. I felt privileged to play a few sets of tennis with this philanthropic war hero at their home in Suffolk.

Dad also became a part-time chairman of the Civil Service Selection Board, and joined Chelmsford Prison's Board of Visitors: he would return with interesting stories of prisoners he had interviewed. I feel shamed by his energy: he also played a central role in setting up and then co-chairing a series of Anglo-Polish round table conferences, involving MPs, academics and journalists. These took place alternately in Poland and the UK.

Back at the Times Diary, my morale eventually began to sag. Varied and enjoyable though it was having good ideas, farming them out, executing some myself, editing the work of others, interacting with various Times specialists, meeting loads of interesting people and being invited to endless openings and launches, diary stories are essentially *hors d'oeuvres*. I had been mainly a diarist for seven years, including two at Printing House Square. It was time for a main course. As often, I was lucky. A substantial and testing assignment was at hand.

Chapter 9

Bonn (1969-1971)

In July 1969, slightly more than two years after my arrival at *The Times*, I was asked whether I would like to take over as the paper's correspondent in Bonn, which was then still very much the capital of the Federal Republic of Germany. The existing correspondent was retiring, and I was on the foreign editor's short list of German-speakers. A general election was due in October, and the Social Democrats, led by the charismatic Willy Brandt, were expected to form the new government for the first time: the three previous Chancellors, Konrad Adenauer, Ludwig Erhard and Kurt-Georg Kiesinger were all Christian Democrats. A time of radical change in West German policy towards eastern Europe was in prospect. My knowledge of Poland, however modest, would be an asset.

Since I had long wanted a spell as a foreign correspondent, this was an opportunity not to be missed – providing Joy was prepared to be uprooted. Prior to Lottie's birth in December 1968, she had been working three days a week back at the *Daily Mail* after a spell at *The Observer*. She did not relish the idea of leaving our house and all her friends, with her freedom of movement further reduced by two very small children (even if we took an au pair girl). But she has a sense of adventure, and could see that the job was just what I needed. So in late August 1969, off we went, having let the house, not easy with a sitting tenant in the middle of it, to two Bohemian but engaging American art historians and their two sons.

Before we departed, I had been to Bonn on an exploratory trip, mainly to find a house. Partly influenced by my colleague Dan van der Vat, who was holding the fort there and whose German was much better than mine, I had decided we should live among Germans rather than in the genteel suburb of Bad Godesberg, home to most diplomats and foreign journalists. I found a pleasantly contemporary house in a newish settlement in Hangelar-Niederberg, on the 'wrong' side of the Rhine. It belonged to a German diplomat serving in Bucharest, one of whose diplomatic friends lived just down the road. All our neighbours were German, and they were not particularly welcoming when we moved in. Joy spoke some German, but – despite her little Renault 4L – felt isolated, as did our (English) au pair. I was frequently away, covering the general election campaign. After a few months, I could see that I had made a serious error of judgement. A move from the estate-like Hangelar-Niederberg became imperative. Happily we found a pleasant though expensive house and garden near the mighty Rhine in the heart of Bad Godesberg, a mere 10 minutes from the office in the elderly but spacious office Mercedes.

Although this was a considerable improvement, Joy – a Londoner for most of her life – was having to adjust to an alien environment while coping with two very small and demanding daughters. It wasn't great for her self-esteem to be regarded principally as the wife of *The Times* correspondent. At dinner parties, she was sometimes asked what her husband thought about such-and-such an issue, rather than for her own view. She eventually generated enough self-confidence to do some freelance journalism about life in Bonn, mainly for the BBC.

The West Germans being sensitive about their image, the government had built an impressive Press Centre for foreign as well as domestic correspondents, within walking distance of the Bundestag (parliament). There was a large room for press conferences, to which ministers came daily to give on-the-record briefings and answer questions. Thanks to my stammer, none came from me. Meanwhile my opposite number from the *New York Times*, the bumptious David Binder, endeared himself to everyone from Willy Brandt downwards with his often cheeky queries. Across a courtyard the latest tapes of the Deutsche Presse Agentur (DPA), the main German news agency, were available. Every half hour or so my secretary would trot across to collect them.

She was competent, slim and attractive. It seems that everyone thought I was having an affair with her. Joy believed them, which did not improve her low morale. Certainly I was fond of this young woman, thanks to the old proximity effect, and had my fantasies, but fortunately I did nothing to implement them. It was not a happy situation.

An office a floor above ours was occupied by an Evangelical (German Protestant) newspaper, with which a highly respected Christian Democratic Bundestag member was involved. He was one of two Germans to whom Dad had given me introductions. His name was Richard von Weizsäcker, and he was later to become arguably the most impressive of West Germany's post-war presidents: certainly the one with the most moral authority. Handsome, soft-spoken, charming and very much on the left of his party, he also had a cutting intelligence. Three minutes spent with him at a CDU party conference was worth 20 minutes with anyone else. It was a privilege to get to know him.

Dad's second introduction was to the legendary banker Hermann Abs, who at 69 was then only just past the peak of his power as chairman of the supervisory board of the mighty Deutsche Bank, of Daimler [Mercedes] Benz, and some 20 other large companies. He was a personification of the West German economic miracle, even if the former economics minister and Chancellor, Ludwig Erhard, was its main architect. Dad had known the very anglophile Abs in Berlin in the 1930s, and had kept in touch.

My credibility at the Press Centre was considerably boosted when Abs arrived to collect me one morning in his huge chauffeur-driven Mercedes 600 (the model in which the Rolling Stones used to tour). A tall and fit-looking man with a handsome head and very good English, he subsequently invited me to dinner at his home in a ritzy suburb of Frankfurt. I had hoped he would take me out to a really good restaurant, but he said: 'I thought it would be so much nicer if my wife cooked us a pork chop at home.' For him, perhaps. As he showed me around his large garden, he bemoaned the amount his gardener cost him: he might soon have to sell some shares to be able to afford him. My heart failed to bleed.

The Press Centre lay on the Bad Godesberg side of Bonn itself, which Adenauer had chosen as the capital of the Federal Republic to emphasise the temporary nature of Germany's division. John le Carré's 'small town in Germany', sometimes known as the *Bundesdorf* (federal village), was charming but unexciting. Contacts between journalists, officials and MPs and its university seemed to be minimal. If there were many concerts in what was after all Beethoven's birthplace, we did not hear of them, and for opera went to Cologne, a mere 25 minutes away by car.

On arrival in Bonn, my chief professional anxiety concerned the adequacy of my German. Even if my passive vocabulary was quite large, I had spoken far less German than French. The language had inevitably changed a great deal. I was nurtured on Goethe and Schiller, Kafka and Thomas Mann. The Social Democratic economics minister, Karl Schiller, used a vocabulary very different from that of Friedrich Schiller, the author of *Don Carlos*. It featured such neologisms as *Konjunktur*, meaning the state of the economy. German political rhetoric involved all sorts of loaded and history-related terms of abuse, such as the *Dolchstosslegende* (stab-in-the-back legend) and *Brunnenvergiftung* (poisoning of wells).

Then there was the challenge posed by accents. The first election rally I covered featured Franz Josef Strauss, head of the Bavarian wing of the Christian Democrats and finance minister in the outgoing Grand Coalition government. Herr Strauss, a demagogic and very rapid speaker, had a strong Bavarian accent. I could understand little of what he said, and there was no transcript of his speech. Had my competitors, notably David Shears of *The Daily Telegraph* and Norman Crossland of the *Guardian*, not helped me out from their own notes, I would have been lost. Of such situations are nightmares made. Without good shorthand, it's hard enough taking notes from someone speaking in English, let alone a foreign language. German is trickier than French, since the crucial verb so often comes at the end of the sentence. In trying to catch up once it drops, you miss the beginning of the next sentence. Although I soon adjusted to the modern German vocabulary, if someone I was interviewing spoke goodish English, I did nothing to encourage him or her to speak German.

Meetings with Willy Brandt

My first close encounter with Willy Brandt, the Social Democratic candidate for the Chancellorship, was in no way anticlimactic. I was already a Brandt fan. His wartime record working for the Norwegian resistance, the courage and intelligence he had shown first as Mayor of West Berlin and then as foreign minister in the Grand Coalition, his known views on reconciliation with eastern Europe, his personal charisma: all fed my admiration. Soon the day came when a group of us foreign correspondents were invited to join an election campaign visit to the university city of Göttingen, set in beautiful countryside near the Harz mountains and the border with the German Democratic Republic (GDR). We were comfortably ensconced in a fleet of high-powered Mercedes and BMWs, and set off northwards at high speed, even if the cars were alarmingly close together. After a couple of hours we stopped in a lay-by, and I found myself peeing next to the great man. It can't have helped my flow, and was clearly not a moment for introductions. Brandt was taller and bulkier than I expected.

Later he joined our table on the election-special train in which we returned in the early hours of the morning. He enjoyed philosophising about politics and life in a very open way, was well-read, had a good sense of humour and spoke excellent English, like many north Germans. Although generally discreet, he said it was rather intolerable that chancellor Kiesinger should have sent emissaries to Moscow without informing his foreign minister, i.e. himself. Brandt seemed much taken by the (to me rather slight) charms of an American woman journalist who had joined our small group: part of his considerable charm was that he was *menschlich, allzu menschlich* (human, all too human).

Shortly after Brandt became Chancellor in early October 1969, I became the first foreign correspondent to be granted an interview with him: whether because he liked me, thought well of my reporting or simply reckoned *The Times* was the most important paper, we will never know. It may have helped that I had written a flattering profile of his chief spokesman, the suave if enigmatic ex-*Der Spiegel* journalist Conrad Ahlers.

For this daunting encounter one Sunday morning at Brandt's residence on the Venusberg, I had bought my first, bulky tape recorder. I was so nervous that I had difficulty setting it up in front of the new Chancellor. But it worked, and Brandt delivered the goods, calling *inter alia* for an early start to talks with Britain about her future membership of the European Economic Community (as it then was), a hot issue. This was aimed at Paris, where there was still little enthusiasm for our entry, and produced a negative response on the following day from the French Foreign Minister, Maurice Schumann: the EEC needed deepening before it was widened, he said. I had helped to make the news. My interview led the front page of *The Times*.

Forays into the GDR

Along with the British government's hopes for West German support for its application to join the EEC, the chief interest in Brandt's chancellorship was its impact on east-west relations. The fall of the Berlin Wall and the demise of communism in the Soviet Union and Eastern Europe were still a decade away. Germany remained a divided country. A repellently repressive regime under Walter Ulbricht ran the GDR, within which West Berlin formed an enclave of freedom, though its autobahn links with West Germany were constantly interfered with. The East Germans had lived under totalitarian regimes since Hitler came to power in 1933. The contrast between the freedom and prosperity of the Federal Republic (and West Berlin), and the GDR's grim poverty and claustrophobic restrictions grew ever more glaring, tempting dozens of East Germans to risk their lives seeking to cross the heavily mined and monitored border strip and the Berlin Wall.

To reunite the two halves of Germany was the unquestioned goal not just of West German policy, but of the free world's – though the French novelist François Mauriac nicely put a different viewpoint when he said '*J'aime tellement l'Allemagne que je suis heureux qu'il y en a deux*' (I like Germany so much I am glad there are two of them). The only difference of opinion was how reunification could best be achieved. Should it, as the Social Democrats believed, be by granting some form of recognition (*Anerkennung*) to the GDR and working towards an unspecified *modus vivendi*, perhaps a confederal structure? Brandt soon made a move in this direction by talking of two German states (implicitly, within one German nation). To most of the Christian Democratic opposition, such concessions to the GDR's craving for international recognition were a dangerous sign of weakness, to some even a form of treason. Because reunification seemed so improbable, there was no discussion of the enormous difficulties it would create, both socially and economically. All parties were for *Wiedervereinigung*. No one thought it would happen any time soon.

No doubt the GDR regime viewed Brandt's talk of closer links between Germany's two entities with mixed emotions. The pressure for some gesture on their part was sufficient to persuade the GDR's nominal leader Walter Ulbricht to summon Western correspondents to a press conference in East Berlin on January 19 1970, a rare event. It was an arctic morning when we traipsed through Checkpoint Charlie into East Berlin – my first visit to Berlin since my early childhood there, of which I had no memory.

Crossing from the animation and bulging material wealth of West Berlin to the gloom, dinginess and poverty of East Berlin was like some exercise in time travel. In East Berlin the shops were scantily provided with shoddy goods, the people poorly dressed, the buildings grimy and still pockmarked with bullet holes, the air heavy with the smell of lignite (brown coal). Ulbricht proved to be a small, plump man with a squeaky voice and zero charisma. The event was more significant for its novelty and for what it suggested about the Brandt-effect than for anything Ulbricht said – which was mostly about the importance of full international recognition of the GDR as a first step to closer relations with the West.

This was not forthcoming. But that March there was a day of high drama when Brandt went to Erfurt in the GDR for the first meeting between the heads of government of the two Germanies, his opposite number being Willi Stoph, the GDR's prime minister. For this I stayed in the charming Elefant hotel in the historic nearby town of Weimar, indelibly associated with Goethe. There most war damage had been sensitively restored.

The Erfurt meeting was historic and moving. The route of Brandt's train through East Germany was lined with waving well-wishers, one of whom cried: 'You have come at last!' Trouble started after Herr Stoph had escorted Brandt across the square between Erfurt station and the Erfurter Hof hotel, where the meeting was to take place. There was an enthusiastic but tightly controlled crowd. Suddenly those permitted to gather down one side broke through the police cordon and started chanting first 'Willy', which could have applied to either leader, then 'Willy Brandt', then *'Willy Brandt ans Fenster'* (Willy Brandt to the window). A young man next to me was one of those who shouted 'Willy Brandt'. A security man tapped him menacingly on the shoulder and said: 'You shouted Willy Brandt.' 'I only shouted Willy', the young man said. Eventually Brandt appeared, and looked down at the forest of waving hands with what seemed a mixture of slight embarrassment and quiet pleasure. For me, it was another page one lead story as well as a memorable day. This Erfurt meeting, along with Brandt's charisma, surely played a small part in undermining communism in eastern Europe, leading to the fall of the Berlin Wall 19 years later.

Two early trips provided painful reminders of Germany's fairly recent past. The first came when I and other journalists accompanied President Gustav Heinemann, a lovely man with an honourable record, on the first visit by a West German head of state to the Netherlands, which Hitler's Germany had so brutally occupied. There were plenty of people to line the streets of Amsterdam, where he inspected a guard of honour, but they stood in palpably hostile silence. The other trip, in February 1970, was to Munich for another first visit, that of the Israeli Foreign Minister Abba Eban. The focal point was his descent by helicopter to the periphery of the former Dachau concentration camp, Hitler's first, where some 28,000 inmates of all nationalists and races were murdered between 1933 and 1945. There had recently been an Arab terrorist bomb attack at Munich airport, and the camp's purlieus bristled with policemen with Alsatian guard dogs straining on leashes. *'Mein Gott, es sieht verdammt echt aus'* ('My God, it looks damned authentic'), commented an Israeli correspondent.

The Polish factor

Brandt was seeking to regularise West German relations with two of Germany's major war-time victims, the Soviet Union and Poland. The Moscow end of the negotiations was covered by our correspondent there, but in 1970 I went twice to Warsaw, first with the genial Foreign Minister, Walter Scheel, leader of the Social Democrats' coalition partners, the Free Democrats (liberals), then with Brandt when he signed the resulting treaty. The Polish capital did not seem to have changed a great deal in the decade since Dad's time, but it was helpful to have been there before and to know something about the country's post-war history. The current British ambassador, the rather patrician Nicholas Henderson (later a much-lauded ambassador in Bonn, Paris and Washington) gave me and a colleague from *Newsweek* magazine, whom I took along, a useful briefing.

Brandt's gift of empathy produced a famous moment. He was already near to tears when he laid a wreath at the tomb of the Unknown Soldier. When he moved to the bronze memorial to the dead of the Warsaw ghetto, he dropped to his knees on the wet flagstones, remaining there for a good 30 seconds. Standing nearby, I was nearly knocked over by photographers trying to get a shot that showed something of the memorial and of his expression. This gesture of atonement went down very well in Poland and across Europe, but in a subsequent poll was found 'exaggerated' by a small majority of West Germans.

For the Brandt visit, most of the press corps stayed in the Europaiski hotel. Seeking some company for the evening, I telephoned the correspondent of a New York tabloid and suggested we went to a restaurant I remembered in the (beautifully reconstructed) old part of the city. Soon after we had settled at our table, a couple of rather professional-looking women took a table nearby and started eying us. As we left, they hastily swallowed their dessert, followed us out into the snow and came up on either flank. 'Hallo, I have a problem,' said the one next to my American colleague. 'I cannot sleep alone.' 'I'm sorry', he rejoined drily, 'I'm afraid I'm going to ruin your night.' No doubt our hotel room phones had been bugged, and this was some crude attempt to compromise one or both of us, a common Communist ploy.

In addition to monitoring the Brandt government's Ostpolitik and its role in the ongoing negotiations for Britain's entry to the EEC, I wrote periodically about the cost and quality of life in West Germany. It helped in making comparisons with the UK that I had lived there so recently. I was struck, for example, by the way the Germans contrived to upgrade jobs that in England were considered low in status: for example, what we have now in the dustbin field they had then, and diesel Mercedes were the norm for the well-dressed taxi-driver. I also harped on the quality in West Germany of trade union leadership and the readiness, reinforced by legal requirements, of management to take trade union views into account (*Mitbestimmung*, or co-determination). British industry was then plagued by strikes. Perversely, an outbreak of industrial strife in the Federal Republic in late 1971 prompted fears that the 'British disease' was proving contagious.

I renewed contact briefly with the same British Army of the Rhine that had first brought me to post-war West Germany at a Press lunch given by the Commander-in-Chief. I was placed next to him – it must have been Sir Peter Hunt – and enjoyed telling him I had once been a regimental office clerk based near Essen.

Some of our friends

Our own quality of life in Bad Godesberg was, in most respects, high. The Rhine, which makes the Thames in London look like a stream, was a few minutes away, ideal for walks along its banks with the girls. There were tennis courts and a swimming pool at the nearby American Club, which was the scene of numerous parties. We had some good friends among the British and American correspondents. They included Norman Crossland, the *Guardian* correspondent, and his wife Kay. Norman spoke excellent German, with a real feel for the language, wrote beautifully, was not notably competitive and gave me much good advice. I sometimes played tennis with the *Telegraph*'s charming and no less helpful David Shears, who was handicapped by his paper's rabidly right-wing leading articles on Germany and east-west relations. I was lucky that *The Financial Times*'s Malcolm Rutherford, a notably heavy smoker, had little enthusiasm for Brandt's policies. Both he and Norman died relatively young after returning to the UK.

Among the Americans our favourite was Joe-Alex Morris of the *Los Angeles Times*, also a tennis partner of mine, and his beautiful German wife Ulla. I did one or two feature-writing trips with Joe-Alex, since we were not in competition and he was excellent company (cigarettes apart). He died young, shot while literally raising his head above a parapet during the Iranian revolution of 1979.

Britain, with the USA, Britain, France and the Soviet Union, retained some sovereignty over the Federal Republic and, more especially, West Berlin. Complex four-power negotiations over the latter's status were ongoing. The Bonn embassy bulged with very able diplomats. The ambassador was not generally held to be among them. Sir Roger Jackling, ironically called Crackling Jackling, was genial, perhaps shrewd but lightweight compared to his No 2, Brooks Richards, and the head of chancery, Christopher Audland, a lynchpin of the four-power talks. As Sir Hugh Greene, until 1969 the Director General of the BBC, commented when he kindly called in at my office to say hello: 'There's no doubt the No 2 is a good deal more impressive than the No 1.' Down the line were, among others, Robin O'Neill, Nicholas Bayne, Nigel Broomfield and Michael Jenkins, all of them notably bright, helpful and, along with their wives, sociable. All went far. We were to see Messrs Audland and Jenkins in Brussels, where they held senior posts in the European Commission. The latter ended up as ambassador in The Hague, and later became President of the Boeing corporation in Europe. For a man of literary and historical bent, he was surprisingly keen on money.

I made some good friends/contacts at the Foreign Ministry (*Auswärtiges Amt*). Chief among them were Gerhard Henze and his wife Juliana, who later stayed with us from time to time in Hampstead. In October 1970 I wrote to my brother: 'Earlier this month we went to an exceptionally pleasant and informal party given by three leading young lights in the Bonn F.O. They were just the sort of people one had hoped to meet in Germany – open-minded, intelligent and even pleasant on the eye. The party was given in an old tower converted into a picture gallery. One tossed meat onto a vast charcoal grill in the middle of the room, and there was dancing and much wine. In fact, there are quite a lot of informal dinners here for around 18, after which one dances. We gave one ourselves recently, practically nothing but Germans, with one or two Americans and a Swedish couple.' We bought in the food and had someone to serve the drinks.

One of our dinner guests was Detlev Rohwedder, a rising star of the economics ministry. He was assassinated by terrorists in April 1991 while overseeing the privatisation of the GDR's industry. I was good at becoming friendly with top-class Germans, but not at wringing news stories, as opposed to guidance, out of them. Among those I interviewed was Ralf Dahrendorf, an ambitious – and bilingual – sociologist who had become a junior minister at the Foreign Ministry. I had dutifully read his classic *Society and Democracy in Germany* (1965). In our interview he assured me there would be a realignment of the political parties in Bonn: it never happened. Dahrendorf was to precede us to Brussels as a member of the European Commission, where he again proved not to be a team player; and then to London, where he was No 1 at last, as Director of the London School of Economics. I liked him, but felt his judgement was affected by his desire to cause a stir, and thus sometimes 'unsound'.

True to stereotype, the Germans were considerably more formal than the British, using surnames and job-related titles at work and even away from the office. I received one invitation on which the host, the proud holder of three doctorates, described himself as Dr Dr Dr whoever (perhaps he should have put a small 3 after just one). They also dressed more formally. On our first Sunday we went off in scruffy weekend clothes to Cologne to see the cathedral and wander around, only to find just about everybody dressed up, at least in the posher areas. For a Sunday walk in the woods, a suit, often green, and matching hat were the norm in autumn and winter.

They had a legalistic streak. One of our Bad Godesberg neighbours summoned me to remove some leaves in his garden because they had come from trees in ours, on the principle: your trees, your leaves. When I was washing our car one Sunday, a neighbour summoned the police: in that Catholic area, such activity on Sundays was against the law. Broadly speaking however, we liked the Germans. Although not notably welcoming, they were generally friendly, helpful and reliable, undoubtedly more serious than the English, yet far from bereft of a sense of humour. For sound historical reasons, they liked to be liked.

They also practised a remarkably open form of government with all those on-the-record press conferences as opposed to off-the-record briefings, British-style. Less democratic perhaps was the tendency to fix the final shape of legislation in all-party committees rather than by debate and votes in the Bundestag itself. On the plus side, this promoted consensus and the national good, and diminished political point-scoring.

Louis Heren ups the pressure

Pressure on me was considerably increased when Louis Heren, who had for many years been *The Times*'s outstanding correspondent in Washington, returned to London as Rees-Mogg's deputy and foreign editor. He had been in Bonn during Konrad Adenauer's long stint as Chancellor (1949-1963), but did not use that against me. He wanted to make his mark, and was keen on contributions from European correspondents on such topics as social services, the generation gap, pollution, driving habits and so on. Less commendably, he always wanted them very quickly, regardless of the pressure of other commitments, running news stories and so on. One involved a day in the life of a steel worker, which took me to Duisburg in the Ruhr; another, German driving habits, which resulted in almost three times the British death toll with roughly the same population. I described the alarmingly long skid marks on the autobahns as 'dramas written in rubber'.

A distressing episode involved my increasingly unreliable secretary. I decided I needed to replace her, and gave her plenty of notice. I had once, probably while on holiday, written her a moderately affectionate note. The day before she left she sent this to the editor with a covering note claiming that she was being victimised. Worryingly, I had no memory of what I had written. Rees-Mogg responded by reassuring me that it was just the sort of note a sympathetic employer should send his secretary. It may have helped that while at *The Sunday Times* he had married his p.a. My new aide, vetted by Joy, was an ultra-competent young woman with excellent English called Wilma von Winterfeld. She even enjoyed my prose style.

In the autumn of 1971, when I had been in Bonn for little more than two years, I was warned that I was to be part of a reshuffle of foreign correspondents. My heart sank when I learned I was destined for Brussels. There was one consolation: I had been working a six-day week, and in Brussels would have a No 2 with whom I could alternate on Sundays. Britain was scheduled to enter the European Economic Community in January 1973, assuming the successful conclusion of negotiations over the coming year. So I would be covering those final negotiations in all their hideously complex detail, and then the first years of our membership. The feeling in Printing House Square seemed to be that Peter Strafford, the vastly knowledgeable former Eton scholar I would be replacing, was not a sufficiently political animal to give the broader picture. I would be able to delegate some of the nitty-gritty to my No 2, notionally leaving me free to write more featurish pieces about the impact and significance of this historic event.

Farewell Willy Brandt: December 1971 (Bundesbildstelle)

In retrospect, I was lucky to have been in Bonn at the height of Brandt's Ostpolitik, for which he received the Nobel Peace Prize in 1971. I was also glad to have been spared the task of charting my hero's downfall: Brandt was obliged to resign in 1974, following the discovery that one of his close aides, Günter Guillaume, was an East German spy. I did not enjoy, or rate highly, Michael Frayn's dramatisation of those sad events in his play *Democracy*. The element of mockery seemed too strong.

Brandt granted me a farewell off-the-record interview before I left Bonn, which was good of him; and I saw him again at a reception in Oxford following the publication in 1980 of the Brandt report on international development (he had chaired the relevant committee). At that party at St Antony's college, he happened to be getting tired when I went over to say hello. 'Why don't we sit down', he said. So we sat down together on a nearby sofa, and I could see the great and good around us wondering: who is that chap with whom Brandt seems so intimate? It was a pleasing coda to my relationship with a great and very human statesman.

Chapter 10

Brussels (1972-1975)

From a family viewpoint, the prospect of moving to Brussels was unappealing. Although Joy had, as mentioned, settled sufficiently in Bonn to do some features for the *Guardian* and the BBC about life in Germany, she felt somewhat trapped by the children and her role as the wife of *The Times* correspondent. There had been some serious strains on our marriage, from which neither of us had fully recovered. As for Brussels itself, the Belgian capital and fulcrum of the European Economic Community had a reputation for miserable weather, long hours of work involving tiresomely technical and complicated subjects such as the Common Agricultural Policy (CAP) and its fisheries equivalent, only partially offset by very good food. Our hearts sank.

On the brighter side, Brussels was considerably more cosmopolitan than soporific little Bonn. It would soon be teeming with Whitehall's brightest and best, and no doubt their equivalents from our fellow new entrants, Denmark, Norway and Ireland (the Norwegians eventually voted against membership). At the professional level, my appointment seemed like a vote of confidence from the editor. William Rees-Mogg, later a convinced Euro-sceptic, was then fervently pro-European. *The Times* devoted a whole news page every day to Europe. Britain's accession to the EEC would be an historic moment. It was something to be invited to record and analyse the events and personalities involved.

Some history

The story of Britain's post-Second World War relationship with our European neighbours, brilliantly chronicled and analysed by our eventual Hampstead neighbour Hugo Young in *This Blessed Plot*, is deeply depressing, as a very brief summary will show.

From 1945 to 1950 Britain was, thanks to its contribution to the allied victory, in a strong position to lead moves towards European reconciliation and cooperation. But most of its politicians and Whitehall mandarins were puffed up with illusions of Britain still being a great power. By all means let the continentals get together, they said: we are too big for any agreements that may result. We have our beloved Commonwealth with all its emotional and commercial commitments. We have our special relationship with the United States.

So we stayed out of the European Coal and Steel Community (1952) and sought only observer status at the talks between its six member states that led to the creation of the European Economic Community, via the Treaty of Rome (1957). Something like panic ensued when successive British governments realised this represented a serious threat to Britain's political as well as commercial interests. So we applied for membership first in 1961 (Harold Macmillan as PM) and 1967 (Harold Wilson). Both bids were scuppered by General de Gaulle, for reasons reflecting Britain's earlier doubts. Following the general's retirement in 1969, negotiations resumed for Britain's membership. These were eventually brought to a successful conclusion in 1972, thanks to a meeting of minds between Ted Heath as PM and Georges Pompidou, de Gaulle's successor.

Having covered some of the earlier stages of those negotiations from Bonn, the prospect of much more of the same in Brussels held little appeal. Nonetheless, I was by background and inclination all in favour of insular old Britain becoming closely involved with its continental neighbours. The big negatives were the Common Agricultural Policy and the Common Fisheries Policy, which respectively encouraged over-production and over-fishing, to the detriment of Britain's budgetary contributions (subsequently reduced by Margaret Thatcher's famous rebate) – and of our fishermen. The CAP was disgracefully protectionist and led to the dumping of food surpluses abroad.

I had little sympathy for the Europhobes, who were keen on free trade but in denial over the need for rules and institutions to ensure a level playing field. Anti-Europeans were to me a breed similar to those right-wing Germans who reckoned Brandt was selling them down the river: short-sighted nationalists. Given Britain's then pathetic economic performance, high inflation and lamentable industrial relations, any loss of sovereignty to the EEC's Council of Ministers, European Commission and Court of Justice seemed to me to promise better management (and delivered it in the environmental field).

Finding a chandelier-free home

Before grappling with such issues, Joy and I had to find a suitable home in the Belgian capital. We went on one or two exploratory trips in November 1971: I was desperate to avoid having to house-hunt from a hotel while starting my new job. Most of the houses we saw had miserably small kitchens, further reduced space-wise by up to four doors, respectively leading, as in one typical case, into the garden, hall, dining and sitting rooms. This seemed surprising in a country so devoted to its collective stomach. Chandeliers and wall-bracket lights abounded. Before long we found a spacious and chandelier-free house with five bedrooms and a small garden in a very quiet street near the charming Parc St Woluwe. It lay a mere eight minutes by car from central Brussels and little more from the British School, unfortunately in the opposite direction, down the chestnut-lined Avenue de Tervueren and past the beautiful beeches of the Forêt de Soignes. Although the house was a touch austere – parquet floors throughout, with a vast sitting/dining room ideal for parties, giving onto a small garden – the location was perfect, and the area decidedly up-market.

Brussels was going to be expensive. The rent was high and, like all Belgian rents, index-linked to inflation. The fees at the (admirable) British School of Brussels also seemed exorbitant. In contrast to its French and German equivalents, it received no government subsidy. And then there were all those delicious restaurants, many of them in a sort of gastronomic zone just off the Grand' Place, itself one of the most beautiful squares in Europe. Sadly, much of historic Brussels had been laid low by insensitive development and road-building.

We moved just after New Year 1972, following a round of heart-warming farewell parties in Bonn. The future President, Richard von Weizsäcker, came to the one we gave, which was partly to introduce my successor Dan van der Vat, a very able operator fresh from South Africa. My No 2 in Brussels, David Cross, had been holding the fort there for a couple of months, following Peter Strafford's reluctant translation to New York (lucky man). David Cross had worked on the foreign news desk in Printing House Square, and was well versed in its predilections. An ambitious and talented No 2 can seem like a threat. David was solid, reliable, very loyal, good company, and no great wordsmith. He already had a good grip on much of the detail of the last lap of our entry negotiations.

Joy, the girls and I were in England for Christmas. Early in January, shortly before my return to Brussels, I had bought a new overcoat in Regent Street. Crossing the road near Liberty's late one afternoon, perhaps in a state of mild shopper's euphoria, I stepped out from behind a parked car, and a taxi ran over my left foot. Although I broke its left wing-mirror as I keeled over, the driver did not stop. The pain was acute, and I was helped by passers-by onto the steps of an adjacent bank. Someone called an ambulance, and I was whisked to the nearby Middlesex Hospital.

There a junior doctor diagnosed a broken ankle, put my lower leg and foot in plaster, gave me some crutches and discharged me. Overnight my injured ankle and foot swelled up, but were imprisoned by the plaster. Result: a lot more pain. Back to the Middlesex, where a consultant cut off the plaster and had me admitted – to a very jolly ward full of men with sports injuries. My leg was put into traction, i.e. raised, and only when the swelling had subsided some four days later was I re-discharged, once again plastered and on crutches. I thus returned to Brussels somewhat restricted in my movements – and on my own. Joy had decided, partly for reasons of health, to spend some time (eventually, several months) in London with the girls, in a flat in Chelsea owned by her ex-*Daily Mail* colleague Judy Innes, who had recently married Michael Astor, brother of David and Bill.

Drama at the Palais d'Egmont

Ted Heath was due to sign the accession treaty in Brussels on January 22: for him, the fulfilment of a dream. The ceremony, in the beautiful Palais d'Egmont, was a major event, with prime and lesser ministers from existing and imminent member states in attendance. There was no special seating for the press, and I found myself next to a genial, youngish Belgian who turned out to be Vicomte Davignon, a diplomat prominent (as I later learned) in the field of political cooperation between member states, and later a Commissioner.

It was a Saturday, and to my delight we were soon joined by Nick Tomalin, then a star of *The Sunday Times*. There was a long delay before proceedings began. It transpired that a disgruntled woman had thrown some printers' ink at Ted Heath as he was about to make his entrance. Nick Tomalin moved off at impressive speed to investigate. Contrary to expectations, the ink-thrower turned out to be a London woman of German origin, protesting not against the EEC but against the proposed re-development of Covent Garden (subsequently rejected). It made a great story for the Sunday papers, which I could cheerfully raid for the facts. A good sleuth I never was. The Germans dubbed the episode the *Tintenattentat*, literally 'ink assassination'. The editor liked my inclusion of that detail.

My friendly competitors

The competition in Brussels promised to be much stiffer than in Bonn. As I wrote to my parents: 'The press corps (British) here is quite dauntingly young, knowledgeable and intelligent. An absolutely brilliant chap of 31 called Andrew Knight has just arrived for *The Economist*. The FT has Reggie Dale, also 31, immensely efficient, accurate and on the ball. The *Guardian* has a very pleasant, relaxed chap of only about 28 called Richard Norton-Taylor, who has been here for years as a freelance and knows it all inside out, yet preserves a good view of the wood as well as of the trees.' We of the posh press thus formed a sort of troika: Reggie, Richard and Roger. There was also a strong BBC contingent, featuring at different times Charles Wheeler and John Simpson among others.

If one could buy shares in people, I would have sunk any spare capital into Andrew Knight, a superb operator with a mind of enviable clarity, with charm and looks to match. He went on to edit *The Economist*, later becoming chief executive first of the Telegraph group and then chairman of Rupert Murdoch's News International. Reggie Dale became a prominent columnist for the *International Herald Tribune*, first in Paris then in Washington. Not for nothing had he been a scholar at Winchester: when there had been some really gruelling, complex and important EEC summit, the clarity of his reportage used to make me feel like weeping. Richard N-T specialised in scoops, extracted from his many contacts with his engaging aura of conspiratorial naughtiness. He later became the *Guardian's* security and defence expert, and has written successful 'tribunal' plays based on the transcripts of investigations and court cases. Fortunately for me, there was also an outstanding head of the Reuter's bureau, Bob Taylor, an engaging man with whom I was not in direct competition. He often explained things to me at ministerial meetings involving economic matters, of which he had a good command.

Both the British and the foreign press corps conformed eerily to national stereotypes. The broadsheet Brits were ex-public school and Oxbridge, unlike the few tabloid correspondents. The Germans were earnest and low profile, the French highly intelligent and aware of it, the Italians charming and, for some reason, notably well-paid.

In most ways it was harder to find out what was going on in Brussels than in Bonn. There was no news agency providing a steady, up-to-the-minute flow of information, as there was in Bonn, Paris or Washington. Everything had to be dug out, all events had to be attended, in case something interesting was revealed. This involved many time-wasting car trips with attendant parking problems. By way of compensation, there was a briefing for the international Press every morning in the bowels of the European Commission building, given by the Commission's chief spokesman, a charming but vapid Italian, and one or more of his fellow porte-paroles of various nationalities, including an American. Much coffee was drunk and gossip exchanged at these convivial occasions.

Also helpful was the daily arrival, by post, of the 15 or so pages of *Agence Europe*, recording in great detail and with some shrewd editorial comment the activities and deliberations of the EEC's various institutions. This agency had been run since 1958 by a redoubtable Italian in his 50s, Emanuele Gazzo, whom I eventually interviewed. He had left home at 16 to become a ship's boy, then studied economics, translated poetry from French and English into Italian, got to know Ezra Pound in his pre-Fascist days, worked in business and became a publisher before settling in Brussels. He claimed that his agency and its six reporters was the first to present news from a European rather than a national standpoint. Their service was invaluable in helping one follow the evolution of a complex decision or negotiation, but arrived a day after the events it described.

When helping cover the EEC's ministerial meetings from Bonn, I had been struck by the collegiate spirit of the Brussels-based journalists. Whatever the venue, the scene was much the same: a large ground floor room in which the press corps swirled around, with a bar at one end (once my undoing), a telephone switchboard and booths off to one side, and a quiet working room with typewriters where we hammered out our version of events. As negotiations proceeded, national press spokesmen, or actual ministers, would descend from on high to describe any progress, usually suggesting that the home team was winning. These briefings would be attended mainly by journalists of the same nationality, but would then be shared with anyone interested. When a British minister was on the record, we would often pool our quotes: essentially, the minister said what we said he had said. If the French and British were known to be aiming for mutually exclusive goals, and both claimed success, we would be suitably sceptical. Officials were reputedly impressed by the extent to which we got the overall picture right.

All 'copy' from such meetings in those pre-laptop days had to be dictated over a telephone to a copy-taker equipped with earphones and a typewriter, a slow process calling for clear enunciation, sometimes eliciting such encouraging comments as 'Is there much more of this?' Some comical errors resulted. I once referred to the 'non-applicant EFTA states', meaning the members of the European Free Trade Area, such as Switzerland, who were not negotiating to join the EEC. This emerged, to general mirth, as 'the non-African EFTA states'. [Much later there was a fine example at the

Independent, when its education reporter dictated a story about the proposed NVQs i.e.national vocational qualifications, only for them to emerge as 'envy queues', which I imagined snaking around social security offices]. During one tense council meeting, when the switchboard girls were getting frazzled, I found I had dictated my long story to *The Financial Times*. Reggie Dale heard my cries of anguish, and was thrilled to find a line still open for him to dictate his own, probably superior version.

Rotating around a void

My first few months in Brussels were far from happy. I missed Joy and the girls dreadfully, was fed up with being asked when they were coming back, and struggled to master the arcane technicalities of existing or mooted EEC directives, plus associated jargon and acronyms. Where was the Berthoud-added-value in what I was writing? I asked myself. There was a kind of void at the heart of the EEC, around which its main institutions orbited. Only a central government would fill it. When hanging around during negotiations, waiting for gobbets of information, one felt utterly peripheral. I contemplated using Joy's absence to ask *The Times* to give me a job back in London.

On the plus side of Brussels was, as expected, the quality of the diplomats and civil servants who had been sent over to defend Britain's interests. Our ambassador to the EEC and head of the large UK mission to the EEC (UKrep) was Sir Michael Palliser. His Belgian-born wife Marie was the daughter of the great Paul-Henri Spaak, a major figure in the establishment of the EEC. Beneath Michael's polished suavity there were wells of warmth and even affection. Happily, the Pallisers also lived in Hampstead, so we continued to see them when he returned to London as head of the diplomatic service.

Under Palliser at UKrep was the larger than life figure of Ewen Fergusson, whose all-round achievements at Rugby I have mentioned. Joy and I saw a lot of him and his amusing wife Sarah, and spent a couple of post-Brussels holidays with them. Ewen is a great wine connoisseur (he was said to have one of the best private cellars in England) and liked to be the centre of attention, all of which made him an excellent host. To tap his considerable brain on a complex topic was a pleasure. His almost too-perfect French must have gone down well when he took over that very grand embassy in Paris. A no less able brain at UKrep belonged to John Weston, a Sinologist and closet poet of dryer and crisper style. He later became the UK's permanent representative at the United Nations. For charm and good looks the palm went to blond, blue-eyed, debonair David Gore-Booth, later an outspoken ambassador in Saudi Arabia and High Commissioner in New Delhi. He died of cancer in 2004, aged 59 and much mourned. All the forgoing received knighthoods.

Britain's two European Commissioners were pleasingly complementary: Sir Christopher ('Fatty') Soames, in charge of foreign affairs, whose wife Mary was Winston Churchill's daughter; and George Thomson, a low-key but much liked and very Scottish former Labour MP, in charge of the contentious regional fund. 'Five of us had a pleasantly unbuttoned lunch with Soames last Thursday', I wrote to my father. 'Although he can be overbearing (once launched on a theme he simply ignores interjections and booms on), there is a certain simplicity and openness about him which seems almost like humility, and he lacks the appalling egocentricity of most politicians…Nor is there anything devious about him, and one can rely on getting gut reactions – from what a gut! – which are often distinctly shrewd.'

Soames's *chef de cabinet* was David Hannay, a refreshingly abrasive diplomat with a legendary grip on the detail of the Commission's directives (it is the Commission's task to draft and implement EEC legislation. The Council of Ministers, representing member states, decides whether to accept, reject or amend the Commission's proposals, a division of labour that many journalists and politicians in London seem unable to grasp). Hannay preceded John Weston to the UN. Later, improbably, he became a 'people's peer' in the House of Lords.

Among other notable characters at the Commission who became friends (of varying durability) was Stanley Johnson, a pioneering environmentalist, his brief there, and under-rated novelist. His first wife Charlotte was an accomplished painter of instantly recognisable portraits. Stanley was no less zanily entertaining and energetic than his then small son Alexander (Al), now better known as Boris. Stanley later became a Conservative member of the European Parliament, but failed to make it to Westminster.

Busy times at NATO too

The EEC was not the only game in town. NATO had its headquarters on the edge of Brussels. For much of my time there, Henry Kissinger was the US Secretary of State and Richard Nixon the President, eventually in the toils of the Watergate scandal. There were divisions of opinion and much mistrust between the US and the Europeans over proposed negotiations with the Soviet Union on forces reductions, over the desirability of super-power summits, and over how to deal with the OPEC cartel following the huge oil price rises of late 1973.

A visit to Brussels from either Nixon or Kissinger, with the formidable White House press corps, was an event, Kissinger being the more memorable. I remember a not-for-attribution briefing from the latter in which he expressed amazement at the strangulated voice of Britain's Foreign Secretary, the very upper-class Sir Alec Douglas-Home, and wondered if he would talk normally if someone jumped on his bed in the middle of the night. I cherished a phrase from a US defence secretary, James Schlesinger, who told a press conference: 'We must not let the adversary have even the perception of a low-risk option.' Some Americans have a weakness for pompous, Latin-derived verbiage.

I had some good contacts at NATO. Brightest and certainly most amusing was Paul Lever, a diplomat in Britain's delegation there. He ended up as our ambassador in (reunited) Berlin. Like a few of the best diplomats, Paul took risks in what he said.

The secretary-general of NATO was the former Dutch foreign minister Josef Luns, who enjoyed being outspoken: a journalist's dream. A huge man of some charm, Luns once gave a talk to the inaugural gathering of the so-called Mid-Atlantic Club, intended to promote US-European relations. Le tout Bruxelles diplomatique was there. I found Luns's speech outrageously pro-Israel (this was soon after the Yom Kippur war of 1973) and when it came to question time, I uncharacteristically stood up to ask what I hoped would be a devastating question. Even as I did so, I saw how easy it would be to answer, and no words emerged from my mouth. My stammer had struck on this most public of occasions. I stood there fishing for breath, with everyone looking at me. Some thoughtful soul said: 'It's rather hot in here. I'll open a window.' I sat down. Bizarrely, I was then seized by a feeling of euphoria. What I had so much dreaded had happened. I was still alive and no one seemed to think the worse of me. It was over. Life went on.

In the spring of 1974 I was told that the newish US ambassador to NATO was a high-powered character destined to go far, and well worth interviewing. His name was Donald Rumsfeld, he had been talked of as a possible Vice-President when Spiro Agnew bit the dust, and was reputed to do one-armed press-ups every morning. I went to see him, disappointingly on a background basis. 'He is about the same age as me, and certainly looks not a day older,' I wrote in my diary (actually he was two years older). 'Dark brown hair, and the sort of clean-cut good looks that used to be fashionable, only marred by rather small and cold grey eyes. A very shrewd operator indeed.' He gave me an hour and a quarter of his time, and showed a cutting intelligence about current tensions in US-European relations. He returned to the USA before long to become White House chief of staff to President Gerald Ford, and then Ford's youthful Defense Secretary – a role he later resumed so disastrously for George W. Bush.

The joys of Belgian politics

Just when the EEC and NATO were firing on all cylinders, there was often a Belgian story to make life more difficult: for example, a threat of development on part of the site of the battle of Waterloo; a fire in a school that killed a dozen children; or a political crisis.

Belgium had become an independent country only in 1830. Of its 10 million or so inhabitants, some 55 per cent live in the northern half, speak a form of Dutch and tend to be Roman Catholic. A further 33 per cent live in the southern half, are known as Walloons, speak French, and tend towards anti-clericalism and socialism. The remaining 11 per cent live in bi-lingual Brussels: predominantly French-speaking, but surrounded by Flemish-speaking villages. There is also a small German-speaking minority near the German border.

The francophone Walloons used to run the country and waxed rich on the traditional industries of coal, steel and textiles. These declined rapidly after the Second World War, and new businesses flourished in the north, with its access to the sea and Europe's great rivers. The three communities had become largely autonomous in cultural matters, but the division of central government's revenue caused much wrangling and fracturing of fragile coalitions. Up to 1830, government was always by a foreign power, usually exercised from afar, and thus suspect. It remained suspect. A Belgian's loyalty is to his commune, where energies were focussed during the centuries of occupation. Localism flourishes, not always productively: for example, while more than 250 people were dying in the Brussels department store fire of 1967, well before my time, members of the Anderlecht fire brigade from southern Brussels were vainly trying to fit their hoses to the water mains of the city centre.

I had a childish weakness for Flemish names, which often ended with an x. At a party I was introduced to a Flem (as we called them), who clicked his heels rather Germanically and said, I thought, if improbably: 'How's things?' 'Fine', I said. 'No', he countered. 'My name is Hustinx.' I visited the village of Erps Kwerps in the hope of finding a postcard bearing its name, in vain.

Once I had a reasonable grip, I found Belgian politics at least as enjoyable to write about as the EEC or NATO: the inferiority complexes of the French-speaking Walloons, long the cocks of the dunghill, vis-à-vis the newly ascendant Flemish majority were genuinely interesting. The Walloons, for example, had not bothered to learn Flemish, long the language of the peasantry. When bilingualism became mandatory for civil servants, they paid the price of their assumptions of superiority (the same happened to those in Quebec who spoke only English). I became friendly with several senior politicians, including Leo Tindemans, a popular prime minister; and Henri Simonet, foreign minister. After Simonet became the European Commissioner for energy, we once found ourselves walking towards each other along a length of carpet. When we shook hands, we both received a strong electric shock, which I naturally attributed to his portfolio rather than the nylon carpet.

Travels within the EEC...

A benefit of the Brussels job was the need to travel within the enlarged community of nations, be it to Luxembourg through the forests and hills of the Ardennes, to Strasbourg for the European Parliament, or to the capitals of whichever country held the six-monthly presidency of the Council of Ministers. Denmark's 1972 referendum on EEC membership took me back to Copenhagen after a gap of 20 years. Willy Brandt had come up to support his fellow Social Democrat, the Prime Minister Jens Otto Krag, whom I interviewed. A few days later Krag amazed everyone by resigning after the Danes had supported him by saying 'Yes', apparently for party political reasons.

At the same time the Norwegians voted to stay out, thanks to an overwhelming No from their rural population. A pro-Marketeer from the governing Labour Party described the outcome to me as "the first successful non-revolutionary attack on the establishment in an industrial country." Here too the Prime Minister resigned. He was Trygve Bratteli, whom I met briefly: a melancholy figure once plucked by liberating troops from a heap of corpses in a German concentration camp. Thanks to its oil fields, Norway has flourished outside the European Union.

Covering the European Parliament in Strasbourg was a mixed pleasure. Best of all was the session in early spring, when much of the Brussels press corps headed down to Alsace on a train nick-named the asparagus special, washing down that seasonal delight with much delicious Alsatian wine. Everyone fraternised in Strasbourg. British members were then Westminster MPs with a so-called dual mandate. It was a good place to get to know Commissioners better, over dinner or a drink in a hotel bar. There were some enchanting interpreters around: I succumbed briefly to the charms of one of them.

In Strasbourg I visited a cousin (on my paternal grandmother's side), Daniel Schlumberger, then professor of archaeology at Strasbourg university, and his wife Agnès. Daniel had once identified the remains of a Greek city in Afghanistan, close to the Soviet border, and later headed the French archaeological institute in Beirut. Writing to my father to commiserate on the early death (at 61) of my uncle Oliver Berthoud, Daniel kindly said of my visit: 'He gave us the impression of a serious, mature, happy man – and that is an impression today's young rarely produce, so one feels comforted when, extraordinarily, one meets one of that quality.' Daniel died a few months later on a visit to Princeton, aged 67.

[Uncle Oliver, who was also my godfather, was a significant person in my life. Like his brothers, he was a first class linguist, served among the code-breakers of Bletchley Park during the Second World War, was the senior army observer at the Nuremberg trials of Nazi war criminals, and translated two books by the French flying ace Pierre Clostermann before ending a good career in education as headmaster for 20 years of Trinity School, Croydon. As a keen viola player (not least for the Croydon symphony orchestra) with a developed interest in contemporary art, he was a source of moral support to me in my early fight against my father's anti-intellectualism. I cherished his sardonic sense of humour, tempered in my case by evident affection. There may have been a touch of the Jekyll and Hyde in him: Clifford Longley, *The Times*'s religious affairs correspondent in the 1970s and a former pupil at Trinity School, told me how Oliver had beaten him with, he reckoned, undue severity. After the death of his wife Celia, Oliver married his secretary, to the family's distress. One of his two daughters, Angela, joined the Scientology cult, not generally a sign of a happy childhood. The other, Diana, married a German school teacher, lives in southern Germany, and proved to be a very good mother.]

...and a major visit to the USA

A priceless perk of being a broadsheet journalist in Brussels was a four or five week trip to the USA, laid on by the Governmental Affairs Institute in Washington – on the basis, presumably, that it was in the US's interests that those who wrote about US/ European relations (as we did) should be better informed about that great country. A few articles were expected in return for this investment. We had to name a theme for the trip, and a couple of sub-themes, around which the itinerary would be planned, all travel and accommodation arrangements being made and paid on our behalf. There were two snags: the trip had to take place, for work reasons, in late July and August, when the EEC's institutions went into their summer recess and much of the USA would be sweltering in high summer humidity; and the first five days had to be spent being briefed by officials in Washington.

I helped the planners devise a programme that would take me to as much as possible of the USA, which I had not visited since my return from Canada via New York and Philadelphia, aged eight. My main theme of US/European relations would be covered by the Washington briefings. My first sub-theme was the recent surge in the value of soya beans (soybeans to the Americans), the USA's second biggest export to Europe, after airplanes. Thanks to excessive demand, the US had controversially imposed restrictions on their exports of this nutritious legume. That topic would get me to Chicago, the mid-West and Colorado, while jazz, my second sub-theme, could at a pinch get me to the West Coast and, on the way back, to New Orleans. A sub-sub theme was race relations.

Washington proved to be as torridly muggy as expected. Even with air conditioning it was a struggle to stay awake, let alone look deeply interested and ask intelligent questions to the 21 senior officials and politicians with whom I spent up to one hour each. Most were impressively high-powered, which implied that I was being taken seriously – though not, detectably, by the elderly, small, bald and rather smug Republican senator Jacob Javits. 'Well, what can I do for you?' he barked before spending four minutes reading memos on his desk, and then repeating the question as if I had just entered. It's no secret that to listen (and take notes) is more tiring than to talk. Those seven days were exhausting, but very interesting. I am the sort of person who is fascinated to learn, for example, that in 1972 the US production of oranges was 9.3 million tons, almost twice the combined production of Spain, Israel, Morocco and South Africa. No wonder the Americans wanted greater access for citrus fruits to the EC market.

A few hours at the Watergate hearings made a change, though the proceedings were considerably less dramatic than the nightly TV highlights complete with dramatic close-ups of witnesses. My evenings were sometimes lonely, though one was spent enjoyably with my old *Evening Standard* colleague Jeremy Campbell, that paper's long-time Washington correspondent, and his wife Pandora; and another at a farewell party given by the BBC's Charles Wheeler, who was heading for Brussels.

After a week in Washington, it was a relief to get to Chicago. There I was an amazed spectator at the Board of Trade, where commodities (including soya beans) are traded with much frenzied shouting, arm-waving – fractures were not uncommon – and the throwing of scribbled notes into a pit. Later I was shown the city's many architectural highlights by a rumpled businessman, and dined at his home overlooking the sea-like

Lake Michigan. My hosts seemed perfect representatives of conservative America. They thought Nixon was being sadistically harried by the press over Watergate, and reckoned his co-accused were 'perfectly wonderful, intelligent and dedicated men.' As for the unemployed, my hostess commented: 'If you find anyone who wants to do some work, please send them along!' I managed to visit the Chicago Art Institute, which on top of its own great collection was showing some 50 of the finest post-Impressionists from the Hermitage and Pushkin museums in Leningrad (as it still was) and Moscow. A visual feast.

My sub-sub theme of race relations took me, courtesy of the Chicago Urban League, to the poverty-stricken black ghetto end of Michigan Avenue. It was quite a revelation: mile on mile of desperate-looking houses with families sitting on the doorstep in the 90°F degree temperature. Had things changed for the blacks in recent years? I asked my guide. 'For a third, the very poor, things have not changed at all. They are as poor as before the 1960s. One third are better off, and the remaining third are doing very well', she said.

From Chicago, on to Omaha, Nebraska, in the heart of the mid-West, with its grid-like pattern of fields. The Cold War was still pretty chilly, and I was committed to writing a piece about the HQ of Strategic Air Command, at a base south of Omaha. As two officers rattled through their briefing, I felt a sense of awe at finding myself at the nerve centre of the US's long-range atomic strike force, with its intercontinental ballistic missiles and 'alert' bombers, plus worldwide reconnaissance operations.

In the subterranean command post from which any nuclear war would be directed, there was push-button contact with all 35 bomber and missile bases at home and abroad. The colonel briefing me pressed the button for Alaska, which responded immediately. 'What's the temperature there?' the colonel asked. 'Fifty one degrees' came the answer. I was told that when President Johnson, who would give the order to fire or take off, visited and pressed the button for the stratotanker base in Spain, he said: 'Good morning, this is President Johnson.' A voice at the other end responded in the coolest tones: 'Good morning, Sir, what can we do for you?' Given that he might have been starting a nuclear war, that was impressive.

In one of those drastic transitions that make journalism stimulating, I was then ferried – via a rodeo, entertaining in small doses – to a family of farmers, the Kellers, near Lincoln, Nebraska. My plan was to describe the impact on this family's income for the dramatic rise in the price of soya beans, in a region where beef had long been king. Harold Keller, gaunt, God-fearing but well-travelled, had been brought up on the same 400-acre farm that he now ran single-handed. Soya beans (contact at last!) were the main crop. These protein-rich beans were, I was told next day by an academic at Nebraska University in Lincoln (the state capital), introduced in the 1800s from China, mainly as a forage crop. The big increase in production came after 1945. Hard-working people like the Kellers have, I imagine, helped make the USA what it is. They passed me on to some only marginally less impressive neighbours, who farmed 1,200 acres with the help of two sons.

The people who smoothed my path across the country, often arranging my local programmes, were mainly female. They worked for the international committees of such bodies as Kiwanis clubs, international visitor centres, international relations councils and so on. Of course I hoped that some of them would be attractive nymphomaniacs, but inevitably they were mostly elderly and motherly. Beth Imig, my guide in Nebraska, was unusual in being youngish and attractive, albeit firmly married with kids, and a devout Christian. She poured out her soul to me about their relative poverty, but contrasted their lot favourably with that of their German-born immigrant parents: her father had gone broke in the Depression, become and remained a garbage collector, but educated all his children at American universities. She said displaced immigrants from the Baltic states had worked up to 20 hours a day after the Second World War, and now owned much of the local real estate.

A pass and a town called Berthoud

Denver next, via Berthoud Pass, at 11,314 feet just within the tree line. A plaque there commemorates the feat of Captain Edward L. Berthoud, once the most famous civil engineer in the West, in engineering the pass in May 1861 while working for the Union Pacific Railroad and searching for a route to the Pacific. His discovery, and the resulting road, shortened the journey west by some 200 miles. Capt. Berthoud was born in Geneva, and came with his parents to New York aged two: a putative forbear, like all successful Berthouds! Berthoud Pass has become a well-known ski resort.

The name also lives on in the small nearby town (pop. around 3,000) of Berthoud, locally pronounced Bur-thud. Before visiting this urban namesake, I spent 24 hours exploring the glorious Rocky Mountain National Park, by car. The highlight was Trail Ridge, 11 miles of which runs above the tree line. At its highest point I was at 12,183 feet, on the same level as the snow-bedecked mountain peaks. The views were staggering. Berthoud itself proved to be a pleasant little town, with its Berthoud National Bank, its *Berthoud Bulletin* newspaper (the office was closed; what a scoop they could have had) and a Berthoud Mill.

It was Sunday, and in the town's small park I found a well-attended picnic in progress. When I revealed my name, I was swiftly made welcome. 'Let Berthoud give unto Berthoud', said one elderly party as he handed me a glass of wine. Most of the inhabitants were, it transpired, of the same German, Swedish and Czech stock as in Nebraska: they had simply pressed on westwards. Gold and silver were the original attraction in the 1860s, replaced by cattle when the precious metals ran out. I was plied with questions: what did I think of the Watergate proceedings? Did Britain also have a colour problem? It made a change from doing the asking.

My next stop was Las Vegas: not to see Elvis Presley or Liza Minelli, who were performing that evening (no tickets available), but to fly – after an evening amid the gaudy tawdriness of the casinos – over the Grand Canyon in a little Cessna with half a dozen other punters. Our pilot swung the plane expertly over the chasm, at the bottom of which swirled the great Colorado River, then landed us at an airstrip on the rim, from which we peered downwards. Majestic it certainly was, but I preferred the more varied splendours of the Rockies.

California, New Mexico and New Orleans

And so to Los Angeles, where Joy joined me at the Beverly Hilton. We had some friends there, Harold and Melody Carlton. Harold, a very amusing man, had spent much time with Joy at the Paris collections as the *Daily Mail*'s fashion artist, and later became a successful author. Despite being basically gay, he had married Melody, and they had gone to live in her native LA. They gave us a wonderful tour of Beverly Hills, including the opulent area where the likes of Paul Newman, Jack Benny, Lana Turner and so on lived or had lived, amid some striking contemporary architecture. Harold told us hilarious stories of his time sewing in Paris for Courrèges. In his apprentice days he was turned loose on the lining of a coat for the Begum Aga Khan, a treasured client. Eventually she came for a fitting. Alas, she could not get her arm through the sleeve, which Harold had inadvertently sewn up. Neither the master nor the Begum was amused.

Off next morning in a hired car to San Francisco by the scenic route overlooking the Pacific, dawdling en route in Santa Barbara (unexpectedly Spanish in feel) and visiting St Simeon Castle, a Gothic folly built atop a hill by the mining and newspaper magnate William Randolph Hearst. Reaching San Fran itself, we were amazed by the skyline, the steepness of its streets, with trolley cars and antique trams plying up and down, and the plunge of the temperature in the evenings, emphasised by a keen wind. After seeing the usual sights there we flew through cloudless skies over the snow-capped Sierra Nevada – a dazzling spectacle – and the Grand Canyon (again) to Albuquerque in New Mexico. Our goal was Santa Fé, of whose attractions we had heard much, with my race relations sub-theme being used to embrace the area's Navajo pueblos. Santa Fé was, then at least, still a simple little town very conscious of its role as a meeting place of Indian, Spanish and American cultures. One-storey adobe buildings predominated: anything over three storeys was banned.

Although the Navajo Indians appeared to be part of the town's life, and not just as peddlers of handicrafts, life in the pueblos seemed bleak. We visited one at San Domingo, some 30 miles out. Photography was banned, reasonably enough, all visitors had to leave by 6pm, and the attitude of the locals to tourists was overtly hostile. They wanted, it seemed, to share some of the white man's prosperity while retaining their old way of life, and they did not want to be stared at like animals in a zoo.

From Santa Fé, Joy headed for Washington, where she had friends. I was at last to see New Orleans, hallowed fount of the music that had given me so much pleasure. It was raining, stickily humid and well after midnight when I ventured excitedly from my hotel in the French quarter onto Bourbon Street, to get an earful of music and an eyeful of the famously balconied architecture. Some of the near-naked girls adorning the many little bars in this area were no less beautifully balconied. Dancing on tables seemed to be their speciality. There was no sense of Soho or Reeperbahn sleaze here. The doormen actually held the door open to give you a better view of the attractions within, saying encouragingly: 'Come on now, it looks much better from close to.' For the $1.50 cost of a beer, young and not-so-young men were sitting at the tables, staring unashamedly upwards.

Next day I headed in a seemingly unsprung Greyhound bus to Thibodaux in the bayou (creek) country, across the mighty Missisippi and through flat, swampy scenery and trees festooned with Spanish moss. The fields were mostly given over to sugar cane or pasture, with white egrets following the cows around. A handsome Roman Catholic priest had gathered half a dozen locals together for me, mainly from nearby Nicholls State University (6,000 students): among them a Catholic sister, an academic with 150 cattle, and a teacher of English, one of the few Jews in town, he said.

The bovinely-endowed academic complained that while the price of beef had soared, so had cattle-rustling. The preferred local method was to paddle up a bayou in a pirogue (canoe), slaughter a cow at the water's edge, and hack off its hindquarters for sale on the local black market. Or a whole cow would be taken off in a larger boat, untraceably. Conversation touched briefly on strange local place-names. Among them was a town called Waterproof. A local newspaper had carried the unfortunate headline: 'Three Waterproof Negroes Drowned.'

On my last evening in New Orleans I visited Preservation Hall, bastion of old-style jazz, where a sadly geriatric band could only sustain an ensemble for a minute or two. By contrast, the Storeyville Band over in Bourbon Street had a brilliant trumpeter and trombonist and an excellent white clarinettist.

My last stop was New York, where the evening temperature was 96°F, my taxi driver cursed me for not getting in quickly enough, broke the handle of my suitcase, and cursed me again for giving him a $10 bill to change: a Pole whom Poland was lucky to lose. I rejoined Joy in a cell-like room at the Barbizon Plaza Hotel. Next morning I spent a couple of hours with the Council on Foreign Relations, who had actually asked to see me. 'I hadn't realised that the EEC was in such bad shape', one of the five Europe specialists said when I had answered their questions. In my remaining two days – Joy preceded me back to Brussels – I visited the Museum of Modern Art, the Guggenheim and Frick collections, and saw a play on Broadway. On my last morning I found a photograph of Joy and me on the front page of a section of the *New York Times*. The article underneath tackled the topic, recently raised, of whether there were sexual overtones to the act of opening a door for a woman. I was shown doing just that for Joy, along with two other men similarly engaged.

It had been a memorable trip. In five weeks I had seen more of the USA than most Americans see in a life time, at virtually no cost to myself. My strongest impression was, perhaps banally, of the splendour and variety of much of the scenery: it was easy to think of the (pre-Obama) USA primarily as a bullying super-power full of over-armed and over-weight religious bigots.

It remained for me to write a substantial feature on the state of US/European relations, drawing on those Washington briefings. I grew increasingly nervous as the features department sat on the resulting opus for a week. It was eventually published on the same day as a major piece on the same theme by the *Guardian*'s then Washington correspondent, Peter Jenkins. We reached virtually identical conclusions. Had features waited a day longer, it would have looked as if I'd copied him – or the piece might have been 'spiked' (killed).

Back to the treadmill

It's hard to adjust to normal life after several weeks of constant stimulus, and the treadmill of Brussels coverage seemed particularly tedious on my return, great though it was to be back with Joy and the girls, who for much of my time in the USA had been with my parents and a niece in Suffolk. True, someone had to assume the burden of explaining the intricacies of the EEC to the British public, but did it have to be me? Joy drew up a list of people she felt we owed dinner, and commented: 'Doesn't that make you want to go back to London?' It did. But the best hope the foreign editor Louis Heren could offer was for changes in 1975.

A modest morale booster in Brussels was at hand, in the shape of 'Europalia', a Ted Heath-inspired festival of British art and music held in October 1973, to celebrate our EEC membership. There were lots of parties to launch its various events. It was good to see old friends from the London art world, and to meet among other notables the charming Peter Pears, who was singing the main role in Benjamin Britten's recent opera *Death in Venice*. Pears was a knowledgeable collector of contemporary British art. He featured also in Britten's songs for tenor and French horn, during which Margaret Thatcher, then Education Secretary, fainted: from heat rather than emotion, it was assumed. Not yet the Iron Lady. This month-long festival climaxed with a barnstorming performance of Berlioz's *Symphonie Fantastique*, with André Previn conducting the London Symphony Orchestra. What other British prime minister of recent times would have thought of such a civilised celebration of Britishness?

Meanwhile Egypt and Syria attacked Israel, launching the so-called Yom Kippur war, the fourth between Arabs and Israelis. In this one, my old boss at the Londoner's Diary, Nick Tomalin, was killed by a Syrian rocket while reporting for *The Sunday Times*, a serious loss in both human and journalistic terms. The war was followed by the OPEC cartel drastically increasing oil prices, which were eventually quadrupled, and the use of oil as a weapon to punish the West for its support of Israel (the Soviet Union was backing and arming Egypt and Syria). An embargo by Arab oil producers on exports to the USA was soon extended to the Netherlands, the most supportive of Israel among EEC countries. Member states faced a dilemma: they wanted to show solidarity with the Dutch, without having the embargo extended to themselves. The EEC was thus thrust into the centre of world affairs as ministers from oil-producing countries hi-jacked a shambolic EEC summit in Copenhagen that December. It was not a happy time for

US/European relations. The following year was marked by American suspicions that the EEC was ganging up against them on trade issues, and attempting to do a separate deal with Arab oil producers. The Europeans for their part felt side-lined whenever Nixon or Kissinger got together with their Soviet counterparts.

It was also a time of discord between Britain and its EEC partners, mainly over the new regional fund and progress towards economic and monetary union. Reporting these tensions was stressfully competitive, sometimes nightmarishly so. After one strenuous day, which included a Pierre Trudeau press conference and ended with a dinner party, Joy and I returned home around 11pm, not entirely sober, to find a message from our Dutch au pair girl for me to call *The Times*'s foreign desk. 'The FT is leading with a story about a new formula for Britain's contribution to the EEC budget', said the genial Ivan Barnes, who was on duty. 'You have 50 minutes to write something for the front page'. The story was also on the front page of the *Guardian*. Ivan did not need to point out that our budgetary contribution was a political hot potato.

The FT's story was by-lined Lorelies Olslager, the German-born No 2 (of three) at *The Financial Times*, so I had to ring her to get the gist of what she had written. Fortunately we were friends. I then hauled the senior Treasury official at UKrep out of bed, or at least onto the telephone, to get some additional spin on the story. He was forbearing. My befuddled brain then had to knock these two elements into a coherent piece and dictate it before midnight, painfully aware that it would look pathetic beside the full FT lead story treatment. I went to bed feeling I had had several years wiped off my life. Lorelies was somewhat depressive, and killed herself a few years later, a sad loss.

Two more cheering episodes stick in the memory. The first involved Bob Taylor, the No 1 at Reuters, whom I overheard in the Commission press room saying to a visiting colleague: 'The nicest writer here, as such, is Roger Berthoud of *The Times*.' The second found me on a train to Paris. Two NATO officials were sitting opposite, reading *The Times*. One of them came to the piece I had written the day before, and said: 'This Berthoud chap has got yesterday's meeting exactly right,' thus disproving the old saw that if you have been involved in anything written up in the papers, it's always inaccurate. I believe I revealed that they were in the presence of this genius. It was also heartening to receive a flow of compliments from Dad about what a credit I was to the family, how highly his friends in the political and foreign affairs worlds rated me etc.

Labour's victory, yet more negotiations

Labour emerged from the February 1974 general election leading a minority government, and more clearly won a subsequent election that October. The change brought a new cast of players to EEC meetings: notably Jim Callaghan as Foreign Secretary, seconded by the genial Roy Hattersley, Peter Shore from Trade and Industry, and Denis Healey as Chancellor of the Exchequer, with occasional sightings of Harold Wilson, once again

Prime Minister. Shore had been consistently hostile to the EEC, often photographed ranting away; but in the flesh turned out to be charming and well able to laugh at himself. Healey was, as expected, an impressive performer.

The aim of the new Labour government was to renegotiate some of the terms of Britain's membership. Oh no! we thought. Are we really going to have to go through that again? The answer, regrettably, was yes. Naturally the French initially ruled out the possibility of any changes, but eventually recognised that a British withdrawal, as threatened, would be damaging. The list of demands was long, led by a partial refund of Britain's disproportionate contribution to the EEC budget, and improved terms for the import of dairy produce from New Zealand.

After 12 months of haggling, the final, minor but face-saving adjustments were agreed at a summit in Dublin in March 1975. It was nice to be in Dublin, staying at the great Shelburne Hotel. On the way in from the airport with my friends and competitors from the *FT* and *Guardian*, our taxi-driver amused us by commenting, as he slammed on his brakes to avoid hitting a nun who had stepped into our path: 'The f...ing bitch wasn't thinking of my insurance premium, was she!'

Life chez Astor

Fortunately life wasn't all work. For holidays, we went several times with the girls to the Ash villa in Cap d'Antibes, sometimes with the current au pair girl, paying only the cost of utilities and cleaning. Once we overlapped with Maurice, who spoiled us by taking us to expensive restaurants. Then there was Joy's friend and ex-*Daily Mail* colleague Judy Innes, former Cambridge belle, briefly an ornament of the Londoner's Diary, and sister of the more famous Jocasta. Judy had, as mentioned, married Michael Astor, and Joy had earlier stayed with them in Chelsea.

The main Astor residence was a smallish stately home, Bruern Abbey, near Burford in Oxfordshire. When I first visited, its Victorian accretions, including a huge entrance hall, were still in place. They were subsequently torn down, and replaced with a single storey courtyard at the rear. The beautiful main façade, facing onto a terrace, large garden and grounds, including a tennis court, remained.

Even as reduced, the house and garden staff ran to some 15 people. There was Mr Boot the butler, Mrs Bliss the chief housekeeper, with an assistant in charge of beds and another for laundry matters, Mr Flatman for cars and machinery, a French chef and sundry lesser luminaries. On one of our visits, Lottie, then five and a great one for chatting up staff, asked a monk-like figure who was cleaning out the swimming pool if he was a gardener. 'Oh no, I'm maintenance', he replied, as if gardeners were way up the hierarchy. To a visitor, the staff seemed to form one big, happy family.

Life at Bruern was lived on a different plane. On one occasion, Michael Astor had been due to go walking in Wales with his great friend, the travel writer Patrick Leigh Fermor, plus Annie Fleming, widow of (among others) Ian Fleming. The walk had to be aborted: Michael had twisted his knee, and la Fleming had just heard that Caspar, Ian's beloved only son, had tried to kill himself on holiday at Goldeneye in Jamaica (he succeeded with a drug overdose the following year; Ann died in 1981). Meanwhile Paddy Leigh Fermor, who had extricated himself from his adopted homeland of Greece with great difficulty – the military junta having just ousted Archbishop Makarios in Cyprus – had arrived by train in the depths of Wales to find no one waiting for him, and was not pleased.

Soon we were joined by David Carritt, legendary expert on Old Master paintings. David on form was the wittiest man I have met. I noted several of his sallies. One concerned the wife of a fellow Christie's director: she was a prolific author, not notoriously monogamous, and apparently an indifferent amateur painter. 'If I were married to ......', David commented, 'I would much rather she committed adultery than painted.' Commenting on a poll that showed Labour's support sharply up, he observed: 'It's all because of Lady Falkender's elevation to the peerage. It's the only real fairy tale of our times.' (Marcia Williams, Harold Wilson's personal and political secretary, had recently and controversially been given a life peerage.)

The focal point of the weekend was a lunch party for the young Maharajah of Jodhpur, his wife, his mother and her secretary/companion. They were staying nearby with Georgie, one of Michael's children by previous marriages, whose husband had been at Oxford with the Maharajah. Georgie explained that the mother should be called Rajmata. 'May we ask where Rajpater is?' David Carritt wondered. On that arctic, rain-swept Sunday morning they arrived, the men in shirts and trousers, the women in saris. The Maharajah was plump, his wife pretty and pregnant. Rajmata was very heavy-going: I was fated to sit next to her at lunch. It seemed they had recently reduced the staff at their palace, where a servant stood behind each guest as they ate, from 900 to 600, and were planning to turn it into a tourist hotel (which opened just three years later, with some 200 rooms). The secretary, who had worked in Paris, was much the brightest member of the group. We escaped after lunch to play croquet on the rain-sodden lawn.

After a spell with my parents on the Essex/Suffolk border, we ended that UK holiday with a few days in Devon chez Maurice and Ruth Ash. The steep slopes leading up from the river Dart to their garden were soon to be clothed in vines producing the excellent Sharpham wine, and milk from a large herd of Jersey cows was being converted into several varieties of very rich, unpasteurised Sharpham cheese (nowadays quite widely available). The Dartington summer music school was in its last week. Imogen Holst, daughter of Gustav, came to supper one evening, and the redoubtable Sir William Glock, former Controller of BBC music and committed advocate of avant-garde composers, to lunch. I sat next to him, and his total lack of interest in me was less than endearing. The Lindsay quartet came to tea, plus violinist Sandor Vegh, who was giving some master classes. Vegh retained a strong Hungarian accent. When I said we lived in Brussels, he said: 'You know the old queen mother, who died last year: I used to teach her violence' (he was, I deduced, referring to his instrument).

163

Stop the world, I want to get off

Before returning to Brussels I had lunch with Louis Heren, *The Times*'s foreign and deputy editor. After a poor start involving a new office car in Brussels, we were getting on pretty well: it can't have been easy for him to adapt to a desk-bound life after many years as a famous foreign correspondent. I put up a case for returning to London with a roving commission in the political and diplomatic hinterland. He thought it a good idea, but warned that it risked being seen to cut across existing patterns of responsibility. There were few if any precedents for foreign correspondents returning home as anything other than specialist leader writers, those grey eminences of the paper. I had been unusual in becoming a foreign correspondent ten years into my career, with a family and a substantial house to re-occupy. Most started young in a number two slot in, say, Paris or Washington, and stayed abroad until retirement. Some, like Charles Hargrove in Paris and Peter Nicholls in Rome, were left *en poste* and went virtually native.

Joy and I were itching to get back to our Hampstead home, to get the girls into the primary school up the hill, and resume a more normal life. The cost of our indexed rent and the fees at the British School of Brussels was rocketing. Our tenants in London had given notice. Social life in Brussels might be pretty good, and Joy was arguably the belle of the British community. But the combination had put some strain on our marriage. So we were delighted when in November 1974 we heard that I could return to London the following spring with a flexible mandate as a reporter, feature writer and interviewer: no fancy title, none of the foreign correspondent's perks like an office and car, just a desk in the home reporters' area. I might even have to do some night shifts. It would be up to me to find my own level.

I had to stay in Brussels until March, when the Labour government's 'renegotiations' were due to be concluded. There seemed to be a case for getting the girls into the popular local Hampstead primary school in January, though Joy's plans to go home just before Christmas were nearly dropped when first Lottie, then Lucy, contracted mumps. What with the mumps and removal men arriving in Hampstead at 7am on a Sunday morning, Joy's return home was a nightmare rather than a happy home-coming.

Meanwhile I had to find somewhere to live for three months, having quit our large house. I ended up staying with Christopher and Mette MacRae and their two daughters. Both Mette, an attractive and very intelligent Dane, and Christopher had been at MECAS (the Middle East Centre for Arab Studies near Beirut, closed in 1978). He had overlapped with me at Rugby, was currently with the embassy in Brussels, and eventually ended his career in Pakistan, where he succeeded my Cambridge friend Nicholas Barrington as High Commissioner. It was very kind of them to take me in. I popped back frequently to see Joy and the girls, and missed them greatly in Brussels.

Despite the MacRaes' kindness, those three months were far from happy. It was a relief to hand over in March to Michael Hornsby, a cool operator who had excelled in reporting the crushing of the Prague spring of 1968. My loyal and supportive No 2, David Cross, stayed on, though he returned to the foreign desk in London before long.

Chapter 11

Back to London, and my first book (1975-1982)

Friends and colleagues alike thought we were mad to want to return to London at a time when the country's fortunes made the Gadarene swine look upwardly mobile. Inflation was around 25 per cent, the unions were demanding pay increases of more than 30 per cent, industry was plagued by strikes, Ted Heath's three-day week of 1974 was still a memory, London was a favoured target for IRA bombs, Harold Wilson's Labour government was riven by a left-right split...In short, Britain truly was the 'sick man of Europe', and its government would soon be applying to the International Monetary Fund for a loan to bail out the economy. Were we masochists willingly to come back to this?

But, as indicated, we had our own family agenda. Joy was a Londoner at heart. I had had enough of being a foreign correspondent in capitals where the main demand was for a nicely wrapped package of the day's news delivered just in time for the first edition: not that I underestimate the value of news, but I often used to wonder 'Wouldn't anyone reasonably intelligent deliver a rather similar package?' I was anxious to evolve a role as a feature writer and interviewer – and also to re-integrate myself into family life. This had, in retrospect, been somewhat fractured by the various strains caused by life in Bonn and Brussels.

'One of my problems', I wrote to my mother a bit later, 'has been thinking for years that I didn't have any problems, refusing in fact to acknowledge my feelings – love, anger and so on – and intellectualising what few emotions I allowed to the surface. The second problem has been compartmentalising things – sex, emotions, intellect. Am now attempting fusion of same, and hope that fission does not take place instead! My work: it is not really a matter of ambition, more of self-fulfilment. This I have not yet achieved – few people probably do.' In other words, I was feeling a bit mixed up, and trying to sort myself out. I ended that letter 'I derive enormous comfort and support from having a mother who has not feared to look deep into herself, and treasure your courage and intellectual honesty more and more.'

The Times's hierarchy as it now was

It made a great difference to morale to feel I had the support of the top troika at *The Times*. William Rees-Mogg was still the editor, Louis Heren the deputy editor and foreign editor, and Charlie Douglas-Home the (suitably named) home affairs editor. A more contrasting trio it would be hard to imagine: Rees-Mogg tall, very much the Roman Catholic, often emotional in his judgements, socially shy but articulate when behind his desk, a fluent, clear and rapid leader-writer, overall a kindly human being; Heren: medium height, chunky build, flattish face reflecting his part-Basque origins, given to *idées fixes* about his colleagues, dangerous when aroused, devoted to his family (his ancient and ailing mother lived with him); Douglas-Home: short, reddish hair, cool brain and manner, wide interests, staggering contacts. All three seemed well disposed towards me. It is hard to exaggerate how much that meant in an office full of jealousies and rivalries. Louis lived near us in Hampstead, and often gave me a lift home in the evening, regaling me with stories of his astonishing rise from East End kid to the most admired foreign correspondent of his generation.

In those days at least, *The Times* seemed to be divided into officers and other ranks. The officer class included the very clever and well-informed specialist leader writers, the features editor – soon to be the engaging Margaret Allen – the political editor David Wood, perhaps the home and foreign news editors (according to personality) and perhaps some members of the 'back bench' (the night editor and one or two others). The reporters, and even the specialists in such fields as science, education and health, were the NCOs and foot soldiers, and none too happy about it. There were one or two special cases, such as Philip Howard, an Old Etonian classicist whose alleged 'light touch' I found ponderous; and the engaging Peter Hennessy, who was laying the foundations of his brilliant post-*Times* career as a political historian by being very kind about Whitehall and all its works ('get it out with an oil can' was his motto then).

Peter and I most enjoyably shared an office for a spell, along with my successor in Bonn, Dan van der Vat, who eventually also became a historian, of the naval variety. It was a challenge to my diplomatic skills to navigate between the various factions. As on the *Daily Express* in Manchester, I drew a line at adjourning to the pub across the Gray's Inn Road after hours. Apart from loathing smoky pubs, I was far too keen to see Lucy and Lottie before they went to sleep. I was and am a doting Dad.

Even if I was in many ways treated as a member of the officer class, it felt like demotion to find myself back, for the first time since Manchester, in the general reporters' room, and even obliged initially to do some night shifts finishing well after midnight: scurrying out to Oxford Street, say, to report on some minor IRA bomb blast. I performed such tasks rather less competently than the reporting staff, whose professionalism – including good shorthand – I much admired, nay envied.

The 1975 referendum

Fortunately there was a major item on the upcoming political agenda for which I was supremely well equipped: the June 5 1975 referendum on whether or not Britain should remain in the EEC (on the marginally better terms negotiated by the Labour government). There was little doubt about which way this would go. All three main political parties were, despite some dissenters, in favour of a Yes vote, as were – hard to believe nowadays – most national newspapers. With Britain in decline and continental West Europe prospering, the case for Britain going it alone, or in some second-class free trade area, looked threadbare.

I had to rein in my tendency to proselytise for a Yes vote, and rather enjoyed describing the Against as well as the For case. In addition to reporting speeches by such opponents as Tony Benn, Enoch Powell and Barbara Castle, I did a lengthy interview with a more moderate critic of membership, the Trade Secretary Peter Shore, who was familiar from his visits to Brussels. In our interview he accused the country's establishment of 'real, rotten defeatism' for not believing that national solutions to the country's problems were possible. He failed to explain why such solutions had not been found before Britain 'collapsed into the EEC', as he put it, and enjoyed untrammelled sovereignty. Charlie Douglas-Home thought the piece had 'a nice dialectical quality'.

Defying my stammer (I was sufficiently angry at his distortion of the facts) at a press conference on the eve of the referendum, I asked another leader of the No camp, the maverick Ulster Unionist and former Tory minister Enoch Powell, how France had contrived to remain so sovereign, economically successful and very French despite 17 years of 'compromised' sovereignty within the EEC. I thought I had him there, but experienced politicians are wonderfully adept at flannelling their way out of tricky questions. Speaking as a passionate Francophile, he said, France was not a parliamentary democracy but a presidential autocracy bent on achieving the hegemony in Europe to which the French believed their culture entitled them. Clever bugger. But the great British public, in a rare bout of wisdom, rejected his views: next day, for every vote against continued membership, two were cast in favour of staying in.

The Ash effect

Looking back on my cuttings from this period, I note a strong Maurice Ash influence. Maurice was not only chairman of the council of the Town and Country Planning Association but also a leading figure in the Green movement, emerging in 1978 as the founding chairman of the Green Alliance pressure group. At Maurice's prompting, I interviewed the economist Dr E.F.Schumacher, whose book *Small is Beautiful*, published in 1973, had made a great impact with its argument that large-scale, oil-intensive technology was increasingly unacceptable on social, human and economic grounds: that was before the oil crisis of the same year proved him so prescient. Already he had a quasi-saintly aura, and with typical modesty he offered to come to *The Times* to see me. Schumacher was then 65, having been born in Bonn, studied at Oxford and emigrated to Britain in 1937, later becoming economic adviser to the National Coal Board. He was a tall, rather shy, seemingly gentle and intensely serious man, but clearly ill, and died only 18 months later. Part of his thesis was that oil-intensive technology produces a dual

167

society: workers who are nothing, and those skilled and rich enough to manipulate it. My interview was lamentably presented, under the feeble headline 'Making the workers happier', with no picture of the great man.

Within a few months of my return, I was doing more or less everything I had hoped to be doing, and felt stimulated by my encounters with men (not many women, regrettably) of ideas. Grasping a concept and endeavouring to put it across in readable prose can be very satisfying. An interview is one of the best vehicles for doing so. William Rees-Mogg seemed pleased with my efforts: in December 1975 he wrote me a short letter, saying *inter alia* 'I should like to give you my very warm thanks for the excellent work you have done for the paper during the past year. I am only writing to a few people whose work has been particularly distinguished. I feel that this has been a year in which we have kept up the best traditions of Times journalism, and you have made a great contribution to that.' I doubt if editors write such letters nowadays. Thank you, William, for being so appreciative. It made a big difference.

In July 1975 Margaret Thatcher, who had unexpectedly been elected leader of the Opposition that February, came to lunch at *The Times*. About a dozen of us were invited to meet this new phenomenon, a female leader of a major party. I disliked her almost immediately. Instead of answering questions, she sought to put down the questioner.

A majority of my features sprang from my own suggestions, to which my father as well as Maurice Ash, among others, contributed. Through Dad's involvement with the Atlantic (international sixth-form) College in Wales, he had become friendly with Lord Mountbatten, the chairman since 1968 of the international council of this spreading chain of colleges. Dad's role was partly to drum up scholarships from West and East European governments, and partly to help set up the national committees that would help choose and fund the lucky students. When he had done the donkey work, Mountbatten would pay a quasi-viceregal visit to endorse the whole exercise, with suitable pomp and government presence.

Why not interview Mountbatten just ahead of his upcoming 75th birthday, Dad suggested: it would be useful publicity for the Atlantic College. Mountbatten, who was not exactly publicity-shy, agreed. The ensuing interview in his Knightsbridge *pied-à-terre* was fun, despite being punctuated by endless phone-calls and a medical inspection by his doctor, for which interruption Mountbatten apologised, appearing at the sitting room door stripped to the waist, doubtless to show how firm and bronzed his torso was. His charm was as legendary as his egocentricity. I was thoroughly shocked when, on a family holiday in 1979 staying with Swiss cousins, I bought a copy of *Le Monde* in Neuchâtel and read of his assassination by an IRA bomb on his sailing boat off the coast of Ireland.

Political and arty interviews

On March 16 1976 Harold Wilson astonished the nation by announcing, a few days after his 60th birthday, that he was resigning as Prime Minister (probably, it was later thought, because of incipient Alzheimer's). Six contenders for his job emerged: Jim Callaghan, Denis Healey, Roy Jenkins, Tony Benn, Michael Foot and Anthony Crosland. My idea of interviewing all six was given the nod. The last three, whose chances looked dim, swiftly agreed. Jim Callaghan, the favourite, ruled himself out, but allowed his press secretary Tom McCaffrey, whom I knew well as head of the Foreign Office's news department, to give me a detailed briefing about his domestic life, habits and predilections. Roy Jenkins said he would participate if Denis Healey would, but unfortunately Healey said No. So much for our friendly encounters in Brussels. However, three was deemed a quorum, and I enjoyed my encounters with each of them, concentrating on their views rather than their personalities. Benn produced his own tape recorder, which was unnerving (fortunately I had mine), but subsequently rang *The Times* to say he thought my piece very fair and accurate, 'as I indeed expected': a kind gesture. All three interviews were handsomely presented on the 'op-ed' page.

Not long afterwards Louis Heren asked if I would like to be among those considered for the job of political editor, from which the rather grand David Wood was retiring. I was flattered, but hated the idea of the long hours closeted in Westminster that would be demanded should I be offered the job. Joy nobly reckoned I could not pass up such an opportunity, and I persuaded myself it would be a valuable and interesting experience. The obvious candidate was Fred Emery, who had replaced Heren as Washington correspondent. He had compounded that serious handicap (few people want their successor to do well) by disagreeing with both Heren and Rees-Mogg over the desirability of impeaching President Nixon over Watergate. He was proved right (hard to forgive) and they were wrong. Happily, Rees-Mogg admitted his error and gave him the job in 1977. Wood was persuaded to soldier on till then.

I was, on balance, relieved. Good note-taking is of the essence in reporting parliament, and it was my weakest suit. Furthermore, I did not enjoy intense pressure, nor did I have a cool head in a crisis. A major threat to my domestic life had been removed, and I would continue to enjoy the glorious variety of my role as a wide-ranging reporter and feature-writer. This was further expanded in February 1976 when the Arts editor, John Higgins, knowing my enthusiasm for contemporary art, asked me if I would interview a topical painter or sculptor (of my own choice) every six weeks or so. Higgins was an opera buff, and recognised that classical music received disproportionate coverage on his pages, as it had under his predecessor.

I was thrilled to achieve this re-entry into the art world, from which I had been professionally absent for seven years. My first subject was Eduardo Paolozzi, the sculptor and graphic artist. He was a bull of a man, and not specially articulate. Fortunately his Italian-Scottish background and his career in the vanguard of Pop art more than compensated. Next came Keith Vaughan, a painter I greatly admired and one of whose gouaches I had bought in the 1960s, a melancholy and sensitive soul and illuminating about the pains of the creative process. Vaughan was already suffering from the cancer that led him to take an overdose some 18 months later. There followed David Hockney, the West German Horst Antes, Lis Frink, the Australian Arthur Boyd, the Americans

R.B.Kitaj (then London-based) and Larry Rivers; Peter Sedgley, John Piper, Louis le Brocquy (Irish), who became something of a friend – and so on.

I was also lucky to interview the great painter Paul Klee's son Felix, whose life seemed to encapsulate the tragedy and irony of being a good German in the Third Reich. I had learnt of his visit to London through a picture dealer, Wolfgang Fischer, to whose gallery the 69-year-old retired stage producer had lent some of his father's works. Not the least bizarre of ex-gunner Felix Klee's experiences was to have been in a prisoner of war camp in 1945, which the Russians had put under the command of a German communist: Willi Stoph himself, later the long-serving Prime Minister of the German Democratic Republic. Stoph had behaved 'impeccably', Klee said. Felix subsequently came near death twice in captivity in the Soviet Union, from pneumonia and typhus, but eventually made it back to his wife and son in Wuerzburg in Bavaria – to find their house had been flattened by an allied bomb; and thence to Switzerland, where his father had died in 1940. Some of the Klee estate had been misappropriated and sold, some entrusted to a foundation in Berne. He effectively became the curator of the 1,400-odd items that remained. That interview was pure joy, and brought together my interest in art and Germany.

Thanks to my three years in Bonn and my role as part-time diplomatic correspondent, I had a good relationship with the West German embassy in Belgravia, and especially with the then ambassador, Karl-Guenther von Hase, whom I had known as the state secretary at the defence ministry in Bonn. He once asked me to lunch à trois with the *Guardian's* then editor, Peter Preston, a shy man who said very little. Von Hase was not loved within the embassy (they found him too Prussian) but highly-regarded outside it, an interesting combination. When I interviewed him before his departure for Brussels, his main theme was that, for all its prosperity, West Germany's psychological burdens from its past weighed more heavily than Britain's economic woes. Several of his successors turned out to be acquaintances from Bonn.

I examined the economic performance of the two countries and the contributory institutional factors in a full-page article in late 1977. How was it, I asked, that 62 million West Germans produced more than twice as much in value terms as 56 million Britons? I examined the parliamentary, constitutional, financial, industrial, tax, pension, educational and training arrangements in both countries. I showed that in virtually all of these the organisational structure in West Germany promoted compromise and cooperation, whereas Britain's tended to promote confrontation and short-term decisions, to the detriment of consumers and workers. The Anglo/US economic model, with its emphasis on short-term profits, returns to shareholders, highly leveraged takeovers followed by asset-stripping (my pet hate), continues to compare unfavourably with Germany's emphasis on long-term investment and ploughing back profits.

A great trip down under

Although I had travelled a fair amount when based in Brussels, it was usually on EEC business. In my new role, wider horizons were opened. Best of all was a three-week trip in 1977 to cover the Queen's jubilee visit to New Zealand and Australia and write as many features as I could manage.

Thanks largely to a very efficient Press counsellor at the New Zealand High Commission in London, my ten days in New Zealand were as fruitful as they were enjoyable. Apart from covering the Queen's half dozen more important or colourful engagements, I managed a similar number of features. I spent 24 hours with some farmers in the Thames Valley, home to more than one million sheep and cattle, and was impressed by the austerity of their way of life: one of them, who managed 2,700 sheep and 170 beef cattle on 1,000 acres by himself (shearing and fencing apart), said that any show of affluence would produce instant ostracism. I interviewed among others the Prime Minister, Robert 'Piggy' Muldoon, and the genial and very impressive Sir Edmund Hillary, first conqueror (with Sherpa Tensing) of Everest.

I had not found time to look up the recent cuttings on Sir Edmund, who was then 57, before leaving London, but read his autobiography on the long flight. So I was alarmed when the taxi-driver taking me to the Hillary residence in a pleasant Auckland suburb said: 'Terrible thing about his wife, wasn't it?' 'Oh, what was that?' I asked. Sir Edmund's wife and one of his daughters had been killed two years previously, it transpired, when a small plane in which they were travelling crashed on an airstrip in Nepal where he was waiting for them. Ignorance of that tragedy, which happened post-autobiography, would have dented my credibility. Sir Edmund was forthright about Prime Minister Muldoon. 'I don't like and never have liked noisy and abusive people', he said.

Like most visitors I fell in love with New Zealand's scenery. I was mainly on the temperate North Island, and interviewed Muldoon in Wellington, where the Queen had opened a new parliament building designed by our own Sir Basil Spence, of Coventry cathedral fame. Someone suggested I might get a good feature from landing in a ski plane on a glacier or two in the Mount Cook sector of the (dramatically beautiful) Southern Alps on the South Island. At 12,349 feet, Mount Cook is New Zealand's highest mountain. The area is noted also for its green alpine parrots, called keas, whose noisy antics I enjoyed watching from my hotel window. They seemed to have a great sense of fun. It included sliding down corrugated iron roofs and tweaking off the rubber from windscreen wipers in the hotel car park.

Before long I was aloft in a little Cessna six-seater. Our goal was one of several glaciers at some 7,500 feet, according to landing conditions. It was, I soon discovered, far from easy to take notes on the geology as well as the drama of what we saw as we soared, swooped and banked over the braided, milky blue waters of the River Tasman, the serrated ridge known as the Minarets, and the crumpled chaos and ice pinnacles of the Hochstetter Icefall. Eventually we landed – it felt as if it was on corrugated iron – and emerged in hot sunshine to stand on the snow-covered ice some 3,000 feet deep of the Franz Josef glacier. It was an overwhelming experience. Trying to write my piece that evening, I realised my notes were inadequate (I had been taking photographs at the same time). So I rang our charmingly androgynous young pilot, Teri Cusack, and he kindly took me up alone at dawn the following morning, an even better experience which helped me sort out the geology as well as the splendour of what I was seeing. He came to see us in Hampstead a few months later.

Could I maintain the pace in Australia? The answer was No. The country was not designed for quick trips, and my visit coincided with a strike back in London involving printers' ink. Several days of publication were lost. In Canberra, however, I managed to interview the Prime Minister Malcolm Fraser, a coldish fish but an articulate one; in Brisbane, the notoriously reactionary Joh Bjelke-Petersen, Premier of the immensely rich state of Queensland; and in Sydney, Prof. Charles Birch, a leading opponent of plans to mine uranium, mainly in the Northern Territory.

My arrival at Canberra airport produced one of my most remarkable 'small world' experiences. In the Arrivals area a female voice behind me said: 'Roger! What are you doing here?' I turned around, and there was Romola Clifton, the only Australian I had ever taken out in London. She was a portrait painter, lived in distant Perth, and was paying her first visit to the Australian capital, mainly to see her sister Angela, who was married to a senator, Fred Chaney. Fred turned out to be youthful, charming, very bright and a rising star in the governing Liberal party. He and Angela soon appeared to collect Romola, pressed me into the senatorial car, dropped me at my hotel, invited me to dinner that evening, introduced me to much of the government and several ex-Prime Ministers at subsequent parties for the Queen and, best of all, invited me for a weekend picnic in the eucalyptus-covered hills not far from Canberra, along with some academic friends.

All this was informative as well as fun, since much politics was talked. They were amused that when, at that opening party, I told ex-PM John Gorton I hoped to do more interesting things than covering the Queen's activities, such as interview Mr Fraser, Gorton replied: 'Whatever makes you think that would be more interesting?' He had a point: Fraser was stiff. At a Press lunch in Canberra, I sat next to a youngish woman reporter (Australian). I said it was nice that in Oz the women said 'Yes' rather than 'Yeez', as in New Zealand. 'Did they never say 'Naw'?' she asked with a laugh.

Australia's capital may be a parochial place to live, but it was unexpectedly attractive. Designed in the early 20th century by the Chicago architect Walter Burley Griffin, it is full of parks and vistas, with a huge jet of water emerging from a lake as a focal point. Beautiful parrots flitted between the many pine trees. After heavy rain, the parks and surrounding foothills of the 'Australian Alps' were agreeably green. As we approached the Governor-General's residence for a reception for the Queen, I admired a bush seemingly covered with large pink blossoms. Then the blossom flew off: it was (no, not the Queen Mother, as a gay friend nicely suggested) a flock of cockatoos.

It rained during much of my short stay in unlovely Brisbane, where I communed with some koala bears in a park as well as with Bjelke-Petersen, and things began to go wrong. When I reached Sydney I was slow to discover that printers' ink was once again flowing and the Times was back in business. I allowed myself to be swept off to lunch with Jack Lee, the film director brother of Laurie (Cider with Rosie) Lee -- lovely house and people, too much wine – while the biggest anti-Queen demonstration was taking place in the Botanical Gardens, and our sovereign allegedly winced when a placard was thrown into her car.

I caught up with her at a subsequent engagement, at which no one seemed very troubled by the placard episode, and I gave it merely a passing mention in my report. But the news agencies went to town on it. That night I was wrenched from my hung-over slumber at 2.30am and asked to put a new 'nose' on my story; so I had to phone the news agency to find out what they had said, and cancel plans for that day in order to attend the court case involving the demonstrator. If 'you're only as good as your last story', I wasn't very good.

The Queen's engagements included a performance at Sydney Opera House of Britten's engaging comic opera, *Albert Herring*. It was interesting to see that iconic building's cut-price interior, subsequently restored to fulfil the Danish architect Jørn Utzon's original plans. Wanting to see a bit more of the area, I hired a car before leaving and drove up the Hunter Valley to a couple of impressive wineries, a rough trip but worth it for the scenery, the parrots and insights into cutting-edge wine-making technology.

My return ticket enabled me to stop off in Bangkok for a couple of days. So humidly hot was it there that when I stepped out of the plane I thought my trousers were on fire. I did the usual tourist things, partly with a very bright banker, Anthony Loehnis (later a director of the Bank of England) and his wife Jenny, whom I had encountered at the baggage carousel. He was typical of a certain type of very bright Old Etonian: amusing, slightly eccentric, shrewd. I had decided to push out the boat and stay – at my own expense, for once – at Somerset Maugham's favourite hotel, the Oriental, as had the Loehnises. There I was given a magnificent suite on the 14th floor (two rooms, two bathrooms, a kitchen) for the price of a single room, and found a note from the manager on a large bowl of fruit, bafflingly saying 'Welcome back'. Whoever they thought I was, I was grateful to him. I shared the journey back with an attractive German woman I had met at the Oriental's swimming pool. What a life.

I had been away three weeks, and received a heart-lifting welcome back. Lucy and Lottie came out first and leaped into my arms, prompting my taxi-driver to comment: 'and to think there's Mummy to come'. Joy had been somewhat overwhelmed by the response to a business venture she had started with an American friend. Called At Home in England, it involved placing American visitors with suitable British hosts. Joy was to vet the hosts, her friend, recently returned to New York from Hampstead, would recruit the American punters. Initial publicity in the UK elicited 800 letters from would-be hosts. The venture proved to be very hard work, only modestly profitable (via a percentage), and fatally vulnerable to exchange rate fluctuations. But it lasted several years and was in sometimes hilarious ways instructive about national characteristics: American kids racing around silver-laden dining tables in baseball caps, and so on. During this time Joy also managed to complete an English degree.

Finnish highlights

My trip down under was not my only debt to Her Majesty. In late May 1976 she was due to visit Finland, where brother Martin was No 2 at the embassy. I didn't expect Louis Heren to give me the OK to cover such a minor royal visit, despite the brother factor, but he did. Learning that several other organs were planning similar coverage, the Finnish embassy in London organised a preliminary informational trip in April for five of us, and Louis OK'd this too. My companions were Alexander Macleod of the Scotsman and BBC, a New Zealander who became a friend; Paul Neuburg, a bright, leftish freelance; Lajos Lederer of *The Observer*, who like Paul was of Hungarian origin but somewhat egocentric; and Norman Kirkham of *The Sunday Telegraph*. Our guide was the Finnish embassy's press counsellor, one Kristopher Graesbeck, who was garrulous and smoked, as did Lederer.

Helsinki, where our modern hotel overlooked a frozen bay, gave a more east European impression than I had expected. Our two Hungarian expatriates confirmed that parts of the city resembled Budapest; and that the two famously related languages sound similar and share many words, though with different meanings. In Helsinki we took in the fine Sibelius monument, on the theme of organ pipes; and Alvar Aalto's severely graceful Finlandia Hall, on seeing which President Giscard d'Estaing is said to have commented: *'Tiens, ça de la gueule'* ('goodness, that's got class' would be a possible translation). Aalto was surely among the 20th century's greatest architect/designers.

The journalistic high point was a lengthy session with President Urho Kekkonen, who enjoyed power comparable to that of an American president. In those Cold War years, Finland had a controversial relationship with its mighty neighbour, the Soviet Union: the term 'Finlandisation' was associated with excessive subservience to Moscow. Finnish nervousness was historically based. The country had been ceded to Russia by the Swedes in 1809, gaining independence only in 1917, after enduring a period of 'Russification'. A vicious civil war ensued in 1918. The Soviet invasion of 1939/40 was heroically resisted and independence preserved, but important territory, including much of Karelia, was lost to the Russians. Kekkonen, president from 1956 to1981 and in charge of foreign policy, aimed for a compromise between conciliation and independence, sometimes called 'active neutrality': Finland became an east-west go-between, witness the Helsinki declaration on human rights, and many negotiations on arms reductions.

My brother Martin once commented that the Finns sometimes brought the silence of the forests to the dinner table. Graesbeck was a notable exception, but even he fell silent as we were ushered into the presidential residence. It was on the edge of a lake on which the 75-year-old President skied in winter, accompanied by an ADC (on holiday, he would apparently notch up to 40km a day). A noble saluki barely raised its head from near the fireplace as we entered the sitting room. There were lots of sculptures around, of moose, lynx and other Finnish fauna. After a 10-minute wait, in came the great man, bald head gleaming in the sunlight, walking briskly with the forward-leaning stance of – it seemed to me – a man surging on skis through the flat Finnish countryside. We later agreed he had a devilishly strong presence.

The highlight of the Queen's subsequent visit was the arrival of the royal yacht *Britannia*, for which every street, balcony, window and even rooftop was festooned with Finns. It was a glorious May day, and police put the crowd at 20,000. Martin, who was No 2 in the embassy, had been away during my first trip. When the Queen reached him in the reception line, she paused and said: 'I understand your brother is behind me.' An alarming thought for the Queen, perhaps, but evidence of good briefing. There was a similar exchange when I was presented to her and Prince Philip at an enjoyable press reception on board *Britannia* that evening. To think I call myself a republican!

At one stage I joined a group in which Philip was holding forth. Not everyone who does boring jobs realises they are boring, he claimed. Had any of us had direct experience that enabled us to know? he asked a touch aggressively. I should have said yes, doing fatigues in the army. *Par contre*, Martin said Philip was very good at talking to shy staff members rather than pushy ones when he visited the embassy; and at adjusting his vocabulary to his interlocutor's. When I wrote that Prince Philip took a sauna (Martin contrived to sit next to him, reporting favourably on the ducal chassis), some craven *Times* sub-editor changed it to 'visited a sauna bath'. Would the idea of Philip naked have been too much for *Times* readers? The royal visit to Finlandia Hall for a concert (inevitably Sibelius, whose work I love) was rendered the more moving by the death of Alvar Aalto, its architect, a couple of weeks earlier.

The best moments of my Finnish experience came after the Queen's departure, when Martin drove us to a lodge on the edge of a lake in central Finland. There we cooked a delicious steak washed down with good claret and watched the sinking sun dapple the lake with pink and purple reflections, like a series of vibrant paintings by Paul Rothko. It never got truly dark, and as we went to bed around 1.45am after many a whisky, a couple of cuckoos were calling to each other.

A more stressful assignment in 1976 was to cover a general election in Malta. There the feisty Labour Prime Minister Dom Mintoff, who saw the island as a bridge between the Arab world and Europe, beat off a challenge from the Nationalist party under the veteran Dr George Borg Olivier. The Maltese were friendly enough, though not to each other: election tactics involved some judicious arson. Their food and housing were depressing reflections of Britain's colonial legacy – and the Catholic church loomed large. The second, less crowded island, Gozo, had better vibes and landscape.

A handful of freebies, and back to L.A.

Trips categorised as freebies (i.e. financed by the host) often spring from the desire of small geographical entities to keep themselves in the public eye. Hong Kong, then still a British colony, was one such. I had not been there since returning by ship from Korea in 1954, so was delighted to fill one such slot in March 1978. I couldn't avoid writing about HK's trade and its small but complex dosage of local democracy, and had added (knowing something about Harlow New Town) housing development as a theme, to get me about in the New Territories on the mainland. I was thoroughly spoilt over the next five days: met at the airport, put up at the plush Mandarin Hotel, driven to all appointments. But the programme was packed.

The colony had of course changed beyond recognition. There were now high-rise blocks *passim*, new roads, glittering shops, teeming people, flaunted wealth as well as shanty towns, a chorus of pneumatic drills: the energy of the place was exhilarating yet exhausting. Only the weather was disappointing: grey and too often wet and misty. As often, fellow journalists helped leaven the diet of briefings. I had several meals with David Bonavia, former *Times* correspondent in Moscow and Peking, now in HK with the *Far East Economic Review*, and his wife Judy. She did not accompany us on a jolly tour of topless bars one evening. At David's suggestion I contrived a trip (just over an hour by jet hydrofoil) to what was still the Portuguese colony of Macao, some 40 miles to the south-west. With its peeling façades and avenues lined with banyan trees, it seemed a world away from Hong Kong. In the 21st century its revenue from casinos has outstripped Las Vegas's.

As usual my diplomatic connections were helpful. The respected Governor, Sir Murray Maclehose, had worked for Dad in Whitehall. He welcomed me warmly, as did his political adviser David Wilson, a friend of Martin's and later himself Governor. The Wilsons invited me to an interesting dinner party with a cross-section of the HK (mainly white) establishment.

Sir Murray reckoned the Governor had three constituencies: Whitehall and Westminster; Peking; and Hong Kong itself (where he had latterly had difficulties with police corruption). One needed backing in at least two of these to have a chance of success. He saw no reason why an ex-politician should not cope as well as a diplomat. [With hindsight, Chris Patten, the last Governor, subsequently alienated at least the first two constituencies, though not necessarily to HK's disadvantage].

Divided Cyprus

The Greek Cypriots also liked to remind the world of their existence. Hence the convening, in May 1978, of a *soi-disant* Commonwealth Communications Conference in Nicosia, organised by the Cyprus High Commission in London: an unvarnished propaganda exercise. I was happy to go, and could take Joy for £89. To reduce the risk of orphaning the girls, she came a day later. It proved to be a high-level yet jolly affair.

Divided Nicosia still bore the scars of battle from the Turkish invasion of 1974, following a coup backed by Greece's military junta. The Turks seized the northern 38 per cent of Cyprus, with much bloodshed. We heard a lot about how the Greek Cypriots had made good the economic loss of the most productive part of the island, and about their progress in rehousing refugees from the north: both genuinely remarkable feats. We were treated to an impassioned harangue by President Kyprianou about the monstrousness of the island's division and of the suicidal terms for a settlement proposed by the Turks – but nothing about the sufferings of the Turkish Cypriots in inter-communal strife in the 1960s, or about the military coup that had precipitated the Turkish invasion.

As a Turkish Cypriot minister I visited across the 'green line' remarked, the Greek Cypriot government seemed to suffer from a 'psychosis of forgetfulness.' For them, history began with the Turkish invasion. 'The nub of the matter', I wrote in my subsequent feature, 'is that the Turkish Cypriot community, which for the first time feels really secure behind the "Attila line", is most unlikely to make any concessions which will be politically acceptable to the Greek side.' As I write some 30 years on, the island remains divided, despite Cyprus's accession to the EU. A recent United Nations plan for a confederal solution was accepted by the Turkish Cypriots in a referendum, but rejected in the south.

Foreign journalists were allowed to visit the north, so Joy and I headed through golden fields of corn, olive, lemon and orange groves past Turkish military cantonments to coastal Kyrenia. Much of the citrus crop was rotting on the ground, and in the villages men were sitting around doing nothing. One could understand the bitterness of former Greek Cypriot owners. The atmosphere was dispiriting. In Kyrenia, where many buildings were pockmarked with bullet holes and there was some destruction in evidence, we were hailed by a couple of resident Brits who had clung on, with tales of the horrors of the invasion. We also visited the village of Bellapaix, immortalised in Lawrence Durrell's then popular memoir *Bitter Lemons*. Our trip ended next day on a low note: the taxi-driver who took us to the airport was the most dangerous I have encountered, overtaking on the brow of hills at 85mph, an experience as frightening as it was enraging. I was in the front seat. So much for not orphaning the girls.

To California via a house-swap

For our main family holiday in 1978, a record year for travel, we did a house-swap with a colleague of American friends in California, Arthur and Elaine Alexander. They had been living in Hampstead while Arthur did a stint at the International Institute for Strategic Studies in London, and Joy had become close to Elaine. Arthur had recently reverted to the Rand Corporation, a defence-oriented research institute in Santa Monica, and had put up a notice there asking if anyone would like to do a house-swap with friends in London. Of the three respondents, he chose the one with the biggest swimming pool, in Pacific Palisades, a smart suburb of Los Angeles, not far from the sea and their own home.

Our swapping partners, the Grahams – he was a brilliant aeronautics engineer with Rand – stayed on for our first night to show us how the house worked, and invited some neighbours to meet us. Their house was so ideal it made us feel guilty about the inadequacies of our Hampstead home, especially its tiny kitchen. We used their huge

Ford estate wagon to visit Disneyland, Universal Studios, the Hollywood Bowl for a concert, the beach of course – and finally friends in San Francisco, the Napa Valley's wineries and Yosemite national park. The girls were then 11 and nine, perfect ages for maximum enjoyment of such pleasures. I gave a talk at Rand on the EEC, interviewed Stephen Garrett, the British director of the then small but overpoweringly wealthy Getty Museum, wrote an LA Diary for *The Times*, and played some tennis. It was a great experience.

....and to the two Germanies

My contacts with the West German embassy resulted in an invitation to pay a return trip to the Federal Republic in October 1978. This took me to Bonn, Ludwigshafen, Munich and Stuttgart, which I had never visited. My guide there was a towering law student, Jürgen Schwab. He took me for a tour of the Black Forest area, including his own Tübingen university: charming city, great landscape in all its autumn glory, and unexpectedly good food. Our driver remarked laconically: '*Essen tut man gut fast überall hier*' (literally 'eating one does well practically everywhere here'). As for the local Swabians, they were notoriously *sparsam*, economical, he said: the Scots of Germany. Many were *heimlich reich* (secretly rich). He told the story of a dying man who asked his wife for a *pretzel*, a Swabian speciality. As he seemed near his end, she put some butter on it for once. 'Ah, I haven't even closed my eyes, and the fat living has begun', he said.

I also visited the headquarters of the *Stuttgarter Zeitung*, a much-admired leftish daily, which had gone over to the new computerised, direct-input technology. It took Eddie Shah and Rupert Murdoch a further eight years and much strife to reach the same point in England. The human highlight was an interview with Manfred Rommel, Stuttgart's mayor and chief executive, and son of the legendary General Erwin Rommel, the 'Desert Fox'. Rommel *fils* was a genial, plumpish, pipe-smoking Christian Democrat, of liberal persuasion. Then 51, he was 15 when his father died aged 52, but remembered his interest in mathematics and engineering, and his practical and ascetic streaks. He received many letters about his father, and requests from historians. 'I am responsible to history to help historians', he said. 'But history is responsible to me to let me have a little peace!'

I wanted to balance this trip with one to the German Democratic Republic, which I had visited only fleetingly while in Bonn. The aim was to spend some nine days in East Berlin, Weimar, Dresden and Leipzig, looking into various aspects of the GDR's development, possibly including agriculture and sport (I had recently interviewed a charming GDR sprinter, Marita Koch, in London).

I was met at East Berlin's Schönefeld airport and taken in a Russian Lada through grey industrial suburbs to a new and sparsely populated International Press Centre. There I found my programme to be long on tourism and short of human encounters, even with officialdom; and it had a sting in its tail. Thanks to the inclusion of unwanted items such as a minder and a driver, and adhering to the official exchange rate, my costs were put at the equivalent of £727, without hotel bills. Half was to be paid up front in convertible currency. Having brought less than that for my total expenditure, I said I would have to take the next plane home unless the bill was drastically slashed. Both my organiser and I said we would consult. That evening I wandered along Unter den Linden, feeling pessimistic, and next morning was told no reduction was possible. *The Times's* foreign desk advised a swift return. I was happy to oblige, and wrote a scathing piece on my return, which I was asked to regurgitate for West German radio. I was sad to miss seeing more of that time-warped Stasiland, where oppression and mutual suspicion had been the norm since the 1930s.

'Anna'

At around this time a chance encounter led to an episode that caused both me and Joy much anguish, though it ultimately led to a belated grasping of marital nettles. It was Yevgeny Yevtushenko who indirectly introduced me to 'Anna'. I was asked to cover a recital by the Russian poet at the Wigmore Hall. Joy couldn't come, so I had a spare ticket, which I gave to the most attractive woman in the queue, a tallish, blonde American, who thus sat next to me. Despite having to write most of my piece during the interval, there was a strong sense of mutual discovery. She was a psychiatric social worker based at the Tavistock clinic, with a daughter of Lottie's age, a separated husband in Birmingham, and an informed interest in the arts. She had seemingly had a fling some time back with Yevtushenko on the QE2. We saw a good deal of each other over the next three months. She seemed torn between wanting to help me improve my relationship with Joy and the hope that I might come to live with her. I too felt torn, our marriage being in an unhappy state. Even though, amazingly, Anna and I never slept together, she seemed to offer a chance to become a whole and fulfilled person again.

As part of that process, she urged me to go and see a shrink, which I did, with on the whole helpful results. Among the problematic factors the psychologist diagnosed were: a sense of rejection resulting from my evacuation to Canada; a consequent reluctance to make a heavy emotional investment in any one woman; a desire for security typified by attachment to home and objects (pictures etc); a dominant and critical father (hence my stammer); ten years in boarding schools and resulting failure to achieve equal relationships with women; and a tendency to hero-worship older men (Tim Tosswill, Maurice Ash, Charles Wintour). None of this surprised me, but it was interesting to hear it from an objective outsider.

To test my feelings toward Anna, I decided to stop seeing her for a trial month, during which it became clear to me that my love for Joy, not to mention Lucy and Lottie, was considerably stronger and more enduring than my feelings for Anna. She was deeply upset when I told her I did not want to see her any more, and I felt a worm – but also a great sense of relief, and my relationship with Joy improved rapidly.

One of my more bizarre assignments came in May 1977. I was in the office finishing off a story about a NATO summit in London that had brought President Jimmy Carter to Europe for the first time. Louis Heren came over and said: 'Keep this to yourself until it's announced in about 10 minutes, but Peter Jay is going to be ambassador in Washington.' Jay, son of the former Cabinet minister Douglas Jay, was the economics editor of our Business News section. I was to go over there, interview him, and then write a profile for the all-too-imminent first edition. I found him wearing a yachting tie and a sheepish smile, saying: 'Sorry to have got you into this rather strange situation.' I left him at 5.50pm, and had written 1,000 words by 7pm. Incredulity at the appointment was general, not least because Peter was married to Prime Minister Callaghan's daughter Margaret, producing cries of 'nepotism!' I had enormous pleasure in spreading the news at a largely diplomatic party to which I then headed, on a distinct high. In the office someone quipped: 'How about consul general in Ulan Bator for you then, Roger?'

Family developments

Parental morale at this stage was at a low ebb. Thanks to medical incompetence, my father had endured three prostate operations: the first two, in Colchester, failed to relieve the blockage, so he was sent by ambulance to a leading specialist in London, who was more successful. Meanwhile my mother had broken a finger, which made caring for Dad difficult. Feeling that the great reaper might be beckoning, he spent several weekends telling me about his life, with me taking notes. His opening words were: 'One thing you must bear in mind – Mother and I were both the product of incompatible marriages.' It made me realise how lucky we had been that there was so much genuine love and tenderness between him and Mother, despite their differences in temperament. Fortunately Dad lived another 12 years, long enough to write his own memoirs, even if too long for his own and everyone else's good.

I took a sabbatical month off in early 1978 (a recently introduced reward for 10 years service), and used it partly to help decide the question of Lucy's secondary education. Should she go from her goodish local state primary up the road at New End to a private or state school? Lucy, a typical No 1 child, was naturally hard-working, keen to excel and socially confident, so could have flourished at a comprehensive. By far the best in the locality was Camden, a former grammar school that Joy had attended. Its intake was drawn from three ability bands: 25 per cent from bands one and three, 50 per cent from band two. Siblings of former pupils had priority. Since Camden had taken girls on a competitive basis, their siblings tended to mop up most of band one. The remaining half dozen or so places were allocated mainly on the basis of geographical proximity, and we were miles away. Extreme social factors were also taken into account, leading Tony Arlidge, a rising barrister and fellow New End parent, to comment: 'But you're obviously too selfish to divorce or commit suicide, Roger!'

So Camden was out, leaving Haverstock, Hampstead and Parliament Hill comprehensives: at the latter, which then had the best reputation, the headmistress

Lucy and Lottie in their teens

With Lis, Binnie and Martin, probably 1970s

addressed prospective parents with a cigarette in one hand, an ash tray in the other. There were also two accessible private girls' schools with excellent reputations: South Hampstead and North London Collegiate. The former was nearby, and handy for making local friends, but was on a cramped site with poor sports facilities. N. London Collegiate had an even better academic record and superb facilities of all sorts, but was out at Edgware, involving a Tube journey and a long walk from Edgware station. With Lucy's encouragement, we opted for NLC, and she sailed in. The fees were a fairly modest £800 a year.

We were worried about Lottie, who didn't seem to be learning much at New End from a rather wet teacher, with the prospect of a disagreeable and unstable one the following year. Lottie had a strong personality, was dominating some of her weaker classmates, and sided with the more rebellious ones. Miraculously, we found a vacancy at a good local independent primary, St Christopher's. I could walk her there in the mornings, and she settled in quickly. Once, when I picked her up from a friend's house in ritzy Chalcot Square, she asked me what I thought about money. 'Well', I said, 'I think that if you have too much of it, or a great deal, it can be dangerous because it cuts you off from other people – you forget how other people live.' She pondered this awhile, then said: 'I think we have just about the right amount of money, don't you?' I said that sometimes I felt we could use a bit more, but on the whole I thought she was absolutely right. Worried by the gap between her paper work and her powers of expression, we had referred her to an educational psychologist. She scored 146 on the Wechsler scale, which the psychologist said was higher than any other child she had tested. The potential was clearly there. But it was tough having a sister who was such a paragon.

The great Times *suspension*

Back at the office in the unlovely Gray's Inn Road, a crisis loomed. For months the management of *The Times* and its sister publications had been trying to negotiate terms for an end to trade union stoppages and for the introduction of the new direct-input printing technology – which would make most printers redundant. To increase pressure, management had set a deadline of 30 November 1978 for a settlement, failing which production would be suspended: printers would be made redundant, but journalists would, as innocent parties, remain on full salaries. The print unions dug in their trotters, and *The Times*, *The Sunday Times* and their various supplements were suspended on the appointed day. To be paid for doing nothing, or very little, might seem an ideal situation. But it was not so simple. There were fears that the closure might become permanent, and that some 400 journalists would find themselves out of a job at the same time. Without the stimulus of regular work, some colleagues became depressed and found their powers of concentration waning. We had to show up at the office once or twice a week, in rotation, to maintain some sort of *esprit de corps* and in case there was a sudden settlement; and there were endless meetings of our 'chapel' (branch) of the National Union of Journalists, which was deeply divided over the desirability of showing solidarity with the locked-out print unions.

It was unfortunate that the 'father' of the NUJ chapel and future president of the NUJ itself, Jake Ecclestone, was of the militant left, as was a key supporter of his, the Times's labour editor, Paul Routledge. Both were natural class warriors, and they had an ideal antagonist in Marmaduke Hussey, the managing director and chief executive of Times Newspapers Ltd, and main architect of the lock-out. With his great height and patrician manner, 'Duke' Hussey – who went on to become a notorious chairman of the BBC's governors – seemed to embody the ruling class. I had a bit of a soft spot for him: he was a larger than life character, and his charming and amusing wife Susan (née Waldegrave), a lady-in-waiting to the Queen, had been helpful to me on royal tours. [Having been badly wounded in the Second World War, Hussey had a prosthetic leg. Once, the story goes, he fell downstairs at Buckingham Palace. When someone suggested getting a doctor, his wife reputedly said: 'It's not a doctor we need, it's a blacksmith!'] On most issues, such as whether or not to cross picket lines or cooperate with a management scheme to print a weekly edition of *The Times* in West Germany, we 'moderates' fortunately had a small majority.

Although my own morale fluctuated, it was sustained by freelance commissions, *inter alia* for the *Spectator*, *Le Matin de Paris* and *Die Zeit*, longer term projects for *The Times*, and a somewhat alarming idea put to me by Charlie Douglas-Home, who was now foreign editor. Would I like to go to Jerusalem for six months as a stop-gap correspondent once re-publication seemed certain? The editor wanted someone who could convey the 'full cultural interest' of Israel. I could also spend some time in Cairo (there was the prospect of a treaty between Israel and Egypt, which President Carter helped become a reality). My family could be flown out at half time to spend a holiday with me. But why, I asked Charlie, did they not use this caesura in the paper's affairs to make a final decision on whom to send to Jerusalem? He looked a bit sheepish, then admitted he had wanted to send David Watts, but the editor considered him too pro-Arab – so for God's sake don't tell William your sympathies are similar, he added with a laugh.

After discussing the pros and cons with Joy, I decided with a heavy heart that I should accept. The idea of spending so long away from the family was upsetting, but it would be a fascinating, and perhaps career-enhancing, experience. So I started wading through such books as the prolix memoirs of Israel's former foreign minister Abba Eban. Fortunately, as the prospect of *The Times* reopening on the new target date in April 1979 receded, it was decided to send the more news-oriented Christopher Walker, who had been reporting ably from the front line in Belfast. Once again I felt a great sense of relief.

The genesis of my Sutherland biography

A tiresome feature of the stoppage was to be asked the same two questions by all and sundry: 'When is *The Times* coming back?' and 'Are you writing a book?' For years I had not merely fancied the idea of authorship, but been pained by the number of books by friends and colleagues (notably from *The Sunday Times*) that thrust themselves on my attention in bookshops. The stoppage was an ideal opportunity to get something going. Freelance commissions were enjoyable, but an evasion. Moreover, I had a valid idea. Shortly before the suspension, in July 1978, I had interviewed Graham Sutherland for the arts page, just before his 75th birthday.

Graham was at the time in his beloved Pembrokeshire. 'It's one of the reassuring things in life that Roger always looks the same', he charitably observed to his wife Kathy when I arrived by train. Graham was a wonderful interviewee, expressing himself in vivid and jargon-free language in a voice of great charm. 'Has anyone tried to write your biography?' I asked before leaving Haverfordwest. 'Well, someone [Leslie Frewin] did try, but I got an injunction to stop publication', he replied. Yes, Graham could be difficult. I never learned the grounds for that injunction, but I filed the idea of a Sutherland biography away – before returning to it in the spring of 1979, when Graham agreed to cooperate, albeit without great enthusiasm. 'I think it is a disability on your part that you don't know more about painting', he said – meaning, I like to think, the act of painting. 'It makes it more difficult to describe what I have been trying to do, which I think I am beginning to understand more clearly in my old age.'

A positive response to the idea from my childhood friend Giles de la Mare, of Faber and Faber, helped get me going. Sutherland was a good subject, both as man and artist. He was still pretty famous, and he and his wife Kathy, a former fashion artist, were a glamorous couple. They lived in some style in the south of France and when in London, stayed at the discreetly opulent Connaught Hotel, where they treated Joy and me to a delicious meal. Although Graham was, for a biographer, disappointingly monogamous, he had an endearing talent for alienating his friends and supporters, notably the art historian Douglas Cooper. The beautiful Kathy, a Cerberus with a waspish if often amusing tongue, sometimes played a helpful role in these rows.

Graham's life seemed to divide naturally into chapters. As an artist, he had been in turn a successful etcher, a leader of the neo-Romantic movement in British painting, a distinguished war artist, a controversial portrait painter of famous people (Somerset Maugham, Lord Beaverbrook, Winston Churchill, Helena Rubinstein among many others), and a not much less controversial religious artist (the Northampton Crucifixion, the vast Coventry Cathedral tapestry). My preference was for his Welsh landscapes of the 1935-1950 period, often seen as his most enduring and influential achievement.

I needed a literary agent to ensure the best possible publishing deal. An office colleague recommended Michael Sissons of A.D.Peters (as it then was), a daunting but highly-rated operator leading a very successful agency. He agreed to take me on, and urged me to write a synopsis of the book as I envisaged it. He then put this to several suitable publishers. Faber made the first bid of £4,000, which Weidenfeld and Nicholson matched. Jonathan Cape also showed interest. After an exciting week, I was thrilled to hear it had gone to Faber for 'seven five'. This advance (against royalties) would be payable in three slices: the first on signing the contract, the second on delivering the text, the third on publication.

Given the uncertainty about the length of *The Times* stoppage, and the difficulty of eventually combining research with a return to full-time work, I launched straight into a series of interviews with Sutherland's friends and family, and with Graham himself. He had a charming house in Kent, but lived most of the time in tax exile near Menton. Among my first interviewees were his delightful brother Humphrey, keeper of coins at the Ashmolean museum in Oxford, whose every word I could have used; the Rev. Walter Hussey, former Dean of Chichester Cathedral, who had commissioned Sutherland's great wartime Crucifixion for a church in Northampton; and the gossipy King's Road framer Alfred Hecht.

The latter nearly caused Sutherland to cancel the whole project. He told Graham that I had asked him what impact he thought the death in infancy of the Sutherlands' only child had had on Graham and Kathy. Graham deduced from this admittedly prurient-seeming question, and perhaps my past on the Londoner's Diary, that the book was not going to be as serious as befitted an artist of his status, and wondered whether he should call it off. It required all my powers of reassurance to keep the show on the road.

Sutherland-related travel

I recorded most of my interviews, with 70 or 80 of Graham's relatives, friends and associates, on an elegant little Japanese tape-recorder ('What a pity you don't have good shorthand, Roger', said Graham, in his typically unsettling way. 'I always feel self-conscious in front of a tape-recorder.' He soon got over it). I transcribed virtually all these tapes verbatim, a very tedious activity, but it does get them into one's memory. If they covered different phases of Graham's life, I cut up the transcripts, plopping the relevant passage into the relevant chapter file. I also spent many even more tedious hours in the libraries of newspaper offices, photocopying useful press cuttings.

Two interviews took me abroad. The first was to meet Graham's greatest fans of his later years: Pier Paolo and Marzia Ruggerini, who had more than 100 items by Sutherland (it has since risen to 600-plus), some of them ravishing. They lived in a handsome house ('Il Castello') on the Lombardy plain, whose interior courtyard was guarded by three fierce Dobermanns. Marzia, a beautiful woman, told me not very reassuringly that she had once caught these dogs shredding her favourite cat, tried to save it, fell over and was attacked herself. Her shoulder was lacerated, her nose almost severed. The scar was visible. Later, when a servant was grating a truffle on our pasta, one of these alarming beasts got into the dining room. I feared it was going to identify me as an alien and have a go at me, but all was well. In a very Italian way, Pier Paolo combined being an art dealer with a licence to sell nationalised gas. Quite how he acquired so many of Graham's war drawings has never been explained.

The second trip was to Montreux, to meet two Sutherland portrait subjects, Wendy and Emery Reves, who were staying in a grand hotel on the lake of Geneva. Emery was a Hungarian émigré who had made a lot of money as an anti-fascist literary agent in pre-war Paris. Among his clients was Winston Churchill, of whose war memoirs Reves subsequently acquired the foreign rights. In 1945 he had published a book called *The Anatomy of Peace*, which Albert Einstein recommended to listeners in his first radio interview after the USA's nuclear bomb wiped out Hiroshima. It subsequently sold 800,000 copies in 30 languages. Wendy, by origin Texan, had been a fashion model in New York, was warmly effervescent and had retained her pert good looks. Among her admirers was Churchill, with whom Emery had remained in touch. With his retinue, Churchill spent some 400 days of his increasingly senile retirement at the Reves' villa in Roquebrune between 1955 and 1960: a sort of flattering nightmare.

Emery was a remarkable collector of just about everything, and commissioned Graham to paint both his and Wendy's portrait. In the flesh, he seemed as melancholy as Wendy was bouncy. Next day, on a balcony overlooking the lake of Geneva (it's a tough life), I debriefed him about his career. A few weeks later, I was on duty at the renascent *Times* when news came through that he had died. I sped home to collect the relevant notebook, and wrote a quick feature about this strange man. Wendy thought it wonderful, and when she was subsequently touting the Reves collection around various U.S. and international museums, she would slap a photo-copy of my piece in front of the visiting museum director and say proudly: 'That's who Emery was!' Eventually the collection went to the chief gallery in her native city, the Dallas Museum of Art.

Graham himself, with whom I had had only three or four interviews and exchanged a few letters, died aged 76 in February 1980, considerably sooner than I (as well as he!) might have wished, stricken by galloping liver cancer. His last days were spent tantalisingly close, at the Royal Free Hospital ten minutes' walk from our Hampstead home. He wished to be visited only by those closest to him: it was subtly humiliating to have one's subject dying down the road without being able to see him. I sent him some tulips, with an affectionate message. At one stage, Kathy rang to say, rather ambiguously: 'Graham's on the way out.' Not long after, it was: 'Graham's gone.' The news was soon on all radio bulletins, and naturally I wrote a tribute in *The Times* (not the rather dry obit).

'When I die, I want you to stay at the Connaught', Graham had told Kathy. Did he mean for a few nights, or for good? Probably the former, given that it is one of London's most expensive hotels, but Kathy thought the latter. So, once she had sorted things out at their home in Kent, to the Connaught I regularly went. She took me through their lives together, and eventually I showed her what I was writing: I like to think it was a therapeutic process for her. She was far more generous in giving me access to Graham's letters, pocket diaries and photographs than he probably would have been, and much less critical of what I wrote. Difficult as he was, Graham would have challenged every remotely unflattering paragraph, with the threat of denying copyright for illustrations. His death spared me a nightmare.

The last straw for Lord Thomson

To revert to the suspended *Times*: in June 1979, any sympathy the proprietor, Lord Thomson, may have felt for us frustrated journalists must have vanished when the NUJ chapel put in a claim for a pay rise of 61 per cent, this despite our having been paid for the last six months for doing very little. I was among the few who voted against such a bid. Management had already indicated a willingness to give us a 40 per cent rise on resumption, taking putative savings on new technology, parity with *Sunday Times* salaries and other factors into account. Who would want to own a newspaper staffed by such ingrates? As it transpired, *The Times* re-emerged after an 11-month absence on November 13 1979, without the management having achieved a satisfactory agreement with the print unions – or indeed with its journalists. They, almost incredibly, went on strike over pay for a week in August 1980. This must have been the last straw for Ken Thomson. That October, Thomson British Holdings announced it was 'withdrawing from the publication of *The Times, The Sunday Times* and their associated publications'. If they were not sold, they would be closed.

Back at work in the edgy interim, I had found it quite hard to re-establish my old combination of the political, the diplomatic and the cultural – though I contributed numerous London Diaries, an enjoyable reversion to an old role, and signed at last with my name. I also spent a stimulating fortnight in September helping to cover a general election in West Germany, visiting Bonn, Essen, Kiel, Bremen, Hamburg, and the beautiful town of Duderstadt, near the GDR border.

Perhaps the feature of which I was proudest involved spending some 40 hours, spread over a week, at a psychiatric hospital in Essex. Such institutions tended to be written about only when something had gone wrong. My idea was to portray an average hospital in a state of normality. I asked Tessa Jowell, then assistant director of the mental health charity Mind, to recommend one such, not too far from London. She came up with Goodmayes, near Chelmsford. I explained to a managerial meeting there what I wanted to do, they said OK, and gave me carte blanche to talk to anyone I liked: from patients, consultants (it was an enclave of South African Jewish exiles) to nurses, social workers and cleaning staff. No doubt I undertook to show them what I wrote, to ensure accuracy and no breaches of privacy.

Rarely in my career have I felt I was learning so much so quickly. Perhaps I was most shocked by the length of time many of the patients had been there: for one it was 73 years (since she was five), for another 70 years. Two had been there for 65 years and 19 for 50 years or more. And then there were the smells and the noise. Who was that shouting all the time, I asked the amazingly spirited nurse in the long-stay, psychogeriatric ward? 'That's Eddie', she said, 'a chronic schizophrenic who has been in since 1934. He's talking to his voices. He takes on the identity of past patients. Mr Green wants a cigarette, he will say. He is still in touch with reality: you can hold a fairly reasonable conversation with him.'

I think I had hoped to reveal something shocking about the excessive use of drugs. But two consultants unhesitatingly admitted that drugs were administered for the benefit of staff as well as patients: with more staff to keep an eye on patients, fewer drugs would be needed. Nurses complained that keeping tabs on 'wanderers', who might be depressives bent on suicide, imposed the greatest strain. My piece was given an entire page, illustrated with a brilliant photograph by Brian Harris. It had some impact. 'Perhaps we should do this sort of thing more often', the Social Services Secretary, Patrick Jenkin, was said to have commented, though 'we' had done nothing to initiate it.

For a separate feature, I attended a clinic at Goodmayes where electro-convulsive therapy (ECT) was being administered to depressives who had more or less withdrawn from the world. To prevent them convulsing too violently, they were injected with a 'muscle-relaxant' so powerful that their lungs ceased to operate, requiring them to be given oxygen. Even so, they twitched. Although I could accept that these people needed shocking back into reality, I found the spectacle so disturbing that I felt faint and had to be helped into a chair.

I was now in my mid-40s (was it my prime?), rising at 6am to make progress on the Sutherland book before a family breakfast, working a full day back at *The Times*, often putting in a couple of hours on the book in the evening and around eight hours at weekends, squeezing in Sutherland-related interviews on the way home, writing countless letters, and so on. All this put an extra strain on Joy, who was struggling with At Home in England and her difficult American partner, as well as the girls. We were also worried about the future of *The Times* and the propensity of new owners to seek new staff.

With publication of the Sutherland book due in 1982, I decided to risk taking nine months off to finish research and do the actual writing. It was just after I'd finished the third chapter that we heard that Rupert Murdoch had acquired the whole *Times* stable, with various unconvincing guarantees about editorial independence. I was not cheered to hear that he had appointed Harry Evans, editor of *The Sunday Times*, as editor vice Rees-Mogg. 'The new editor resembles a fox terrier, constantly yapping and flushing journalists from their comfortable bolt-holes. An enthusiast!' I wrote to a cousin after I'd put in a few days at the office. With staggering naiveté, I thought this might be the moment to secure my ambition to be features editor (a senior but actually rather horrible, nerve-racking desk job). Like most new editors, Harry preferred to have his own creatures around him. He didn't bother to answer my letter, and gave the job to Tony Holden, with Peter Stothard, then not an obvious future *Times* editor, as Holden's deputy.

I felt it wise to attend a sort of inaugural meeting of the home staff, with bustling Harry in the chair. He went around the boardroom table, asking each of us in turn what we wanted to contribute to the 'new' *Times*. Cue emetically bright-eyed, bushy-tailed responses. By the time Evans got to me, about three-quarters of the way around the table, I couldn't resist saying: 'Well, Harry, from what I've heard, some much-needed languor, and perhaps a bit of style.' This endeared me to my colleagues, but not to the great enthusiast. That WOSB spirit rode again.

Sutherland: publication and the dreaded reviews

Career considerations aside, I was under some pressure to finish Sutherland, since a retrospective of his work had been fixed for May 1982 at the Tate Gallery (now Tate Britain). It was more exciting than I expected to go through my file for each chapter, listing everything I had to get in and making unexpected connections. I showed a few chapters to Giles at Faber. He urged me to cut down on detail and dates, to stand back a bit more, and remind the reader of the broader picture. I realised that a newspaper feature has to carry a reader for only a short burst, so one can pack in the facts. The reader of a book is potentially with you for longer stretches, so the text must be less dense. Inevitably at first I wrote too much, horrified at the idea of wasting material so arduously garnered. Averaging about 2,000 words a day, my first draft ran to 625 typed A4 pages. These I reduced in six weeks to 400 simpler, clearer, faster-paced ones, with shorter sentences: a concentrated burst of effort that gave the book a consistent tone and enabled me to catch those repeats to which authors are prone. Inside every fat chapter a thin one lurked. It was a challenge to release it.

There remained much to be done with the illustrations, but initial reactions to the text from Faber were encouraging. A few months later I was able to hold in my hand the dust jacket, with which I was delighted, as I was subsequently with the binding and spine. It was a dream realised. There was moreover thrilling news on the serialisation front, thanks to the legendary skills of Pat Kavanagh of A.D.Peters: *The Sunday Telegraph*, then bracing itself for competition from the new *Mail on Sunday*, bid £20,000 for three extracts. Since the higher tax rate was then 60 per cent, I would lose much of that. But at least my nine months loss of salary would be more than made good.

A week or so before the first serialised slice was published, huge posters went up around London. They showed a large gilt picture frame enclosing a Churchillian hand with index and second finger parted in the well-known V gesture, with the caption (if I remember it correctly): 'This is what Churchill thought of Sutherland's portrait of him', and urging everyone to read more about it in the first instalment of a new biography of the painter. All very gratifying – except that nowhere was the author's name mentioned. It was however prominent in the very well edited extracts in *The Sunday Telegraph*.

There came the dreaded moment of the first reviews. Of these, someone once advised: 'Don't read them, measure them!' By that criterion I did well. The book was taken seriously: my chief fear was of being dismissed as a superficial journalist unequal to the task. The first review was by J.W.Lambert, *The Sunday Times*'s literary editor.

He first raised what was to be a frequent, not unreasonable complaint: that the book was over-detailed. Like most reviewers, he devoted much of his considerable space to a judicious summary of the book's contents. I winced only once, when he wrote: 'He sets out the stations of the charming but fretful pilgrim's progress in serviceable prose.' Serviceable?! One critic kindly referred to the 'easy elegance' of my style, while another said its banality was 'occasionally downright hilarious'. Ouch!

Lambert was a good deal kinder than the poet Stephen Spender in *The Listener*, the BBC's classy but long since defunct weekly journal. Spender accused me of separating Sutherland's life from his art, adding: 'The biographer of an artist is a critic or he is nothing.' Don't worry, said a literary friend. To be reviewed at length by Spender is far more important than what he says. It means your book matters. In fact Spender was not alone in considering the book short on critical evaluation. With hindsight, I should have made my views on the various phases of Graham's work clearer. It was a case of misplaced diffidence. In *The Times* Richard Holmes called my book a 'marvellous introduction' to the Sutherland retrospective that had just opened at the Tate Gallery, a kind but rather short-term view.

Graham Sutherland: A Biography was published in May 1982, price £12.50 (I argued hard against £15). I had returned to the 'new' *Times* in August 1981, somewhat nervously, albeit more or less recognised as the chief feature writer. Tony Holden was all charm as features editor, but it soon became obvious that his loyalty was to Harry Evans rather than to some relic of the Rees-Mogg era, as he doubtless saw me. Peter Stothard, the deputy features editor, also ex-*Sunday Times*, was a tougher character. In a letter to my brother I described him as 'an arrogant if intelligent thug'. Intelligent certainly, but curiously inarticulate: he had difficulty outlining what he wanted from a feature, though less in later describing how I had failed to deliver it.

The Harry Evans factor

As for Harry Evans, he was in some ways a breath of fresh air, and his generally social democratic views were much closer to mine than Rees-Mogg's. But he was having difficulty adjusting to the very different rhythms of a daily as opposed to a weekly newspaper, causing chaos and printing delays by wanting to rewrite pieces late in the evening. At the adjacent *Sunday Times*, there had been strong men, generally hired by his predecessor Denis Hamilton, who could help Harry sort good ideas from bad. At *The Times*, there was a tendency to defer to the new editor.

Harry was keen to sustain his image as a campaigning journalist, and asked me to write a strong piece about the unsexy subject of non-tariff barriers to trade within the EEC, i.e. ways, other than import duties, of keeping out competitive goods from other member states. I was happy enough to find various, often amusing examples, such as the French (inevitably the worst offenders) insisting on metal balls being bounced against imported wooden doors: if the balls left a dent, the doors were banned. Unfortunately, everyone I talked to said NTBs were really a minor problem compared with fluctuations in the exchange rate. When I turned in my nuancé feature, Harry summoned me and said: 'I'm afraid this isn't the sort of campaigning piece I was looking for.' I replied that I had shown it to the MEP who had suggested the idea to him (Basil 'Boz' de Ferranti, a typical wealthy Evans friend) and he thought it excellent. I don't suppose Harry was too thrilled that I had thus protected myself.

Two other episodes left a bad taste. I had written a piece (which Tony Holden had actually liked) about the Liberal Party's doubts about allying itself with the Social Democratic Party, and was subsequently asked to write a leader on the same theme. At the last minute, Harry said he wanted Bernard (later Lord) Donoughue to write it. Donoughue had been a senior policy adviser to Prime Minister Harold Wilson, and played a shadowy role at Evans's elbow. I winced when I read his hostile leader: all my Liberal contacts must have thought I was a two-faced shit.

Something similar happened when Charlie Douglas-Home asked me to do a farewell interview with Denis Hamilton, who was stepping down as editor-in-chief of Times Newspapers. I knew Sir Denis quite well, and went happily up to his eyrie. Some 15 minutes into our chat, in burst Tony Holden, explaining a trifle sheepishly that Harry had wanted him to be in on the exercise. Such touching faith, I thought. I was so disgusted that I left Tony to write the piece, having fed him a bit of what he'd missed, and rejected his suggestion of a joint byline. He inserted a (gratuitous) flattering reference to Rupert Murdoch.

Taking the Murdoch shilling

A few weeks later Tony, a man whose later career as a versatile biographer I admire, invited me for a drink, rarely a good sign. He told me that generous redundancy terms were on offer: four weeks salary for every year served, 15 in my case, plus six months in lieu of notice, tax-free. Harry Evans, he indicated, had been disappointed by my work, and would not be distressed if I left. If I decided to stay, some other role would be found for me, which sounded ominous. Since I was finding it increasingly hard to get my stuff into the paper, I favoured departure.

Before accepting, I looked around for another job, and within a couple of days had a promising offer. Thus emboldened, I applied for the redundancy package. Similar terms had also been put to my colleagues and friends David Spanier and Marcel Berlins. They too decided to take the Murdoch shilling. We were lucky: that offer was rescinded a few days later. Only seven of us had got under the net. Murdoch soon called for 600 redundancies, mainly from clerical and printing staff, the entire package to be agreed before anyone benefited, and 'within days rather than weeks', failing which he would close the paper down.

Would we get our cheque before Murdoch pulled the plug? I then banked with Williams and Glyn's. They sent a special messenger with my cheque to Barclay's

(Goslings branch, ironically), and the money was secured. Messrs Berlins and Spanier beat me to it. Only then did we feel able to celebrate with a farewell party. When Peter Stothard came in, I said to him: 'Oh, Peter, thank you for making it so much easier for me to leave *The Times*'…'.because I found you so obnoxious' were the unspoken words, but I think he took it as a compliment. Harry Evans survived only a few weeks longer. His social democratic sympathies seem to have played a part in his dismissal (they were scarcely a secret, so why did Murdoch appoint him?). Subsequently there were farcical scenes at *The Times*. On March 11 1982, Charlie Douglas-Home was telling staff he had been appointed editor, while Evans remained in his office trying to edit, with the staff divided into supporters of one or the other. I was relieved not to be there.

For me, it was the end of a golden era in which I was given a great deal of freedom to choose my own subjects. Newspaper journalists come to identify with their title: for 15 years I had been 'Roger Berthoud of The Times', and *The Times* had been a highly respected, pro-European newspaper for which I was proud to work. I was sad to be leaving. Just how important the support of my superiors had been was shown by the rough ride I had under Messrs Evans, Holden and Stothard. Harry Evans was wont later to describe me as having been 'bone idle', so I suppose I succeeded in adding that touch of languor, deceptive of course.

How would I have fared had I stayed on to serve under my friend Charlie? Probably I would have been alienated by his increasingly right-wing, perhaps opportunistically Murdochian views. I'm glad I was spared that dilemma. The way he fought his cancer, attempting to edit the paper from the Royal Free Hospital, was widely admired; and the turnout at his memorial service in St Paul's, which I attended, was evidence of the esteem and affection in which he was held by a vast range of people. At *The Times* he was succeeded by one Charlie Wilson, a Scot with a short fuse who would probably have loathed me.

Chapter 12

The *Illustrated London News*, Henry Moore, and freelancing (1982-1988)

Rarely did I feel more fortunate than on leaving *The Times* in February 1982. Not only was I escaping that slough of despond, clutching a cheque for some £24,000 (worth double nowadays), but I had the promise of a job at my old salary. On top of that, in two months my first book would be published, and I would receive the third slice of my advance from Faber plus the £20,000 serialisation fee (less agent's commission) from *The Sunday Telegraph*. So when, just before I quit Printing House Square, Joy phoned to say the garden wall had fallen down, I was able to assure her we could afford to have it rebuilt.

The new job was as deputy editor of the *Illustrated London News*. The *ILN* belonged to a small group of magazines still owned by the same Thomson group that had just shed *The Times* and associated publications. The *ILN* had been edited for the past 11 years by a former features editor of *The Times*, James Bishop. Jim, a bustling, energetic and rather cheerful former foreign correspondent, lived near us in Hampstead, and had been friendly and helpful during my two years editing the Times Diary. He mentioned to our mutual neighbour Louis Heren (who had himself hoped to edit *The Times*) that he was looking for a new deputy at the *ILN*, and Louis said: 'How about Roger Berthoud?' I owe a lot to that Hampstead network.

Although I would be a bigger fish in a much smaller pond, the *ILN* job was perfect for that stage of my evolution – especially since, encouraged by Maurice Ash, I was hoping to follow up my Sutherland biography with one on Sutherland's more famous contemporary Henry Moore. The *ILN* at this stage had a circulation of some 60,000 a month, in 160 countries. It had a glorious past, reflected in its valuable archive. First published in 1842 by a former newsagent, Herbert Ingram, it was one of the world's oldest continuously published magazines. In the wake of the Crimean war, to which Ingram sent six war artists and the world's first war photographer, its circulation rose to 310,000 copies a week. Its subsequent contributors included Sir Arthur Conan Doyle, R.L.Stevenson, Thomas Hardy, J.M.Barrie and Rudyard Kipling. It currently featured a monthly contribution from that all too patriotic and very ancient historian Sir Arthur Bryant.

The growing post-Second World War ubiquity of television had killed off most general magazines (including *Picture Post*). The *ILN* was saved by being bought in 1961 by the Thomson Organisation. It went from being published weekly to monthly when Jim Bishop took over as editor ten years later.

I had three months off before starting at the *ILN* on June 1. I used this partly to launch the Sutherland book, which was launched in early May with a party at the Redfern Gallery in Cork Street, W.1; partly to persuade Moore to accept me as his biographer and then write a synopsis; and partly to take the family in our new Vauxhall for a week's holiday in April to Brittany, which I hadn't visited since a teenage exchange. For once we stayed in hotels rather than with friends, a sure sign I was feeling flush. The food was delicious, the hotels variable, the weather perfect, the menhirs (standing stones) striking.

Nigel and Maude Gosling with Henry Moore, probably 1960s (detail, Jane Bown, *The Observer*)

Although 1982 was a sort of *annus mirabilis*, it was tinged with sorrow by the death of my cousin and godfather Nigel Gosling. He had been the art critic of *The Observer*, and also its ballet critic along with his wife Maude Lloyd, a former ballerina of high standing, under the joint byline Alexander Bland. When Rudolf Nureyev defected from the Soviet Union in 1961, Nigel and Maude took him under their wing at their Kensington home (Nureyev used their basement flat), and vastly broadened the dancer's intellectual horizons. Nigel was as gentle as he was erudite, as amusing as he was wise, and had a voice of particular charm. Few critics can have been as widely loved. To me he epitomised all the values I most cherished. Even my somewhat philistine father recognised his qualities, though he disliked having to listen to Maude's views on current affairs. We continued to see Maude intermittently after Nigel's death. She remained remarkably serene and beautiful, and was widely cherished into her semi-blind old age, dying in 2004 aged 96. Dad would have been distressed that her obits were considerably longer than his.

One highlight of 1982 was my first trip back to Canada. Why had I left it so long? I had told Joy and the girls so much about my war years there, and they were excited at the prospect of seeing where I had spent those long summer holidays. The Keyserlingks' log cabin overlooking Lac Labelle had given way to a substantial family home, and the lake seemed to have shrunk. To my childish eyes it had seemed huge, but soon after we arrived Lucy, then 15, swam to the far shore and back. I had seen a great deal of Bob in Europe, and we had had the occasional visit in London from the Keyserlingk parents. It was great to see them in their own setting, yet with the independence of staying in one of their sons' houses on the edge of the lake. It was a Proustian experience, complete with the sound of loons calling in the night, and many a squashed porcupine on the rough local roads. Sadly, no skunks were in evidence.

From Labelle we headed by car down to New England, staying with various friends amid glorious landscape, and then up to Buffalo, where we visited the stunning Albright-Knox Art Gallery, which had bought its first Henry Moore in 1939, and on to Toronto via the Niagara Falls, where Lucy picked up a nasty chill from the spray. The Art Gallery of Ontario in Toronto, and the city itself, had played a significant role in Moore's life, and in two days I interviewed six of the main players involved in the (locally controversial) acquisition of a large bronze for a new civic square. I also paid my respects to Kenneth (Lord) Thomson, a passionate art collector who had once been notably kind to me when still proprietor of *The Times* (he gave me a lift home in his Rolls when I had that broken ankle).

Pinning down Henry Moore

Henry Moore had not been exactly enthusiastic about the idea of my writing the first full biography of him: although his fame was past its peak, there was already a vast literature about his work and, to a lesser extent, his life. In my favour was our long acquaintance, my friendship with his friend Maurice Ash, my career as a journalist (which he seemed to have followed as a *Times* reader), the extensive coverage given to my Sutherland biography, and the fact that he liked me, or so his long-time secretary Betty Tinsley told me. He was however anxious that I might take up too much of the shortish time he might expect to go on being productive: he was 83 and none too fit.

To test me he asked me to draft a statement he wanted to contribute to the battle against the expansion of Stansted airport, which was not far away and then the subject of a lengthy inquiry. That wasn't difficult. I called Maurice Ash, who as chairman of the Town and Country Planning Association knew all about Stansted, marshalled a few environmental arguments, and mimicked Henry's speech patterns, all within a couple of hours. He was impressed, and before long rang me at home to say 'Carry on!' He also asked me if I could identify a framed drawing on a bookshelf in his sitting room, of a

195

nude figure. 'It's not easy', he said. 'It's by somebody after somebody else.' 'Could it be Cézanne?' I asked tentatively. 'Jolly good!' he said. 'Cézanne after a drawing by Rubens.' By some freak of chance I had seen a few Cézanne drawings recently and noticed a form of hatching within the outline to which he seemed addicted.

Two months later Moore tried to call the whole exercise off. Laid low by stomach problems, he had actually read my Sutherland book, and had – I deduced – been alarmed by the clinical way in which I had shown Graham's weaknesses: that rather unctuous desire to please the powerful and wealthy, his talent for alienating his friends, and so on. The general message was: I don't want to be portrayed like that. I hastened on a rescue mission to Perry Green, near Much Hadham in Hertfordshire, where Henry had lived since 1940. With me came Giles de la Mare of Faber & Faber, who would be editing the book and whose illustrious family lived nearby. We assured Henry that since he was a totally different character to Sutherland, the tone would also be totally different. He accepted our assurances, and the show was back on the road.

There was another crisis that November, when I was well into the project and discovered that William Packer, the respected art critic of *The Financial Times*, had been signed up to write the text for a short pictorial biography of Moore. I wrote the sculptor a stern-yet-wounded letter indicating that I regarded this as something of a betrayal. I was told this angered him considerably: no doubt he was not used to being ticked off. I would have done better to remonstrate in person, and when I did so, he saw my fear of being undercut, assured me no other such books were in the pipeline, and our good relationship was restored. With hindsight, Bill Packer's addition to Moore literature did mine no harm.

A dilemma confronted me on my weekly visits to the Henry Moore Foundation at Perry Green. It had been set up some five years previously, in part to save Moore from paying around £1m a year in tax. It owned enough of Moore's work to mount a retrospective exhibition. Contributing to, and helping organise, major Henry Moore exhibitions around the world were a large part of its staff's activities. It was run (under a more famous director) by David Mitchinson, whose knowledge of Moore's work was encyclopaedic. Also present at that stage, in a nebulous role, was Henry's niece Anne Garrould. She and David did not get on, yet both were important to me. If I saw too much of Anne, I risked alienating David. But Anne could deliver much crucial information about Henry's family, facilitating access, for example, to his surviving sister. Anne clearly liked me, and I took the risk of frequently lunching with her at the local pub before returning to my desk at the *ILN*. If David held this against me, he did not show it. Our relationship warmed up when Anne departed the scene.

The one family member Anne could not deliver was Henry's daughter Mary, a contemporary of my sister Belinda (they had mutual friends). It can't have been easy being the only child of someone vastly famous who was also somewhat possessive, dogmatic and in many ways conservative in his views. Mary had rebelled, and remained prickly to deal with. Leaving aside any light she might have shed on her relations with Henry and her Russian-born and not very maternal mother Irina, I knew Mary had some valuable early letters from Henry's friends. I asked her whether I might have access to them. 'Only if I can control the book' was the unacceptable response.

The Foundation, housed in custom-built premises next to the Moores' home, Hoglands, and surrounded by studios and gardens studded with Henry's bronzes, was a glorious place to work. There was even an archivist, and it was daunting, on my first visit, to see banks of filing cabinets full of Moore's press cuttings, all in date order. I spent much of my Friday mornings there flogging through them and photocopying the most relevant. At some stage I would spend an hour or so with Henry, often trying to knock him off his standard responses by seeking a reaction to something one of my 70-odd interviewees had said. Generally Irina was present, and would add her own quite sharp memories. With her high cheek bones and slightly oriental eyes, she looked like an icon, an impression diminished by her heavy smoking – a habit Henry should have discouraged. He had after all been gassed in the battle of Cambrai in the First World War, and she suffered from osteoporosis.

My role at the ILN

Although everything initially seemed to move rather slowly at the *Illustrated London News*, it was a soothing place to work. I had my own office, and the staff was largely female. It included the beautiful Jeanette Collins, the chief designer, whom Jim Bishop had brought over from *The Times*. The *Burlington Magazine*, with its erudite focus on Old Master paintings, was part of the same group and shared our premises. It was then edited by Neil MacGregor, later the hugely successful director of the National Gallery and, subsequently, of the notoriously intractable British Museum, which he put back on its enormous feet. No less charming than Neil was the *Burlington*'s manager Kate Trevelyan, of the illustrious Cambridge family.

My tasks included commissioning a good deal of material in consultation with Jim Bishop, and then sub-editing it: I was amazed how badly some quite well-known journalists wrote. A conspicuous exception was my old *Times* colleague Marcel Berlins, who was always readable, accurate and literate. He wrote a particularly enjoyable piece about French truffle hunters and their porcine and canine sleuths.

Jim wanted me to contribute a monthly column of two or three interviews. We agonised over what to call it, plumping eventually for 'Encounters' in large type, followed by 'with Roger Berthoud'. Perhaps 'by' would have been better, since 'with' suggested I was being encountered, rather than doing the encountering. Circulation-wise, I should probably have encountered more very famous people, including film stars. But they tend to be plugging their latest product, and say much the same thing to every interviewer. The less famous, the little known and the unknown were to my mind more interesting.

I aimed at variety. One typical Encounters involved an interview with Teddy Goldsmith, the pioneering environmentalist brother of the entrepreneur Sir James Goldsmith and founder of *The Ecologist* magazine (latterly edited by his nephew Zac). Just about everything Teddy foresaw in our interview, improbably at Aspinall's gaming club, has come to pass: 'Serious climatic changes are inevitable, triggered by deforestation and pollution of the atmosphere...the world is being desertified.' He inveighed particularly effectively against big dams, and the replacement of traditional subsistence farming in the third world with cash crops.

I balanced him with Joan Washington, voice (that is, accent) coach at the National Theatre, RSC and so on. She reckoned she could place anyone with a regional accent to within 10 miles of their provenance. Americans speak with a far lower tongue position than the English, she said, and emphasise words by lengthening the vowel sounds rather than changing the pitch. French and Italian have a repetitive tune: hence all the body language to emphasise a point. The tight jaws observed in once heavily polluted cities lead to greater nasality (e.g. Birmingham and Liverpool): the sort of information I find fascinating. Another Encounters involved the actor Denis Quilley, a Hampstead neighbour, and Jacquetta Hawkes, archaeologist, author and widow of J.B.Priestley: I had interviewed the latter at their home in Stratford-on-Avon just before his death two years previously, in 1984.

As may be imagined, in five years, with two or three interviews a month, plus some longer ones presented as features, I got through a lot of people. Among the better known were the actors Judi Dench (not yet a national treasure) and Sheila Hancock; the opera singers Rosalind Plowright, Frederica von Stade and Robert Lloyd; the author Peter Ackroyd (how did he write so much while drinking so much?); architects Richard Rodgers and Terry Farrell; and various politicians, notably John (later Lord) Biffen, a man of real quality despite his negative views on the EEC. The jazz clarinettist and cartoonist Wally Fawkes was an ideal subject: quite well known but rarely interviewed, and I'd always wanted to meet him. The actress-singer Patti LuPone and the mezzo soprano 'Flicka' von Stade (both American) were among my most engaging subjects. Von Stade had fans who followed her around the world. One of them, presumably a dentist equipped with binoculars, wrote to her saying: 'You have marvellous fillings – who does your dentistry?' As I observed: a whole new approach to opera-going opened up.

LuPone, then appearing in *Les Misérables*, had huge brown eyes and wonderfully sensuous lips, on which I commented – and which she allowed me to kiss lightly on departure. As for Rosalind Plowright, I saw her a day after marvelling at her voice and beauty as Desdemona in Verdi's *Otello* at the Coliseum. She was staying at her sister's mews cottage in London, and we had to sit on a bed together for the interview. On a bed with the fair Rosalind! So near yet so far.

I spent most of a day down in Ditchling, Sussex, with Rowland Emett, creator of that hit of the 1951 Festival of Britain, the Far Tottering and Oystercreek Railway, and many other wonderfully whimsical machines, both working and merely drawn. I was greatly impressed by his blend of imagination and engineering skills. He was a gentle man of enormous charm. His wife Mary was his business manager, a pillar of supportive strength.

Contrary to most journalistic practice, when possible I gave my interviewees a chance to check the accuracy of what I had written. I was prepared to delete a sentence if, seeing it in print, an interviewee reckoned it might hurt a family member. One unexpected reaction came from Alan Davie, a painter I had long known and admired. 'Is this something you dashed off?' he asked down the phone in his strong Glaswegian accent. 'I mean, it reads like something by a local reporter.' 'Are you being serious?' I replied incredulously. 'Would you care to be more specific?' He mentioned a couple of sentences that were perhaps a touch compressed. I resisted the temptation to make the interview less complimentary.

The two pieces of which I was proudest at the *ILN* were a feature on the Japanese community in London; and a last-minute leading article on President Reagan's bombing of Libya. In 1983 there were an estimated 16,000 Japanese living in London. I interviewed some 16 of them, chosen for their closeness to the culture gap (interpreters, translators, journalists) and the variety of their activities (martial arts instructor, musician, ikebana teacher, fashion designer, businessman etc). The clearest common factor was their enjoyment of the space and freedom they found in London. Japan, they said, is a crowded island where cramped living conditions lead to considerable social pressures, anxiety about the reactions of others, and conformism ('If a nail sticks up, knock it in'). In London they had the freedom and space to develop their personalities. On the negative side were England's class antagonisms, bad industrial relations, poor service, resistance to change, some inconsiderateness (e.g. litter), weather and food: a longish list, yet many were keen to stay. As the cover story, my piece was headlined 'The British through Japanese eyes'.

Jim was away and the magazine was about to be printed when in April 1986 Reagan unleashed bombers, some UK-based, on Tripoli and Benghazi, in revenge for terrorist attacks on Americans attributed rightly or wrongly to Colonel Gaddafi's agents. I scrapped the existing leader and waded into Reagan. 'Israel's example' I wrote, 'has shown that terrorism cannot be bombed out of existence. Violence breeds more violence, and terrorism is a many-headed hydra hungry for martyrs….The world's most powerful democracy must set an example of self-restraint. If every country affected by terrorism reached for its bombers, the world would be in flames.' One American reader telephoned to say that he was cancelling his subscription. Maybe others did the same. I shouldn't have been pleased, but I was.

Two-pronged trips

Jim Bishop generously allowed me to combine *ILN* business with research for my Moore biography, which had the benefit of getting me out of London. For example, I needed to visit Moore's birthplace, the mining town of Castleford near Leeds, partly to meet any surviving contemporaries. So I arranged to do a Yorkshire Encounters, featuring among others Tom Laughton, brother of the actor Charles Laughton. Like his brother,

Tom was a major picture collector (he had more than 100 works by our friend Zdislaw Ruszkowski), and until his retirement was one of the last working proprietors of a large hotel, the Royal Hotel overlooking Scarborough bay. I did similar two-pronged trips to West Berlin, to visit Moore's main bronze foundry; to New York, where he had had his first one-man exhibition at the Museum of Modern Art in 1946; and to Dallas and Houston, where a number of his major patrons and bronzes were to be found.

My trip to New York was nerve-racking. I had only a few days there, had unwisely not fixed interviews in advance, and soon discovered that New Yorkers don't like to be thought available at short notice. After wondering whether I would land anyone for my Encounters column, I ended up – thanks to various friends – with a nice mix: Brian Urquhart, the outspoken British deputy director general at the United Nations, the beautiful fashion designer Diane von Fürstenberg, and the art historian John Rewald.

The *ILN* was doing a (rather self-serving) series on great hotels of the world, which I was to start off on that trip with a night at the Pierre. I was impressed to find Albert Finney and Tom Courtenay breakfasting there together the following morning. Next night, being by then on Moore business, I stayed at my own expense at the very modest Pickwick Hotel, next to a sex-shop called The Come-Again Erotic Emporium.

From New York I took a four-hour bus journey to Lenox, a small town of clapboard houses west of Boston, to interview and stay with Stefan Lorant, founder in 1938 of that great magazine, *Picture Post*. Stefan was the father of my great friend Robin Hooper's sister, thanks to an affair with their mother Alison Blair, who had worked with Lorant in the 1930s as the editor of the pocket-sized *Lilliput* magazine. After leaving his native Hungary, Lorant had worked in Germany editing the *Münchener Illustrierte Presse*, a pioneer of photo-journalism, before fleeing to London (via Budapest and Paris) after six months in prison following Hitler's rise to power in 1933.

In London he founded first *Weekly Illustrated*, then *Lilliput* and, in 1938, *Picture Post*. They were all hugely successful. But although his autobiographical book *I was Hitler's Prisoner* had sold almost 500,000 copies as a Penguin Special, when war broke out he was obliged to report to Bow Street police station every week to have his Alien's Certificate of Registration stamped. His efforts to become a naturalised Briton failed, and in the summer of 1940 he sailed in high dudgeon to the United States in a ship full of children (not including me) being evacuated to the United States. His deputy, Tom Hopkinson, took over as *Picture Post*'s editor, subsequently garnering much of the credit for the magazine's superlative qualities. In the USA, Lorant later wrote and self-published half a dozen heavily illustrated and very successful books on great American presidents and cities.

There he was when I arrived in Lenox, a large, rather untidy figure looking less than his 82 years, waiting for me at the bus stop in a biting January wind. He greeted me warmly, his voice still redolent of his native Hungary, and off we went to his book-lined old farmhouse set in 60 acres. Hopkinson, in his autobiography, had portrayed Lorant as an inspired but chaotic genius, and no doubt his working methods may have been taxing to his colleagues. But in his study were 50 filing cabinets documenting his life and work.

A better organised man I have rarely met. I spent many hours debriefing him about his life. The long piece I subsequently wrote as a one-person Encounters read more like an obituary than an interview, always a danger when chronicling a complex life, though he kindly sent me a postcard saying it was 'excellently written.'.

To justify a later trip to Texas, where Moore had numerous important collectors, I planned a feature for the magazine chronicling the cultural rivalry of Dallas and Houston. This was largely architectural: while Philip Johnson's work dominated Houston, I.M. Pei was the presiding genius in Dallas, though there was some overlap. I was fixing this up when a call came through from Wendy Reves, inviting me to come to Dallas for the opening of the Reves collection which, as mentioned, had ended up at the Dallas Museum of Art. I'm already coming over, I said. Perhaps I could use the ticket for my wife? So Joy came with me.

We started in Houston. Coming in from the airport, a blood-red sunset threw the city's staggering downtown skyline into dramatic relief. Over the next 36 hours a charming guide from the Houston tourist board took us around the city in a stretched limo (not the best vehicle for peering upwards) and introduced us to key players on the cultural scene. He also took Joy off to NASA, where she interviewed Christa McAuliffe, the schoolteacher-turned astronaut killed soon afterwards in the Challenger space shuttle disaster.

Proceeding to Dallas, a marginally more human city than Houston, the challenge was to grip the cultural scene while interviewing Moore's collectors and enjoying as much as possible of the programme laid on for the Dallas Museum's guests. Because of Emery and Wendy Reves's connections with Churchill, some of the great man's family members were present, along with his biographer Martin Gilbert, with whom we were already friendly. We were all put up in the magnificent Mansion at Turtle Creek, a hotel of rare perfection, and our trips (by coach) included one to the great Kimbell Art Museum at Fort Worth, some 25 miles away. The Kimbell is venerated for the purity of its design, by Louis Kahn, as well as the quality of its paintings and artefacts: masterpieces only, in just the right quantity.

At the newly enlarged Dallas Museum, the Reves collection was displayed in a re-creation of six rooms of La Pausa, their villa at Roquebrune which the Duke of Westminster had built for Coco Chanel. To celebrate the opening, a glitzy ball was held at the museum. On the Moore front I met, among others, the diffident and charming Margaret McDermott, the grand patron of the arts in Dallas: her late husband Eugene was one of the three founders of Texas Instruments. Everything in her beautifully designed house was quiet, understated perfection, down to the last Monet. We lunched with a small alabaster Moore carving on her dining table, and a stunning Braque on the end wall. It was time to modify a few clichés about Texas.

Moore's Tuscan bungalow

A Moore-and-friends-related holiday in Paris, Provence, Tuscany, Bonn and the Netherlands (the girls were now in their mid-teens) took us to Henry's villa in Forte dei Marmi. The sculptor had discovered this smart resort on the Tuscan coast in the mid-1950s, while working on his giant reclining figure for Unesco's headquarters in Paris. The marble for that commission came from the nearby Apuan mountains, and the figure was roughed out by artisans based at a nearby marble depot-cum-quarrying company (Henraux) at Querceta. The Moores took to holidaying in Forte dei Marmi, eventually acquiring their own shack there, and then commissioning a small and not very inspiring bungalow. When I explained to Henry that I needed to interview the artisans and experience the overall marble-working set-up, he kindly said we could stay in the (by then little used) villa.

Though my expectations were low, its iron beds, tweed-covered sitting room furniture and general austerity were disappointing. But the marble floor was deliciously cool, the beach only a few minutes walk away, and the Italian tourists handsome. One of the artisans I interviewed escorted us to an excellent restaurant, and the managing director of the Henraux works led the way in his VW on perhaps the most frightening drive I have experienced. This was to a quarry near the summit of Mount Altissimo, where the travertine marble is cut with rotating wires, water and abrasive sand, as if with a giant cheese-cutter. From ground level, what looks like snow up there is really chips of marble. Driving up the vertiginous track with my precious cargo (wife and daughters), there was a sporting chance of being brushed off by one of the lorries thundering down, with tons of marble doubtless diminishing the effectiveness of its brakes. My knees felt like jelly, but the views from the top were inspiring.

Fortuitously, a hunk of travertine stone had recently arrived at the Henraux works, from which a Henry Moore Madonna and Child destined for St Paul's Cathedral was beginning to emerge. I was encouraged to take a few chips out of it with a hammer and chisel. An American sculptor nearby commented: 'You've already done more than many sculptors'. It was quite normal for sculptors to send over little maquettes (models) which were then grossed up by the artisans without the artist so much as visiting Querceta. At the Madonna's subsequent unveiling at St Paul's, I could have claimed – and probably did – to have carved more of it than Henry. But the concept, crucially, was his.

In mid-1983, shortly after that trip, Henry nearly died. This was worrying as well as distressing: publication was not due until 1987, and some rival author might have pipped me to the biographical post. The cause of near-death was a prostate operation that went wrong, as they often do. But Henry pulled through, thanks largely to daughter Mary, who rushed over from her home in South Africa. She took him back to Hoglands from Addenbrooke's hospital in Cambridge, where his will to live seemed to have faltered. Back in his familiar surroundings, he was installed in a bed in his beloved sitting room, with its large Degas pastel and other masterpieces acquired from his main dealers, Marlborough Fine Art.

It was there, in bed, that he later received a visit by helicopter from President François Mitterrand, who made him a Commander of the Legion of Honour (the German Chancellor Helmut Schmidt had preceded him). Thanks to a bomb scare at the French embassy a couple of days earlier, security at Hoglands was tight: police, sniffer dogs, long-handled mirrors to search under cars, fire engines standing by. To general amusement (I was there), local garbage collectors effortlessly penetrated this *cordon sanitaire* on their weekly round. Asked by the President which French sculptor had influenced him, Henry replied a touch ungraciously: 'Rodin, of course.' Was there someone more recent, perhaps? 'Giacometti; but he was Swiss, of course.'

Sherwood buys the ILN

In February 1985, about three years after I had joined, the *ILN* changed hands. The redoubtable new owner was James Sherwood, who as a young man had founded Sea Containers, soon to become the world's largest lessor of container ships. He is better known for his revival of the luxury Orient Express train service and ownership of the Cipriani hotel in Venice, among others. The *ILN* was making a slight profit, but Sherwood hoped to increase its circulation from 60,000 a month to 100,000. Jim Bishop was, thank goodness, to remain as editor.

There were pluses and minuses in this. The big plus was moving from modest if cosy premises in Bloomsbury to Sea Containers House, a modern if unlovely office block on the south bank of the Thames hard by Blackfriars bridge. At first I had an office to myself overlooking the river, but was soon joined by Alex Finer, congenial, efficient, ambitious, who was in charge of the expanded section listing forthcoming arts events. Another new recruit was a former picture editor of *The Observer*, Bryn Campbell, himself a top class photographer and for me a twin soul in matters both aesthetic and political (we only disagreed about the abilities of one of my favourite photographers, Nancy Durrell McKenna). We were both well to the left of Jim Bishop, whose father had been a Tory MP, and neither of us liked the hard-nosed new 'publisher' (commercial manager), Tony Price. As for Jim Sherwood, a bulky man with cold, light blue eyes set in a ruddy face, he seemed like capitalism made flesh.

We should have been grateful to him for pumping money into an essentially unviable concern. The pressure on us to be more commercially-minded increased, and a focus group was consulted for its views on various *ILN* features, including my Encounters column, about which its members failed to enthuse adequately. Editorial matter likely to attract advertising was encouraged. Some 'advertorials' (ads that looked like ordinary features, discreetly labelled as advertisements) made their unwelcome appearance.

The virtually insoluble problem was how to sell a monthly general interest magazine in an era of Sunday newspaper magazines, specialist publications and saturation television coverage. Bryn and I reckoned it could only be done with photo features striking enough to become addictive and a talking point. Such a magazine would have been very expensive to produce, and the 'lead' time for printing of two or three weeks would tend to make topical pictures seem out of date. No less intractable was the difficulty of persuading newsagents to display the magazine adequately ('racking').

The girls rise, the parents sink

Looking back on this period when I was working on the Moore biography for long hours at home, Lucy commented: 'It was a bit frustrating for us, Dad, as you were there, and yet you weren't there.' I feel guilty about that now, and very grateful to Joy for shouldering the extra burden. It's a problem faced by most authors. I remained a doting dad, and we had some lovely times on Hampstead Heath, playing catch, or tennis on various local courts. Lucy had inherited my enjoyment of eye-and-wrist games (tennis, hockey, badminton), Lottie had Joy's athleticism and excelled at lacrosse, the long-jump and sprinting.

Academically, Lucy set a high standard by gaining 8 As and a B at O-level, and was thinking of becoming an engineer. Although she excelled at the humanities, for A-levels she took both maths and further maths, plus physics and German. I sat with her on her bed when she opened the fateful envelope giving her results. To her grief, she had notched an A only in German, a B in ordinary maths, and Cs in physics (then badly taught at NLCS) and further maths. It was enough to secure her place at Bristol university, her first choice, to study mechanical engineering. She had already, pre-A-levels, been offered university sponsorships by Rolls Royce, the Ministry of Defence and British Aerospace, and had accepted BAe. Her subsequent career as Dr Lucy Berthoud, high-flying space scientist and engineer, helped demonstrate how poor a guide A-level results are to later achievements.

We thought the less diligent Lottie might follow her sister to Bristol, but she did unexpectedly well at A-level (two As and a B). Joy thought: Gosh, that's good enough to try for Oxford. Thus she came to read French and German at Wadham College at 'the other place', which was good for her morale.

As for my parents, having both been born in 1900, they were by 1985 well into the sad decline of old age. After 21 years at Gaston House, they had from 1967 lived successively in two smaller, though by no means small houses near the Essex-Suffolk border, then in Gosfield Hall, a large mansion near Dunmow converted for crumbling gentlefolk. Their last move was to a retirement home near Uckfield in Sussex, some five miles from our elder sister Lis, who bore the main burden of their decline. Mother was OK mentally, as was Dad initially: his chief problems were the lack of compatible company and his fading eyesight. All but one of the dozen or so inmates were female, and Dad felt a competitive dislike for his rival male, known as the Commander, who failed to acknowledge Sir Eric's manifest superiority.

Although he and I got on pretty well at this stage, old age seemed to exaggerate his weaknesses and prejudices. He had always been reluctant to admit he might be wrong: probably a sign of insecurity. He was now liable to get into a rage if his rightness was not acknowledged, even on the most trivial matters; and as his short-term memory faded, he became increasingly fussed about who was coming to see him and when. Plans, always a preoccupation, became an obsession. 'What am I doing tomorrow?' he might ask five times within ten minutes. Fading faculties reduced his ability to read, watch TV and listen to the radio. His frustrations took their toll on Mother, who was in constant pain from arthritis. Dad was very conscious of his decline. 'I must say, I never thought I would end up like this', he once poignantly told me. For a proud man, it was hard to bear, even if by most standards he was being very well looked after.

His reactions to Martin being dubbed KCVO after a visit by the Queen to Trinidad and Tobago, where Martin was to spend six years as High Commissioner, were amusingly ambivalent: pride that another family member had been knighted was sicklied o'er by knowledge that most ambassadors who handle a royal visit competently receive this royal gong, which was of course not to be compared with his KCMG, the serious Foreign Office knighthood – though most people, gallingly, would not know the difference.

Moore's thoughtfully-timed death

I strove to keep in touch with the art world. One memorable private view led to Joy and I giving a lift, on the way to a dinner, to Francis Bacon and William Scott. Rarely can a Vauxhall Astra have carried so precious a freight. Bacon was entertainingly malicious en route about Moore's work. Henry had done some good work early on, he conceded, but latterly he seemed to lack any sense of scale: some of his big things were like grotesque balloons. As for the much-vaunted Shelter drawings, he expected larvae to come creeping out of them any minute. The diminutive Scott, a painter's painter, kept discreetly silent.

As I re-wrote my Moore biography, generally simplifying my over-stuffed first draft, my subject's grip on life was visibly weakening. My visits to him on a Friday mornings were now largely social. Occasionally there would be a burst of the old inquiring spirit, as when he asked me to dig out some information about narwhals, one of whose unicorn-like tusks graced his long coffee table. All too often he fell asleep in front of me, a feat many may have wished to emulate.

In the event, his death could, unlike Sutherland's, scarcely have been more considerately timed. It came on Sunday August 31 1986, just after I had handed in my more or less complete typescript. I had only to make some small adjustments to the prefatory material and the last chapter, and the story was complete. By chance, a journalist who had until recently been the tenant of our basement flat had just started work as deputy features editor of the *Daily Mail*. He rang me for an instant piece about Moore, to run alongside one by, for no obvious reason, William Rees-Mogg. I negotiated a fee of £750, pretty good for an afternoon's work (albeit one with four years of toil behind it), and they were so pleased with my effort that they ditched Rees-Mogg's.

It was sobering next day to read the obits, which spoke of Henry as a great Englishman as well as a great artist: a leader in *The Daily Telegraph* called him 'the most internationally acclaimed Englishman' since Winston Churchill. Had I done him justice, I wondered? The 'service of thanksgiving' at Westminster Abbey three months later raised the same question. Sir Stephen Spender (would he write another nasty review?) gave the largely inaudible address, Dame Peggy Ashcroft and the Duke of Gloucester read the lessons, Sir Georg Solti conducted the Royal Philharmonic, Dame Felicity Lott sang, Prime Minister Margaret Thatcher was there – and so was *meine Wenigkeit* (little me), feeling daunted amid this cross-section of the establishment, but proud to be the great man's biographer.

Moore-wise there was still plenty of tedious work to do that autumn, rounding up illustrations and writing captions. It proved impossible to find a reasonably up-beat colour shot of Henry with one of his works for the jacket: he never seemed to smile in such a context. We made do with one of him looking glumly through a two-piece figure. Faber proved to be having an economy drive, and used cheap paper for the text, which eventually yellowed. All this was put right in 2003, when Giles de la Mare published a second edition under his own imprint, as described later.

Meanwhile we helped Lucy settle into Bristol University, in a pleasant but noisy hall of residence in Clifton. Since we had by this stage some spare cash and much surplus furniture from my parents, for her second year we bought a two-bedroomed flat in a mansion block in the less smart end of Clifton, which she shared with a friend. It had been repossessed, and needed a lot done to it. We chose an incompetent builder, and much hassle ensued. The end product, complete with antiques, was about as far removed from your average student's digs as could be imagined.

Another door marked Exit

About two years into the Sherwood era at the *ILN*, there were some unsettling portents. One morning Bryn Campbell, the picture editor, opened a packet mistakenly included in his post. It contained details of a head-hunt for a new editor. This was news to Jim Bishop who, it transpired, was to become editor-in-chief. My head was, needless to say, not among those being hunted. I felt I had to write a letter to James Sherwood putting forward my claim to the job and my concept for the magazine's future, as did Alex Finer.

Knowing that my age, 53, was not on my side, I decided to try freelancing. In this I could not fail, I was assured by a Hampstead neighbour and former *Evening Standard* colleague, Andrew Duncan. He had been sufficiently successful as a freelance – notably interviewing famous people for the *Radio Times* – to send his kids to private schools. I was stupid enough to believe him, not realising that for all his innocent, pink-cheeked looks he was a ruthless operator. My naïve confidence was also boosted by the low quality of work proffered by freelances to the *ILN*. If that's typical, I thought, how can my finely-honed prose and extreme reliability fail to be greeted with rapture?

I was not told I'd got the chop from the *ILN* until early May 1987. I couldn't complain: my five-year stint there had significantly subsidised my Moore biography, and the job had been thoroughly enjoyable, thanks in part to my freedom to interview anybody I chose. I had had a pleasant relationship with the editorial staff, and appreciated Jim Bishop's support and friendship. The man head-hunted to succeed him was Henry Porter, formerly of *The Sunday Times*. I was offered three months notice/salary as compensation, and trebled that after consulting the Institute of Journalists, which I had recently and presciently joined, having had enough of the far-left politicking of the National Union of Journalists.

Porter, then aged 34, was a very able and energetic journalist (and, subsequently, successful thriller writer), but the sort of thruster to whom I am temperamentally averse. He attempted to change the old warhorse into something sexier and more gossipy, more akin to the *Vanity Fair* whose London editor he later became. He thus alienated old subscribers without attracting enough new ones. He, and the *ILN* itself as such, lasted just two years.

Caribbean consolation in T & T

A few weeks before the expected axe fell, Joy and I spent a great fortnight in the Caribbean, most of it with Martin and Marguerite in T and T, as they called it. The highlight was a 24-hour trip to the Asa Wright Nature Centre in the rain forest in the north of Trinidad, about 75 minutes drive from the capital, Port of Spain. The centre was named after the Icelandic-born widow of a British barrister: in 1967 she had converted their 200-acre citrus, coffee and cocoa estate and its colonial-style plantation house into a wildlife trust.

Hardly had we stepped onto the plantation house's balcony, marvelling at the view down the valley, than a magnificent toucan – channel-billed, Martin assured us – flew across our field of vision. Even if the rain forest was more open and less steamy than the Amazonian affair of my imagination, it was exciting enough, with lianas hanging from the canopy 100 feet above. Among the many avian attractions were the lovely blue-crowned motmot, or king of the woods; the nicely named violaceous euphonia, and the little white-bearded manakin, which somehow clicks its wings and dances when sexually aroused: apparently most of the time. Orange-winged parrots screamed as they climbed skywards with bat-like wingbeats before planing noisily downwards. A manicou, or black-eared opossum, fled through a grove of bananas, and a black squirrel watched us warily.

Another of the great sights of Trinidad is the evening flight of the scarlet ibis into the Caroni Marshes barely 20 minutes from Port of Spain. This we observed from a punt in which we puttered to a series of large, mangrove-girt lakes. Our guide pointed out four-eyed fish, bulging eyes protruding from the water, and fiddler crabs waving their single big claws from the sand in unison, like an orchestra of rude gesturers. Many of the ibis had selfishly repaired to the Orinoco delta across the sea in Venezuela, to which Trinidad was once attached. Even seeing 80 of them rather than the full complement of around 6,000 coming in to roost in the mangroves was thrilling enough. It's the keratin in their food that turns them scarlet, our guide explained: a much brighter shade than flamingos.

On a Trinidad beach we admired the mixture of races (Afro-Caribbean, Tamil Indian and Chinese, though few of the latter were about) and spotted a familiar compatriot, the abstract painter John Hoyland with his beautiful black partner: another small world moment.

Tobago, some 20 minutes flight away, is far less developed and more picturesque than Trinidad, full of deserted bays with little horseshoe-shaped beaches. One of our highlights there came when, after a delicious seaside lunch of lobster with garlic sauce, a local ornithologist showed us a ruby topaz hummingbird sitting on a tiny nest of lichen. Could this diminutive, fragile creature be related to the astonishingly aggressive hummingbirds that contested the nectar-feeders as we took breakfast on Martin's veranda?

India, courtesy of the British Council

Shortly before my Moore biography was published in October 1987, the British Council invited me to give two lectures on the sculptor in India. The Council, which had done so much to promote Moore's work abroad, was staging a big Moore exhibition in New Delhi and a smaller one starting in Chandigarh. With me would travel a couple of art critics, the loquacious John Russell Taylor of *The Times*, whom I knew, and Michael Shepherd of *The Sunday Telegraph*, plus a charming and very efficient minder from the British Council, Nigel Semmens.

Soon after our arrival in New Delhi we went for a walk in a temperature of around 100°F, being pestered much of the time by touts trying to flog us useless trinkets, postcards etc. A shoeshine boy said to me: 'Shit on your shoe, Sir: me clean?' Since I had just put on clean shoes and noticed no dog poo around, this seemed unlikely. But looking down, I saw a splat of greyish turd on my right shoe. Certainly, clean if off, I said – but I had no rupees yet to give him. When the same thing happened to JRT, we realised that while one tout pestered us with postcards ('Looking is free!'), another squirted shit onto our shoes via one of those devices used to decorate cakes. One admired the teamwork and spirit of enterprise, but what a welcome.

There ensued several congenial if slightly frustrating days of openings, briefings, drinks, dinners and sightseeing. The Prime Minister Rajiv Gandhi, son of Indira and soon also to be assassinated, opened the handsome Moore show with a very good speech; and we went by coach to the miraculous Taj Mahal some four and a half hours drive away, and on to the abandoned and monkey-ridden city of Fatehpur Sikri: a long and exhausting day.

My lecture in Delhi went OK, though I stammered badly once. The one in Corbusier-designed Chandigarh was preceded by a nerve-racking four-hour journey in a British Council car, with drivers in opposite directions playing chicken on the crown of the road (India's traffic is rated among the deadliest in the world). I liked Chandigarh's modernist domestic architecture, but not the civic buildings. My lecture went less well. For the sake of the slides, the only light in the hall was on my lectern and I had no contact with the audience.

I took advantage of this trip to fulfil a whimsical ambition involving a quick visit to Bombay (now Mumbai). Seaching a few months back for Lord Jellicoe's entry in *Who's Who*, I had been captivated by an adjacent one:

JEJEEBHOY, Sir Jamsetjee, 7th Bt cr 1857; b 19 April 1913; s of Rustamjee J.C. Jamsetjee Jejeebhoy (d1947), and Soonabai Rustomjee Byramjee Jejeebhoy (d 1968); S [succeeded] cousin, Sir Jamsetjee Jejeebhoy, 6th Bt, 1968 and assumed name of Jamsetjee Jejeebhoy in lieu of Maneckjee Rustomjee Jamsetjee Jejeebhoy...

It was love at first sight as the glorious litany rolled on through the list of charitable institutions of which the seventh baronet was chairman. Seventh! Who had founded this dynasty, and how? Should I not share my findings with a wider public in, perhaps, an epistolary interview in my *ILN* column? Sir Jamsetjee took my overtures in a friendly spirit, and sent me a copy of a flowery biography of the first baronet ('Frowns of fortune were no strangers to Jamsetjee...'), a Parsee trader, mainly with China, who became enormously rich and a pioneer philanthropist. In 1842 he was the first Indian to be knighted, and in 1857 was made the first baronet in the empire East of Suez.

I felt guilty when telephoning the 7th baronet from New Delhi, since I no longer had my *ILN* column as a guaranteed outlet for an interview. But he was happy to see me and, when I said it would be helpful for my article, to put me up for a night. His house on the sea front was gloomy, with 25 grandfather clocks chiming through the night and many relics of his forbears' trading days in

The 7th baronet

evidence. Sir Jamsetjee himself, then aged 74, was as charmingly courteous as his letters suggested. His rather large wife Shirin, also a Parsee, was harder work, and it was she – voluminously clad in pink – who next morning drove us, very slowly in the fast lane, to the fury of taxi drivers, for a tour of the city's flamboyant Indo-Victorian architectural highlights, and to the various institutions that the first baronet had founded. These included the first hospital in Bombay for the poor of all classes and races, the first art college in India, and sundry schools.

Sir Jamsetjee also took me to the most striking feature of the Parsee religion: the Towers of Silence, on the top platform of which the naked bodies of the dead are placed, to be picked clean by vultures. The bare bones are then swept into a central well or ossuary. The three or four towers were well screened by trees from curious eyes. It was enough that many vultures wheeled overhead (they have subsequently become a threatened species). Were body parts sometimes dropped onto the balconies of nearby high-rise apartments, I wondered? I was not surprised to learn that there was a movement among Parsees for cremation, a logical solution since the Parsees, originally Zoroastrians, worship God through fire. The original sandalwood fire brought over by immigrants from Persia some 1,400 years ago still allegedly burns in Udvada, in the Gujurat, where they formed a small agricultural community. Many moved to Bombay in the 17th century. Their zeal and integrity endeared them to the British and eventually brought large fortunes to such families as the Petits, Jehangirs, Wadias and Tatas – as well as the Jejeebhoys.

I was predictably appalled by all the signs of poverty amid the bustle of Bombay: children begging, people sleeping in drainage pipes about to be laid, or under flimsy plastic sheeting, a strong stench of human ordure in some areas. But I was grateful to the British Council for flying me to India and back and putting me up for nearly two weeks. Their modest return was two lectures and a piece in the recently founded *Independent* about the Moore show in Delhi.

On my return just before the publication of *The Life of Henry Moore* (£14.95), the Redfern Gallery once again gave a launch party, mainly for those who had helped, and we had a dinner at home for family and friends. This time I had taken care to include a critical overview of his work, so there was not too much carping on that score in the extensive reviews. I was criticised mainly for excessive detail and failing to penetrate into Moore's emotions and their relationship with his work. Since Henry himself preferred not to peer into that deep well for fear of analysing away the springs of his inspiration, it was tough to expect me to do so, and I was averse to amateur psycho-analysis. My favourite review was by Hilary Spurling, Matisse's biographer, who called the book 'lucid, elegant and shapely' and ' impeccably documented, admirably organised and undeniably gripping ...' Overall, I was a bit disappointed by the reviews, but thrilled to have completed a massive task.

Although *The Observer* showed signs of interest in serialisation, nothing came of it: even serious newspapers were by now only interested in revelations, preferably adulterous, and Henry's sexual life after marriage appeared to have been, from a biographer's viewpoint, distressingly blameless (or very discreet). Even though I had taken no unpaid leave to complete this one, and had had a separate American publisher, I probably made less from it than from *Sutherland: a Life*. The American publishers, Dutton, took a useful proportion of the 16,000 copies that Faber printed. Reviews in the USA were sparse: Canada did better, thanks to Henry's links with Toronto. Our local Hampstead independent bookshop (since expired, like its founder Ian Norrie) put five copies in a window display, which was cheering.

Mother's death

Four months later, at around 1.30am on February 22 1988, Mother died aged 87, the immediate cause being cancer of the liver which, as Graham Sutherland had found, moves very fast. I had visited her and Dad regularly, and had seen Mother in hospital in Tunbridge Wells the day before. She was in a coma, and her chest was rattling horribly, a very distressing sound. The hospital was sensibly not striving to keep her alive, so her death was being accelerated by dehydration, not a pleasant thought but preferable to a prolonged coma.

Some men are shattered by their mother's death, even if it takes place at an advanced age and after a long illness. Does that show emotional depth, or perhaps some kind of failure to come to terms with their own identity and/or the inevitability of death? I was naturally deeply saddened that my mother, whom I loved and in some ways greatly admired, no longer existed. But I think we siblings were relieved that she had been released from the physical pain of her arthritis and digestive problems, and from the mental pain of witnessing the progressive decline of Dad's faculties as well as her own.

It fell to me to give the address at her funeral in the same church in Great Hallingbury where she and Dad, and my two sisters, had been married, and where Gran's funeral had taken place. Material was not lacking, not least thanks to the memoirs she had completed in 1979. But it would be hard to get the balance right between the many elements her life: her interest in Gourdjeff, Ouspensky, Jung and Maurice Nicoll on the one hand, and her founding of village clubs, her work on adoption committees and her love of animals on the other. My big worry was that I would stammer badly in such an emotional situation, and not be able to continue. In the event, I did stammer once, but managed to get going again.

By this stage Dad had rallied somewhat from a phase in which he seemed to be contemplating suicide. He was taken off to a private psychiatric home to see whether he was suffering from some form of dementia or serious depression. He was so horrified to be thrust into these new surroundings that he insisted on being returned next day, unassessed, to his residential home. He seemed to be suffering from a terrifying feeling of inadequacy. Following Mother's funeral, Martin and Marguerite generously took him off to Trinidad, to his great benefit.

The hazards of freelancing

'Felt v. depressed', I noted in my diary some 10 days later. That was doubtless partly a reaction to Mother's death. But I wasn't enjoying freelancing. There were far too many freelances pursuing too few very busy features editors. 'Some fucking freelance for you', a secretary on the *Evening Standard* shouted to her boss when I telephoned, not even bothering to cover the receiver. To think I had once been a golden boy there! That was a nadir. More frequently I would cultivate, say, the features editor of that excellent magazine *Good Housekeeping*, even taking her out to an expensive lunch, only for her to be transferred soon afterwards to a different job. Generally magazines paid better than newspapers, and were less stressful to work for. With newspapers, the classier the publication, the smaller the fee. *The Times* didn't pay too badly, however, and I did numerous interviews with artists for the then arts editor before he too moved on.

Over the years I had developed links with the Hamburg-based liberal weekly *Die Zeit*, and managed to sell them the idea of a monthly Letter from London, of 1,000 or so words which they would translate. I aimed to concentrate on aspects of Britain that Germans might find surprising, or which contrasted sharply with life in West Germany. Thus I interviewed the half-dozen or so members of the Thatcher Cabinet who came from working class backgrounds (including John Major, Peter Walker, John McGregor and Cecil Parkinson); returned to my old boarding schools; and described a splendidly scruffy and unGerman Lurcher Fair in Norfolk. It was great fun, but surprisingly badly paid. My best earner was a piece for the short-lived *Business* magazine edited by Stephen Fay, on the economics of picture-dealing, mainly involving the then ascendant Waddington Galleries.

There was something episodic about freelancing over a wide field, and it was tempting, after finishing a major exercise, to take a day off. Hampstead Heath beckoned from across the road: it was recovering from the great storm of October 1987, which uprooted around 1,000 of its trees (we were afraid the large beech opposite our house might join us in the connubial bed). Happily, Joy had turned her versatile talents to a job administering courses at Westminster University, to the benefit of the family finances. Lucy was firing on all cylinders at Bristol, and even learning to fly. Lottie was on her way to Oxford after a spell working in Germany to get her German up to the level of her French.

I had contemplated attempting a book on the German resistance to Hitler, on which there seemed to be little still in print in English and which I thought deserved to be better acknowledged in Britain. I abandoned this when I discovered there were some 250 books on the subject in German, many very fine-focus: Communist, Catholic, Protestant, military etc. My agent reckoned a mountain of work would produce a financial mouse. Would I be interested, I was asked, to write a biography of Leon Trotsky? Or of Princess Anne? A nice spectrum, but I was ill-equipped for the first, and had no desire to become a royal biographer (during my Sutherland years, the former Press Secretary at Buckingham Palace, the genial Sir William Heseltine, as he became, had asked me if I would like to be considered for the No 2 job in the Palace press office.)

To succeed as a freelance, one needs to be very good at marketing oneself, or an acknowledged expert on a subject in constant demand, preferably both. I was a good salesman of my ideas within an office where I was known and liked. I was not good at making a pitch to very busy people who didn't know me. And I had always preferred not to specialise. So it was a relief when one of my freelance pieces, an interview with the French artist Niki de St Phalle, led serendipitously to another full-time job on a national newspaper.

Chapter 13

The Independent (1988-1994)

The Independent* had been founded in October 1986 by three ex-*Daily Telegraph* journalists: Andreas Whittam Smith, its first editor; Matthew Symonds, deputy editor; and Stephen Glover, foreign editor. Under the brilliant advertising slogan 'It is. Are you?' it had got off to a very good start, positioning itself upmarket of the Murdoch-owned *Times*, and attracting a talented staff, not least from *The Times* itself. I had tried to sell my services as a freelance to the editor of this exciting newcomer's arts page, the youthful Tom Sutcliffe. He expressed enthusiasm for my Encounters column on the *Illustrated London News*, and thought I might perhaps do some TV reviews for his page. Nothing came of that, but the features department accepted my Niki de Saint Phalle interview. In delivering it in June 1988 to the Indie's reassuringly unsmart premises in Old Street, London EC1, I bumped into Peter Jenkins, my contemporary at Trinity Hall, to whom I had often chatted at EEC summits. Peter, whose life was to be cut short by a lung disease four years later, was the paper's much-admired political columnist. 'What are you up to?' he inquired. 'Freelancing, not very happily', I replied. 'I know they're looking for a leader writer here', he said. 'Why don't you apply?'

The vacancy was caused by the impending redeployment of the engagingly cocky and amusing Andrew Gimson. He was and is a stylish writer, but his spiritual home was *The Daily Telegraph*, whose parliamentary sketch writer he later became. The chief leader writer was John Torode, whose political views were further to the right than his previous role as the *Guardian's* labour editor suggested, and certainly well to the right of mine. He was dubious about the EU. I was grilled for the job by Matthew Symonds, who asked me *inter alia* whether I considered myself stronger on domestic or foreign affairs. Which would do me more good, I wondered. I probably replied that I found that hard to answer. According to Torode, Symonds subsequently told him I would get the job over his dead body. But he did offer me a trial period of three weeks, while Gimson was on holiday.

I had written a few leaders on *The Times*, but that was way back. I would have to crank up my sluggish freelance metabolism. These trial weeks would be like doing an exam every day – using direct-input computer technology for the first time (I had remained stuck in the typewriter era, as had my previous employers, the *ILN*.) A friend at the Indie, Michael Church, introduced me to the office's Atex system on my first morning, and Torode, essentially a genial soul, proved welcoming and helpful.

Leaders were written into a tailor-made file, which indicated how many lines one was under or over-length. The screen could be split in half, with the relevant running news agency story on the right. Old-fashioned cuttings from the library were still available. Two leaders (one each, though sometimes a specialist contributed one) were required from us most days, of around 450 words. A single, longer one was needed on Friday for Saturday. Subject to any later developments, the topics were usually fixed at a preliminary meeting at noon. This followed the morning conference, at which each department went through its highlights, with possible leader themes being suggested and sometimes briefly discussed as the last item. On my first trial day, my subject remained to be decided at the 2.30 or 3pm meeting with the editor and/or deputy editor, and possibly a relevant specialist or two.

That left me with a dilemma. I had a long-standing lunch engagement with the Conservatives' leader in the House of Lords, Lord Belstead, an Oxford friend of Martin's whom I had consulted about a recent freelance piece. It would be a struggle to get from Old Street to Westminster and back by 2.30pm, but I thought it worth trying to impress Symonds et al with my connections, and there wasn't any research I could yet do. So off I went anxiously to this otherwise sedative meal in one of those rare places where one can still feel young and promising in one's 50s.

I just made it back for the 2.30 pm meeting, at which it was decided I should write about President Ceausescu's plans to bulldoze villages in Transylvania, home to much of Romania's 1.7 million Hungarian minority: the dispossessed were to be settled in tower blocks. I had loathed Ceausescu since I was in Bonn (when a toadying Romanian correspondent asked me what I thought of the great leader, I replied that I found his mixture of Gaullism abroad and Stalinism at home particularly repellent), and was delighted to be able to wade into him. But first I had to brief myself via the cuttings and an all too lengthy chat with the paper's voluble East European editor, whom I tracked down in Vienna. I was pleased with my first two sentences: 'To be Romanian at this moment of history is a misfortune. To be a Romanian of Hungarian ethnic origin is a double catastrophe.' But before long I found myself over-length, and hard-pressed to achieve the necessary shrinkage by the deadline of 6.30pm. Matthew Symonds made some helpful suggestions, and my first *Independent* leader was born.

A more serious test was a full-length leader (around 1,000 words) on Lord Justice Butler-Sloss's report on child abuse – and the response to it – in Cleveland. This, as I wrote, 'confronts the British public squarely with a number of unpalatable facts: that the sexual abuse of children is widespread; that neither doctors nor social workers nor the police can tackle it effectively without cooperating; and that the line between doing too much too quickly and too little too late is so fine as to be a matter for cautious and anxious debate in each case.' Such leaders tended to be largely analytical, supporting some recommendations, questioning others. Since the report was embargoed for 24 hours, I had a full day in which to write it. Andreas liked the outcome, suggesting only the deletion of a single adjective. It's sad that the same failures of communication between responsible agencies have featured in all too many subsequent child abuse tragedies.

I had been told that Symonds, who took more leader meetings than Whittam Smith, was particularly interested in defence. So before my trial stint began, I had persuaded my old Brussels friend Paul Lever, later ambassador in Berlin but then the leading defence expert in the Foreign Office, to give me a good briefing on current East-West disarmament negotiations. In my third week the topic came up. Matthew, who had a considerable stammer (with which, as an old sufferer, I naturally empathised), gave me his angle. When he later read my effort, with me standing behind him like a nervous schoolboy having his essay scrutinised, he offered not a single suggestion for improvement. I knew I had got the job, as was confirmed at the end of the week, to general rejoicing at home.

Some very classy colleagues

What a pleasure it was to be back in an office full of intelligent and engaging people. Many of Fleet Street's finest had migrated to the Indie. From *The Times* there was Richard Dowden, the leading Africa specialist, and Nick Ashford, the Indie's foreign news editor, though all too soon to die of cancer. From *The Observer*, Neal Ascherson, and from *The Sunday Times* his beautiful and brilliant wife Isobel Hilton, who was fluent in Mandarin as well as Spanish. There seemed to be seriously attractive and very able women in their mid-to-late 30s *passim* on the home front, among them Sarah Helm, Sabine Durrant, Heather Mills (no relation to the ex Lady McCartney), Allison Pearson and Cara Chanteau, with all of whom I periodically had lunch. Heather was my favourite, though I was aware she had a tall and unfairly handsome husband. Sarah later did time in Brussels for the Indie, married Jonathan Powell, Tony Blair's chief of staff at No 10, and contrived to write several successful books as well as bring up two children.

I took to Andreas almost instantly: he and I seemed to be rare among the editorial staff in being interested in what might be called high culture. Football and pop music were more widespread enthusiasms. He seemed pleased to have near him someone who relished writing leaders on such topics as the merits of opera at Wembley stadium, or the relevance of an artist or author's life to his or her work.

As time went on, he took me to lunches to which he had been invited: to Douglas Hurd, then Foreign Secretary; with Ian Jack to John Birt, then the controversial head of the BBC; to a wonderfully unreconstructed ambassador of the German Democratic Republic, on whom a preservation order should have been slapped, as I remarked. I usually sat next to Andreas at the morning conference, with something of the role of licensed jester. He confessed once: 'I know that my whole personality changes for the worse when I get behind the wheel of a car...' 'Are you sure it's a change, Andreas?' I asked, to general laughter. When Tom Sutcliffe said the arts page was doing a piece on the Canadian singer k.d.lang, he turned to me and said: 'You haven't heard of this woman, have you, Roger?' 'Sorry to let you down, Andreas but yes: one of my daughters is a fan, and she's got a wonderful voice,' I replied.

Matthew Symonds was harder to read: he was a more private person, only rarely revealing his enthusiasms (Purcell was one). He could be quite cutting, in a friendly sort of way. When I was floundering around on some topic, he observed: 'Mind like a steel trap'. His own mind was exceptionally clear, especially on economic topics. Crucially he was, like Andreas, pro-European, liberal on crime and punishment, anti-Thatcher but in favour of free-markets, hawkish on defence. Stephen Glover, the foreign editor, further to the right and a Eurosceptic, was involved with leaders only when (rarely) in charge. He was a man of much personal charm: sadly, he descended to some very petty journalistic sniping at Andreas and the Indie when he left the paper after a brief, unsuccessful stint as the first editor of *The Independent on Sunday*.

Some stressful moments

There was something relentless about producing a leader virtually every afternoon, knowing that there was nothing else to fill the allotted space (there is no such thing as a timeless leader). The worst hazards were (a) losing a half-completed draft when the computer system crashed and one had not hit the 'save' button recently: should one try to remember what one had written, or think afresh? And (b) having to switch topics when a major event occurred during the afternoon. That happened soon after I had been taken onto the staff: on August 17 1988, news came through at 5pm that President Zia of Pakistan had been killed in a helicopter crash.

I was three-quarters of the way through a leader on some complex change in the social security system, with which my brain was full, and had only 90 minutes to deal with Zia's demise. Fortunately there were some good cuttings on the top of his fat file, and I squeezed in a phone call to friend Nicholas Barrington, High Commissioner in Islamabad, who seemed to have a lingering admiration for the dead dictator. Matthew Symonds had been friendly at Oxford with Benazir Bhutto, whose father had been executed by President Zia, and who was now leader of the main opposition party. I packed a lot of Pakistan's history into my leader, ending with the sage if not entirely logical observation that 'the path to full democracy will be hard, but the lesson of President Zia's death is that it offers the only safe way forward.'

The worst single instance of having to dump a completed leader and dash off another occurred in January 1992. There had been a seriously complex story in the papers about the trial of a former British Military Intelligence agent in Northern Ireland. The many charges against him included conspiracy to murder, and tipping off Protestant paramilitaries about potential murder candidates. No danger of having to write a leader about an ongoing trial, I thought, and didn't bother to read more than the headlines. So I was horrified when Matthew Symonds emerged at 6.15pm and said he was really sorry, but Andreas wanted a leader about the trial, on the theme that there shouldn't be one law for the province and another for the rest of the UK. 'You can have till 7pm to write it', he added. It took me at least 10 minutes to get my head around the story, and

I feared I was rattling off a pretty vacuous piece. Yet when I read it today, it seems like a lucid, even elegant exposition of the case and issues involved. Matthew gave it a quick read, and said with something like admiration in his voice: 'You did very well to turn that around so rapidly, Roger'. I felt as if three years had been wiped off my life.

Sundays could also be stressful. Only one of us would be on duty, having had Friday off. If there was no specialist around capable of writing a leader on a relevant topic – among those brilliant at doing so were Peter Wilby, the education editor and later editor of the *New Statesman*, and the polymathic Isabel Hilton – one had to write two. On a beautiful sunny Sunday, it could be hard to pin down any outside expert to debrief. To my amazement, on one such summer's day I got hold of, successively, the two leading academic experts on Ethiopia when one of its wars with a secessionist province (probably Tigray) seemed to be over.

Needless to say, I tried to avoid writing leaders on economic topics: it takes confidence to generalise. Luckily Matthew Symonds always dealt with the Budget. In retrospect, given my Brussels background I could have coped with 'Black Wednesday', September 16 1992, when sterling was forced by speculators to withdraw from the (European) Exchange Rate Mechanism and the official interest rate rose to 15 per cent. The specialist targeted to write the leader on that fraught day was the paper's economic commentator, Hamish McRae. There was a problem: no one seemed to know where he was. I felt the cup might pass to me as 4pm approached. My panic subsided when that wise and delightful man was located. He despatched an impeccable piece in short time.

Contacts are everything in the leader-writing business, and I amassed a formidable file of hundreds of experts on a huge range of topics. Many were lecturers or professors: Oxford and the London School of Economics produced far more useful ones than Cambridge. 'It's that parasite Roger Berthoud, leader writer at *The Independent*, anxious to pick your brains on the state of the Russian economy', I might say to one of the nine academics and ex-ambassadors I eventually had listed under Russia. Often they would be unavailable, and I would anxiously wait for them to call me back while I was trying to get someone else. I did feel a bit of a nuisance, but I think they quite liked trying to spot their input in next morning's leader.

Near though they were, there was a problem with in-house experts: if they were having to deal with an important White Paper, not only reading it but attending some ministerial briefing, the last thing they wanted was a leader-writer pestering them for views or information. Sometimes, flatteringly, a ministerial press officer would ring to say: 'You might like to talk to the Secretary of State about today's White Paper'. I was once put on to Michael Howard, the Home Secretary, most of whose views I detested. I opened the bowling by observing: 'I think it's generally agreed that there is a link between crime and poverty'… Howard practically went ballistic: absolutely not, he said at some length and very heatedly. I ended up even more hostile to the White Paper than before, as I told the press officer. (When asked if her husband had a short fuse, Howard's wife, the ex-model Sandra Paul, once said: 'He has no fuse at all').

I was lucky to be writing leaders in the pivotal decade that saw the end of the Communist era in the Soviet Union and eastern Europe, and with that the end of the Cold War. Sometimes the pace of change was dizzying. One Friday, August 23 1991, Boris Yeltsin, then the hero of the resistance against the putsch that had briefly unseated President Gorbachev, was signing a decree suspending Communist activities in Russia. History was being made in front of us all, and it was a tough task to convey the full significance of this running drama. It made me feel very small and inadequate.

A few weeks earlier there had been a heated debate at an enlarged leader conference about the desirability of West European military intervention, in some form or another, in the incipient civil war in former Yugoslavia, as the dominant Serbs threatened to crush the independence of Croatia and Slovenia. I was supposed to write a leader for the front page (our first) calling for action. What form this should take, given American leadership of Nato, the organisation's essentially defensive mandate, and the absence of an effective European Union military entity, was far from clear. But I cobbled together a judicious synthesis of the debate. When I came to write another front page leader a year later, once again calling for action, the Serbs were bombarding Sarajevo and well into their programme of ethnic cleansing in Bosnia. It was a couple of years before NATO did intervene. Andreas distinguished himself by going to Sarajevo, at considerable risk to himself, and writing a very moving full-page piece about its sufferings.

Among other major topics of that era were: Tiananmen Square and its fore-and-aftermaths; the search for peace in Palestine (what's new?); continuing violence in Northern Ireland and on the mainland, and the failings of our own judiciary, notably Lord Lane, over the Birmingham Six and other miscarriages of justice; the demise of apartheid in South Africa; the Gulf War; the death of Ayatollah Khomeini; and Chris Patten's struggle to strengthen democracy in Hong Kong prior to Britain's handover to Beijing in 1997.

Patten's efforts were not only publicly vilified in colourful language by China's overlords, but also undermined by a cabal of Foreign Office China specialists. Patten believed that the more democracy Hong Kong acquired, the harder it would be to reverse. The sinologists argued that it was counterproductive to antagonise Beijing. We called this a policy of 'pre-emptive cringe' (sadly, I did not coin the term, which was probably Matthew's). The leading sinologist was Maggie Thatcher's adviser, Sir Percy Cradock. In an attempt to persuade us we were wrong, he and other Foreign Office specialists took several of us to an excellent lunch at the RAC Club. Their arguments failed to impress, as Sir Percy had expected. We subsequently bit the hand that had fed us with relish. It's one way journalists show their imperviousness to spin.

My debt to Dad

When I was two-thirds through a Friday-for-Saturday leader about the (pre-slaughter) demonstrations in Tiananmen Square in late April 1989, Dad's nursing home in

Tunbridge Wells rang to say he was not at all well. 'Are you saying he may be dying?' I asked. The deputy matron said she feared that might be so. I had been to see him the previous weekend, and had almost gagged on the smell in his room: he had been incontinent and partially paralysed since a couple of strokes before Christmas, and was much of the time in a semi-coma. On one visit in January I had asked him: 'Do you recognise me as Roger, your son?' 'Yes'. 'Are you in a sort of shadowy world down there?' 'No'. But then he would wet his lips and say 'two hundred and sixty three'.

Semi-prepared though I was, it was a shock to learn that the dominant figure in my earlier life was about to be snatched away. Should I finish the leader, or hand it over and head straight for a train, I wondered. I decided to complete it. Fortunately the smell in his room was more bearable this time, and a stiff tot from a handy bottle of Macallan whisky provided solace. I shook his shoulder, but failed to get any reaction. There was not much to do but think and read until Lis, who lived nearby and had borne the main burden of his decline, returned in the hope of seeing him out. I departed around 9.30pm. It was all pretty ghastly, she reported next morning. The nurses had come in every 90 minutes to turn him (he had serious bed-sores), and the smell had again been appalling. At 9am she went home for some breakfast, and he died at 10.20am on April 29 1989 – peacefully, with a big exhalation, Lis was told – before she got back.

I subsequently wrote in my journal: 'I think the reason that none of us (probably) felt any great grief at Dad's death – unless it has yet to hit us, as it probably will a bit at the funeral – is that his decline took so long and was so painful to witness. Had he gone when still entirely on the ball, I am sure we would all have missed in particular the close, if sometimes destructive interest he took in all family affairs. In so many ways he was a very good father. If only he had not got so many trivial things so out of proportion, and been so prejudiced on so much.'

I certainly owed him a huge amount: my interest in foreign affairs, my enjoyment of languages, a whole world of invaluable contacts, his keen interest in my various jobs, his sociability, his generosity with money (which he never used as punishment or reward), his enjoyment of the countryside, his often cutting sense of humour. Typical of the latter was an exchange we had, a few years back, before going out together. He was dithering between his club etc ties, and the others. 'If I had to choose between ties that showed some sort of achievement and ones that showed good taste, I would tend to opt for the latter', I commented. 'My dear Roger', he responded with an anticipatory chuckle, 'if I may say so, you have had little choice.' When asked once by an acquaintance whether he played bridge or golf, he replied: 'No, I live in the country.' No wonder I like people with a cutting edge.

I had to a considerable extent defined my sense of identity against his very strong personality, and I think he respected me for having stood up to him. After coping with his anger and his *idées fixes*, I was not easily daunted by anyone else. I admired him for his energy, and the dedication with which he worked for all those worthwhile causes already mentioned.

A former diplomatic colleague of his Copenhagen days wrote a not very warm obituary for the Times. I was friendly with the deputy obits editor of *The Daily Telegraph*, which still had anonymous obituaries, and he asked me to do one for them. It proved less difficult than I expected. In my only critical sentence I said: 'Berthoud had great charm and energy, even if to his own staff and to visiting Britons he occasionally showed a pompous streak and undue regard for punctilio'.

Martin delivered the funeral tribute: no easy task, since his relationship with Dad had in recent decades been trickier than mine, and he found it hard to give a sufficiently warm impression. But the result was generally commended for its balance. Attendance at his memorial service in St James's church, Piccadilly was greatly reduced by a railway strike.

Grasping the Middle East nettle

As mentioned, my initial admiration for the state of Israel had long since been replaced by indignation at its territorial expansionism and ruthless behaviour in the occupied territories. My first leader on this topic resulted in a sort of mental seizure. I tried to pack in too much history, and just couldn't meld it with the current situation. Our Middle East editor, Harvey Morris, a sound operator but not a natural leader writer, had to be brought in to get me back on track. That was rather humiliating.

It was a different leader of mine on Israel that prompted a note to the editor from Lord Sieff, of the Marks and Spencer dynasty, who was chairman of Independent Publishing's board and an active Zionist. 'How does your leader writer justify his views?' he asked. This was blatant interference, and I toyed with the idea of sending a copy to *Private Eye*. But it could only have come from me, and would have been disloyal to Andreas. I should have replied: '*The Independent*. We are. Is he?' Since the strongly pro-Palestinian Robert Fisk ('a four-letter word beginning with f and ending with k', as one pro-Israel lobbyist described him to me), was hyper-active as our Middle East correspondent, Lord Sieff must often have choked on his breakfast toast.

The Gulf War was tricky, since overnight developments were liable to undercut a leader written the day before. On the morning that President Saddam invaded Kuwait, Andreas, whose reactions were rarely predictable, came into our office and said: 'I hope we aren't going to get too steamed up about one shit invading another', or words to that effect. We had then the part-time services of Richard Davy, a former *Times* leader writer, as also of Godfrey Hodgson, formerly of *The Sunday Times*: both formidably intelligent and experienced. Richard pointed out that a sovereign state had been attacked and invaded by its neighbour, a gross violation of international law and the UN charter. It was thus a matter of the utmost seriousness. Andreas saw the point immediately, as of course did most of the rest of the world.

Perhaps the leader of which I was proudest was one Andreas asked me to write for Christmas 1988 (see Appendix). 'If God's chief motive in bestowing a Son on mankind was to redeem the human race from its sinfulness', I observed, 'no objective assessment could conclude that the mission has yet been successful. At times, He seems to have made matters worse.' When I showed it to Andrew Brown, then the paper's religious affairs correspondent, he exclaimed: 'You mean you got this past the editor!' Paul Oestreicher of Coventry Cathedral told Andreas he found it 'a very sensitive exposition of the secular viewpoint.'

A memorable trip to Pakistan

My relations with Andreas were strengthened by a visit in November 1989 to Pakistan, where his son Ben was doing a stint on an English-language weekly, the *Friday Times*. Andreas was friendly with its courageous founders, the Sethis. Using the excuse of our recent 25th wedding anniversary, Joy and I had accepted an invitation from Nicholas Barrington, who was still our man in Islamabad. Nicholas had previously invited us to stay when he was in Cairo, but thanks to the deadline for my Moore biography, we had been unable to accept.

It was Nicholas's second posting to Pakistan, and he knew everybody. Apart from a slight tendency to over-pack our programme, he could not have been a better host, even meeting us at the airport with the official car at around 6.30am and whisking us through immigration. The embassy residence was a handsome example of contemporary architecture, complete with garden and swimming pool, and ultra-comfortable. The only hazard was being woken by the yelping of jackals and, at 4.45am, by the first of five daily amplified chantings of the muezzin from the nearest mosque, calling the faithful to prayer.

Nicholas had arranged for us to hire a car with driver to take us for three days in the Swat valley, a ruggedly beautiful part of the North West Province governed until 1969 by the last Wali of Swat. Driving was mainly on the basis of 'might is right', brilliantly decorated buses and trucks with people clinging to them being a feature. In what more recently became a war zone pitting the government against the local Taliban, full beards and Islamic clothes were even then the norm. Although Joy was dressed with due decorum, there were few women around, and they were generally wearing burkhas. The vibes from the men felt hostile. But the towns through which we passed, with their mix of goats, cows, buffalo, dogs, occasionally a camel, horse-drawn tongas (traps), auto-rickshaws and so on were a visual riot. In the valleys, the Swat river foamed over boulders, and the autumnal colours of poplars, paddy fields and fruit-laden persimmon trees were heightened by a backdrop of snow-clad mountain peaks.

On our return to Islamabad we found a friend from Nicholas's years in the Tokyo embassy installed as a fellow guest. Tetsuko Kuroyanagi was, in Japan, a hugely famous television chat-show hostess and interviewer, herself a former actress, and had written a best-selling memoir emphasising her debt to her untypical, character-building education. When the Japanese ambassador to Pakistan came to dinner, he seemed almost overwhelmed with excitement at meeting perhaps Japan's most famous woman, royal family apart. When we encountered Japanese tourists, they were soon pointing her out. Tetsuko was very amusing and a great mimic, her mock-Japanese rendering of Elvis singing 'Rub me tender, rub me true' being a high point. She also had some gripping tales (plate-sized spiders etc.) about visits to Africa as a Unicef goodwill ambassador. With her frequent changes of wardrobe and elaborate make-up, it was hard to imagine her roughing it.

She flew with Nicholas and us to Lahore, capital of the Punjab and one of the most beautiful cities of the subcontinent, with its famous mosques, fort and Jehangir's tomb, the latter a miniature Taj Mahal set among gardens full of parakeets and chipmunks. As Nicholas's guests we were invited to a memorable party in a wonderful, rambling house in the teeming old city, where le tout Lahore was gathered – including the unfairly handsome cricketer Imran Khan in a flowing white robe, surrounded by a bevy of English groupies (it was before his marriage to Jemima Goldsmith). In a courtyard with a blazing fire and two musicians playing I had a long chat with the lesser Whittam Smith, a tall young man of some courage. He said that if the *Friday Times* wrote anything too hostile to Islam, hired thugs would appear and break up their computers: it was a very violent society. His own task was to impart a consistent stylistic patina to the prose of Pakistani contributors and staff.

The day the Berlin Wall was breached found us in Peshawar, near the border of Afghanistan and long the focal point for the leaders of the Afghan resistance to communism. The High Commission had a small outpost in a leafy suburb of that rough city, where we stayed. At a party that evening, the sons of one or two mujaheddin leaders were present. When I mentioned the dramatic events in Berlin to one of them, he said: 'Of course it's happened thanks to us.' As my brain did a couple of backward flips, he continued: 'If we hadn't defeated the Russians in Afghanistan, this would never have happened.' I began to see his point: by forcing the Russians to withdraw, the mujaheddin had started the unravelling of the Soviet empire. I would have loved to have been in Berlin for those memorable scenes as East Germans poured through the Wall, watched on television by an incredulous world. But one can't have everything.

We also took a trip up the Khyber Pass, for which a permit from the Ministry of Tribal Affairs and a military escort were required. We were not cheered to learn that one such escort had not long ago been fiddling with his rifle en route and had virtually blown off the head of an English girl. We seemed in the event more likely to be killed by some mad and probably doped-up driver: overtaking on elbow bends was not unusual. The pass was dramatic, studded with fortresses, pickets and the insignia of regiments that had defended it during the Afghan wars. There was a sad coda: when I wrote a piece for the Indie about our trip, I got a letter from the dead girl's father, asking how could I be so positive about such a violent country. It has since got a whole lot more violent.

To Latin America with Jo Frampton

Another major trip, in 1990, took me to Latin America for the first time. My old Cambridge friend Jo Frampton sold colour scanners for a subsidiary of Delarue in that part of the world, and invited me to join him on one of his sales trips: we could share hotel rooms, so I would only have to pay for air fares, internal travel and food. Sometimes I would have to amuse myself while he worked.

We met up in Bogota, where we stayed with the British ambassador, Keith Morris, a Cambridge friend of Jo's, and his Spanish wife Carmen. It was cold in the Colombian capital, which is 8,600 feet above sea level, an altitude that affected Jo but not me. Although Colombia's reputation (for drug wars, kidnappings etc.) was already dodgy, I felt quite unthreatened in Bogota, where I visited the amazing Gold Museum and the outlying salt mines, into one of which an underground cathedral has been hewn. From there we flew to Boca Grande, a resort on the Caribbean adjacent to Cartagena (gorgeous beach, beautiful women in 'dental floss'-style bikinis, brown pelicans bombing the sea), then on to the island of San Andres, which we had to flee after a few hours, ahead of a major storm which would otherwise have trapped us.

The highlight of the trip was the gloriously romantic Mayan site of Tikal in the heart of the Guatemalan rainforest. We got there early, and there were screeching monkeys and little foxes around, but few tourists. Climbing the incredibly steep temples, clinging onto a chain, was quite an experience: one was advised to come down backwards. Our next stop was Merida in Mexico, to visit the great sites of Uxmal and Chichen Itza, where atop a temple I came face to face with one of the Chacmool reclining figures that had so inspired Henry Moore. Finally to smoggy Mexico city, where we stayed with the Swiss ambassador, Paul-André Ramseyer, a very entertaining friend of my picture-dealing first cousin Anne Berthoud. There I visited the great Museo Antropologia, saw Diego Rivera's murals, and went with friends of Jo's through appalling traffic to the outlying pyramids. Coincidentally, my brother Martin was visiting Mexico City at the same time from Port of Spain, and was staying with the British ambassador. I became aware of this too late for us to meet up.

Trouble at the Indie

My admiration for Andreas Whittam Smith was tempered by his essentially hubristic decision in 1990 – he was chief executive as well as editor, a bad idea – to give the Indie a Sunday sister, *The Independent on Sunday*, or Sindie. 'Remember, Roger, all businessmen are monopolists at heart,' this former City editor of *The Daily Telegraph* had once told me. He turned out to have a streak of the monopolist himself. It seemed to rile him that a newish venture, the *Sunday Correspondent*, was successfully wooing the Indie's readers – despite his successful strategy of making Saturday's Indie, with its brilliant magazine edited by Alexander Chancellor, a substantial enough package to last readers through the weekend. *The Independent on Sunday* was launched in 1990, with a view to killing off the 'Corrie' (some of whose financial backers had originally backed the Indie, on the understanding that it wouldn't start a Sunday edition). The Indie had been launched in a favourable economic climate. The Sindie was born in a recession.

Edited by Stephen Glover, it was criticised for the weakness of its news coverage. Some of Glover's senior appointments, such as Sebastian Faulks as deputy editor, had to be expensively replaced. The *Corrie* did indeed fold, and the *Sindie*'s circulation moved upwards – helped by the Gulf War and peaking at more than 400,000. Thereafter sales ebbed, and there was demoralising talk of closure, or making the Indie a seven-day operation (as was successfully done, with some 70 redundancies), and/or sacking Glover, who was indeed defenestrated. As I was getting some coffee one morning in the Sindie area, someone called out 'Looking forward to writing our leaders, Roger?' I winced.

A lesser but deeply unpopular move was to sign up the *Guardian*'s well-known interviewer Terry Coleman, in whose meandering pieces the word 'I' recurred with irritating frequency. There was general outrage at the salary, not to mention the Jaguar, that he was believed to be getting. I had been an admirer of Coleman's earlier work, and he turned out to be a delightful person. But his first two interviews were not a success, and he departed to write some acclaimed biographies (Laurence Olivier, Nelson) and historical studies.

Slightly more than half-way through my time at the Indie, John Torode was moved over to features, and the number of leaders rose, thanks to a questionable redesign, from two to three. 'Does that make me chief leader writer?' I asked Matthew Symonds. 'I suppose it does', he replied: not exactly a ringing endorsement. But I did extract another salary increase. Having, as a freelance, been in a weak negotiating position when I was taken on, my initial salary was low, though I had received a hefty rise when shortlisted for the job of features editor. I had written a number of features myself, notably two long profiles. Both proved tricky for personal reasons: Sir Claus Moser was the Warden of Lottie's Oxford college, Wadham, and Sir David Wilson, the outgoing Governor of Hong Kong, was as mentioned a friend of Martin's. He was being criticised as insufficiently political.

As chief leader writer I was to be endowed with two young neophytes. These were Jack O'Sullivan, former health services specialist, and Tim Jackson, former correspondent in Tokyo and, briefly, Brussels, where he had proved hard to handle. They were both 28, had overlapped at Merton College, Oxford, but in all other respects could not have been more different.

Jack was full of Irish charm, extrovert and supportive. Tim was a geeky loner, thin on collegiate spirit. He wore headphones and took high-speed notes direct onto his own laptop during telephone interviews. I used to upbraid him for coming in late, and was probably more unpleasant to him than I should have been. It transpired he was writing a biography of Richard Branson. If he had told me this, I might have been more sympathetic. On the plus side, he was very intelligent, and a natural and fluent writer, which could not be said of Jack O'Sullivan. I had to plead for the latter's retention when Andreas quite rightly wanted to switch him back to reporting, at which he was very good.

I was supposed to supervise the output of these two while writing my own leaders, a stressful task. Tim evaded scrutiny by writing onto his laptop, transferring the finished product to the office computer at the last minute. Later, during the dot.com boom, he made a lot of money by starting up a British rival to E-bay called QXL.com. This was subsequently merged with a German competitor, and the new entity was sold during the dotcom boom for a reported £1bn. I was not thrilled to see a photograph of him and other 'Global leaders of tomorrow' in the National Portrait Gallery at the peak of his success. Jack O'Sullivan could also be pushy, but eventually left the Indie to co-found Fathers Direct, an organisation aiming to improve family relationships, not to be confused with the stunt-addicted Fathers4Justice.

A strange weekend in Manchester

We leader writers were among a dozen or so Indie journalists despatched to Manchester in 1994 for a weekend, conducted jointly with Granada TV and the Kettering Foundation, to test the value of 'deliberative polling'. Two hundred citizens, selected as a microcosm of the population, had been asked to fill in a questionnaire about their views on crime and punishment. They were then invited to Manchester and exposed for a weekend to the often conflicting views of policemen, ex-prisoners, politicians, legal experts and so on. Finally, they were asked all the same questions again. The aim was to see whether people change their views on a particular topic if given a chance to become better informed about it.

Happily, they did, their views becoming significantly less retributive. For example, support for sending more people to prison as an effective way of cutting crime fell from 57 to 38 percent. Our task was to act as moderators of periodic discussion groups, which were supposed to agree on questions for the upcoming speakers. A tabloid journalist could have had fun with a story headlined: 'Shock and horror as liberal journos meet public': we were appalled by the 'hang 'em and flog 'em' attitudes that the weekend helped to soften. Among my own group of 15, 11 favoured capital punishment, and one (not a Muslim) reckoned burglars should have a hand amputated.

Among those who addressed us was Tony Blair, then the Opposition's home affairs spokesman. 'Blair was very fluent though gutless, notably on the legalisation of drugs (he was dead against). Made me think he was more of an opportunist than I had hoped', I told my journal. Blair was already pandering to the tabloids, one of his most lamentable weaknesses. Of course he did intermittently show courage of a sort: for example in pushing through the abolition of Clause Four, that core Labour commitment since 1918 to the nationalisation of key industries and utilities. And I suppose it took a historically blind form of courage, coupled with poor guidance from God, to commit British forces to his friend George W. Bush's assault on Iraq. But that was well after my time at the Indie.

Painful changes on all fronts

It was on the day Saddam's troops withdrew from Kuwait that Joy withdrew from our house in Hampstead and took a flat across the river in Stockwell, recently vacated by a friend of hers. Our relationship had been afflicted by the empty-nest syndrome, exacerbated by both girls being abroad. Lottie was in Paris, working during her gap year in the library of the *International Herald Tribune*, prior to going to Oxford. Lucy was in Toulouse, qualifying herself for the PhD she was to do there over the next three years (on the impact of space debris on the solar panels of satellites). Joy and I were having communication problems. We had both, separately and together, consulted therapists of various schools. They provided interesting theories, often linked persuasively enough to our childhoods. But it is one thing to understand one's problems a little better, and another to thrash them out in a constructive manner: all too often I would not raise a topic with Joy because I thought I already knew what the answer would be – and that I wouldn't like it.

At some stage I had wondered aloud whether it might be helpful if we spent a few weeks apart, to gain a better perspective. Joy seized the initiative by taking over a flat in Albert Square, Stockwell, being vacated by a female friend. Her friend was moving across this attractive square, which is set in a very mixed area, prompting a Hampstead friend to comment: 'I hadn't realised that living with you was even worse than living in Stockwell!' Joy and I agreed to see each other at least once a week, and did some things together – such as taking Lottie and her possessions up to her first year room at Wadham College, Oxford, where she was to read French and German.

In Stockwell, Joy fell in with a group of ex-services officers and their wives, while I rather enjoyed my new-found freedom. She found it refreshing to be judged purely as herself, rather than partly as my wife. I had a streak of the bachelor in me, no longer held at bay by fatherhood, and got involved with various women, notably a doctor friend who lived up the road. Eventually, to cut a painful story short, Joy came back and I moved out, along with about half my pictures and some furniture – to a spacious and airy first-floor flat in Southwood Lawn Road, Highgate, with a view over what estate agents were pleased to call 'the Cholmeley valley.' Before long I was joined there by my doctor friend. 'How clever of you to have an in-house geriatrician already', someone said.

My move to Highgate, for which my sister Belinda provided some valuable support, coincided with Andreas Whittam Smith's exit from the editorship of the Indie, thanks to sundry morale-sapping changes in the paper's ownership. I was sad to see the driving spirit of what had been a very fine newspaper forced out, and went into his tiny office to say goodbye on his last day. He was staring at the framed front page of the paper's first issue, which must once have thrilled him. His whole body seemed to express sorrow that it had come to this. I really felt for him.

For a fortnight Ian Jack, who had succeeded Glover as editor of the Sindie, took over. Ian was a totally convincing personality. I would have followed him anywhere.

'Our' first leader concerned Winston Silcott, a bearded Afro-Caribbean of troubled past and threatening aspect whom the tabloids loved to demonise. Silcott was one of the 'Tottenham Three' wrongly convicted of the murder of Police Constable Keith Blakelock during the Broadwater Farm estate riot in October 1985. The convictions were quashed in 1991, and Winston had just been awarded £17,000 compensation. I headlined my leader, of which Jack changed not a word, 'Silcott deserves his money', earning a (flatteringly) scornful comment in next morning's *Sun*.

Enter Hargreaves

A week earlier we had heard that Andreas was to be succeeded as editor by Ian Hargreaves, deputy editor of that great source of editors, *The Financial Times*. He took over on August 15 1994, and I immediately sensed I was in trouble. Like Harry Evans, Hargreaves was a shortish north countryman, but – unlike Harry – he turned out to have much of the policy wonk about him. He got us leader writers together and said in as many words: 'I must confess I don't have a very high opinion of the *Independent*'s leaders. It seems to me they too often lack intellectual rigour, and are not prescriptive enough.'

That was hardly my idea of inspiring leadership, and Hargreaves' tendency to look unblinkingly through me was unnerving. Whatever intellectual rigour was, I determined to make it suffuse my leaders, though I remained reluctant to make prescriptive recommendations. I was slow to get off the mark: on two of the three first days of the new era, I was shafted by Jack O'Sullivan and Tim Jackson, who grabbed the suggested topics ahead of me. When I did get going, Hargreaves had a distressing habit of knocking out my last paragraph and substituting his own often prescriptive thoughts. He seemed to have a tin ear for language. The rolling Berthoud periods were followed by the tripping Hargreaves monosyllables, creating a strange effect.

Matthew Symonds had inevitably been swept away by the new broom, to be replaced by Martin Jacques, who had been a successful editor of *Marxism Today*. Jacques was – no doubt still is – an engaging fellow, a natty dresser in sub-Vietcong battledress mode; but he seemed largely unaware of the exigencies of daily journalism. He would be crawling over a leader, perhaps searching for intellectual rigour, while the sub-editors were desperate to get it into the system. Like P. Stothard at *The Times*, he was better at knowing what he didn't want than what he did. Hargreaves imported from the *FT* another ex-communist, Charlie Leadbeater, an archetypal, quietly spoken but pleasant policy wonk, whose role as No 3 and features supremo was not altogether clear.

Another redundancy cheque

The ensuing four months of 1994 were deeply depressing. Messrs Hargreaves and Jacques clearly had little faith in me, and Messrs O'Sullivan and Jackson were good at capitalising on this. To add to the general gloom, the Indie was due to move from Old Street, near Liverpool Street, to Canary Wharf, whither we repaired periodically to be trained on new computers. My level of ineptitude was judged exceptional. I knew the axe was poised, and one Friday in early December I received the expected summons to the editor's office. The message from Hargreaves was: excellent redundancy terms are on offer and you would be well advised to take them. John Torode and a few others, including the admirable though part-time Richard Davy, were similarly extruded.

September marked my 60th birthday. I was quite proud to have remained employed so long in such a young profession, though I hoped to avoid drawing my various pensions until I was 65. My redundancy cheque would help keep me afloat, with some freelancing. 'Silver linings crowd into view', I wrote in my diary. Not least was being spared the vile commute to Canary Wharf, to which my colleagues would be moving 10 days later. Freedom beckoned! Perhaps I could write another book. Meanwhile I had the not exactly morale-boosting experience of 'signing on' for unemployment benefits in darkest Camden Town.

Torode and I gave a farewell party in a local hostelry. David Robson, the features editor, delivered a witty lament at our passing, which played on our contrasting personalities: 'JT, rough-hewn, sartorially challenging, steeped in the history of class war [his father had been a communist], well-versed in self-defence and explosive in offence. And always emblazoned on his kipper tie, *in vino gravitas*. And RB, beautifully turned out, quietly spoken, a patrician among peasants. The conditions that brought together these contrapuntal forces will perhaps never be repeated. The theatre that was big enough to hold them now stands as an epitaph.' What did we do, he wondered, when we disagreed about how to put the world to rights. 'Then presumably RB would raise his eyebrows to his arty postcards, JT expectorate into his cacti.'

I was touched to get a letter from Rosie Waterhouse, the paper's social services correspondent, saying *inter alia*: 'During the leader writer conferences that I attended I came to rely on your consistently wise and compassionate comments. They will be sorely missed in this newspaper.' I liked to feel I had made a bit of a difference on various fronts: where prisons were concerned, I had been consistently in favour of rehabilitation rather than retribution. I had been generally sympathetic to social workers. I had been eloquent in supporting the target of a more united Europe. I had helped make the paper more even-handed in its attitude to Unionists and Republicans in Northern Ireland (i.e. less sympathetic to the Protestants, who were killing as many people as the IRA). And I had been quick to pinpoint the vileness of Slobodan Milosovic's murderous nationalism.

John Torode, who was not friendly with Lord Tebbitt for nothing, went off to his spiritual home, the *Daily Mail*, to write well-paid features. Hargreaves lasted at the Indie but a year, commendably resigning over proposed editorial budget cuts, and became professor of journalism at Cardiff University. Jacques, stricken by the death of his young Malaysian wife in 2000, reverted to his role as columnist, and held various professorships in Asian universities: he presciently, if rather relentlessly, forecast the rise of Asia and decline of the West. Leadbeater became an authority on 'innovation and creativity', described by Demos as 'one of the top management thinkers in the world' and a multiple author of books with titles such as *We-think*. These are seriously intelligent people, but perhaps more academics than daily newspapermen.

So ended my life as an employed journalist. According to the Trinity Hall newsletter of April 1993, my life itself had ended a year earlier: 'Berthoud R.E. [sic] (1954)' was listed among those whose deaths had been reported. Who reported it, I wondered. There was thus considerable amusement – quiet rejoicing? – when I subsequently turned up at a memorial service in Cambridge for Charles Crawley, the college's former Senior Tutor and father of my school friend John Crawley.

Leaving aside those months as a trainee on the *Daily Express* in Manchester, I had served on four publications: the *Evening Standard*, *The Times*, the *Illustrated London News*, and the *Independent*. Undoubtedly the most fun was editing the *Evening Standard's* Londoner's Diary with a generally brilliant staff and a very supportive editor, but there were plenty of highlights on *The Times*. Writing my two biographies in the interstices had been satisfying, if strenuous. Writing leaders for the Indie was intellectually demanding and stimulating. I learned a lot and liked many of my colleagues.

I was supremely lucky to have been a journalist in an era before technology exploded. For most of my time, newspaper journalism involved ballpoint pens, notebooks, perhaps a small tape-recorder, telephones and typewriters (later, computers). True, it would have saved much aggravation and some misunderstandings had one been able to send copy straight from a laptop. But with the advent of websites, podcasts, blogs and sundry other sites, that simple era was replaced by one of ceaseless demands for fresh material. I am therefore amazed at the quality of writing to be found in the *Guardian*, which I read nowadays.

On leaving the Indie I was aware that freelancing would involve using a computer, and with the support of my in-house doctor friend, I bought one. It caused me much anguish, and of course I never used more than a fraction of its potential. Even emails remained beyond me until the Obituaries editor of the Indie insisted on my sending copy electronically. But my new Dell certainly made additions and deletions a great deal easier and swifter. The more demanding challenge of my new freedom was to take some decisions about how I wanted to live the rest of my life.

Chapter 14

Highgate and Wiltshire (1995-?)

Highgate is less cosmopolitan than Hampstead, and has fewer glamorous residents. But it is, away from the roads that feed into it, more tranquil and village-like, and the architecture of the main drag, Highgate Hill, is a cut above that of Hampstead's High and Heath streets, with their boutiques, restaurants and estate agents. If it is a bit further from the Heath, it is much nearer Kenwood and most of the ponds, and has near its heart the beautifully landscaped Waterlow Park. In 1862, one Frederick Prickett, a surveyor, called Highgate 'a justly celebrated and truly healthful hamlet…situate on a lofty eminence' – though its healthfulness may have been diminished by its large number of pubs, many still in evidence. These were no doubt attributable to the tollgate established in the 14th century at the top of what became Highgate Hill, through which all north-south traffic had to pass, with long delays calling for refreshment.

If Southwood Lawn Road was architecturally a touch suburban, it was quieter than our old home 25 minutes walk across the Heath in Christchurch Hill, over which Joy now presided. I was made to feel welcome in SLR by my immediate neighbour, Douglas Maxwell, a versatile designer-artist-writer-photographer and his less exhausting wife. I soon introduced myself to a number of other residents, some of whom I asked for a drink or meal, thus apparently setting a new and infectious standard of sociability in the street.

Before long Douglas suggested we might collaborate on a short book on Highgate: he would take the photographs and I would write an introduction and captions. I had my doubts about his skills as a photographer, but decided I would take the risk. Among the 80-odd images that we eventually selected from his endeavours, a good two thirds were of buildings or locations requiring captions of an historical nature.

My nine-page introduction touched on such matters as Coleridge's 18-year sojourn, the history of Highgate Cemetery and of the more ancient Highgate School, founded in 1565 by Sir Roger Cholmeley, the biggest landowner in the area. In addition to plundering earlier publications, I spent hours amid the archives of the Highgate Literary and Scientific Institution, and talking to such local figures as the chair of the Friends of Highgate Cemetery. Overall, it was an enjoyable and educational experience. The upshot was a slim but quite elegant floppy-back of 40 pages entitled *Highgate: a Tranquil and Salutary Place*. It was published by the Asian owner of the local Post Office-cum-store and sold quite briskly in local outlets.

A propos Highgate School: I once commented to one of its teaching staff on the scruffiness of its then exclusively male pupils. He told me they dressed like that to avoid being verbally or physically abused on public transport: a national phenomenon, no doubt.

My doctor friend, let's call her M, moved in with me, but kept her cottage in Hampstead. The length of her stay was not discussed. She was both intelligent and amusing, though I sometimes felt I was a bit of a substitute for her beloved brother, who had recently died after wrapping his car around a tree. I much enjoyed preparing our evening meal, and smiling down at her as she walked up the short front garden path on her return from her work in the public health sector. She loved eating out, and had her 'pleasure per pound' principle: better to spend more on a good meal than less on an indifferent one. She was quite techie, and helped me come to terms with that first computer.

I had one or two friends and acquaintances in Highgate. First among these were Ivo and Rosemary Bondy. Ivo, who was of Czech Jewish origin, had started a china and glass importing business, then did an M.Phil. in law, later supervising the same subject at various Cambridge colleges and lecturing at Middlesex University. For 20 years he was also an increasingly senior London magistrate. Rosemary was the daughter of an eccentric and much-loved Tunbridge Wells GP, once an Irish boxer of some note. She rose from the local Citizens' Advice Bureau to chair the Barnet Health Trust.

Apart from their substantial home in Highgate, the Bondys acquired a house near Framlingham in Suffolk, to which I was periodically invited. On one occasion I arranged for us to visit the well-known architect H.T. (Jim) Cadbury-Brown, best known for his Royal College of Art building adjacent to the Albert Hall. Back in the 1960s I had, rather improbably, had an introduction to him from Dad: they had met thanks to the theatre that Cadbury-Brown had designed for Essex University. Long ago Jim had invited Joy and me to dinner in London with Ernö Goldfinger, the famous modernist architect (Trellick Tower) who lived down the hill from us in Willow Road in a small terrace of houses he had designed. Goldfinger was a bit of a bruiser, and not amused when I referred to his terrace as 'flats'.

Cadbury-Brown and his American-born wife Betty, also an architect, lived in Aldeburgh in a house filled with light that they had designed together, featuring floor-to-ceiling doors and many sky-lights, all brilliantly integrated into the garden. As a couple, they had a blend of innocence, integrity and ever-youthful charm that was unique in my experience. It was enhanced by Betty's famous whisky sours (at noon!) and much talk of jazz. At lunch with the Bondys afterwards in an excellent Aldeburgh restaurant someone crossed the floor to ask me: 'You of the resonant voice, are you by any chance a TV chef?' I was surprised by the adjective, but had to disappoint him.

In Highgate, Ivo started a monthly discussion group of generally genial souls, to which I contributed a couple of short papers. One was entitled 'What is art?' and was indebted to E.H.Gombrich's *The Story of Art*, which I read for the first time. I had once interviewed Gombrich in his Hampstead home, which was only sparsely hung with pictures: he seemed, like many a Viennese Jewish émigré, to be far more interested in music. With his usual no-nonsense clarity, he opened what must be the best-selling book in its field with the words: 'There really is no such thing as Art. There are only artists.' The definition I offered was: 'Art is what a significant number of people of influence agree it to be.'

Gombrich taught me something I hadn't appreciated: that the Reformation raised the question in non-Catholic Europe of whether art should continue to be so fixated on religion. In came secular and intrinsically banal subjects, previously shunned: portraits, land and seascapes, still lives and so on. The Dutch artists who painted these with such virtuosity were emphasising treatment rather than subject matter, the decreasing importance of which is a key feature of the last century of art history. Marcel Duchamp, with his famous urinal of 1917, controversially extended the range of art to articles selected rather than created by the artist. Those who followed his cue widened the gap between avant-garde art and the general public.

Those who nowadays moan about the Damien Hirsts and Tracey Emins of the art world seem unaware that there is a lot of seriously good painting and sculpture around that draws on the history of art and is executed with great skill in traditional media. Art critics perpetuate this by reviewing only blockbuster exhibitions: there are no more 'gallery round-ups'. As a result much excellent work shown in commercial galleries gets no publicity in the serious press, while the tabloids sensationalise the works of the BritArt pack. As for museums such as the various Tates: following their past mistakes and omissions, they are so anxious not to miss the *avant-garde* that there is no longer any *garde* to be *avant*.

My own tastes have inclined towards mainstream modern British art: neo-Romantics (Sutherland, Keith Vaughan, David Blackburn), others more in the St Ives tradition, such as Patrick Heron and Ben Nicholson; Celtic artists, among them Alan Davie, William Scott and Ceri Richards; and various Polish-born painters, for example Josef Herman and our friend Zdzislaw Ruszkowski. I have known few greater pleasures in life than buying a new painting, drawing or original graphic. One of the pains of marital separation was leaving behind almost half of those I had acquired, usually and no doubt selfishly without consulting Joy, because I feared she would say no. I remember the exact circumstances of almost every acquisition.

One I retained is a delicate watercolour landscape by Louis le Brocquy, a leading Irish painter (of Belgian extraction). After I had interviewed him for *The Times*, he offered me a small work, as was normal in France, where he lived. It's not normal here, I said gently: I would feel I was abusing my position. We later visited Louis, a man of great charm, and his wife Anne Madden, also a successful painter, at their home inland from the French Riviera, and he came at least once to our house in Hampstead. There, some 15 years after my interview, he said: 'Roger, I really would like to insinuate something I've done into your collection, and have brought this along, inscribed to you...' How could I hold out against that, particularly his use of the word insinuate? Thus I acquired a treasured watercolour, *Farm Buildings near Dublin* (to which city he and Anne had returned), with the legend 'To Roger in admiration and friendship, Louis, London April 1991.'

Happy times with Ken Draper

My time in Highgate was enriched by contact with two engaging creative spirits: the painter and sculptor Ken Draper, and the ceramicist Ewen Henderson. I met Ken thanks to that virtuoso pastellist David Blackburn, a Yorkshireman. David saw himself – as the art historian Kenneth Clark also saw him – as part of the great tradition of English landscape artists, including Graham Sutherland in his Pembrokeshire period. Because we knew each other slightly and because of my biography of GS, David suggested to his dealer, John Hart of the Hart Gallery in Islington, that I might 'open' a retrospective show of his work in the Djanogly Art Gallery at Nottingham University. It was a flattering invitation, but a daunting experience: at the due moment all those attending the private view, among them the city's mayor in full fig, surged towards me to hear my faltering speech about the artist.

I had not previously met John Hart, who was then still working part-time as a GP and had only recently started his London gallery with his wife Kit. They lived outside Nottingham, and invited me to stay for the night. Their converted barn was naturally well hung with pictures, and I kept on saying: 'Gosh, I really like that'. In most cases, the response was 'It's by Ken Draper', a Hart Gallery artist of whose work I had seen little. John Hart added: 'We need a book about him. Perhaps you should write it.' He later added: 'I'm sure you'll get on, as you both like women.' The Hart Gallery had already commissioned two handsome books about gallery artists, and was among the first to develop this promotional tool.

I was looking for a project, and this seemed ideal: close involvement with a sympathique artist who considerately lived in Menorca (with another gifted artist, Jean Macalpine). A mere 50,000 words were required, and the research would largely involve debriefing Ken and to a lesser extent his friends in London, doing a bit of 'contextualising', the trickiest bit, and visiting the sources of his inspiration in Menorca. The fee was modest, but one of Ken's pictures would be part of it.

The man himself turned out to be as engaging as I had expected. Like Henry Moore, he was a Yorkshire miner's son, but very differently hewn. Ken is tall, handsome, generous-hearted and extrovert, one of the great huggers of our time and very good company. He was a joy to debrief over perhaps half a dozen long tape-recorded sessions in my Highgate flat. His childhood had been much more testing than Moore's. When he was eight years old, his back began to arch, and his parents were told he had a suspected TB spine. For eight months he was kept in bed in a hospital on the outskirts of Sheffield, strapped down on his back, head held rigidly in a harness with boards on either side, weights hanging over the back of the bed to keep him absolutely still. During the day he and other patients would, in suitable weather, be wheeled onto a verandah, so his only view was of a ceiling or the sky. He became an expert on the play of light, with enhanced peripheral vision. (The American painter Sam Francis told me that something similar had happened to himself as a child, but unfortunately he spoke in Californian psycho-babble, rendering the interview unuseable).

When released from his bondage, Ken had to learn to walk again, was taught initially at home, excused games when he went back to school, and like Moore found a wonderful art teacher, a woman fresh from Goldsmiths' College in London who encouraged his artistic talents. At 15 he went to Chesterfield College of Art, thence to Kingston's and finally to the Royal College of Art in Kensington. From there he emerged primarily as a sculptor, and made a considerable name for himself up to the mid-'80s. A first visit in 1985 to Menorca, with whose landscape

Ken Draper at work

he and Jean fell in love, prepared the way for a switch of emphasis to landscape-based drawing, mainly in pastels. Before settling out there, they enjoyed a spell surrounded by the dramas of the sea in Portland, to whose austere charms Ken introduced me. I have not forgotten the sound of the pebbles of Chesil Beach being ground together by the incoming waves. For Ken, the marine sunsets were inspirational.

My visit to Menorca was the high point of my relationship with Ken and Jean. They put me up in a flat belonging to a friend near their own small property at Es Castell, a village close to the picturesque capital, Mahon, a flourishing and historic port. Although the island is less than 30 miles long, its terrain ranges from rolling pastureland to coastal cliffs. Exposed trees are bent over by the ferocious *tramuntana* winds that periodically strike. The island's features include huge, mainly disused limestone quarries, some dating back to Roman times; T-shaped megalithic monuments called *taulas* and conical ones called *talyots*, around 3,000 years old; virtuoso drystone walls; and gorges and crests of limestone and whorled red sandstone.

I was conscious of the need to gather material for my book from my week on the island, and did much scribbling in my notebook. That apart, what a delight it was to be taken around by Ken and Jean and shown the many sources of Ken's inspiration: a fresh layer upon many previous layers formed by his travels around England, the USA and Asia. Quarries featured prominently. Many of the older ones were carved into hillsides in the usual way. A few more recent ones had been cut straight down into a field.

One such, only recently abandoned, was like a giant vertical tomb 80 or so feet deep, its saw-scarred walls reflecting the sun's dazzling light. Ken had spent many hours trying to capture its magic. As we peered over the protective wall, we saw a scene of desecration. Rubble had been dumped in the two far corners: to the left quarry rubble, to the right builders' rubble. Even as we stood there, the silence was shattered as a truck tipped a huge load onto the builders' pile, with much crashing and rumbling as it landed and settled. Ken noted that the two piles formed near-perfect cones, one light, one dark. Soon, he reflected, this whole chamber of light would disappear, and eventually cattle would graze again atop his memory of space. The Fall would be redeemed. When he had digested what we had seen, he set to work to capture those cones in a pastel of great subtlety called *Aftermath*.

It was exciting to see him at work in his huge hangar-like studio out in the country. Pastels come in both oily and dry versions. Ken would put layer upon layer, often scraping away the latest to reveal one beneath, and occasionally creating a fine mist by grinding a chalky pastel, then securing it with fixative. He could also relax there, and we played a lot of ping-pong and some snooker. In the evenings we ate very well, in or out, and usually drank rather too much.

A separate pleasure of the Draper exercise was to debrief a few of his closest friends. Notable among these were Nigel Hall, an abstract sculptor of world-wide reputation and enormous charm; and the no less distinguished John Carter, whose austere and minimalist work hovers between painting, sculpture and mathematics. Nigel Hall kindly said that my Draper text read like a novel. I was pleased with the title I dreamed up, *Transience Captured: the Life and Art of Kenneth Draper*, and with its coffee table format and 64 colour plates.

Getting to grips with a leading potter

It was also cheering to be contacted by the eminent ceramicist Ewen Henderson, with a view to my writing an introduction to a major exhibition of his work at the Midlands Art Centre in Birmingham. I had been interested in pots since my days in Copenhagen. Latterly I had been writing the occasional review for a ceramics magazine based in Exeter, and had met numerous collectors. I think Ewen picked me because he also did rather good landscape watercolours, thought I would appreciate both sides of his output and wasn't part of the sometimes bitchy world of ceramics.

He lived and worked in Camden Town in a slightly gloomy house – African carvings in the sitting room did nothing to lighten the mood – and was an engaging if potentially tetchy personality. Tallish, bearded and around 60 years old, he was well read, and passionate about classical music. In both fields he much admired the Russians: from Dostoevsky and Shostakovich to the pianist Sviatoslav Richter, of whom I am also a fan. Ewen was a great conversationalist, and turned out to have had a remarkable life.

His father was the resident GP at a large, red-brick psychiatric hospital in Staffordshire: Ewen called it 'a frightening place designed to keep people mad'. His family lived in a staff house, with inmates acting as servants. After grammar school he endured National Service – in the ranks, thanks to his bolshy streak – mainly in North Germany, where his interest in music was sparked by seeing Furtwängler conduct the Berlin Philharmonic in Kiel. After demob, he took up an apprenticeship in a chemical company in Castleford, Yorkshire (Moore's home town), and soon found himself managing a branch in Cardiff specialising in impregnating timber. He commented very typically: 'I was guilty of making timber unrottable in a series of revolting houses in Newport which should have been allowed to rot very quickly.'

After six or seven years, art belatedly called. He took local evening classes then, aged 29, the foundation course at Goldsmiths' College in London, where he was first seduced by clay. Those twin ceramic deities, Hans Coper and Lucy Rie, were among his teachers when he moved to Camberwell School of Arts and Crafts, as it then was. He rebelled against both of them, started to build vessels freely rather than on the wheel, and subsequently helped push ceramics in the direction of sculpture. I loved most of his work, and he generously gave me a tea bowl to say thanks for what I had written.

When I mentioned my contacts with Ewen to daughter Lottie, she cried: 'Not Mr Henderson! He was our art teacher at school' (i.e. North London Collegiate, part time). It was a nice bond. To celebrate the opening of the show in

Ewen Henderson in his studio

Birmingham, Ewen hired a bus and invited several dozen friends to travel up with him to the Midlands Art Centre. Champagne and smoked salmon sandwiches were laid on. Among his friends was Geoffrey Smith, the American-born, swooping-voiced presenter of Jazz Record Requests on Saturday afternoons, to which I listen. It's always good to put a face to a BBC voice. Away from the mike, he spoke quite normally.

What with the champagne and the jiggling of the bus, after an hour or so I needed a pee more urgently and painfully than ever before or since, and eventually persuaded the driver to stop at a motorway services station. I feared I might have done myself an injury. Ewen's show looked wonderful, and was opened by a distinguished fan, Sir John Drummond, former director of the Edinburgh Festival and BBC 3: he was presented by the BBC with a Henderson ceramic torso at the Last Night of the Proms on his retirement as director of that much-plugged BBC festival. I had seen Drummond periodically since Cambridge days: he was a close friend of our neighbour John Tusa, who also later became Sir John. Drummond was famous, but not always loved, for his prodigious energy, scathing wit and encyclopaedic knowledge of the arts and their practitioners. He died in 2006, aged 71. I had enjoyed interviewing him for my column in the *ILN*, torrentially articulate though he was.

A Caribbean cruise

One day in 1995, Brian MacArthur, an old colleague who had risen to be an associate editor at *The Times*, rang to ask if I would like to go on a cruise around the Virgin Islands in the Caribbean in three days time (a staff reporter had fallen ill). Travel arrangements were swiftly made, and I joined four other journalists and a PR minder at Gatwick, whence we flew to Puerto Rico. There we eventually boarded MS *Seaward*, a ten-decker 700-foot long liner of the Norwegian Cruise Line. The 1,350 punters on board were, unexpectedly, mostly youngish Americans including honeymooning couples. At the first evening's 'singles' dance I was lucky to meet an entertaining and slimly shapely woman called Gay, of whom I was to see quite a lot. I like to think I helped her recover from an alcoholic husband, whom she had left.

Given the number of people on board, and a crew of 630 from five nationalities (as the captain told us), the food was astonishingly good: if you asked for rare beef, you got it rare in a restaurant serving hundreds for dinner in two shifts. Food could be consumed in numerous other locations. In addition to breakfast, lunch and dinner, there was tea, an ice-cream stall and a midnight buffet, plus 24-hour room service, all (except drinks, expensive) included in the price. A number of the Americans were already grossly obese.

As I wrote in my eventual piece, the greatest joy was to lean on the ship's rail, rum punch in hand, chatting to friends or a new acquaintance as the setting sun transformed the vast sky into a Turneresque drama of pinks, dark blues and reds, followed by a moon that turned the water silver. We visited some stunning beaches in our eight days, not least in the Dutch Antilles. My only gripe was that where I had written 'My encounters suggested that far more of those aboard were employed in business than in the professions: I did not meet one lawyer', 'business' was changed to read 'trade', a mischievous attempt to make me sound snobbish. Freelances are not in a strong position to protest about such matters.

Another travel commission from *The Times* – 'Tunisia as a weekend destination' – took me to the wonderful Roman site of Dougga, about two hours drive from Tunis and poised 2,000 feet above a fertile valley; to Carthage (disappointing); and to the Bardo museum and its unrivalled collection of Roman mosaics. A not so funny thing happened to me on the way to the forum in Carthage: I lost my footing on a raised path, and keeled slowly over onto my left temple. Result: some abrasion, and eventually a classic black eye. I was taken for an X-ray, which revealed no internal damage. Among the small and sympathetic press party was Sally Weale, then of the *Guardian*, a charismatic woman married to an architect. Perhaps I literally fell for her.

For the arts page of *The Independent* I contrived a trip to Luxembourg, where an old Brussels friend, Nick Elam, was ambassador: 'a small seat, but in the front row', as a predecessor had dubbed it, Luxembourg being one of the founder members of the EEC. Nick and his delightful wife Helen shared my enthusiasm for contemporary art, and the Foreign Office had, thanks to that very civilised Foreign Secretary Douglas Hurd, OK'd their idea of having artists in residence in the (embassy) residence for several weeks each. Luxembourg's ministry of culture was among local financial supporters of the scheme. The artist when I was there was a painter, Gavin Maughfling, who found it pleasant to be treated 'as if what one is doing is important.' It made a nice piece. One evening we memorably visited Liliane Heidelberger, a French-born sculptor who lives in Luxembourg. She was impressive both as a woman and as a sculptor (mainly in stone), and deserves to be much better known. I have coveted the work of few sculptors as ardently. The Elams have remained cherished friends.

Where travel-writing was concerned, I preferred to write about trips for which I had paid. One such took Jo Frampton and me in May 1996 through the Pelepponese to the Mani region in the deep and arid south of the (underrated) Greek mainland, memorably described by Patrick Leigh Fermor in his eponymous travel classic. We spent a couple of nights in his adopted village of Kardhamili. I had written to the great man, mentioning a couple of mutual acquaintances and hoping to say hello as an admirer. When I telephoned on our arrival, his housekeeper said he was in London. It may even have been true.

Back to South Korea

My last significant trip for *The Times* was my own initiative, but I could not conceivably have afforded it myself. I had long hankered to return to South Korea and witness the transformation of the country since my military service there in 1953-54. Then it was in a state of ruin following the end of the Korean War: the capital, Seoul, virtually destroyed and with a population of little more than one million, its hills stripped of trees, its people destitute, a corrupt dictator, Syngman Rhee, its US-backed president. When I returned in 1997, courtesy of the South Korean National Tourism Organisation and KLM and with *The Times*'s blessing, Seoul's population was around 10 million, the country's economy 11th in the world, its educational standards among the highest, and its democracy pretty robust. Surely no other country has achieved a more comprehensive transformation: one that would no doubt be drastically set back if the peninsula was reunited.

The tourist board was generous: I was provided with a car, guide and driver, neither of whose English was wonderful – but the driver, an amusing fellow, was a great gastronome, so we ate consistently well, largely along Japanese lines. My first priority was to revisit the site of my old regiment, somewhere between the Imjin river and mount Kamaksan. Brigadier Colin Parr, defence attaché at the British embassy, helped me pinpoint it on a wall map, not far from the town of Choksong. There I somewhat incredulously stood next day. Where once had been our mainly tented camp and an adjacent minefield, there were now fields of ginseng.

Too much of the next six days was spent in our comfortable car flogging down, across and back up the often beautiful and mountainous terrain, visiting here a national park, there – in the Buddhist south, in and around Kyongju – temples, pagodas and remarkable museums. The spring weather was deeply disappointing: wet and misty. Journalistically the high point was a few hours at Panmunjom in the so-called demilitarised zone on the 38th parallel, where around 600,000 North Korean and 400,000 South Korean and American troops faced each other across the demarcation line, not far north of Seoul. Bizarrely, it had been turned into a tourist attraction, complete with American military briefings for visitors in a conference room, through whose northerly windows North Korean soldiers peered, a surrealist spectacle. There was even a souvenir shop selling everything from jewellery to chocolates.

Korea revisited: Panmunjom

Virtually every touristic spot in South Korea was overrun with coaches, disgorging Koreans, whose motto seemed to be 'me first', plus hordes of schoolchildren. For a Westerner, the sheer number of people could be oppressive, not least on Seoul's thronged pavements. I was surprised by how much make-up the young women wore. It often seemed to be aimed at covering spotty complexions. But which came first?

In my Kyongju hotel, a bathroom card offered massages day and night. What delights might be on offer? After a good dinner, I summoned a masseuse. When I opened the door, there was not the young beauty of my dreams, but a middle-aged and wholly blind woman. I had forgotten that in South Korea only the registered blind can be officially licensed as masseurs (though that leaves plenty of unofficial, sighted ones). Humour has been defined as the gap between expectations and reality. I laughed inwardly, and submitted myself to her treatment. This included walking on my back, which seemed to do more harm than good.

My move to the South West

My return trip to Korea had brought back the Korean dimension of my life. Interesting though the trip had been, I almost wept with pleasure when I emerged from my plane at Bristol airport on a golden evening to the music of blackbirds, robins and thrushes in full song. Bristol, not Heathrow or Gatwick, because six months earlier, in September 1996, I had moved from Highgate to the village of Turleigh, near Bradford on Avon in Wiltshire. My doctor friend had long since returned to her Hampstead cottage. She was succeeded in my affections by a Japanese woman, divorced from an academic English husband and living nearby in Highgate with her young son. We had first met when she worked for a Japanese newspaper in an office opposite mine at *The Independent*. Her love for me was touching, and I felt deeply guilty when I told her that I was thinking of getting back together in some form or another with Joy.

Of course I felt guilty towards Joy as well. We had been seeing more of each other, and thought some new element in our lives might help renew our relationship, with the help of a cottage in the country. I would spend more time in the country, she more time in London, where she planned to convert the top three floors of our house into a separate and lettable unit, retaining the ground floor, basement and garden. Why not the south-west? We had ex-Hampstead friends near Bradford on Avon in Wiltshire, with whom we had stayed. The scenery was ravishing, Bath was a mere 15 minutes away with all its architectural beauty and culture, London 80 minutes by train. Our friends alerted us to a cottage in Turleigh, a charming village built in a horseshoe overlooking the Avon valley. The cottage was rather small, with a precipitous garden.

We decided on a larger house in the same lane, but there was a hitch in securing it. After we had agreed the price, the vendor, a retired civil servant, died very suddenly outside the gates of Twickenham after watching a Rugby match. His traumatised widow found it hard to decide whether to stay in the vicinity. It took almost a year overall to complete the deal, but was well worth the wait. The house lies at the end of a no-through lane, half way up a hill facing south across the valley with the river Avon and the Kennet and Avon Canal to a sheet of trees. It has an 80-foot terrace perfect for parties and eating outside, and more than half an acre of gently sloping garden. The loudest sound comes from the weir at Avoncliff, at the bottom of a steep meadow. Avoncliff boasts an aqueduct carrying the canal over the Avon and, quaintly, a request-stop for designated trains on the line connecting Cardiff, Bristol and Bath with Portsmouth, Weymouth and Brighton.

It was a thrill to be back in the country. I had been hankering for such a change of life. The yen reached back to my childhood in rural Essex. I had loved working in our little garden in Hampstead, and now had a much larger area to play with. I loved birds, in which this pastoral bit of Wiltshire was well endowed. And I loved walking. Hampstead Heath had been fine, not least for birds: I once practically trod on a woodcock there, and one of the ponds had sedge warblers aplenty. Now I had a canal towpath and the banks of the Avon within a few minutes, replete with kingfishers, herons, even the occasional goosander. Add the nearby beauties of Bradford on Avon and Bath, and you have something hard to beat. I fell in love with this house, its quiet, its garden, its birds, its view, the changing light on the trees across the valley – and its sheer practicality. Whenever I return, even from Bath or Bradford on Avon, I marvel at how fortunate I am; and when I come back from abroad, I want to kiss the ground, even after a dozen years of living here. When the moon is full, it always seems to be opposite my bedroom window precisely at 11pm, and on a clear night the stars are a joy. From my bath, I can observe buzzards cruising on the thermals.

On the exciting day of my arrival, the keys had been left with neighbours in a handsome Georgian house up the lane. When I collected them I was urged to come back for a drink, and then, after three whiskies, to stay for dinner, during which I drank an entire bottle of wine. My hosts were Dr Derek Heap, retired, and his wife Ann, a former nurse. Derek, it soon transpired, had also been at Rugby, had left just before I arrived, but remembered Martin. 'I'm sure you'll shake up the village' he told me a trifle ambiguously.

A few hours after my arrival I saw a beautiful woman parking a Volvo a few houses from mine. She told me she was Anna Tham, Swedish-born and a psychotherapist. 'Good God!' I cried. 'I've just come from Hampstead, which is full of psychotherapists!' She invited me to dinner with friends from the village a couple of days on. I rang an art-world friend, Liese Thynne, an ex-model who worked at the Beaux Arts Gallery in Bath, and she said: 'There's a very nice woman in Turleigh who is a serious collector, called Sheila Day. Why don't you contact her?' So I did, and Sheila, another retired doctor, asked me for a drink with several local artists. So it went on, very encouragingly. In making such contacts it helps to have been a journalist and accustomed to picking up a phone to ring strangers. The days when to do so took a major psychic effort, as when I joined the *Daily Express* in Manchester in 1960, seemed aeons ago.

Labelle revisited: Bob Keyserlingk in his 60s

This house consists of three one-up, one-down cottages dating from around 1700, knocked into one long unit, probably in the 1930s, with a 1950s wood-clad extension, in which I first established myself. Most of my furniture went temporarily into the garage. The ground floor proved to be lined with asbestos cement tiles: not harmful in themselves when painted, but I was advised to have them removed, an expensive specialist operation for men in white coats and masks. A visit to the Keyserlingks in Canada while that was going on seemed a good idea, and it was great to see them

My view across the Avon valley

Turleigh Croft, watercolour by my army friend Bernard Hickey, 2003

again. Eventually the very thick stone walls, having been cut back to the rubble, were replastered, to excellent effect.

I did much of the redecorating myself, helped in short bursts variously by daughter Lucy, back from the European Space Agency in the Netherlands, working for Matra Marconi Space in Bristol and waiting for a visa to spend nine months at NASA in Houston; a decorator who did such tricky tasks as relining ceilings; and the son of a friend. After a day's decorating, I would often walk the mile and a half to Bradford, swim in the distressingly tepid town pool, then walk back. Where did I find the energy?

Lucy and I were strolling by the Avon one fine day in late January when she told me that she had decided she was gay. Although she had had several boyfriends, she was also friendly with one or two seemingly gay women, so this came as no great surprise. I accepted it as a fact of life. Unfortunately neither Joy nor I particularly liked her first gay partner, who visited her when she was settled in Houston.

Just before Lucy returned to Bristol after her nine months in Texas, we had a very bonding experience, meeting up in Seattle and spending a week in the North West Pacific, hopping from island to island northwards. Although it was June, the mountain ranges inland from Seattle were still capped with snow. Apart from enjoying the spectacular scenery, which included island rain forests – 'You are in Cougar Country', said the signs alarmingly – and those famous giant sequoias (conifers), we went whale watching (orcas) and sea-kayaking, and ate a lot of delicious wild salmon.

Lucy cut down by M.E.

The strain of 'coming out' probably added to the pressures that were to ground our high-flying daughter and for a long time cloud my happiness in Turleigh. One December evening in 1997 she telephoned me to say that she had collapsed at work at Matra Marconi Space and had been taken by ambulance to Southmead Hospital in Bristol, with what was suspected to be M.E. (myalgic encephalopathy, aka post-viral fatigue syndrome). Could I, she asked weakly, collect some things from her flat in Clifton and bring them over? Feelings almost of panic, certainly of deep gloom, seized me as I raced over. I had great difficulty finding the hospital, where her (admirably supportive) consultant and various ancillary services were based.

Misleadingly, Lucy was soon up and about. But over the next few years her symptoms worsened and multiplied. They included acute pain in her thighs, jumpy legs, adrenaline on fast forward, hunger every two or so hours (but she did not put on weight), insomnia linked to all these, hypoglycaemic episodes, terrible headaches if she read or listened to music – and of course chronic fatigue that eventually prevented her from walking more than a few yards and made a wheelchair essential outside. Her ability to work at home declined from a couple of hours a day to zero. Talking taxed her, listening even more so. After much complex form-filling, she was deemed eligible for disability benefits, and her employers eventually gave her a not ungenerous disability pension.

M.E. being largely unfathomed by conventional medicine, no help was available from her GP save Amitriptylene, an anti-depressant often used to treat insomnia. But her GP was, unlike some others in similar circumstances, supportive. When approached, purveyors of most forms of alternative medicine were confident they could help. Lucy tried virtually all of them. Each reckoned that within a few weeks or months she would be restored to health. Those she tried included faith-healing, acupuncture, Chinese herbal medicine, Reiki, colonic irrigation, kinesiology, homeopathy, and endless diets, one of which restricted her to bananas for a week. My favourite panacea involved moving her bed so she avoided sleeping above an underground river, located by dowsing. All these cost money, and many required me to ferry Lucy around Bristol and environs, which I did willingly but sceptically. Each one at least gave her hope, but none produced a detectable improvement. Naturally she spent a good deal of time with me in peaceful Turleigh. One of the few gains was that we became extremely close.

Lucy bore her deprivations with remarkable fortitude. To salvage something from the wreckage, she decided to learn the guitar. In the process she became a close friend of her guitar teacher and his partner, a very good singer. She soon had two sets of friends: the high-flyers, mostly from school and university, who worked too hard and had plenty of money but no time; and her impoverished new friends, with less exacting jobs, more time and too little money. While still very weak, she met a potential partner, Kate Donoghue, who soon bravely moved in with her. Kate is a child psychologist with huge blue eyes, a very warm personality, and a great sense of humour.

Only when someone recommended a relatively new approach called Reverse Therapy, a cousin of Cognitive Behavioural Therapy, did her recovery – from a very low point – begin. It is possible that after some seven years, the average duration of this scourge, Lucy's body was ready. But judging by the response to an article in *The Daily Telegraph* at about this time, numerous other sufferers have also found Reverse Therapy helpful. Lucy had been a classic over-achiever, constantly looking for new challenges, a perfectionist at work, reluctant to say No, determined to overcome her few weaknesses. She had probably pushed herself too hard, and her body seemed to have said: take seven years off, Lucy. Reverse Therapy helped to heal the rift between mind and body.

Her recovery began after half a dozen sessions with a therapist in Clevedon, a seaside town not far from Bristol. Within a year, she could walk for several hours in, say, the Brecon Beacons, and do some work. She now puts in two or three days a week at Explore! a kids-oriented science museum in Bristol, and periodically lectures on space matters for the engineering faculty at Bristol University. It's quite a change.

Lottie's new life

Earlier during Lucy's illness her sister Lottie had moved to Bristol with her husband-to-be, and was able to give valuable support. She had met her partner, Nick Lawson, while living in East London. Around ten years previously he had been ordained by his teacher, the founder of the Friends of the Western Buddhist Order. That remarkable man, whom coincidentally I had interviewed while at the *ILN*, was known as Sangharakshita. Nick was in turn given the name Amarajyoti (meaning undying light). Ordination seemed to represent only a small step on the path to enlightenment via a spell in a retreat centre in Spain. No celibacy was involved, and as far as the gentle, handsome Nick was concerned, no robes or shaven heads. He had done various jobs for the FWBO, which has a commercial wing, and he and Lottie met via its headquarters in the East End.

In 1995 Amarajyoti had gone to study at Norwich School of Art and Design, while Lottie found a job first in the FWBO's publishing wing, then at Waterstone's. They moved to Bristol after four years, and stayed for 18 months. Lottie is a talented organiser, and in Bristol she found a council-related job helping to run an international millennium project for teenagers interested in the environment. Subsequently she has worked at the interface between health and education for two other councils and the NHS: first in and around Brighton and then for South Gloucester Council. They have settled in Nailsworth, an old mill town near Stroud, and have two daughters: Isla, born in 2003, and Lois, born two years later. Lottie has been the main bread-winner, Amarajyoti a wonderfully patient house-husband. Now that Lois has joined Isla at school, he is moving into teaching

As for Lucy and Kate, they have a very lively daughter, Eva, born to Kate in 2005. Their donor, Mark, is a London-based engineer in the oil industry with several children of his own. He comes to family events with his own family. Both Lucy and Lottie live within 50 minutes of Turleigh, which is great for us all. The grand-daughters love tumbling around my garden together.

That bachelor streak

Unfortunately it did not prove easy to evolve a pattern of life in which Joy was sometimes here (generally at weekends) and sometimes not here. As I became more and more embedded in the country, London came to seem more and more stressful, and my visits dropped from a couple of days a week to perhaps one a fortnight. Eventually Joy sold the Christchurch Hill house at the top of the market, and acquired her own residence in Bath, to be near Lucy, Lottie and the granddaughters, a small flat around the corner in Hampstead, and a newish apartment down the hill near the Royal Free Hospital, which she lets: it is effectively her pension. We lunch together and remain good friends.

There is, as mentioned, an element of the bachelor in me. I like being able to relate to people one-on-one, without that feeling of being monitored. I love being able to invite anyone I meet for a meal, perhaps that same evening. I love being able to play music when and at the volume I want, to go for a long walk alone without feeling I'm being selfish, and garden for as long as I fancy. Living with someone involves endless compromises.

Lottie and Amarajyoti

Lucy and Kate

My friends come variously from Turleigh and outlying villages, from Bradford on Avon and Bath. Not long after I arrived, several of them helped me form a support group to raise funds for the Medical Foundation for Victims of Torture, to which I had periodically contributed. I had always hated the idea of fund-raising, thinking I would be useless at asking for money. The Medical Foundation was looking for volunteers to start up regional support groups, and I thought: 'Come on, Berthoud, do something useful!' There are, I discovered, enjoyable if strenuous ways of raising funds. We gave the odd paying lunch and a dinner-dance at a local village hall; organised a *soirée musicale* at Corsham Court, a stately home belonging to the Methuen family, even a botanical walk; and we took part in charity sales in Bath. Over four years we raised £12,000 before deciding we had exhausted the good will of our friends. My siblings have been even more active as fund-raisers: Martin for Prisoners Abroad, Binnie for Hope and Homes. Lis is a pillar of support for the elderly in her old village near Taunton. In our different ways, we have been belatedly following the example of our public-spirited parents.

In Turleigh I helped edit a classy millennium book about the village, elegantly illustrated by our only Old Etonian, for which someone from each of Turleigh's 55 households contributed a brief account of their family and home. I wrote the introduction and postscript, and edited their contributions. Since the millennium, more than half the houses have changed hands, some twice, and there is pressure for a new edition. Eventually I became chairman of the village trust committee, which decides how to spend the modest income from a bequest. In 1920 a certain Major Leverson Scarth so loved the village that he left it a capital sum and a house to act as a focal point. The house was sold when television seemed to make a village centre redundant, thus increasing the capital. We spend most of the money on such ventures as the millennium book, and on an annual picnic ('Summerfest') in June, with a marquee and free drink: people bring their own food. Consequently we all know each other. The village has got progressively younger, as I had predicted in the millennium book, and there is a party for the now numerous children each September.

Updating Henry Moore

After a couple of years, something dangerously like work intruded upon this idyll (Lucy's traumas apart). I had been distressed that my biographies of Moore and Sutherland had gone out of print without being paperbacked. One person who could help put this right was Giles de la Mare, my old friend and former editor at Faber, who had set up his own eponymous imprint after leaving Faber. A launch party in 1999 for one of his books found him in a receptive mood, as far as the Moore biography was concerned. Sir Alan Bowness, a former director of the Tate Gallery and of the Henry Moore Foundation, kindly joined me in suggesting a new edition. Another serious supporter was Peter Osborne of the Berkeley Square Gallery (later Osborne, Samuel), who loved the book and said he might purchase two or three hundred copies, as did the Henry Moore

Foundation. The latter also provided a subsidy towards production costs and again gave me free access to their photographic archive. That alone was worth thousands of pounds.

Giles was thus emboldened to give me the go-ahead for an updated and revised version. Fortunately there was some valuable new material to incorporate, notably 17 illustrated letters that Moore had written to his last girl friend before he fell for another student, his eventual wife Irina Radetzky. She was called Evelyn Kendall, and Henry had kept notably quiet about her all his life. Her daughter had found the letters in her basement, shown them to BBC TV's *Antiques Roadshow*, and then auctioned them at Sotheby's in London. The foundation had photocopied them, and the anonymous purchaser gave me permission to quote from them. In addition, I thought I should amplify my arguably inadequate coverage of one or two aspects of Moore's work, such as his debt to surrealism, a movement I had never taken to; and append a chronology of the main events involving the Henry Moore Foundation since the sculptor's death.

This included a short summary of the complex legal action brought by Moore's daughter Mary against the foundation, contesting the interpretation of her parents' legacies. Had Mary won, she could have claimed around two-thirds of the foundation's collection of Moore's sculptures and many of his drawings. Much of the case hinged on the question of whether so-called 'artist's copies' are personal to the sculptor, or part of the normal process of producing an 'edition': for example, six bronze casts plus one called an artist's copy. After five weeks of hearings, which I did not attend, the judge found in favour of the foundation, a verdict upheld three years later by the Court of Appeal.

Happily, the rift between Mary and the HMF was later bridged. She is a difficult woman, but it can't have been easy to be the only child of someone so excessively famous, who was also a somewhat possessive and prescriptive father. Her Russian-born mother Irina, traumatised by her childhood experiences in revolutionary Russia, was by contrast not very maternal. Unsurprisingly, Mary again declined to make available to me any of the archival material in her possession, but did point out one or two small errors in the first edition.

In September 2001 I was nearing the end of my labours on this project when I had a visit from a Canadian specialist in Moore's drawings, Dr Alan Wilkinson, whom I knew well: he had played a key role in securing a large haul of Moore's work for his former employers, the Art Gallery of Ontario in Toronto. We spent a long day, punctuated by a walk, discussing Moore and a book Alan was preparing on Moore's writings. It wasn't until around 11pm that we switched on the TV and learned of the mesmerisingly appalling events soon dubbed 9/11.

Giles and I agreed that the new edition of my biography should have its illustrations integrated into the text where relevant, rather than in blocks. Although they at first seemed rather smaller, I was delighted by the finished product with its vastly more appealing cover, and by my major opus's renewed availability. I gave half a dozen lectures to help publicise it, an exercise I enjoyed. My fee ranged from zero, not even travel costs, to around £120.

Giles ordered a print run of 3,065 copies. Too late to add to this, there came an order for 1,000 copies from Book Club Associates, which had to be printed separately, at some loss to Giles. I was thrilled to hear of the book club order, imagining a large cheque heading my way (I had had no advance). In fact I received a miserable £350: book clubs demand huge discounts, so the author usually gets much less than his or her standard percentage of the retail price. Nowadays big bookshops also expect large discounts, pointing out that they are in competition with supermarkets and Amazon. In retrospect, I much regret the leaders I wrote at *The Independent* in favour of the abolition of RPM for books (the Net Book Agreement), the effects of which were all too accurately predicted by those who opposed it.

At about the time I moved to Turleigh, Joy too had flowered into authorship with *Pecking Order: How Your Place in the Family Affects Your Personality*, published by Gollancz. It was largely inspired by the similarities she detected between her own experience as a first child with a younger sister, and the relationship between our own two daughters. A shadow hovered over her researches: an American academic was known to be preparing a much larger survey on the same theme. So she was under considerable pressure from Gollancz to adhere to a very tight schedule. In the event her study, published as an original paperback, received a good deal of publicity, and was compared favourably with the American academic's heavy-weight and more historical tome by one respected reviewer.

The curse of Yellow Nail Syndrome

I had moved to Turleigh just before my 63rd birthday. Physically I was in reasonable shape, though I had a history of sinusitis, and the beginnings of a chest problem. X-rays revealed some damage to my right lung, impairing its ability to process the mucus that gets generated in that region. When Joy and I were staying with Ewen and Sarah Fergusson in 2001 at their house not far from Mont Ventoux in the Lubéron, my ankles started getting puffy. I dismissed this as a by-product of the heat. But they stayed swollen even on return to England, then the swelling spread to my legs: a clear case of lymphoedema (retained fluid). Finally, my finger and toenails started discolouring and crumbling. A chest consultant from the Royal United Hospital in Bath was the first to suspect Yellow Nail Syndrome.

This is a rare and 'medically interesting' condition combining my four problems: sinusitis, bronchiectasis, lymphoedema and disintegrating nails, in varying degrees of severity. It is thought, not conclusively, to be caused by a recessive gene, sometimes affecting whole families. But none of my siblings show any sign of it, nor did my parents. My case could have been much worse. I can, for example, walk up steep hills without difficulty, which is fortunate as I live on one. I am however liable to have half a dozen chest infections a year, for which I have stand-by antibiotics.

At the time of writing Joy is in good shape, as are my sisters Binnie and Lis. Binnie oscillates between her home near Hungerford and her studio off Kensington Church Street, and is devoted to her two granddaughters, two Burmese cats and one black Labrador. Lis has had the toughest time. Her first husband died of cancer. Then she heroically oversaw our parents in their declining years. After a period of respite, her second husband began to succumb in his early 80s to dementia, aggravated by late-onset Huntington's, and died after several distressing months in nursing homes. My brother Martin's health has been good, but his greatly loved wife Marguerite has had three operations for cancer, and has endured years of chemotherapy at the Royal Marsden Hospital in London. Her courage and resilience have been remarkable.

Being a habitudinarian, I have established a daily – though not inflexible! – routine: up around 7.15 am, read much of the *Guardian* over breakfast and listen to Radio 4 until around 9.30am, peck at the computer till 12.30pm or so; walk for up to an hour and garden in the afternoon, followed by a bit of a read; in the evening, I sometimes go to a concert or film, more rarely the theatre, entertain or am entertained, or watch TV or a DVD and/or read with CD accompaniment. *A propos* the theatre: there are to my mind few things worse than a bad play or a badly acted play, especially a so-called comedy during which people laugh inanely to show they are getting their money's worth. The sense of release when walking out in the interval is blissful.

Grandchildren are proverbially one of the joys of advancing years, and Joy and I see a lot of our three, albeit most often separately. Kate and Lucy's Eva has exceptional energy levels and is a great charmer. Lottie and Amarajyoti's Isla shows a keen interest in music and dance. Her sister Lois wants to do everything Isla can do, and often gets frustrated. Their visits are a joy if sometimes tiring, as visits from old friends for the weekend can also be.

I sometimes lunch or spend a night in London. One irresistible invitation was to a lunch hosted by Nicholas Barrington for 'some of his more literary friends'. It was held in a book-lined private room at his club, the Athenaeum. Among those present were Michael Holroyd and his partner Margaret Drabble, V.S.Naipaul and his Pakistani-born wife Nadira; Michael Frayn and Claire Tomalin; Bamber Gascoigne and his wife Christina; Julian Pettifer; and Victoria Schofield, an expert on Pakistan and author of a recent biography of Lord Wavell. I sat next to Michael Holroyd: a more delightful famous author it would be hard to find. Messrs Frayn, Gascoigne and Pettifer were Cambridge contemporaries of mine, as of course was our generous host.

I am fortunate in my local friends, whose names I will not drop, high achievers though some of them are. We are a bit of a gang, and support those among us who are active in the musical and art worlds. We are lucky to have in Bath a seriously good art cinema, the Little Theatre cinema; a seriously good theatre, the Theatre Royal; three seriously good art galleries, the (council-backed) Victoria Art Gallery, the (commercial) Beaux Arts Gallery and the Adam Gallery and many others; plus a vibrant classical music scene, with two major music festivals a year and regular concerts in the beautiful Bath Abbey, whose acoustics are alas well short of ideal. All that's missing is a custom-built concert hall. As for Bath, just to drive down into the city and see those glorious Georgian terraces laid out below is to have one's heart lifted.

Bird-watching holidays

Much as I like living alone, holidays are a problem for single people. One solution is to travel with a group. My first such venture was to Hungary with Ornitholidays, whose ingenious name apparently discourages obsessive twitchers scornful of the concept of holidays. They are called listers in the USA, and can be a menace: their main interest is in ticking off a species new to them, so they want to move on rather than observe and enjoy. In the autumn of my life, my interest in cities and museums has waned, while landscapes and birds have grown in appeal. The Hungarian trip was spectacular. The highlight came when we stood in a carefully chosen field as an estimated 20,000 migrating cranes flew in against a brilliant sunset, the air filled with their bugling calls, and landed in marshy terrain around us. As a bonus, a white-tailed eagle dived in among them, killing one and causing a picturesque panic.

We were in the strikingly flat Hortobagy national park some 200 miles east of Budapest. This protected but partly agricultural *puzsta* has huge skies, a wonderfully subtle range of browns and greens, and very sculptural wells. Huge fish farms (for carp) flanked by marshland are widespread – perfect for geese, duck, herons, egrets, all manner of waders, and much else besides. After a few days, we barely looked up when our Hungarian guide said 'hen harrier' or indeed 'marsh harrier', so common were they. The many raptors, for me the most exciting birds, included four species of eagle, at least four different falcons, a goshawk and several varieties of buzzard. During one picnic lunch – the late October weather was consistently sunny – we watched a family of four white-tailed eagles soaring above us, swooping playfully at each other.

In the more banal setting of a small town garden, 55 long-eared owls were roosting in three trees. Most were quite well camouflaged: spotting them became a bit of a game. One was sitting on a branch in the open, and set our cameras clicking. It was the first time I'd seen a camera slotted onto a telescope, resulting in one shot of a single glowing yellowy-orange eye. Telescopes with tripods are bulky but invaluable on such trips. Luckily for those of us with mere binoculars, several of our party had them and allowed us to have a peer when they had lined up, say, two distant red-breasted geese. At one stage I thought our leader called out, pointing skywards: 'Y-fronted geese'. A nice concept, but of course they were white-fronted.

Other excitements included two dozen very shy great bustards. Hungarian Grey cattle, large beasts with magnificent horns, were a feature of many of our stops. We visited a farm that bred another Hungarian speciality: woolly pigs, variously off-white, black and chestnut coloured. They had quite shaggy, curly coats, and rushed to the fence to commune with us. Subsequently, whenever we were served pork the cry would go up: 'Woolly pig!'

My street cred was raised in one posh *czarda* (restaurant) where we were tackling the usual goulash soup and trying to discourage violinists from serenading us with such Hungarian classics as *My Bonnie Lies Over The Ocean*. A stunningly beautiful woman came over to me and said 'Hello! Good to see you again.' The penny dropped: she was the Hungarian-American behind me in a long queue for the loo on the flight to Budapest, and we had chatted for about 15 minutes. It seemed quite a coincidence, considering we were 200 miles from the capital, albeit in the touristic town of Hortobagy itself.

My second trip with the same company took me in April 2007 to the Aegean island of Lesbos (or Lesvos), from which Turkey is easily visible. We were a smaller, more cohesive group of five, one woman, no spouses, plus a leader, Roger Lawrence, who was as delightful as he was knowledgeable. Our hotel in Skala Kalloni, the coastal townlet near which we stayed, was full of birders from England. One could see why: this beautiful island was awash with spring migrants, and an Englishman had written a book about birding there. We were greeted on arrival by the hotel's resident nightingale, which seemed to sing night and day. Warblers were the Lesbos speciality, and on the saltpans near the hotel were flamingos, glossy ibis and much else besides. Subsequent trips have taken me to Romania (a floating hotel on the Danube and brown bears in the Carpathians) and the ancient forest of Bialowieza in north-east Poland.

Maurice Ash dies

In January 2003, my old friend and to some extent mentor, Maurice Ash, died aged 86. My debt, indeed the whole family's, to him was enormous. He greatly widened my cultural horizons from the age of 16, not least by introducing me to contemporary art and Henry Moore. He helped me decide to become a journalist, and later taught me much about the environment and Buddhism. For a year or so he let me his flat off Portland Place for a song, thus increasing my spendable income. He and his wife Ruth entertained the four of us at least once a year at their wonderful home near Totnes, made Dartington as well as their Sharpham estate part of our lives, and allowed us to use their villa in Cap d'Antibes for two or three family holidays. Their daughters Kate, Maryon and Clare also become friends.

As soon as it became clear that Maurice would not long survive (Ruth, the main source of his wealth, had died of motor neurone disease in 1986), I decided I must do his life justice in a substantial obituary. He helped me fill in some gaps in my knowledge, I wrote it well in advance, and the finished product appeared over three full columns in *The Independent* the day after his death. It must have been pretty convincing, since the other broadsheets gave him the same sort of attention several days later. I felt I had repaid a small part of my debt to him, as I had in a minor way with my art dealer friends Andras Kalman of the Crane Kalman Gallery, Peter Gimpel of Gimpel Fils, and his brother Jean, medievalist and promoter of appropriate technology.

A wake was held for Maurice at Sharpham, a crowded occasion on and around that wonderful cantilevered staircase. I felt honoured to be one of the four speakers. The occasion was a reminder of how widely loved he was, especially within the large Dartington community.

Granddaughters and great nieces at a family party 2008:
Lois on left, Isla holding finger-sucking Eva in the middle (Tessa Smith)

There was a time when we Berthouds seemed to meet mainly at weddings and funerals, at which proper conversation is difficult. So we decided to have a family party every summer, with rotating hosting alleviated by contributions on the food front. Usually we invite cousins, including first cousins from Switzerland, with numbers ranging up to 45. Sometimes we have just us four siblings, our spouses if any, our offspring and grandchildren. It's a great opportunity for the young to get to know each other better, and for us to get to know our great nephews and nieces better. There is a large preponderance of the latter.

For my most recent birthday, marking three quarters of a century on this much-abused planet, I invited my two daughters, their partners and their three offspring; my three siblings; a handful of friends from Cambridge days; and 20-odd local friends and neighbours. The sun shone for most of the time, as it often does in mid-September. After drinks on the terrace, we ate lunch under a large apple tree on the upper garden: sirloin of beef and poached salmon, plus various salads, virtually all my own work. Martin made a heart-warming speech, Lucy and Lottie read out a touching ode, and I thanked everyone for their love and affection, which I had felt welling up towards me.

In the course of my career, I sometimes paused to wonder whether, or when, I had peaked. In terms of happiness, I think it may be now.

November 2009

THE INDEPENDENT

40 CITY ROAD, LONDON EC1Y 2DB (telephone 01-253-1222; telex 9419611 INDPNT)

In the name of Christ

CHRISTMAS is a time for reflection as well as for gifts and celebration. We give to celebrate Christ's birth. If that motive has been somewhat lost to view in Western Europe in this era of lapsed or non-practising Christianity, most people are at least aware of the origin of the Christmas festival; and they are generally all the better for the excuse it provides to bring families together and strengthen the bonds of love or affection with gifts and good cheer.

Many of those who pause to reflect on the legacy of Christ's birth may wonder whether their celebration is justified. If God's chief motive in bestowing a Son on mankind was to redeem the human race from its sinfulness, no objective assessment could conclude that the mission has yet been successful. At times He seems to have made matters worse. Millions have been slaughtered, tortured and persecuted in the name of Christianity. The victims have been followers of other gods, Christians who dissented from the prevailing orthodoxy, and innocent tribes whom invading Christians sought to convert or eliminate: the Crusades, the colonisation of the Americas, and the Inquisition were simply highlights. Even such mass slaughterers as Stalin and Hitler, who may seem to represent the anti-Christ, were the product of Christian civilisation; and Communism in its purer forms was based on Christian ideals. When Western, Christian civilisation points its collective finger at the followers of other gods and prophets, it does well to consider its own grisly record.

Yet the Christian ideals of love, compassion, sacrifice, justice and peace have inspired much that lifts mankind above the crude struggle for survival and domination, from centuries of courageous, selfless struggle on behalf of the deprived, the suffering and oppressed to great architecture, music, art and literature. Whether or not the Christian world still goes to church, it remains heir to these ideals and committed to spreading them as widely as possible.

The past 12 months have given cause for optimism, with moves towards peace in Afghanistan, the Gulf, southern Africa, to some extent in Cambodia, and perhaps in the Middle East. President Gorbachev's espousal of internationalism and his unilateral arms reductions inspire hope that the barriers between the peoples of Eastern and Western Europe will be reduced to a point where we can share our European heritage together. Against that must be set the continuation around the globe of torture, arbitrary imprisonment, unfair trials and mass political executions. Nearly one-fifth of humanity lives in abject poverty, and some 12 million refugees are wandering across borders from countries racked by civil war or persecution.

It is tragic, but far from coincidental, that the same Palestine where Christ was born should for the past half-century have been the seat and source of bitter conflict. Centuries of persecution of Jews by Christians, inspired by a vengeful and utterly unChristian reading of history, culminated in the unprecedentedly well-organised evil of the Holocaust, which in turn led to the creation of the state of Israel and the dispossession of Arab Palestinians. No dispute is harder to resolve than one in which each side is widely agreed to have much right on its side. Despite recent concessions by the Palestine Liberation Organisation and the positive American response to them, the prospects for peace in the crucible of Christianity do not look bright. Until it is achieved, it will be hard to contemplate the story of Christ's birth in Jerusalem without a sense of searing irony.

As we prepare to enjoy Christmas in the security of our homes, we may spare some thoughts for those who are hungry or suffering around the world, for those who have no family and no adequate support, and for those whose loved ones have been torn from them. The Armenian earthquake was a humbling reminder of man's puniness in the face of natural disasters; the Clapham Junction train crash of his fallibility in controlling his inventions; and the Lockerbie jumbo jet disaster — if it was caused by a bomb — of the deadliness and ruthlessness of human hatred. The Western hostages in Beirut are victims of the same evil. Christian churchmen have shown increasing courage and imagination in combating the forces of darkness and fighting for freedom and basic rights. If the Western world as a whole is to justify the nobler aspects of its heritage, it should strive as hard for an end to hunger, torture, gross injustice and the abuse of the environment as it does to maintain its own prosperity.

24 December 1988

THE INDEPENDENT

40 CITY ROAD, LONDON EC1Y 2DB (telephone 01-253-1222; telex 9419611 INDPNT)

Lord Mackay and the Antichrist

BIGOTRY and intolerance have driven the Lord Chancellor, Lord Mackay of Clashfern, from the Church which he once described as manifesting "the most tender love that has ever been described". Lord Mackay's announcement yesterday that he was no longer a member of the Free Presbyterian Church of Scotland was the right response to the decision, taken by the Church's synod on Thursday, to suspend him from his position as a senior elder and from Communion for attending requiem Masses for two legal colleagues who were also friends.

It is nowadays considered odd that someone of outstanding intellect should belong to a tiny fundamentalist sect. Could Lord Mackay really have shared his church's (and the Rev Ian Paisley's) view of the Pope as "Antichrist, that man of sin, that son of perdition, that exalteth himself in the church against Christ, and all that is called God"? Presumably not, if he felt able to attend those funerals. While the fundamentalist wing of the Free Presbyterian Church regards the papal Mass as "the most blasphemous form of religious worship that Satan ever invented; an offence unto God and destructive of the souls of men", the more moderate consider it "positive testimony of man's relationship with God if he stands among idolatrous worshippers and refuses to become involved with their practices", as a recent pro-Mackay pamphlet put it.

The Lord Chancellor was no convert, but born into the faith. He came, like the Prime Minister herself and so many members of her Cabinet (including Kenneth Clarke, Cecil Parkinson, John Moore, John Major and Peter Walker), from a modest working-class background. His father, a railway signalman from Ballerno, just outside Edinburgh, was a Free Presbyterian, and young James Mackay was brought up to strict observance of the Sabbath, which he maintains, and belief in the verity of the Bible. He turned out to be a brilliant mathematician, becoming a lecturer at St Andrew's University and completing the mathematics tripos at Cambridge before turning to the law.

To succeed both in mathematics and the law demands a rigorous mind, and James Mackay's is evidently an outstanding instrument. If such an intellect were addressed to his religious beliefs, would it not inevitably expose them as in many respects anachronistic, not to say grotesquely intolerant? Could any reasonable man today support, as the Free Presbyterians do, the Westminster Confession of 1643, with its central belief that "some men and angels are predestinated unto everlasting life, and others foreordained to everlasting death"? Or believe that the world was actually made in six days, complete with fossils?

Yet John Calvin, the French-born religious reformer on whose teachings the wider Presbyterian Church bases its beliefs and practice, was a classical scholar before introducing heretic-burning to Protestantism. He was also, as Lord Mackay has pointed out, trained as a lawyer. When Calvin fled to Switzerland, the puritanism he imposed in Geneva proved highly unpopular, leading to riots organised by a faction called the Libertines. Calvinism eventually prevailed; and the hard work, thrift and sobriety which it enjoined brought Geneva great wealth. If capitalism has a spiritual father, he is Calvin.

Although Mrs Thatcher cites her father, Alderman Alfred Roberts of Grantham, rather than any foreigner, in her own advocacy of hard work and thrift, it is appropriate that one of Calvin's spiritual descendants should grace her Cabinet. No doubt his background and beliefs helped to convince the Prime Minister that he would make a suitable successor to Lords Hailsham and Havers. Mrs Thatcher also greatly admires those other believers in thrift, hard work and sabbatarianism, the Jews.

Not even during Lord Mackay's troubles with his intolerant co-religionists has anyone suggested that his good nature or his powers of judgement have been affected by his religious beliefs: on both counts he compares favourably with that much more orthodox Christian, Lord Hailsham. Lord Mackay was not only the most prominent of the Free Presbyterians' elders, but also an impressive advertisement for their faith. The synod has shot itself in the foot with its harsh decision. No doubt Lord Mackay will adhere to his convictions: in an age of relativism, ecumenism and permissiveness, Presbyterianism has a not unappealing austerity. Its good name was impugned by the intolerance of those from whom the Lord Chancellor has now wisely parted company.

27 May 1989

Remembering the good Germans

THE GERMANS are often portrayed as having been virtually unanimous in their support for Hitler after he came to power in 1933 — at least until it became clear that Germany was likely to lose the war. The truth is more complex, as today's 50th anniversary of the most famous plot to assassinate him reminds us.

From Hitler's rise to power in 1933 onwards, his persecution of the Jews and other policies of racial "purification", the brutal behaviour of his henchmen and police, and his suppression of all forms of dissent, disgusted large numbers of decent Germans. It is hard for Britons, who have never lived in a police state, to imagine the courage required to perform even minor acts of resistance in one so complete as Nazi Germany. Yet many found the nerve to do so, and died as a consequence.

The Communists were among the first to suffer. Many were rounded up in 1933. Others tried parading their opposition on the streets, with often fatal results, before choosing the path of emigration to Moscow. The inclusion of Communist leaders in a new exhibition in Berlin devoted to the resistance has prompted outspoken protests from Franz Ludwig von Stauffenberg, youngest son of Claus von Stauffenberg, the colonel who planted the bomb that almost killed Hitler 50 years ago. His reaction is surely misplaced: loathsome though their post-war actions were, the Communists, especially those who stayed in Germany, were as much a part of the resistance as the aristocratic army officers prominent in the 20 July plot.

The officers' heroism, heightened by the grisly fate they and many of their relatives suffered when Hitler survived, should not obscure the courage of all those other Germans, be they Protestants, Catholics, Social Democrats, trade unionists, students or ordinary people from all levels of society, who risked their lives in active or passive forms of opposition. Some sheltered Jews, others helped prisoners used as slave labour.

These were the "good Germans", whose existence the Allies found it inconvenient to recognise, let alone support. There were good arguments for the policy of unconditional surrender agreed at the Casablanca conference of 1943. But Britain's leaders had been deeply suspicious of the German opposition from its first formal pre-Munich approach in 1938 onwards. Ultimately, it was simpler to paint the German people as a collective enemy, and one deserving to be bombed into the ground. Today is a good moment to recall that this was an injustice to many brave men, women and children.

20 July 1994

Notes and References

Chapter 1

An article in the *Reader's Digest* of November 1955, 'The Secret Voyage of Britain's Treasure' was very useful.

The Britten quotes are from Humphrey Carpenter's *Benjamin Britten: A Biography* (Faber & Faber 1992)

Much of the information about my father's life throughout the book comes from his autobiography *An Unexpected Life* (privately printed by The Anchor Press 1980). My mother's memoir was called *My Childhood, my family and other adventures* (from the same source, 1979)
My guide to the life of my great grandfather was *The Life Story of Sir Charles Tilston Bright*, by (his son) Charles Bright (Constable 1908). Some details of the Gosling tribe came from *My Grandfather and Other Goslings*, by Sarah F. Courage (privately printed *circa* 2005 by the Lavenham Press), a lavishly illustrated and fascinating chronicle.

Chapter 2

The obituary of Fanny Blankers-Koen was in the *Guardian* of 26 January 2004.

For a good account of Michael Straight at Cambridge, see *Anthony Blunt: His Lives*, by Miranda Carter (Macmillan 2001). For the Elmhirsts, see *The Elmhirsts of Dartington*, by Michael Young, Routledge & Kegan Paul 1982.

Chapter 3

My Territorial Army unit was No 1 Prisoner of War Interrogation Unit, based in Balham: a noble attempt by the army to use my German, but my stammer rendered me a hopeless interrogator. I only had to report a few times.

Chapter 4

Graham Storey, my tutor, became more widely known as the editor of Dickens' letters.

Chapter 7

John Herbert's *Inside Christie's* was published by Hodder & Stoughton in 1990. The photo is opposite p268.

Chapter 10

Hugo Young's *This Blessed Plot* was published by Macmillan in 1998. Hugo kindly sent me a copy inscribed 'To a European of much longer pedigree than me', an allusion mainly to my father's involvement with the Marshall Plan, I think.

Also useful: Piers Brendon's *The Dark Valley: a Panorama of the 1930s* (Jonathan Cape 2000); Peter Hennessy's *Having it so Good: Britain in the Fifties* (Allen Lane 2006); Andrew Marr's *A History of Modern Britain* (Pan Books 2008).

Index

Note: page numbers in *italics* refer to illustrations